Nazi-Looted Art and the Law

Bruce L. Hay

Nazi-Looted Art and the Law

The American Cases

Springer

Bruce L. Hay
Law School
Harvard University
Cambridge, Massachusetts
USA

ISBN 978-3-319-64966-5 ISBN 978-3-319-64967-2 (eBook)
DOI 10.1007/978-3-319-64967-2

Library of Congress Control Number: 2017948667

Printed on acid-free paper

This Springer imprint is published by Springer Nature
The registered company is Springer International Publishing AG
The registered company address is: Gewerbestrasse 11, 6330 Cham, Switzerland

For Nathaniel

Preface

The subject of Nazi-looted art and its restitution has attracted interest in many domains—legal, political, cultural, academic, and popular—in recent years. Plundered artworks and the conflicts over them have become a principal "site of memory," to use Pierre Nora's term, of the Holocaust and its aftermath. To the rapidly growing literature on the topic, this book adds an account of the American judiciary's treatment of restitution claims that, for one reason or another, the parties have been unable to settle without resort to litigation. It is written in a descriptive rather than a prescriptive register, with the purpose of explaining the complex legal issues the courts have faced in adjudicating disputes that stretch across decades and continents. My hope is that it will be of use to readers in a variety of fields.

I thank David Chai, Chloe Do, Medha Gargeya, Victoriya Levina, Isabel Marin, Erin Thomas, Catherine Wiener, and Zachary Steele for their assistance.

Cambridge, MA, USA | Bruce L. Hay

Contents

Chapter 1
Introduction

1.1 Restitution Litigation in American Courts

In late 1997, a newspaper article revealed that the Museum of Modern Art in New York was exhibiting a painting that the Nazis had confiscated from its Jewish owner in Vienna in 1938. The painting, Egon Schiele's *Portrait of Wally*, was on loan from the Leopold Museum in Vienna, whose founder, the article indicated, had falsified the work's provenance to conceal its history.[1] Just before its scheduled return to Austria, the painting was seized by authorities in New York, who launched a judicial proceeding to have it declared stolen property and returned to the original owner's family. The case drew international headlines and sent shockwaves throughout the art world, which until then had mostly turned a blind eye to the traffic in Nazi-looted art and to many museums' practice of collecting artworks that had suspiciously changed hands during the Holocaust. It also helped inaugurate a series of American court cases over what have been termed "the last prisoners of war"—artworks that claimed to have been taken from victims of Nazi persecution and never returned to their rightful owners.[2]

The cases that have gone to court, nearly twenty in number, fall into three general groups: suits involving claims against public museums; suits involving claims against private collectors; and suits involving claims against foreign states. Let me begin with a brief introduction of each.

---

[1]Dobrzynski (1997).

[2]On Holocaust-era looting and destruction of art, see Nicholas (1994), Petropoulos (1996), Feliciano (1997), Simpson (1997), Müller and Tatzkow (2010), Hopp (2012), Ronald (2015), and Huyssen et al. (2017). The prisoner reference was coined by Elan Steinberg of the World Jewish Congress. See Dellheim (2013), which also discusses Pierre Nora's concept of "sites of memory," mentioned above in the preface.

B.L. Hay, *Nazi-Looted Art and the Law*, DOI 10.1007/978-3-319-64967-2_1

1.1.1 Claims Against Public Museums

United States v. Portrait of Wally In the *Portrait of Wally* case,[3] following the painting's seizure in New York, the heirs of Lea Bondi, the original owner of the Schiele, intervened to claim it, as did the Leopold Museum. The litigation lasted for twelve years, producing a number of published judicial opinions, before finally settling as a trial was scheduled to begin. Under the settlement, the Leopold Museum agreed to purchase the work from Bondi's family.

Rosenberg v. Seattle Art Museum In *Rosenberg v. Seattle Art Museum*,[4] heirs of Paul Rosenberg claimed that the Nazis had stolen a Matisse painting from him in France in 1941, which was later sold in New York and eventually donated to the Seattle Art Museum. Upon receiving the results of a commissioned investigation, the museum concluded that the work was stolen and returned it to the family.

Grosz v. Museum of Modern Art In *Grosz v. Museum of Modern Art*,[5] the family of artist George Grosz sought to recover paintings of his that, they asserted, were stolen by the Nazis from his dealer following the artist's flight from Germany and were later acquired by the Museum of Modern Art. The museum contested the claim, having concluded from a commissioned investigation that the paintings were not stolen. The courts ruled that the lawsuit was barred by the New York statute of limitations.

Museum of Fine Arts, Boston v. Seger Thomschitz In *Museum of Fine Arts, Boston v. Seger-Thomschitz*,[6] the heir of Oskar Reichel claimed that in Vienna in 1939 Reichel had sold, under duress, a Kokoschka painting that was later sold in America and eventually donated to the Museum of Fine Arts in Boston. The museum disputed the claim, having concluded that the sale was voluntary, and brought an action for declaratory relief on the theory that the action was time-barred. The courts ruled in the museum's favor under the Massachusetts statute of limitations.

Detroit Institute of Arts and Toledo Museum of Art v. Ullin In *Detroit Institute of Arts v. Ullin* and *Toledo Museum of Art v. Ullin*,[7] heirs of Martha Nathan claimed

---

[3]United States v. Portrait of Wally, a Painting by Egon Schiele, No. 99-Civ.-9940 (S.D.N.Y., filed Sep. 22, 1999). The case is examined in Chap. 2.

[4]Elaine Rosenberg et al. v. Seattle Art Museum, No. 98-cv-1073 (W.D. Wash., filed July 31, 1998). Because the case produced no written opinions (except concerning an ancillary dispute between the museum and another defendant), I do not examine the case in this book. For a summary, see Lee (1999).

[5]Martin Grosz et al. v. Museum of Modern Art, No. 09-cv-3706 (S.D.N.Y., filed April 10, 2009). See Chap. 8.

[6]Museum of Fine Arts, Boston v. Claudia Seger-Thomschitz, No. 08-cv-10097 (D. Mass., filed Jan. 22, 2008). See Chap. 10.

[7]Detroit Institute of Arts v. George Ullin et al., No. 06-cv-10333 (E.D. Mich., filed Jan. 24, 2006); Toledo Museum of Art v. George Ullin et al., No. 06-cv-7031 (N.D. Ohio, filed Jan. 24, 2006). See Chap. 13.

that in 1938, shortly after fleeing Germany for France, she had sold paintings by Gauguin and van Gogh under duress to a group of dealers in Paris, which were later acquired by the Detroit and Toledo museums. The museums took the position that the sale was voluntary, brought actions for declaratory relief, and won the cases on the ground that the Michigan and Ohio statutes of limitations had expired.

Schoeps v. Museum of Modern Art In *Schoeps v. Museum of Modern Art*,[8] heirs of Paul and Elsa von Mendelssohn-Bartholdy claimed that the couple had sold several Picasso paintings under duress in Berlin in 1935, two of which were later acquired by the Guggenheim Museum and the Museum of Modern Art in New York. The case settled on the eve of trial, with the museums keeping the paintings in exchange for an undisclosed payment.

Von Saher v. Norton Simon Museum of Art In *von Saher v. Norton Simon Museum of Art*,[9] the family of Jacques Goudstikker seeks to recover a Cranach diptych taken from his Amsterdam gallery by Hermann Göring, which eventually made its way to the Norton Simon Museum in California. The museum has contested the claim, and the case is still pending at the pretrial stage after several rounds of appeals.

1.1.2 Claims Against Private Collectors

Goodman v. Searle In *Goodman v. Searle*,[10] the family of Friedrich and Louise Gutmann claimed that the Nazis had seized a Degas painting that the couple had shipped to Paris shortly before they were deported from the Netherlands and murdered in concentration camps. The work made its way through Switzerland to the United States and was eventually purchased by a collector in Chicago. In a settlement reached shortly before trial, the parties agreed to jointly sell the painting to the Art Institute of Chicago.

Orkin v. Taylor In *Orkin v. Taylor*,[11] heirs of Margerete Mauthner claimed that the Nazis had taken a van Gogh painting from her before she fled Germany in 1939, and sought its return from film star Elizabeth Taylor, whose father had purchased it

---

[8]Museum of Modern Art and the Guggenheim Museum of Modern Art v. Julius Schoeps et al., No. 07-Civ.-11074 (S.D.N.Y., filed Dec. 7, 2007). See Chap. 11.

[9]Marei von Saher et al. v. Norton Simon Museum of Art at Pasadena, No. 07-cv-2866 (C.D. Cal., filed May 1, 2007). See Chap. 6.

[10]Nick Goodman et al. v. Daniel Searle, No. 96-cv-6459 (N.D. Ill., filed July 17, 1996). Because the case produced no written judicial opinions, I do not examine it in this book. The case is discussed in Dobrzynski (1998) and Trienens (2000).

[11]Sarah Adler et al. v. Elizabeth Taylor, No. 04-cv-8472 (C.D. Cal., filed Oct. 13, 2004). Andrew Orkin was later substituted as lead named plaintiff. See Chap. 5.

in London in 1963. The courts entered judgment for the defendant, ruling that the suit was barred by the California statute of limitations.

Bakalar v. Vavra In *Bakalar v. Vavra*,[12] heirs of Fritz Grünbaum claimed that after his 1938 arrest in Vienna the Nazis seized his art collection, including a work by Egon Schiele that passed through Switzerland before being purchased by a collector in New York. The courts ruled that the suit was barred by the equitable doctrine of laches.

Dunbar v. Seger-Thomschitz In *Dunbar v. Seger-Thomschitz*,[13] the heir of Oskar Reichel sought to recover a Kokoschka painting that, she claimed, was sold under duress in Vienna in 1939 and later acquired by a collector in New Orleans. The courts ruled that the suit was barred by the Louisiana statute of limitations.

Vineberg v. Bissonnette In *Vineberg v. Bissonnette*,[14] trustees of art dealer Max Stern's estate sought to recover a Winterhalter painting the Nazis had forced him to sell along with the rest of the inventory of his Düsseldorf gallery in 1937. The courts ordered the painting returned to the estate, in what to date is the only final judgment on the merits of a Nazi-era art restitution claim.

1.1.3 Claims Against Foreign States

Altmann v. Republic of Austria In *Altmann v. Republic of Austria*,[15] the heirs of Ferdinand Bloch sought to recover six Klimt paintings that the Nazis had confiscated from him after he fled Vienna in 1938, several of which were later placed in state museums. Following an unsuccessful attempt to recover the paintings from Austrian authorities in the late 1990s, the heirs filed suit against the Republic of Austria in the United States. After five years of pretrial proceedings and a ruling by the Supreme Court allowing the case to go forward, the parties agreed to have the matter resolved by an arbitration panel, which ordered five of the paintings returned to the family.

---

[12]David Bakalar v. Milos Vavra et al., No. 04-cv-3037 (S.D.N.Y., filed Mar. 21, 2005). See Chap. 9. Another case brought by Grünbaum heirs, Timothy Reif et al. v. Richard Nagy et al., No. 161799/2015 (N.Y. Sup. Ct., filed Nov. 16, 2015), is pending.

[13]Sarah Dunbar v. Claudia Seger-Thomschitz, No. 08-cv-711 (E.D. La., filed Jan. 22, 2008). The case is briefly discussed at the end of Chap. 10, which focuses on Seger-Thomschitz's claim against the Museum of Fine Arts, Boston.

[14]Robert Vineberg et al. v. Maria-Louise Bissonnette, No. 06-cv-211 (D.R.I., filed May 8, 2006). See Chap. 14.

[15]Maria Altmann v. Republic of Austria, No. 00-cv-8913 (C.D. Cal., filed Aug. 22, 2000). See Chap. 3.

Westfield v. Federal Republic of Germany In *Westfield v. Federal Republic of Germany*,[16] the family of Walter Westfeld sought compensation from the Republic of Germany for his lost art collection in Düsseldorf, which the Nazis confiscated and auctioned off before deporting him to Auschwitz. The courts entered judgment for the Republic of Germany, ruling that the suit was barred by the doctrine of foreign state immunity.

Orkin v. Swiss Confederation In *Orkin v. Swiss Confederation*,[17] an heir of Margerete Mauthner claimed that in Berlin in 1933 she had sold, under duress, a van Gogh drawing to a private collector who donated it to a state-owned museum in Switzerland after the war. The courts ruled in Switzerland's favor on the ground of foreign state immunity.

Cassirer v. Kingdom of Spain In *Cassirer v. Kingdom of Spain and Thyssen-Bornemisza Collection Foundation*,[18] heirs of Lilly Cassirer seek to recover a Pissarro painting seized by the Nazis in Munich in 1939, which was later sold in the United States and was eventually acquired by the Spanish government and placed in the Thyssen-Bornemisza Museum in Madrid. The case, still in the pretrial stages, is currently pending before the United States Court of Appeals for the Ninth Circuit.

De Csepel v. Republic of Hungary In *de Csepel v. Republic of Hungary*,[19] heirs of Erzsébet, András, and István Herzog seek to recover the family's art collection, which was seized by the Nazis in Budapest in 1944 and later placed in several museums and university collections in Hungary. After a protracted, unsuccessful attempt to recover the collection in the Hungarian courts, the heirs filed suit against the Republic of Hungary in the United States. The case, still in the pretrial stages, is currently pending before the United States Court of Appeals for the District of Columbia Circuit.

1.2 This Labyrinthine Proceeding

The term *labyrinthine* appears more than once in the judicial opinions in these cases. "This labyrinthine proceeding," one trial court describes the case before it, resuming work after reversal by the court of appeals on choice-of-law grounds; another struggles with "the labyrinthine arguments" of the parties concerning

---

[16]Fred Westfield et al. v. Federal Republic of Germany, No. 09-cv-204 (M.D. Tenn., filed Mar. 2, 2009). See Chap. 4.

[17]Andrew Orkin v. Swiss Confederation et al., No. 09-cv-10013 (S.D.N.Y., filed Dec. 7, 2009). The case is briefly discussed at the end of Chap. 5, which focuses on Orkin's claims against Elizabeth Taylor.

[18]Claude Cassirer v. Kingdom of Spain and Thyssen-Bornemisza Foundation, No. 05-cv-3459 (C.D. Cal., filed May 10, 2005). See Chap. 7.

[19]David de Csepel et al. v. Republic of Hungary et al., No. 10-cv-1261 (D.D.C., filed July 27, 2010). See Chap. 12.

fragments of evidence from war-torn Europe. It is an apt adjective, indeed, for the cases as a group—for their legal and factual intricacies, for the circuitous paths they have followed between trial and appellate courts, and for the procedural and jurisdictional barriers that forestall adjudication of a claim's merits.[20]

In large part, the complexity of the cases is due to the sheer passage of time since the initial events underlying them, many of which occurred in the 1930s and 1940s. There are various reasons the litigation has been so long delayed: Holocaust survivors often lacked the financial or psychological resources to pursue a claim, or believed it futile to do so; necessary information was sometimes hidden away in archives that have only recently been opened; the internet has eased the difficulties of tracking down missing works and supporting documentation. The time lag makes of each case a long, complicated narrative—a labyrinthine narrative—in which families are dispossessed, postwar restitution proceedings are unsuccessful, missing artworks change hands in several countries, statutes are enacted and repealed, evidence disappears and reemerges, and heirs learn decades later of claims they knew nothing about.

The questions confronting courts are correspondingly complex, bringing into play an array of laws from multiple jurisdictions and levels of government. Though Congress has passed some legislation on the subject, there is no comprehensive American statute governing Nazi-era art restitution claims. Claims are instead governed by a patchwork of state, federal, and transnational legal materials—American common law, statutory law, and constitutional law, along with public and private international law and the substantive laws of European countries. Here, in schematic form, are some of the questions courts have had to confront.

1.2.1 Domestic Law

Statutes of Limitations Virtually all of the claims filed in court have been met with defenses based on state statutes of limitations, which typically require property restitution claims to be brought within three years after they materialize. The principal problem for the courts has been to determine at what point a claim accrued, and the limitations period began running, during the long interval between the artwork's wartime loss and the filing of the claim in court. For example, in the *Orkin* case, the missing work was acquired by the defendant in 1963, but its location was unknown to the original owner's heirs until it was advertised for sale in 2002. The issue for the courts was whether the case was governed by a "discovery rule," according to which the limitations period begins running when the claimant should have discovered the missing property's whereabouts; and if so, when Margerete

[20]The quotations in this paragraph are from Bakalar v. Vavra, 819 F. Supp.2d 293, 294 (S.D.N.Y. 2011), and United States v. Portrait of Wally, 663 F. Supp.2d 23, 264 (S.D.N.Y. 2009).

Mauthner's heirs should have located the artwork she parted with in 1939.[21] Variants of these questions emerge in many of the cases.

Equitable Time Limits Courts have also been asked to use their equitable powers to allow claims that would otherwise be barred by the statute of limitations or, conversely, to bar claims that would otherwise be allowed by the statute of limitations. In the *Grosz* case, for example, the claimants filed in court after negotiations broke down with the museum, and were met with the defense that they were too late under the applicable statute of limitations. The question for the courts was whether the statute, otherwise fatal to the claim, should be "equitably tolled."[22] And in the *Vineberg* case, Max Stern searched extensively for his confiscated art collection in the years following the war but eventually gave up in the mid-1960s after his efforts had proved fruitless. When his estate sued four decades later to recover a missing work that had resurfaced, one question for the courts was whether the claim was barred by the equitable doctrine of laches, which precludes claims that have been unreasonably delayed.[23] This too is a recurrent issue.

State Restitution Measures The California legislature extended the statute of limitations for Nazi-era art claims against museums and galleries in 2002, proclaiming the state's interest in providing a "reasonable opportunity to commence an action in court" for Holocaust "victims and descendants [who] are investigating the whereabouts of artwork that rightfully belonged to their families."[24] The law was challenged on constitutional grounds in the *von Saher* case, leading the courts to rule that state-level Holocaust restitution legislation of this type impermissibly encroaches on the federal government's exclusive authority over foreign affairs.[25] A revised version of the time extension, which does not single out Holocaust-era claims, has so far withstood constitutional challenges on federalism, due process, and freedom of expression grounds.

Federal Restitution Measures In the Holocaust Victims Redress Act of 1998, Congress endorsed the principle that "all governments should undertake good faith efforts to facilitate the return of private and public property, such as works of art, to the rightful owners in cases where assets were confiscated from the claimant during the period of Nazi rule."[26] The United States is also a party to several international conventions on the subject: the Washington Conference Principles

---

[21]Orkin v. Taylor, 487 F.3d 734 (9th Cir.), cert. denied, 552 U.S. 990 (2007).

[22]Grosz v. Museum of Modern Art, 772 F. Supp.2d 473 (S.D.N.Y.), aff'd, Grosz v. Museum of Modern Art, 403 Fed. Appx. 575 (2d Cir. 2010), cert. denied, 565 U.S. 819 (2011).

[23]Vineberg v. Bissonnette, 529 F. Supp.2d 300 (D.R.I. 2007), aff'd, Vineberg v. Bissonnette, 548 F.3d 50 (1st Cir. 2008).

[24]2002 Cal. Legis. Serv. Ch. 332 (A.B.1758).

[25]Von Saher v. Norton Simon Museum of Art, 592 F.3d 954 (9th Cir. 2010), cert. denied, 564 U.S. 1037 (2011).

[26]Holocaust Victims Redress Act, Pub. L. No. 105-158 § 202, 112 Stat. 15, 17–18 (1998).

on Nazi-Confiscated Art, the Vilnius Forum Declaration, and the Terezín Declaration on Holocaust Era Assets and Related Issues, all of which urge signatory governments to implement measures for resolving Holocaust-era art restitution claims on their merits.[27] Claimants have invoked these provisions in an effort to avoid enforcement of state statutes of limitations, presenting the courts with the question whether state time limits should be deemed preempted because they conflict with federal policy. The issue has apparently been settled for future cases by the Holocaust Expropriated Art Recovery Act of 2016, which creates a special federal statute of limitations, and displaces state limitations periods, for claims that are filed or pending after 2016.[28]

1.2.2 International Law

Foreign State Immunity The claims against foreign governments have all met with the defense of sovereign immunity, raising a series of interpretive problems for the courts. One question, eventually resolved by the Supreme Court in the *Altmann* case, was whether the Foreign Sovereign Immunities Act of 1976 applies retroactively to lift foreign states' immunity for events that occurred in the 1930s and 1940s.[29] Other questions have included whether Nazi art expropriations fall under the Act's "commercial activity" exception to immunity; whether they fall under the provision lifting immunity for takings of property in violation of international law; and whether one country's taking of an artwork in violation of international law exposes another country to suit for recovery of the work.

Effect of Foreign Restitution Proceedings In several cases, claimants unsuccessfully brought restitution proceedings in other countries, either in the immediate postwar period or more recently, before filing their claims in the American courts. A resulting question for the courts is whether, under the doctrine of international comity, they should consider further litigation foreclosed by the foreign proceedings.[30] In the *de Csepel* case, for example, the Herzog heirs brought a protracted lawsuit in the courts of Hungary to recover their family's art collection, in which the judiciary initially ruled in their favor but ultimately dismissed the suit. In the

[27]U.S. Dept. of State, The Washington Conference on Holocaust Era Assets, Washington Principles on Nazi-Confiscated Art (Dec. 3, 1998); Vilnius International Forum on Holocaust-Era Looted Cultural Assets, Vilnius Forum Declaration (Oct. 5, 2000); Prague Holocaust Era Assets Conference, Terezín Declaration on Holocaust Era Assets and Related Issues (June 30, 2009).

[28]Holocaust Expropriated Art Recovery Act, Pub. L. 114–308 (Dec. 16, 2016), § 2(6), discussed in Chap. 15. Because it only applies to claims filed or pending after its enactment, the Act does not affect past cases in which courts have ruled claims time-barred.

[29]Altmann v. Republic of Austria, 142 F.Supp.2d 1187 (C.D. Cal. 2001), aff'd, 317 F.3d 954 (9th Cir. 2003), aff'd, 541 U.S. 699 (2004).

[30]A related recurring issue in the cases is whether a matter should be dismissed under the doctrine of forum non conveniens or some similar principle.

pending American proceeding the government of Hungary has argued that the earlier judgment precludes the new litigation, to which the claimants have responded that the Hungarian proceedings did not comply with international standards of due process. The matter remains to be decided.

Acts of State Along similar lines, defendants have argued that certain postwar dispositions of artworks by European governments constitute "acts of state" that, under the eponymous principle of international law, may not be reviewed or set aside by American courts. In the *Portrait of Wally* case, for example, the painting was recovered by Allied forces after the war and turned over to Austrian authorities, who determined that it belonged to someone other than Lea Bondi, the dispossessed owner. When Bondi's heirs sought the work's return in the American litigation, they were met with the argument that the courts could not revisit the Austrian authorities' earlier decision. The problem for the courts, in this and other cases, has been to determine the degree to which foreign restitution decisions of this type fall under the act of state doctrine.

International Treaties Several cases have also raised the question whether any of a series of postwar international accords have the effect of extinguishing later restitution claims. In the *de Csepel* case, for example, the courts have had to determine the effect of the 1947 allied peace treaty with Hungary, as well as a 1973 treaty between the United States and Hungary regarding property taken in the postwar Soviet era, on the availability of relief in the American courts.

1.2.3 Conflicts of Law

Another persistent issue is the problem of selecting the applicable substantive law to govern ownership disputes. A missing work has been bought and sold in a series of countries, each with different rules for determining the rights of original owners and current possessors; which country's rule should be applied? The question arises over and over. In the *Bakalar* case, for example, Fritz Grünbaum's art collection disappeared in Austria, was later sold in Switzerland, and was purchased by the current possessor in New York; these jurisdictions' laws diverge considerably with respect to a purchaser's ability to acquire good title in stolen art; the courts had to choose among them. (Generally speaking, continental laws offer more protection to purchasers of stolen property than do Anglo-American laws.) Or consider the *Cassirer* case, in which the number of candidates is even greater: seized by the Nazis in Germany, the contested work changed hands in the Netherlands, California, and New York, spent twenty-five years in Missouri, was sold to a collector in Switzerland, and is now in Spain. The heirs' right to recover the work will depend on which of those jurisdictions' laws is ultimately applied.

1.2.4 Substantive Law

Having decided to apply a given jurisdiction's substantive law, a court must then determine the content of that law. This itself can be a contentious matter, particularly when a foreign country's law is at issue. The *von Saher* case, for example, turns in part on whether, under Dutch law, title to the stolen artwork reverted to the government of the Netherlands after the war, and was effectively passed on to the current possessor. The *Cassirer* case, to take another example, turns in part on the interpretation of the Spanish law of adverse possession, which is disputed by the parties and has involved conflicting expert testimony.

1.2.5 Questions of Fact

Intertwined with the legal questions are the factual uncertainties present in many of these cases. In a few, the central facts are clear. In the *Westfield* case, for example, there was no doubt that the Nazi government took Walter Westfeld's art collection in Düsseldorf and kept the proceeds from its sale before murdering him at Auschwitz; the Reich carefully recorded it all.[31] In others, the facts are murkier. In the *Seger-Thomschitz* cases, for example, the parties vigorously disputed whether Oskar Reichel's sale of art to a longtime associate in 1939 occurred under duress, and there was little documentary evidence to illuminate the question. The courts went out of their way to highlight the lack of evidence supporting the claims in ruling that the claims were time-barred.[32] This is a repeated pattern in the cases: the courts' resolution of procedural and other "technical" issues is influenced by their perceptions of the underlying merits of a given claim. "We need not, and we do not, resolve [the] factual disputes in this appeal," reads one opinion, "because the issues before us are purely legal."[33] The opinion nonetheless proceeds to demonstrate that "what transpired with the painting during the 1930s in Berlin is clouded in uncertainty," leaving the firm impression that this has something to do with the ultimate ruling.[34] In this way, factual questions may exert a kind of gravitational force on the "purely legal" aspects of the cases.

[31]The location of most of the art nonetheless remains unknown.

[32]Museum of Fine Arts, Boston v. Seger-Thomschitz, 2009 WL 6506658 (D. Mass. 2009), aff'd, 623 F.3d 1 (1st Cir. 2010); Dunbar v. Seger-Thomschitz, 615 F.3d 574 (5th Cir. 2010).

[33]Orkin v. Taylor, 487 F.3d 734, 736 (9th Cir.), cert. denied, 552 U.S. 990 (2007).

[34]*Id.* at 737.

1.3 Approach of this Book

This study undertakes an in-depth examination of the written judicial rulings in these disputes, with a view toward producing a sort of jurisprudential narrative of the cases. It looks at the questions the courts have confronted, the answers they have arrived at, and the legal and evidentiary materials they have rested their decisions on. I quote liberally from the judicial opinions, both published and unpublished, letting the courts speak for themselves when possible. As is typical in the American common law system, the courts rely heavily on earlier lines of decision, which I summarize and synthesize in the discussion of each case. Where necessary, I also refer to the litigation documents submitted by the parties in the multiple rounds of trial and appellate litigation in many of the cases. My objective is to draw together these disparate threads to create a coherent, accessible account of each case.

The cases themselves represent one thread of a much larger, unfinished story. The vast plunder and destruction of property during the Holocaust, central to the Nazis' program of erasing even the memory of Jewish life in Europe, has been the subject of renewed attention in recent years after decades of neglect.[35] (An emerging legal view, as one court recently observed, is that the property seizures, being designed to deprive Jews "of the resources needed to survive as a people," constituted acts of genocide.[36]) The restitution campaign that began in the 1990s has led to diplomatic accords, national commissions, and class action litigation over stolen bank accounts, insurance policies, and other plundered financial assets.[37] Victims' families in Europe continue to seek the return of homes seized long ago, as well as communal property such as synagogues and cemeteries.[38] With respect to confiscated art, some 47 countries have signed international pledges, as yet only partially kept, to seek "just and fair solutions" to the problem of locating and returning pieces still missing, estimated by experts to number a hundred thousand or more.[39] The reckoning with the past, of which the cases examined here are a part, remains a work in progress.

---

[35]In addition to the works cited in note 2 above, see Aly (2007), Dean et al. (2007), Dean (2008), and Huener and Nicosia (2009).

[36]Simon v. Republic of Hungary, 812 F.3d 127, 142–43 (D.C. Cir. 2016) (emphasis in original). See also Abelesz v. Magyar Nemzeti Bank, 692 F.3d 661, 675 (7th Cir. 2012). The designation is important for purposes of determining whether a particular expropriation violated international law. See Section 12.3.1 below.

[37]See Eizenstat (2003), Bazyler (2003), and Bazyler and Alford (2006).

[38]See European Shoah Legacy Institute (2017), Siegel (2017), and Zieve (2017).

[39]See Schnabel and Tatzlow (2007), Campfens (2012), Fisher and Weinberger (2014), and Voss (2017).

References

Aly, Götz. 2007. *Hitler's Beneficiaries: Plunder, Racial War, and the Nazi Welfare State*. Translated by Jefferson Chase. New York: Metropolitan.

Bazyler, Michael J. 2003. *Holocaust Justice: The Battle for Restitution in America's Courts*. New York: New York University Press.

Bazyler, Michael J., and Roger P. Alford, eds. 2006. *Holocaust Restitution: Perspectives on the Litigation and Its Legacy*. New York: New York University Press.

Campfens, Evelien, ed. 2012. *Fair and Just Solutions? Alternatives to Litigation in Nazi-Looted Art Disputes: Status Quo and New Developments*. The Hague: Eleven International Publishing.

Dean, Martin. 2008. *Robbing the Jews: the Confiscation of Jewish Property in the Holocaust, 1933-45*. New York: Cambridge University Press.

Dean, Martin, Constantin Goschler, and Philipp Ther. 2007. *Robbery and Restitution: The Conflict over Jewish Property in Europe*. New York: Berghahn Books.

Dellheim, Charles. 2013. Framing Nazi Art Loot. In *The Art of Being Jewish in Modern Times*, ed. Barbara Kirshenblatt-Gimblett and Jonathan Karp. Philadelphia: University of Pennsylvania Press.

Dobrzynski, Judith H. 1997. The Zealous Collector—a Special Report: A Singular Passion for Collecting Art, One Way or Another. *New York Times*, December 24.

———. 1998. Settlement in Dispute over a Painting Looted by Nazis. *New York Times*, August 14.

Eizenstat, Stuart. 2003. *Imperfect Justice: Looted Assets, Slave Labor, and the Unfinished Business of World War II*. New York: Public Affairs.

European Shoah Legacy Institute. 2017. *ESLI Immovable Property Restitution Study*. Accessed July 20, 2017. http://shoahlegacy.org/restitution-of-immovable-property.

Feliciano, Hector. 1997. *The Lost Museum: The Nazi Conspiracy to Steal the World's Greatest Works of Art*. New York: Basic Books.

Fisher, Wesley A., and Ruth Weinberger. 2014. Holocaust-Era Looted Art: A Current World-Wide Overview. Claims Conference/WJRO. Accessed July 15, 2017. http://art.claimscon.org/our-work/looted-art-report.

Hopp, Meike. 2012. *Kunsthandel im Nationalsozialismus: Adolf Weinmüller in München und Wien*. Wien: Böhlau Verlag.

Huener, Jonathan, and Francis R. Nicosia, eds. 2009. *The Arts in Nazi Germany: Continuity, Conformity, Change*. New York: Berghahn Books.

Huyssen, Andreas, Anson Rabinbach, and Avinoam Shalem. 2017. Nazi-Looted Art and Its Legacies: Introduction. *New German Critique* 130: 1–6.

Lee, Felicia. 1999. Seattle Museum to Return Looted Work. *New York Times*, June 16.

Müller, Melissa, and Monika Tatzkow. 2010. *Lost Lives, Lost Art: Jewish Collectors, Nazi Art Theft*. London: Frontline.

Nicholas, Lynn. 1994. *The Rape of Europa: The Fate of Europe's Treasures in the Third Reich and the Second World War*. New York: Knopf.

Petropoulos, Jonathan. 1996. *Art as Politics in the Third Reich*. Chapel Hill: University of North Carolina Press.

Ronald, Susan. 2015. *Hitler's Art Thief: Hildebrand Gurlitt, the Nazis, and the Looting of Europe's Treasures*. New York: St. Martin's Press.

Schnabel, Gunnar, and Monika Tatzlow. 2007. *Nazi-Looted Art: Handbuch Kunstrestitution weltweit*. Berlin: Proprietas-Verlag.

Siegel, Nina. 2017. Holocaust Survivors in Poland Find Restitution Claims "Like a Carousel." *New York Times*, May 10.

Simpson, Elizabeth, ed. 1997. *The Spoils of War: World War II and Its Aftermath: The Loss, Disappearance and Recovery of Cultural Property*. New York: H.N. Abrams.

Trienens, Howard J. 2000. *Landscape with Smokestacks: The Case of the Allegedly Plundered Degas*. Evanston, IL: Northwestern University Press.

Voss, Julia. 2017. Have German Restitution Politics Been Advanced Since the Gurlitt Case? A Journalist's Perspective. *New German Critique* 130: 57–73.
Zieve, Tamara. 2017. European Parliament President Urges Post-Holocaust Restitution Progress. *Jerusalem Post*, April 26.

Cases

Abelesz v. Magyar Nemzeti Bank, 692 F.3d 661 (7th Cir. 2012)
Sarah Adler et al. v. Elizabeth Taylor, No. 04-cv-8472 (C.D. Cal., filed Oct. 13, 2004)
Maria Altmann v. Republic of Austria, No. 00-cv-8913 (C.D. Cal., filed Aug. 22, 2000)
David Bakalar v. Milos Vavra et al., No. 04-cv-3037 (S.D.N.Y., filed Mar. 21, 2005)
Claude Cassirer v. Kingdom of Spain and Thyssen-Bornemisza Foundation, No. 05-cv-3459 (C.D. Cal., filed May 10, 2005)
David de Csepel et al. v. Republic of Hungary et al., No. 10-cv-1261 (D.D.C., filed July 27, 2010)
Detroit Institute of Arts v. George Ullin et al., No. 06-cv-10333 (E.D. Mich., filed Jan. 24, 2006)
Sarah Dunbar v. Claudia Seger-Thomschitz, No. 08-cv-711 (E.D. La., filed Jan. 22, 2008)
Nick Goodman et al. v. Daniel Searle, No. 96-cv-6459 (N.D. Ill., filed July 17, 1996)
Martin Grosz et al. v. Museum of Modern Art, No. 09-cv-3706 (S.D.N.Y., filed April 10, 2009)
Museum of Fine Arts, Boston v. Claudia Seger-Thomschitz, No. 08-cv-10097 (D. Mass., filed Jan. 22, 2008)
Museum of Modern Art and the Guggenheim Museum of Modern Art v. Julius Schoeps et al., No. 07-Civ.-11074 (S.D.N.Y., filed Dec. 7, 2007)
Andrew Orkin v. Swiss Confederation et al., No. 09-cv-10013 (S.D.N.Y., filed Dec. 7, 2009)
Timothy Reif et al. v. Richard Nagy et al., No. 161799/2015 (N.Y. Sup. Ct., filed Nov. 16, 2015)
Elaine Rosenberg et al. v. Seattle Art Museum, No. 98-cv-1073 (W.D. Wash., filed July 31, 1998)
Marei von Saher et al. v. Norton Simon Museum of Art at Pasadena, No. 07-cv-2866 (C.D. Cal., filed May 1, 2007)
Simon v. Republic of Hungary, 812 F.3d 127 (D.C. Cir. 2016)
Toledo Museum of Art v. George Ullin et al., No. 06-cv-7031 (N.D. Ohio, filed Jan. 24, 2006)
United States v. Portrait of Wally, a Painting by Egon Schiele, No. 99-Civ.-9940 (S.D.N.Y., filed Sep. 22, 1999)
Robert Vineberg et al. v. Maria-Louise Bissonnette, No. 06-cv-211 (D.R.I., filed May 8, 2006)
Fred Westfield et al. v. Federal Republic of Germany, No. 09-cv-204 (M.D. Tenn., filed Mar. 2, 2009)

Chapter 2
United States v. Portrait of Wally

2.1 Background

Lea Bondi (1880–1969) was a Jewish art dealer in Vienna known for her patronage of Egon Schiele and other Austrian expressionist painters. In the mid-1920s she acquired Schiele's 1912 work *Portrait of Wally*, which depicts his lover Valerie Neuzil, and kept it in her private collection at her home. Following the Anschluss in 1938, her gallery was aryanized and sold to a Nazi functionary named Friedrich Welz. In 1939, after taking control of the gallery, Welz visited her apartment and, seeing *Wally* hanging on the wall, demanded that she surrender it to him, claiming he was entitled to it as part of the sale. Fearing that Welz could prevent her planned emigration from Austria, Bondi turned over the painting to him. Soon afterward she fled to London, where she settled permanently.

At war's end, U.S. military forces arrested Welz for war crimes and seized the artworks in his possession, including *Wally*. Not knowing its owner's identity, the military authorities mistakenly concluded that *Wally* belonged to the family of Heinrich Rieger, a well-known Jewish collector of Schiele's works who had died in Theresienstadt after being forced to sell his collection to Welz. The painting was combined with the rest of Rieger's collection and handed over to Austrian authorities. Following a restitution proceeding to recover the collection, Heinrich Rieger's heirs, now settled in the United States and unaware of the authorities' mistake, agreed to sell most of the collection to the Austrian Gallery Belvedere in 1950. *Wally* was among the items shipped to the museum as part of the sale.

Bondi recovered her gallery in her own restitution proceeding in 1949, and set about trying to track down *Wally*. In 1953, she was visited in London by a young Austrian art collector named Rudolf Leopold, who sought her assistance finding Schiele works to add to his collection. Asked by Bondi if he knew the whereabouts of *Wally*, Leopold informed her that it was at the Belvedere. Bondi told Leopold that *Wally* had been stolen and asked him to explain to the Belvedere's management that the painting belonged to her, promising in return to inquire about Schiele works

B.L. Hay, *Nazi-Looted Art and the Law*, DOI 10.1007/978-3-319-64967-2_2

he might purchase in London. A year later, Leopold acquired *Wally* from the Belvedere in exchange for other artworks. Rather than return it to Bondi, however, Leopold kept the painting for himself.

In 1957, Bondi learned that Leopold had the painting and, through a lawyer, asked him to return it to her. Leopold replied that because Bondi had failed to pursue the matter with the Belvedere, it was "clear that she no longer had an ownership right" to *Wally*, and it now belonged to him. Bondi declined her lawyer's advice to sue Leopold, convinced that Austrian judges would favor their countryman over an expatriate and, as she wrote to the lawyer, "if the lawsuit is lost, I have lost my picture forever."[1] Over the next decade she attempted various measures to shame Leopold into returning the painting, which were unsuccessful. Bondi died in London in 1969.

Leopold sold his collection in 1994 to the Austrian government, which built a private museum in his honor and named him director for life. In late 1997, the Leopold Museum loaned *Portrait of Wally* to the Museum of Modern Art in New York as part of an exhibition entitled "Egon Schiele: The Leopold Collection." The exhibition catalogue, written by Leopold, contained a fictitious provenance for *Wally*, inventing nonexistent names and locations for supposed preceding owners.[2] As the exhibition drew to a close, Lea Bondi's nephew, acting on behalf of Bondi's heirs in the United States and England, contacted the Museum of Modern Art, informing it that *Wally* had been stolen and asking it not to return the painting to the Leopold Museum until its rightful ownership had been settled. The Museum of Modern Art refused, stating that it was contractually obliged to return the painting. The heirs then contacted the New York district attorney's office.[3]

2.2 Proceedings

In January 1998, just before *Wally* was to be shipped back to Austria, the district attorney's office served the Museum of Modern Art with a subpoena, demanding that the painting be delivered to a grand jury convened to investigate whether the museum was in possession of stolen property. The museum filed a motion in court seeking to quash the subpoena. Following proceedings in the trial and appellate courts, the case arrived at the state's highest court, which in September 1999 invalidated the subpoena under New York's Arts and Cultural Affairs law, which insulates from seizure works of art sent to the state by nonresidents for purpose of a

---

[1] United States v. Portrait of Wally, 663 F. Supp.2d 232, 245 (S.D.N.Y. 2009).

[2] See Dobrzynski (1997).

[3] A documentary film, *Portrait of Wally: The Face that Launched a Thousand Lawsuits* (P.O.W. Productions, 2012), tells the story of the case and the events underlying it.

museum exhibition.[4] This effectively brought the state-level proceedings to an end.

The matter was then taken up by federal authorities. Immediately after the state court subpoena was quashed, the United States Attorney's office in New York obtained a warrant for the temporary seizure of *Wally*, and brought a civil forfeiture action in federal court seeking to permanently confiscate the painting.[5] The legal basis invoked by the government for confiscation was that the Leopold Museum, at the direction of its namesake, had violated federal law prohibiting the importation of property known to have been stolen.[6] The Leopold Museum and the administrators of Lea Bondi's estate both joined the proceeding, each claiming rightful ownership of the painting. The Leopold Museum then moved to dismiss the case on a variety of jurisdictional and procedural grounds, as well as denying the truth of the government's allegations.

The district court initially granted the motion to dismiss in July 2000, ruling that the painting did not qualify as stolen property.[7] According to the court, the painting lost its status as "stolen" when it was recovered by the U.S. armed forces after the war and transferred to the Austrian government for restitution to the owner. Following this ruling by the court, the United States Attorney's office successfully moved to amend its complaint;[8] the amendment clarified that the army officials who recovered the painting did not realize *Wally* had been stolen, and also stated that the painting was never the subject of a restitution proceeding.

In April 2002, the district court held that the amended complaint should not be dismissed.[9] Reversing its earlier decision, the district court ruled that *Wally* remained stolen property when it was imported to the United States. In addition, the court rejected the Leopold Museum's other proposed grounds for dismissing the case. The Austrian State Treaty of 1955 did not give the courts of that country exclusive jurisdiction over the *Wally* dispute, the court held; nor did considerations of international comity require dismissal out of deference to the Austrian restitution process. The act of state doctrine also did not prevent the case from going forward, because a determination that the painting was unlawfully imported would not require invalidating any act of the Austrian government.

[4]In the Matter of the Grand Jury Subpoena Duces Tecum Served on the Museum of Modern Art, 93 N.Y.2d 729 (N.Y. 1999). On loaned art's immunity from seizure, see Kaye (2010) and van Woudenberg (2012).

[5]In federal forfeiture actions, which are considered *in rem* rather than *in personam* proceedings, it is customary to designate the contested property as the nominal defendant. The federal government's case was accordingly styled "United States v. Portrait of Wally, a Painting by Egon Schiele."

[6]National Stolen Property Act, 18 U.S.C. § 2314. Items that are imported to the United States in violation of this law are subject to forfeiture. See 19 U.S.C. § 1595a.

[7]United States v. Portrait of Wally, 105 F. Supp.2d 208 (S.D.N.Y. 2000). This was the first of four opinions the district court issued in the case. To distinguish it from the later opinions, we will refer to it as "*Wally I.*"

[8]United States v. Portrait of Wally, 2000 WL 1890403 (S.D.N.Y. 2000) ("*Wally II*").

[9]United States v. Portrait of Wally, 2002 WL 553532 (S.D.N.Y. 2002) ("*Wally III*").

Finally, the district court rejected the museum's laches defense and its contention that confiscation in a civil forfeiture proceeding would unconstitutionally deprive it of property without due process of law.

For the next six years, the parties conducted extensive pretrial discovery of documents and witnesses, at the close of which both sides filed cross-motions for summary judgment. In 2009, with a different judge now presiding,[10] the district court denied the motions, ruling as follows. First, the documentary evidence demonstrated that *Wally* was stolen from Bondi in 1939, and in addition that it remained stolen when it was shipped to the United States in 1997. The evidence was so clear that no trial was necessary on these issues. Second, to succeed in the forfeiture action, the United States would also have to prove that the Leopold Museum knew, or deliberately avoided knowing, that *Wally* was stolen when it was shipped to the United States. A jury trial was needed on this issue because its resolution depended on witness credibility. Accordingly, the court ordered a trial limited to the issue of the museum's knowledge of the painting's status as stolen property.

The case settled shortly before trial was to begin.

2.3 Threshold Questions

Among the myriad legal issues that the *Wally* litigation presented, there were numerous arguments that the district court could not, or should not, reach the merits of the government's claim that the painting had been unlawfully imported and was subject to forfeiture. We will consider these in turn.

2.3.1 Treaty Obligations

The State Treaty of 1955, entered into by Austria and the United States along with the three other occupying Allied powers, ended the postwar occupation and established an independent civilian government for Austria. Article 26 of the treaty obliged Austria to return property that had been the subject of forced transfer or control on account of the owner's religion or racial origin and, in the case of property that remained unclaimed or heirless after six months, required the government to take control of it and distribute it to "appropriate agencies or organizations" in order that it "be used for the relief and rehabilitation of victims of persecution."[11]

---

[10]United States v. Portrait of Wally, 663 F. Supp.2d 232 (S.D.N.Y. 2009) ("*Wally IV*"). In 2006, the judge originally assigned to the case, Michael Mukasey, retired from the court, and the case taken over by Judge Loretta Preska.

[11]Austrian State Treaty of 1955, art. 26(2).

Relying on this language, the Leopold Museum argued that "the Treaty expressly designated the sovereign Republic of Austria as the sole authority responsible for the disposition of property improperly seized during Nazi rule."[12] Given Bondi's failure to reclaim *Wally* within six months of ratification, the museum contended, the treaty "vested the Austrian Republic with sole responsibility for disposing of the unclaimed painting."[13] Further, the museum argued, the treaty's ratification by the United States "recognized that the disposition of property was expressly entrusted to Austria, and neither this nor any other United States court has jurisdiction to consider or decide issues relating to Austria's disposition of property covered by Article 26."[14]

The court rejected this argument. For one thing, the court stated, the treaty said nothing about stripping other countries' court systems of jurisdiction over cases involving Holocaust-era art looting. "Article 26 on its face does not state that the Austrian government has exclusive jurisdiction over such property, and the Leopold provides no case law from any country in support of its novel interpretation," the court noted; "[n]othing in the Treaty suggests that this court is without jurisdiction to hear a forfeiture case which includes issues of ownership of property taken by the Nazis."[15] For another thing, Austria had not disposed of *Wally* in the manner prescribed by the treaty, which required that unclaimed property be "used for the relief of victims of the Holocaust," not placed in the hands of private collectors such as Leopold or placed in a museum named in his honor.[16] Because the purpose of Article 26 "was to restore property to its true owner, an exercise of jurisdiction in this case would seem to be unobjectionable under the Treaty."[17]

2.3.2 International Comity

The Leopold Museum additionally argued that the case should be dismissed under the doctrine of international comity, which involves "a discretionary act of deference by a national court to decline to exercise jurisdiction in a case properly adjudicated in a foreign state."[18] The doctrine, the district court explained, "requires a balance of interests of the respective forums and of international policy," keeping in mind that mutual recognition "fosters international cooperation and encourages reciprocity."[19]

---

[12] *Wally III*, 2002 WL 553532 at *7.

[13] *Id.*

[14] *Id.*

[15] *Id.*

[16] *Id.*

[17] *Id.* at *8.

[18] In re Maxwell Communications Corp., 93 F.3d 1036, 1047 (2d Cir. 1996). On international comity in American law, see generally Dodge (2015).

[19] *Wally III*, 2002 WL 553532 at *9 (quoting Spatola v. United States, 925 F.2d 615, 618 (2d Cir. 1991)).

The museum's claim to comity rested on the property restitution system enacted in the wake of the 1955 treaty. Its argument, as the district court summarized it, was that "the court should defer to the Austrian restitution system, which was enacted with the approval of the Allies and is thus consistent with both United States and international policy," and in addition that "Austria's interest in the subject matter of this litigation is paramount."[20]

The fatal flaw of this argument, according to the court, was that "there is no pending action, proceeding or decree relating to this case in Austria to which this court could defer."[21] It might well be true, the court stated, that the laws and procedures of the Austrian restitution system were fully compatible with the "laws and interests of the United States and international law"; nonetheless, "the principle of comity does not act as a pre-emption doctrine, barring this court from hearing a valid forfeiture action merely because there are foreign laws that might also apply."[22] Rather than give due weight to Austrian proceedings, the museum was effectively asking the court to give that country complete control. "The mere existence of the Austrian restitution system," the court declared, "does not vest exclusive jurisdiction in Austrian courts to hear all issues touching upon Holocaust-related property."[23]

The court also denied that Austria's interest in terminating the case outweighed America's interest in adjudicating it. "The Leopold argues," according to the court, "that Austria has a greater interest in this case because of acts taken by Austria with respect to the painting, the existence of its restitution system, and its responsibility under the Austrian State Treaty."[24] Yet because "there has been no formal or purposeful act of the Austrian judiciary, executive, or legislature with respect to the painting rising to a level that would implicate international comity," the museum had failed to demonstrate how a proceeding in the United States would impair the interests served by Austria's restitution system.[25] At the same time, the United States has a strong interest in enforcing its own laws as applied to conduct on its own soil; the ownership of *Wally* under Austrian law was only one part of the case, which revolved around trafficking laws that the United States had a powerful stake in enforcing. "The basis for this forfeiture action," the court declared, "is the alleged importation of *Wally* into the United States in violation of the National Stolen Property Act," under which it is "United States law and policy to prohibit transportation of stolen or converted goods into the United States."[26] Because ordinarily "United States courts will not yield in the name of comity if doing so

[20]*Wally III*, 2002 WL 553532 at *9.

[21]*Id.* at *10.

[22]*Id.*

[23]*Id.*

[24]*Id.*

[25]*Id.*

[26]*Id.*

conflicts with the law or policy of the United States," the court concluded that dismissal was not warranted.[27]

2.3.3 *Laches*

A further issue was whether to dismiss the case under the equitable doctrine of laches, which courts have "discretion to apply ... in light of the equities of the parties."[28] Generally, the district court noted, "laches is applied where it is clear that a plaintiff unreasonably delayed in initiating an action and a defendant was unfairly prejudiced by the delay."[29] The museum argued that the doctrine should bar *Wally*'s forfeiture because no claim to the painting had been made by either Bondi or her heirs in the forty years since Bondi's lawyer had last corresponded with Leopold, and the delay had "substantially prejudiced" the museum because nearly all the principal witnesses to the events in question were long dead.[30] The museum also noted that Bondi had made a conscious decision not to sue Leopold for fear that, as she wrote in a 1965 letter, "if the litigation was lost, the picture would irrevocably be taken from my possession."[31]

The court rejected the argument because the *Wally* litigation was a forfeiture proceeding brought by the federal government to enforce the laws against trafficking in stolen property, and not a private claim brought by the Bondi heirs. There was no authority, the court held, suggesting that the laches defense was available against the federal government in civil forfeiture cases. Moreover, even if such a defense were available in theory, it would not apply in the present case because the United States brought the action promptly after *Wally* had been imported. The doctrine would not, therefore, prevent the court from reaching the merits of the case.[32]

2.3.4 *Fair Notice*

The museum also argued that the proceeding violated due process because the museum had been deprived of fair notice of its legal obligations, in that the museum

---

[27]*Id.* Employing this reasoning, the court later ruled that international comity did not warrant summary judgment in the museum's favor. *Wally IV*, 663 F. Supp.2d at 248–49.

[28]Robins Island Presidential Fund, Inc. v. Southold Development Corp., 959 F.2d 409, 423 (2d Cir. 1992) (internal quotation marks omitted), quoted in *Wally IV*, 663 F. Supp.2d at 274.

[29]*Robins Island*, 959 F.2d at 423, quoted in *Wally IV*, 663 F. Supp.2d at 274.

[30]*Wally IV*, 663 F. Supp.2d at 274.

[31]Quoted in *id.* at 275.

[32]To be sure, Leopold's long undisturbed possession of the painting was relevant to the merits of the case, being part of his claim to having acquired ownership by prescription. See Section 2.4.3 below.

could not have reasonably anticipated that *Wally* would be subject to forfeiture if imported to the United States. The district court rejected this argument because knowledge of the painting's stolen status was an element of the government's legal basis for bringing the action. According to the government's complaint, the museum had imported *Wally* knowing that it was stolen. If that allegation turned out to be true, the district court reasoned, the museum could hardly assert that it lacked fair notice of the risk of forfeiture. Any concerns about fair warning would be accommodated by the proceeding, the court concluded, because the museum would have a full opportunity to show that it did not know the painting was stolen.[33]

2.4 Merits of the Forfeiture Claim

With the foregoing threshold issues resolved in the government's favor, the central issues in the *Portrait of Wally* litigation became predominantly factual ones, concerning the circumstances of Lea Bondi's loss of the painting after the Anschluss, its arrival at the Belvedere after the war and subsequent acquisition by Leopold, and its eventual shipment to the United States. Analytically, the court was confronted with three overriding questions: (1) whether the painting was stolen from Bondi by Welz, the dealer who aryanized her gallery; (2) if so, whether it remained stolen property after the war, despite its recovery and disposition by government authorities and Leopold's long possession of it after 1954; and (3) if so, whether Leopold knew it was stolen when he and his museum imported it into the United States.

2.4.1 Burdens of Proof

Before considering the court's treatment of those three questions, we should remark on the burdens of proof employed by the court in the proceeding. In its complaint, the United States sought to confiscate *Wally* pursuant to the federal civil forfeiture statutes, which provide that stolen merchandise shall be "seized and forfeited" if it "is introduced or attempted to be introduced into the United States contrary to law."[34] The government's position was that the painting had been introduced contrary to the National Stolen Property Act, which is violated by anyone who "transports, transmits, or transfers in interstate or foreign commerce any goods" worth more than $5,000, "knowing the same to have been stolen, converted or taken by fraud."[35] Under the applicable legal standard, the district court explained, the

[33] *Wally IV*, 663 F. Supp.2d at 275–76.

[34] 19 U.S.C. § 1595a.

[35] 18 U.S.C. § 2314. On civil forfeiture of stolen art, see generally Kreder (2005, 2011). See also Spiegler (2007).

government must come forward with evidence that the painting had been imported in violation of the Act; if it does so, the burden of proof would be on the museum to establish it had not.

More precisely, the statute governing the burden of proof in civil forfeiture actions, since repealed but nonetheless applicable to the *Wally* proceeding, stated that "where the property is claimed by any person, the burden of proof shall lie upon such claimant; ... Provided, that probable cause shall be first shown for the institution of such suit or action, to be judged of by the court."[36] As the district court explained, this statutory framework created a complex structure of shifting burdens of proof. The government bore the initial burden of "making a showing of probable cause," meaning that "the Government must show 'reasonable grounds, rising above the level of mere suspicion' to believe the property is subject to forfeiture."[37] Once the government has done this, "the burden shifts to the claimant to show, by a preponderance of the evidence, that the property is not subject to forfeiture."[38] Finally, if "the claimant meets this burden, 'the government must provide evidence of its own to the contrary that is at least as persuasive and credible.'"[39] Thus, the court held, if the United States could establish probable cause to believe that the painting had been unlawfully imported, the ultimate burden of proof would be on the museum to show that, more likely than not, the importation was in fact lawful.

The Leopold Museum argued unsuccessfully that this assignment of the burden of proof violated the constitutional requirements of due process. This argument, as the court observed, had been considered and rejected in previous cases by numerous courts, which had "all explicitly upheld the constitutionality of the probable cause standard in civil forfeiture cases."[40] In an earlier case, for example, it was unsuccessfully argued that the seizure of money in a narcotics-related forfeiture proceeding was tantamount to a criminal penalty, and therefore should be governed by the procedural protections applied to criminal cases, including the requirement of proof beyond reasonable doubt.[41] The Second Circuit court of appeals rejected the argument on the ground that forfeiture served a number of non-punitive purposes, including defraying the government's expenses of combatting drug trafficking and

---

[36] 19 U.S.C. § 1615. In a 2000 amendment to the civil forfeiture laws, the government's initial burden of proof was raised from "probable cause" to "preponderance of the evidence," the standard a plaintiff must meet in most civil actions. See Civil Asset Forfeiture Reform Act of 2000, Pub. L. No. 106-185, 114 Stat. 202, codified at 18 USCA § 983. This amendment was ruled inapplicable to the Wally proceeding because the case had been commenced in 1999, before the amendment's effective date. *Wally IV*, 663 F. Supp.2d at 251 n. 12.

[37] *Wally IV*, 663 F. Supp.2d at 251 (quoting United States v. An Antique Platter of Gold, 991 F. Supp. 222, 228 (S.D.N.Y. 1997)).

[38] *Wally IV*, 663 F. Supp.2d at 251.

[39] *Id.* (quoting United States v. Parcel of Property, 337 F.3d 225, 232 (2d Cir. 2003)).

[40] *Wally III*, 2002 WL 553532 at *29. On constitutional aspects of civil forfeiture, see Bridy (2014) and Piety (1991).

[41] United States v. $2,500 in U.S. Currency, 689 F.2d 10, 13–15 (2d Cir. 1982).

reducing its profitability. Such remedial and regulatory purposes, the court of appeals noted, are often pursued by the use of civil sanctions imposed with less than proof beyond reasonable doubt. Moreover, as another court upholding the forfeiture statutes stated, "Congress may alter the traditional allocation of the burden of proof without infringing upon the litigant's due process rights unless the statute is criminal in nature."[42] Declaring that these courts' decisions "will not be disregarded here,"[43] the district court concluded that the museum could constitutionally be required to bear the ultimate burden of proof in the case, provided that the United States could establish probable cause that *Wally* had been imported in violation of the National Stolen Property Act.

2.4.2 The Painting's Theft

The first of the three questions for the court was whether the evidence supported the government's contention that the painting had been stolen from Lea Bondi by Friedrich Welz, who purchased and aryanized her gallery. More precisely, the question was whether, as the government alleged, Welz had forced Bondi to relinquish the painting from her personal household collection after the sale of her gallery was complete.[44] As the district court noted, the National Stolen Property Act did not define "stolen," but previous decisions had established that it should be construed broadly. In one earlier decision, the Second Circuit court of appeals had stated that the term should be understood to include "all felonious takings ... with intent to deprive the owner of the rights and benefits of ownership, regardless of whether or not the theft constitutes common-law larceny."[45] The term's application, according to that earlier decision, should not be made to depend on "the archaic distinctions between larceny by trespass, larceny by trick, embezzlement and obtaining property by false pretenses," but should instead on the common sense determination of "whether there has been some sort of interference with a property interest."[46] Thus, an "item is stolen," the district court explained, "if it 'belonged to someone who did not ... consent' to its being taken."[47]

---

[42]United States v. $250,000 in U.S. Currency, 808 F.2d 895, 900 (1st Cir. 1987).

[43]*Wally III*, 2002 WL 553532 at *29.

[44]If Welz had acquired *Wally* as part of the gallery purchase, the painting might still have qualified as stolen on the ground that the sale had been under duress. However, the government did not pursue this theory; its argument was that *Wally* was not part of the gallery inventory but rather was in Bondi's private collection, and that Welz had pressured Bondi into giving it to him under the implied threat that he would prevent her emigration from Austria.

[45]United States v. Long Cove Seafood, Inc., 582 F.2d 159, 163 (2d Cir. 1978) (quoting United States v. Turley, 352 U.S. 407, 417 (1957)), quoted in *Wally IV*, 663 F. Supp.2d at 252.

[46]*Long Cove Seafood*, 582 F.2d at 163 (2d Cir. 1978), quoted in *Wally IV*, 663 F. Supp.2d at 252.

[47]*Wally IV*, 663 F. Supp.2d at 252 (quoting United States v. Schultz, 333 F.3d 393, 399 (2d Cir. 2003)).

The government pointed to a series of documents indicating that *Portrait of Wally* had once been part of Bondi's personal collection. The catalogue for an exhibition of Schiele works held at her gallery in 1925–1926 listed the painting as being from "private collection L.B."; the catalogue for a Schiele exhibition held at another Vienna gallery in 1928 listed the painting as belonging to "Lea Bondi, Vienna."[48] The first catalogue raisonné of Schiele's works, Otto Kallir's *Egon Schiele Persönlichkeit und Werk*, published in 1930, also listed "Lea Bondi, Vienna" as the most recent owner in *Portrait of Wally*'s provenance.

There was also a set of documents indicating how Bondi had lost the painting. Welz was an art dealer who, in his application for membership in the Nazi party, boasted that "I made my gallery available solely to Aryan artists" and "always stocked pictures of our 'Führer' (even during the prohibition period)."[49] Following the German annexation of Austria, Bondi's gallery, known as the Würthle, was designated non-Aryan and made subject to confiscation. To salvage some of its value, Bondi agreed to sell the Würthle to Welz, who obtained permission to aryanize it in March 1938. Bondi and her husband made arrangements to emigrate the following year. Explaining later in a letter to Otto Kallir how she surrendered *Wally* to Welz, Bondi stated that on the eve of their departure, Welz appeared at their apartment to discuss the Würthle, and discovered the painting in her possession:

> [He] saw [*Wally*] hanging on the wall and demanded the painting. I explained that the painting is my own private property and that it had nothing to do with Würthle. He kept pushing in the unpleasant way it was done at that time until my husband who was also present told me to give in and that we probably already wanted to leave the country tomorrow, don't make any trouble you know what the man could do.[50]

Another letter written by Bondi to Kallir in the 1960s, and an undated writing found among her papers, told the same story, adding that Welz had paid her nothing for *Wally*. And in a 1948 decision returning the gallery to Bondi, the Restitution Committee noted that Welz had wrongfully demanded "a Schiele from the claimant."[51]

The museum contended that Bondi's writings were inadmissible as evidence because, it argued, they had not been authenticated. The court rejected this position, ruling that the documents met the standards of authentication set forth by the

---

[48]Quoted in Amended Memorandum of Law of Plaintiff United States of America and Claimant Estate of Lea Bondi Jaray in Support of their Joint Motion for Summary Judgment (filed February 26, 2009), United States v. Portrait of Wally, a Painting by Egon Schiele, No. 99 Civ. 9940 (S.D.N. Y.), at 11.

[49]Quoted in Amended Statement of Material Facts in Support of Joint Motion for Summary Judgment by Plaintiff United States of America and Claimant Estate of Lea Bondi Jaray (filed February 26, 2009), United States v. Portrait of Wally, a Painting by Egon Schiele, No. 99 Civ. 9940 (S.D.N.Y.), at 4.

[50]Letter to Otto Kallir (dated August 22, 1966), quoted in Amended Statement of Material Facts, note 49 above, at 5.

[51]Quoted in Amended Statement of Material Facts, note 49 above, at 9.

Federal Rules of Evidence. Those rules state that to "satisfy the requirement of authenticating or identifying an item of evidence, the proponent must produce evidence sufficient to support a finding that the item is what the proponent claims it is."[52] In the case of what the rules term "ancient documents," the authentication requirement is met by evidence that a challenged document "is in a condition that creates no suspicion about its authenticity, was in a place where, if authentic, it would likely be, and is at least twenty years old."[53] Otto Kallir's granddaughter, a director of the New York gallery he had opened after escaping Nazi-controlled Vienna, testified that the letters were drawn from a gallery file containing Kallir's correspondence with Bondi. Another director of the gallery, who had once worked as Kallir's secretary, testified that she had created the file many years earlier. "This testimony," the district court ruled, "is sufficient to show that the letters are in fact what they purport to be."[54]

A closer issue was presented by the "typewritten, unsigned, undated, and admittedly incomplete" document in which Bondi recounted turning over *Wally* to Welz. Bondi's great-great nephew testified that he had found the document in a desk at the London residence that had belonged to Bondi and in which, after Bondi died, his grandmother lived. He had lived in the residence during the 1980s, and testified that Bondi's belongings had been kept there long after her death in 1969. Sometime in the late 1980s, he testified, while helping his grandmother organize the desk, he had discovered this document among other papers in one of the drawers. It was typed on "L.B.J." letterhead (for Lea Bondi Jaray). This testimony, the court ruled, sufficed to establish the document's authenticity, because the document "contains a first-person narrative in English typed on Bondi's personal letterhead, using a typeface similar to that used by Bondi in other correspondence with Kallir, some of which she wrote in English," and "was found in a likely place—namely a bureau at her residence in London."[55] The museum's assertions that these writings were not credible, the court stated, could not affect this conclusion. Any doubt about the credibility of a document's contents, the court noted, "goes to the weight the trier of fact chooses to accord to the document, not to its admissibility."[56] The court also rejected the museum's argument that the writings must be excluded as inadmissible hearsay, noting that under the Federal Rules, items that are authenticated as "ancient documents" are exempt from the prohibitions on hearsay evidence.[57]

Having decided that the writings were admissible evidence, the court ruled that the United States had met its initial burden of proof on the theft issue. According to the court, a verdict that Welz stole *Wally* would be proper under the National Stolen

---

[52]Federal Rule of Evidence 901(a). See generally Mueller and Kirkpatrick (2012), pp. 999–1064.

[53]Federal Rule of Evidence 901(b)(8).

[54]*Wally IV*, 663 F. Supp.2d at 254.

[55]*Id.*

[56]*Id.* (quoting 5 Weinstein's Federal Evidence § 901.11[2]).

[57]See Federal Rule of Evidence 803(16).

Property Act if it were proved that Welz "demanded the painting from Bondi in the face of a claim that it was part of her private collection and thus unconnected to Welz's Aryanization of her gallery."[58] In light of the documentary evidence, "which consists of letters, the [undated] Bondi statement, documents from Bondi's post-war restitution proceedings, and catalogues showing that *Wally* was not part of the Würthle Gallery," all viewed "against the historical backdrop of the Anschluss," the court declared that "I conclude that there are ample grounds to believe that this indeed occurred."[59] The government had therefore "met its threshold burden of showing probable cause to believe Welz stole *Wally* from Bondi by demanding it from her at a time when she could not refuse."[60]

The burden then shifted to the museum to show, by a preponderance of the evidence, that Welz in fact had not stolen the painting. The museum attempted to show that Bondi's story about surrendering *Wally* in 1939 was a fabrication, and that she had in fact sold the painting along with the rest of the Würthle inventory the previous year. To support this contention, it pointed to the following five items of evidence:

(1) An entry in a 1943 government auditing report indicated that, according to a 1939 letter, the painting had been acquired for 200 Reichsmarks. The court found this very weak, noting that the letter to which the entry referred could not be found, and "this uncorroborated entry, prepared by an unknown individual years after the vent in question, is insufficient to counter Bondi's multiple written statements."[61]
(2) A 1966 letter from Otto Kallir to Lea Bondi stated that "You wrote that . . . the painting was first 'bought' by Welz from you against your will," which indicated, according to the museum, that Welz had paid Bondi for the painting. The court rejected this argument, declaring that "the cited passage clearly contradicts the Museum's interpretation," because the fact "Kallir put the word 'bought' in quotes indicates that he either suspected or had been told otherwise, and the remainder of the sentence clearly indicates that Welz took *Wally* against [Bondi's] will."[62] If anything, stated the court, the letter "tends to strengthen the Government's case rather than the Museum's and does nothing to controvert the Government's showing that Welz stole *Wally*."[63]
(3) At the 1949 restitution proceeding in which Bondi recovered the Würthle, Welz's relatives and one of his employees had testified that Bondi was not coerced into selling the gallery. The court responded that these statements "are irrelevant insofar as they discuss only Bondi's sale of her gallery, the

[58]*Wally III*, 2002 WL 553532 at *16, quoted in *Wally IV*, 663 F. Supp.2d at 256.

[59]*Wally IV*, 663 F. Supp.2d at 256.

[60]*Id.*

[61]*Wally IV*, 663 F. Supp.2d at 257.

[62]*Id.* at 257–58.

[63]*Id.* at 258.

Aryanization of which is undisputed, and say absolutely nothing about *Wally*."[64]

(4) In a letter to Bondi, her lawyer stated that she had "entrusted" *Wally* to Welz, which the museum urged the court to read as indicating a voluntary transfer. "This tortured reading," the court replied, "is belied by the letter's recommendation that Bondi sue Leopold for the Painting because it belonged to her rather than Welz or anyone else."[65]

(5) Finally, there was an inconsistency in Bondi's written accounts from the 1950s and 1960s, some of which claimed that Welz took her painting in 1938, others in 1939. The court replied that this discrepancy was insignificant, given that all of the accounts "indicate that Welz took *Wally* from Bondi's apartment after she told him that it was her private property apart from the Würthle Gallery," and the fact that "the incident may have occurred in 1938 rather than 1939 is immaterial."[66]

From this analysis of the evidence, the court concluded that the museum had failed to rebut or disprove the government's demonstration that Welz had stolen *Wally* from Bondi. Indeed, so strong was the evidence of theft that "no reasonable trier of fact could find that the Museum has met its evidentiary burden of showing by a preponderance of the evidence that Welz did not steal *Wally*."[67] Accordingly, the court ruled that as a matter of law, *Wally* was stolen before Bondi emigrated to London in 1939, and no jury trial would be necessary on the issue.

2.4.3 Postwar Transfers

The court next had to confront the museum's contention that the painting could no longer be considered stolen after the war, even if it were true that Welz had once stolen it. The museum made a number of alternative arguments to this effect. It argued that the painting lost its status as "stolen" by virtue of its seizure by the U.S. military and transfer to Austrian authorities; that Bondi's rights to the painting were extinguished by the settlement of her 1949 restitution proceeding against Welz in which her gallery was restored to her; that the Austrian authorities' decision to transfer the painting to the heirs of Heinrich Rieger, and to approve its subsequent sale to the Belvedere, constituted an act of state beyond challenge in American court; and finally, that Leopold had acquired ownership of the painting by operation of the Austrian law of prescription.

---

[64] *Id.*

[65] *Id.*

[66] *Wally IV*, 663 F. Supp.2d at 259.

[67] *Id.*

2.4.3.1 Recovery by Occupation Forces and Transfer to Austrian Authorities

Upon their occupation of Austria in May 1945, United States armed forces arrested Welz and detained him for two years on suspicion of war crimes. His property was seized pursuant to a denazification decree authorizing seizure of all property belonging to the Third Reich and individuals "held under detention or any other type of custody by Military Government or the Allied Military Forces or by their order."[68] Responsibility for tracking down the art in his possession was given to the army's Reparations, Deliveries, and Restitution Division (RDR), which was charged with taking custody of artworks and returning each "to the government of the country from which it was taken . . . upon submission of satisfactory proof of its identifiability by the claimant government."[69] In 1947, the RDR delivered the Welz art it had recovered, including *Wally*, to the Austrian Office for the Preservation of Historical Monuments. The question for the court was whether, under the so-called recovery doctrine, *Wally* lost its status as "stolen" as a result.

The recovery doctrine is a principle derived from the English common law according to which "one cannot be convicted of receiving stolen goods if, before the stolen goods reached the receiver, the goods had been recovered by their owner or his agent, including the police."[70] The doctrine, which the American courts have incorporated into the nation's criminal law, is applied to police recovery of stolen property on the basis of "agency principles, which imply a principal-agent relationship where government officials are deemed to act on the owner's behalf."[71] The theory, as the district court in the *Wally* proceeding explained, is that "stolen property, recaptured by the police, no longer has the status of stolen goods but, rather, is held by the police in trust for, or for the account of, the owner."[72]

Earlier in the proceeding, at the pleading stage, the district court had refused to dismiss the case under this doctrine, reasoning that the allegations in the government's amended complaint established that the painting remained stolen even after its recovery by U.S. forces and transfer to the Austrian government.[73] According to

---

[68]Supreme Headquarters Allied Expeditionary Forces, *Provisional Handbook for Military Government in Austria*, Decree No. 3, "Blocking and Control of Property," Article I (April 1945), quoted in Third Amended Complaint, United States v. Portrait of Wally, a Painting by Egon Schiele, No. 99 Civ. 9940 (S.D.N.Y.), ¶ 5(f). On American armed forces' recovery of Nazi-looted art, see generally Kurtz (2006).

[69]Message from War Department to U.S. Forces in Austria, No. WARX 99226 (March 4, 1946), quoted in *Wally IV*, 663 F. Supp.2d at 239.

[70]United States v. Muzii, 676 F.2d 919, 923 (2d Cir. 1982), quoted in *Wally IV*, 663 F. Supp.2d at 259. The doctrine is usually traced to two nineteenth-century English cases, Regina v. Schmidt, L.R. 1 Cr. Cas. Res. 15 (1866), and Regina v. Dolan, 29 Eng. Law & Eq. 533 (1855).

[71]United States v. Muzii, 676 F.2d 919, 923 (2d Cir. 1982), quoted in *Wally IV*, 663 F. Supp.2d at 259.

[72]*Wally I*, 105 F. Supp.2d at 293.

[73]As noted above, the district court initially ruled that the case should be dismissed under the recovery doctrine (*Wally I*), but allowed the government to file an amended complaint (*Wally II*).

the amended complaint, the armed forces personnel who seized *Wally* following Welz's arrest had no reason to know that *Wally* was stolen, or to doubt Welz's ownership of the work; the same was true, the government alleged, of the Austrian officials to whom it was handed over. If these allegations were correct, the district court ruled, the recovery doctrine was inapplicable to the case because neither the U.S. armed forces nor the Austrian authorities were acting as Bondi's agent when handling *Wally*. They neither knew it was stolen nor had any duty to return it to its owner, and this "lack of both knowledge and duty makes this case unlike every other case cited to the court that applied the recovery doctrine to the police or other implied agents."[74] The U.S. and Austrian officials could hardly be viewed as agents of Bondi if, as the government alleged, they were "not required, or even authorized, to return *Wally* to its true owner."[75]

Following discovery, the court ruled that the government's allegations in this regard had proved true. "The Government has provided ample evidence," the court stated, "that United States forces did not know *Wally* was stolen": when the war ended, the military seized millions of items pursuant to decrees that "authorized seizure of all property of persons, like Welz, who were detained by the military, regardless of whether such property was stolen," and the "sheer volume of such seizures provides ample reason to doubt that United States forces had any real knowledge of *Wally*'s history."[76] Nor was there any evidence that the Austrian Monuments Office to which U.S. forces sent *Wally* knew that the painting was stolen, or that it had "a legally enforceable duty to return the Painting to Bondi." Indeed, the court pointed out, it would be quite inappropriate to consider the Monuments Office as standing in an agency relationship to *Wally*'s owner in London, given its institutional mandate to prevent objects like it from leaving the country: "the Government has shown (and the Museum has offered no evidence to rebut) that [the Monuments Office's] primary interest was in keeping Austrian cultural objects in Austria rather than in restitution."[77] Under these circumstances, the recovery doctrine had no application to the case.

2.4.3.2 Restitution Proceeding Against Welz

An additional question for the court arose out of the administrative proceeding Lea Bondi brought to recover the Würthle gallery from Welz. Following the war, Allied occupation forces forced Austria to enact a series of laws to restore Nazi-seized

In light of the new allegations in the amended complaint, the court rescinded its earlier ruling (*Wally III*).

[74] *Wally III*, 2002 WL 553532 at *15.

[75] *Wally IV*, 663 F. Supp.2d at 260.

[76] *Id.*

[77] *Id.* at 261.

Jewish property, administered by a restitution commission.[78] One of these denazification laws created a restitution commission charged with restoring stolen property to the original owners. In 1948, Bondi brought a claim before the commission to undo the 1938 sale of her gallery to Welz. "Although the exact claims and evidence she presented to the Restitution Commission are unknown," as the district court pointed out, a written decision survives in which the commission ordered Welz to return the gallery, despite his protestation that the sale had been fair.[79] "During the course of the evidentiary procedure," the commission's decision stated, "no facts of the case could be determined that showed that [Bondi] would have sold [the Gallery] without being persecuted due to the national socialist seizure of power."[80] The commission further explained that Welz "did not always conduct himself in a fair and generous manner, e.g., ... when he demanded ... a Schiele" from Bondi.[81] Welz appealed the decision; in documents opposing the appeal, Bondi argued that Welz had "beat down even the low price" she had asked for the gallery, and that he had "demand[ed] objects from [Bondi's] private assets ..., the handover of which had never been discussed."[82] Bondi and Welz subsequently reached a settlement agreement, the terms of which remain unknown, which the commission approved in 1949 with the statement that "all mutual claims" had been resolved.

The Leopold Museum argued in the district court that this proceeding terminated Bondi's ownership of *Wally*, with the result that thereafter it could no longer be considered stolen. The court rejected this contention because there was no evidence that Bondi had sought the painting in the proceeding, having been told by Welz that the painting was no longer among his possessions; the U.S. military had mistakenly bundled it with the collection of Heinrich Rieger and handed it over to the Austrian Monuments Office in 1947. The court noted that the decision of the restitution commission was limited to restoring the Würthle Gallery to Bondi, and made no reference to *Wally* except to note, as an indicator of Welz's unfair dealings with her, that he had taken a Schiele belonging to her. Contrary to the museum's argument, the court stated, this apparent reference to *Wally* did not establish that the painting was the subject of the restitution proceeding. It could just as easily be read as signifying that the restitution commission "was distinguishing [*Wally*] from property belonging to the Gallery," which was the focus of the proceeding.[83] Because the museum could not establish by a preponderance of the evidence that Bondi had actually filed a claim for *Wally* in the proceeding, the decision of the restitution commission could not be viewed as having terminated her ownership of the painting, or having ended its "stolen" status.

[78]See generally O'Donnell (2011), pp. 62–63; Presidential Advisory Commission on Holocaust Assets in the United States (2000) at SR23–SR25.

[79]*Wally IV*, 663 F. Supp.2d at 242.

[80]Quoted in *id.*

[81]Quoted in *id.* (internal quotation marks omitted).

[82]Quoted in *id.*

[83]*Id.* at 262.

2.4.3.3 Transfer to the Belvedere

Analytically, the next question for the court was whether the Austrian authorities' handling of *Wally* after its recovery by Allied forces constituted an "act of state" that extinguished Bondi's ownership of the painting, effectively ending its status as stolen.[84] The relevant facts were these. As it prepared to hand over to Austrian authorities the art it had seized from Welz, the army's Reparations, Deliveries, and Restitution Division received a list of works, including several Schieles, that Heinrich Rieger had surrendered to Welz before being sent to his death at Theresienstadt. The list included a picture known as *Portrait of His Wife*, which (because Schiele did not inscribe titles on his works) RDR officials mistakenly concluded must refer to *Portrait of Wally*.[85] The officials accordingly combined *Wally* with the Rieger collection and, in December 1947, released it to the Austrian Monuments Office along with other works.

A few months later, as the RDR continued to search for items still missing from the Rieger collection, an army officer spotted the mistake after being informed by Welz that *Portrait of Wally* did not depict Schiele's wife. The RDR sent a letter to this effect to the Monuments Office, which ignored it. Following a 1950 proceeding before the Austrian restitution commission, the Rieger heirs received from the Monuments Office a number of works that, shortly afterward, they agreed to sell to the state-owned Austrian Gallery Belvedere. Though not referred to in the sale contract or the official documents approving the transaction, *Portrait of Wally* was among the works delivered to the Belvedere. The director of the Gallery, Karl Garzarolli, recognized the painting, writing "Wally Neuzil from Vienna" in his notes; despite the painting's absence from the list of works that were part of the transaction, Garzarolli added it to the Gallery's collection without notifying anyone of the mistake.[86]

In denying the museum's motion to dismiss at the outset of the case, the district court rejected the museum's contention that to adjudicate the action would impermissibly entail "revisiting and invalidating Austria's disposition of the painting to the Belvedere together with other property given to the Rieger heirs."[87] To begin with, the court declared, "it is far from clear that the doctrine applies to the act in question," because an "'act of state' must be a formal or official act by an actor with sovereign authority," and "*Wally* was never legally transferred to the Rieger heirs pursuant to an official Austrian government determination of ownership."[88] The

[84]The court addressed this issue in the portion of its opinion devoted to jurisdictional issues rather than the merits of the case. I discuss it here because the museum's act of state defense essentially required the court to decide whether it could consider the painting stolen in spite of the Austrian authorities' actions. On the act of state doctrine, see generally Harrison (2016); Keitner (2013).

[85]Schiele married Edith Anna Harms in 1915. *Portrait of Wally*, painted in 1912, depicts Valerie Neuzil.

[86]The intricacies of this course of events are recounted in the Amended Memorandum of Law, note 48 above, at 14–20, and in *Wally IV*, 663 F. Supp.2d at 239–42.

[87]*Wally III*, 2002 WL 553532 at *8.

[88]*Id.*

Monuments Office never "purposefully placed *Wally* with the state-owned Belvedere in derogation of Bondi's interest," but rather "erroneously attributed it to the Belvedere with the Rieger collection."[89] Such an inadvertent mistake, the court reasoned, did not qualify as one of the deliberate "public acts of a sovereign" to which the act of state doctrine applies.[90] Moreover, the court noted, the Monuments Office had no authority to make ownership determinations, as "Austrian law provided that the Restitution Commission would govern the return of property to its rightful owner."[91] There was good reason to believe, then, that the mistaken disposition of *Wally* was neither an "act" within the meaning of the act of state doctrine, nor one officially ratified by the "state" as the doctrine requires.[92]

Whether or not the formal prerequisites for the doctrine's application were met, its motivating objectives would not be served, continued the district court, by a ruling in the museum's favor. According to the Supreme Court, "the policies underlying the act of state doctrine should be considered in deciding whether, despite the doctrine's technical availability, it should nonetheless not be invoked."[93] In the present case, the district court declared, "the balance of interests counsels against applying the doctrine," because "there is no possible interference with the executive branch in its conduct of foreign relations."[94] This was so, in the court's view, for the simple reason that the executive branch was itself the plaintiff in the litigation, whose aim was nothing more than the implementation of Austrian law's own aim of restituting stolen artworks to their rightful owners. "An inquiry into the [Monuments Office's] shipment of a painting under the post-war Austrian regime would not impinge upon the executive's preeminence in foreign relations, particularly where the restoration of ownership has always been a professed goal of Austrian law and where it is the executive branch itself that brings this forfeiture action under United States law."[95]

After the completion of discovery the museum renewed its position, arguing that the act of state doctrine called for summary judgment in its favor. It pointed to several documents of official acts—approvals of the restitution of Rieger's collection to his heirs, of the Belvedere's acquisition of art from the Riegers, and of the later transfer of *Wally* to Leopold—and argued that these acts would in effect be set aside by *Wally*'s forfeiture, in violation of the act of state doctrine's command that the American judiciary avoid invalidating the public acts of foreign sovereigns. The district court disagreed, stating that "the Court is not being asked to *invalidate* any

---

[89] *Id.*

[90] *Id.* The court found it unnecessary to rule on the contention of the United States that, during the Allied occupation that lasted until 1955, the Austrian authorities lacked the requisite sovereignty to qualify as a "state" for purposes of the act of state doctrine.

[91] *Id.* at *9.

[92] *Id.*

[93] *Kirkpatrick*, 493 U.S. at 409.

[94] *Wally III*, 2002 WL 553532 at *9.

[95] *Id.*

action by an Austrian governmental authority, but only to determine the effect of such action, if any, on *Wally*'s ownership."[96] The act of state doctrine, the district court noted, "does not establish an exception for cases and controversies that may embarrass foreign governments, but merely requires that, in the process of deciding, the acts of foreign sovereigns taken within their own jurisdictions shall be deemed valid."[97] Here, the court stated, there was no indication that the official actors in question had either the intention or authority to extinguish Bondi's claim to ownership of *Wally*, so the court could assume their acts were valid while still allowing the litigation to proceed. Moreover, the court declared, the documents unearthed by the museum did not affect its earlier "determination that the balance of interests favors adjudication of this action," given that "the executive branch actively seeks adjudication of its claim and Austrian law favors restoration of ownership."[98]

2.4.3.4 Prescriptive Possession Under Austrian Law

The Leopold Museum's final argument that the painting could no longer be considered stolen rested on the principle of ownership by prescription, which provides that ownership of property may be acquired by virtue of its continuous good-faith possession for a specified period of years. This argument brought into play the property law of Austria, which as the district court noted was relevant to the determination of *Wally*'s "stolen" status, because "although federal law determines whether property has been stolen, local law 'controls the analytically prior issues of (a) whether any person or entity has a property interest in the item such that it can be stolen, and (b) whether the receiver of the item has a property interest in it.'"[99] Under the Austrian law of prescription, as the court understood it from an expert opinion, "a possessor of property may acquire title to that property if the possession is based on legal title (purchase or exchange) and extends throughout the statutory period"—at least three years—"accompanied by the possessor's belief that the possession is lawful."[100] The museum made two arguments: first, that the Belvedere acquired ownership of *Wally* through prescription, conferring good title which was then passed on to Leopold; second, even if the Belvedere did not do so, Leopold himself acquired ownership of the painting through prescription after taking possession of it.

The district court rejected both arguments because, in its view, neither the Gallery nor Leopold could satisfy the requirement of good faith. That requirement cannot be met, the court noted, "if, at any time during the prescription period, the

[96] *Wally IV*, 663 F. Supp.2d at 248.

[97] *Kirkpatrick*, 493 U.S. at 409, quoted in *Wally IV*, 663 F. Supp.2d at 248.

[98] *Wally IV*, 663 F. Supp.2d at 248.

[99] *Wally III*, 2002 WL 553532 at *16 (quoting *Wally I*, 105 F. Supp.2d at 292), quoted in *Wally IV*, 663 F. Supp.2d at 262.

[100] *Wally III*, 2002 WL 553532 at *17, quoted in *Wally IV*, 663 F. Supp.2d at 263. There were several possible prescription periods applicable to the case, the shortest of which was three years. See *id.* at 265.

possessor had any objective reason to doubt his claim, or if he was negligent in maintaining his belief of lawful possession."[101] In the event that "the possessor has an objective reason to doubt his ownership, he may regain confidence by performing an investigation sufficient to remove any such doubt, at which point the statutory period begins to run anew."[102] The Belvedere had ample reason to doubt its ownership of *Wally*, the court ruled, because the painting was nowhere listed among the works it was acquiring from the Rieger heirs, either in the purchase agreement or in the documents the Gallery submitted for approval of the purchase. The handwritten notes of Gallery director Garzarolli concerning the painting indicate that he "knew it depicted 'Wally Neuzil from Vienna' and no painting matching this description had been restituted to the Rieger heirs."[103] In addition, according to her written statement discovered among her papers after her death, during a 1948 trip to Vienna "Bondi visited the Belvedere and claimed ownership of *Wally*, thereby providing an independent objective reason for the Belvedere to doubt it owned the Painting."[104] While not providing conclusive proof of the matter, her statement was in the court's view "sufficient to satisfy the Government's threshold showing of probable cause to believe the Belvedere lacked the requisite confidence to acquire title to *Wally* by prescription."[105]

With the burden of proof thus shifted to the Leopold Museum, the court next ruled that the museum had failed to disprove the government's case by a preponderance of the evidence. Indeed, one of the principal pieces of evidence the museum submitted in its favor actually supported the government's case. The evidence in question was a 1950 letter from the Riegers' lawyer to a Belvedere official purportedly indicating, according to the museum, that *Wally* belonged to the Rieger collection. However, as the court noted, that same letter expressly refers to an earlier determination that the painting belonged to Bondi's collection, and states that the letter's author is "unable to examine the accuracy" of that determination.[106] "That alone should have been sufficient cause for the Belvedere to suspect that *Wally* was not part of the Rieger collection," the court declared; and yet "the Museum cites no evidence indicating that the Belvedere conducted any type of follow-up investigation or contacted Bondi."[107] Throughout its possession of the painting, therefore, until its 1954 transfer to Leopold, the Gallery was on notice that the painting may have belonged to Bondi.

The court also rejected the museum's argument that Leopold himself had acquired prescriptive ownership of the painting. "Under Austrian law," the court stated, "even slight negligence by an acquirer (through either *bona fide* purchase or

[101] *Wally III*, 2002 WL 553532 at *17, quoted in *Wally IV*, 663 F. Supp.2d at 263.

[102] *Wally IV*, 663 F. Supp.2d at 263.

[103] *Id.*

[104] *Id.*

[105] *Id.* at 264.

[106] Quoted in *id.* at 264.

[107] *Id.*

prescription) destroys the confidence necessary to gain title," meaning that if a purchaser should "have reason to suspect the seller's ownership, he is required either to return the item in question to its true owner or to conduct a reasonable investigation sufficient to 'credibly remove' any ownership doubts."[108] By Leopold's own admission, during their meeting in London "Bondi told him in 1953 that 'she had a claim to the picture' and asked for his help regaining it."[109] Later that year, when Leopold informed Belvedere director Garzarolli of Bondi's statement, the latter said he knew nothing of her purported ownership and repeatedly insisted that the painting had belonged to the Rieger heirs. Informed of these conversations in a 1954 meeting with Leopold, Bondi replied that she did not wish to discuss the matter further. That was the extent of Leopold's inquiry into her claim to the painting, the court declared, finding "his cursory investigation inadequate."[110]

In acquiring the painting, the court noted, Leopold had relied on Garzarolli's self-serving word alone and "sought no documentation whatsoever regarding *Wally*'s provenance, even though the last catalogue addressing the issue listed Bondi as its owner"—a catalogue which Leopold admitted to having studied.[111] "Nor did he contact either the Rieger heirs or their lawyers," and he "did not even ask Bondi why she thought the painting was hers or how she had lost it to begin with."[112] Rather, the court continued, "he simply asked the party from whom he hoped to acquire *Wally* to deal with the issue and looked no further."[113] Being an experienced art collector who knew Bondi was Jewish and was well aware of the Nazi traffic in stolen art, the court stated, Leopold "cannot be said to have reasonably dispelled any ownership doubts by relying solely on the seller's uncorroborated word."[114] His failure to look further into the matter "was plainly negligent and serves to vitiate any claim to good-faith acquisition he might otherwise have had."[115]

Furthermore, the court continued, Leopold never conducted an adequate investigation after acquiring the painting in 1954. In 1957, he engaged in an exchange of letters with Bondi's lawyer which, he argued, settled any doubts an owner in his position would reasonably have had concerning its ownership. This argument, the court responded, "makes little sense."[116] Upon learning in 1957 that he had bought *Wally* from the Belvedere without telling her, Bondi had her lawyer write Leopold that the painting belonged to her. Leopold replied that he had inferred from her inaction that she had no valid claim to the painting, and that Garzarolli had assured

---

[108] *Id.* at 265.

[109] *Id.* at 266 (quoting declaration of Rudolf Leopold).

[110] *Id.* at 267.

[111] *Id.*

[112] *Id.*

[113] *Id.*

[114] *Id.*

[115] *Id.* at 268.

[116] *Id.*

him that it had belonged to the Rieger heirs. In response, her lawyer wrote that Bondi had not waived her ownership rights and that the Rieger heirs had obtained *Wally* through a mistake. At this point Leopold arranged for Garzarolli himself to write the lawyer, reiterating the position that the painting had been lawfully acquired from the Riegers and Bondi had never laid claim to it before.

That brought the exchange to an end but, in the court's view, hardly settled the question of ownership. "That [Bondi's lawyer] did not send Dr. Leopold further correspondence on the matter does not mean that the doubts were laid to rest," the court declared.[117] Nor did the fact that Bondi never sued have any bearing on the ownership question, the court stated, because it knew of "no authority indicating that a possessor thus aware of an adverse ownership claim nonetheless holds the property in good faith unless the adverse party then sues for it."[118] The 1957 correspondence sufficed to perpetuate the doubts surrounding *Wally*'s ownership, which could only have been resolved by further inquiry by Leopold, who "admittedly investigated the matter no further."[119] As a result, he did not acquire ownership by prescription at any time during his subsequent possession, and *Wally* remained stolen property when it was imported to the United States in 1997.

2.4.4 The Museum's Knowledge

The final question for the court was the problem of *scienter*, one of the elements of a violation of the National Stolen Property Act. It was not enough for the government to show, as it had, that the painting was stolen property; the government, the district court stated, "must also show that the Museum imported *Wally* into the United States *knowing* it was either stolen or converted."[120] The museum had conceded, and the district court agreed, that the knowledge held by Leopold, its director, could be imputed to the museum itself.[121] The question therefore was whether Leopold knew the painting was stolen or converted.[122]

---

[117] *Id.*

[118] *Id.* at 269.

[119] *Id.*

[120] *Id.* at 269 (emphasis in original).

[121] *Wally III*, 2002 WL 553532 at *24. The court declined the museum's later request to revisit this issue. *Wally IV*, 663 F. Supp.2d at 273–74.

[122] As the district court noted, the National Stolen Property Act applies to property known to have been "stolen or converted," where conversion is defined as "the 'unauthorized exercise of dominion and control over another's personal property, to exclusion of or inconsistent with the rights of the owner.'" *Wally IV*, 663 F. Supp.2d at 273 (brackets omitted) (quoting United States v. Smith, 686 F.2d 234, 242 (5th Cir. 1982). The government argued both that the museum knew *Wally* to have been stolen and that it knew the painting to have been converted. The court devoted most of its analysis to the former contention, giving only passing attention to the latter (see note 137 below).

The court began its analysis by describing the nature of what must be proved in this context. On one hand, the court noted, negligence is not the same as knowledge, and establishing *scienter* requires more than showing a lack of due care. The court's earlier conclusion that "Leopold did not perform an adequate investigation to obviate reasonable suspicion that *Wally* belonged to Bondi" did not "compel a finding that he knew someone stole it from her."[123] On the other hand, it was not necessary for the government to show that Leopold knew with certainty that the painting had been stolen. "The Painting is also subject to forfeiture," the court stated, "if Dr. Leopold was aware of a high probability that *Wally* was stolen and deliberately looked the other way."[124] An earlier decision had stated that "deliberate ignorance and positive knowledge are equally culpable," and that "to act 'knowingly,' therefore, is not necessarily to act only with positive knowledge, but also to act with an awareness of the high probability of the existence of the fact in question."[125] Further, the court noted, the government could "rely on circumstantial evidence to show that Dr. Leopold had the requisite knowledge to render *Wally* forfeit."[126]

The Government's Evidence The government directed the court's attention to several clues that Leopold knew, or strongly suspected and intentionally refrained from verifying, that the painting was stolen. Some of this evidence we have already encountered in the preceding discussion, including the fact that Bondi informed Leopold in 1953 of her position that the painting, then hanging in the Belvedere, was rightfully hers; Leopold's awareness that Jewish art dealers like her had seen their collections looted by the Nazis and placed in circulation on the market; Leopold's refusal to look into *Wally*'s provenance when purchasing it from the Belvedere in 1954, beyond accepting at face value its director Garzarolli's self-serving assurance that its chain of title was clean; and his failure to even minimally investigate when Bondi's lawyer informed him in 1957 that the painting belonged to her. There were, however, other indicators, not yet discussed, of what the government termed "Leopold's guilty knowledge" of the painting's stolen status.[127]

There was, first, the haste with which Leopold acquired *Wally* for himself after Bondi entrusted him with recovering it for her. Rather than slowing down his purchase of the painting, learning of Bondi's claim seemed to make him move more quickly, as if he knew there was a problem and wanted to get hold of the painting before anyone realized it was not the Belvedere's to sell. A government document approving the exchange of *Wally* for art owned by Leopold indicated that the transaction was to be expedited, and that Leopold had threatened "to withdraw

[123] *Wally IV*, 663 F. Supp.2d at 269.

[124] *Id.*

[125] United States v. Reyes, 302 F.3d 48, 54 (2d Cir. 2002), quoted in *Wally IV*, 663 F. Supp.2d at 269.

[126] *Wally IV*, 663 F. Supp. 2d at 269.

[127] *Wally IV*, 664 F. Supp.2d at 270.

his offer if the exchange were further delayed."[128] The government contended that Leopold's "rush to conclude the exchange" was, as the court stated, evidence of "his awareness that he doubted whether the Rieger heirs, and thus the Belvedere, really owned *Wally*."[129]

There was, second, Leopold's evasiveness toward Bondi after he had acquired the painting. After learning in 1957 that he had gotten the painting from the museum, Bondi encountered him at an exhibition in London. She "asked him at once," she later reported in a letter, "whether he had brought [the] picture with him. He was very self-conscious and said that must be settled in some way, but unfortunately he was called away immediately."[130] Afterward he did nothing to verify the provenance of the painting, and in correspondence with Bondi's lawyer offered nothing but Garzarolli's unsupported statements on the subject.

Third were the shifting stories Leopold told in his published writings about *Wally*'s provenance. In a 1972 book about Schiele, which professed to offer the complete provenance of the works it discussed, Leopold listed only one person (Emil Toepfer) as having owned *Wally* before he did.[131] No mention was made of the Rieger family in connection with *Wally*, even though the book contained an extensive discussion of the Schiele paintings and drawings that had belonged to Heinrich Rieger. Then, in 1995, as the Leopold Museum was being created, Leopold wrote an updated provenance for *Wally* in which for the first time he listed Rieger and his heirs as being among the painting's previous owners. This alteration of the provenance, the government contended, was "an overt attempt to legitimate his ownership through sheer fabrication."[132] Had he genuinely believed the Riegers to be in the chain of title, the government asserted, Leopold would have included them in the 1972 book. That he did so only in 1995 indicated, the government claimed, that Leopold "knew *Wally* never belonged to the Rieger heirs but wanted to forestall any uncomfortable questions about the Museum's title to the painting."[133]

These items of evidence, the court concluded, were "sufficient to establish probable cause to believe that Dr. Leopold knew, or consciously avoided knowing, that *Wally* was stolen."[134] The burden then shifted to the Leopold Museum to disprove the government's case by a preponderance of the evidence.

---

[128]Quoted in *id.* The offeror was not identified by name, but the government argued that it must be Leopold.

[129]*Id.*

[130]Quoted in *id.*

[131]In his *catalogue raisonné* of Schiele's works, Otto Kallir listed Emil Toepfer as *Wally*'s first owner, followed by Richard Lanyi and then Lea Bondi. Kallir (1966). Leopold's 1972 book claimed to correct errors in the Kallir catalogue. See *Wally IV*, 663 F. Supp.2d at 270.

[132]*Wally IV*, 663 F. Supp.2d at 271.

[133]*Id.*

[134]*Id.*

The Museum's Evidence The museum offered three types of evidence in support of its position. First and foremost was the testimony of Leopold, the only participant in the underlying events who was still alive, to the effect that he genuinely believed *Wally* was not stolen. In his declaration offered in connection with the parties' summary judgment motions, Leopold stated that Bondi never told him the painting was stolen; that he arranged for Bondi to meet with Belvedere director Garzarolli, but she failed to do this or take any other steps to recover the painting from the museum; that when he asked her why not, in 1954, she told him to drop the subject; and that he believed Garzarolli's assurances that the Gallery had acquired the painting from its legitimate owners, the Rieger heirs. This course of events, Leopold claimed, convinced him that his title to the painting was good.

Second, the museum pointed out that Leopold made no attempt to hide his possession of *Wally* after acquiring it. He displayed it at numerous exhibitions in multiple countries; indeed it was at one such exhibition in 1957 that Bondi first learned he had obtained the painting. Had he believed the painting was stolen, the museum argued, he would hardly have called so much public attention to his possession of it.

Third, the museum pointed to explanations Leopold offered for the discrepant provenances he had created for *Wally* over the years. The list of *Wally*'s owners in the 1972 book was not intended to be complete, but only to list the first owner followed by the most recent owner. When he added the Rieger heirs to the chain of owners, he did so at the urging of an assistant who suggested expanding the written provenance to include intermediate owners; he "was not looking to falsify *Wally*'s history, but rather added information he sincerely believed to be true."[135]

The Need for a Jury Trial Given the conflicting evidence, whose evaluation presumably depended on determining Leopold's credibility as a witness, the court held that a jury trial was necessary on the question whether he knew, or consciously avoided knowing, of the painting's stolen status. Neither the government nor the museum was entitled to summary judgment on the issue, for each had come forward with evidence that, if credited by a jury, would warrant a verdict in its favor. "If, as the Museum contends, Dr. Leopold actually believed that the Painting was not stolen," the court remarked, "he cannot be said to have consciously avoided that fact. If, on the other hand, he purposely rushed his acquisition of *Wally* because he knew it belonged to Bondi and sought to conceal this fact in his later publications, Dr. Leopold undoubtedly had the requisite knowledge to render *Wally* forfeit."[136] Each side had adduced sufficient evidence that, according to the court, "I cannot say that, making all reasonable inferences in favor of the nonmoving party with respect to each motion [for summary judgment], there is only one choice for a reasonable trier of fact on this issue," meaning that "the question is properly one for the jury."[137] Therefore, because "the Government has met its threshold burden of

---

[135] *Id.* at 272.
[136] *Id.* at 272–73.
[137] *Id.* at 273.

showing probable cause to believe Dr. Leopold knew *Wally* was stolen, the Museum will bear the burden of proving at trial that he did not."[138]

2.5 Epilogue

The trial of *United States v. Portrait of Wally* was scheduled for July 26, 2010. Rudolf Leopold, director for life of the Leopold Museum, died in June 2010. Shortly after his death, the board of the Leopold Museum contacted the Bondi heirs and offered to buy *Wally* from them for $19 million, following an appraisal that had put the painting's value at approximately that amount. The offer was accepted, and the government, the museum, and the heirs agreed to settle the forfeiture action a few days before trial was set to begin, bringing nearly thirteen years of litigation to a close. Schiele's *Portrait of Wally* was sent back to Austria in August 2010 and hangs in the Leopold Museum.[139]

References

Bridy, Annemarie. 2014. Carpe Omnia: Civil Forfeiture in the War on Drugs and the War on Piracy. *Arizona State Law Journal* 46: 683–628.

Dobrzynski, Judith H. 1997. The Zealous Collector—a Special Report: A Singular Passion for Collecting Art, One Way or Another. *New York Times*, December 24.

Dodge, William S. 2015. International Comity in American Law. *Columbia Law Review* 115: 2071–2104.

Harrison, John. 2016. The American Act of State Doctrine. *Georgetown Journal of International Law* 47: 507–571.

Henry, Marilyn. 2010. Justice Is Done, Finally. *Jerusalem Post*, July 24.

Hickley, Catherine, and Zoe Schneeweiss. 2010. Leopold Pays $10 Million to Keep Schiele's "Wally." *Bloomberg News*, July 21.

Kallir, Otto. 1966. *Egon Schiele: Oeuvre Catalogue of the Paintings*. New York: Crown.

Kaye, Lawrence M. 2010. Art Loans and Immunity from Seizure in the United States and the United Kingdom. *International Journal of Cultural Property* 17: 335–359.

Keitner, Chimène. 2013. Adjudicating Acts of State. In *Foreign Affairs Litigation in United States Courts*, ed. John Norton Moore, 49–66. Leiden: Martinus Nijhoff.

Kline, Thomas R. 2010. Portrait of Notoriety. *Wall Street Journal*, July 27.

Kreder, Jennifer Anglim. 2005. The Choice Between Civil and Criminal Remedies in Stolen Art Litigation. *Vanderbilt Journal of Transnational Law* 38: 1199–1252.

———. 2011. Executive Weapons to Combat Infection of the Art Market. *Washington University Law Review* 88: 1353–1363.

[138] *Id.*

[139] On the settlement, see Henry (2010), Hickley and Schneeweiss (2010), and Kline (2010). Details of the case's resolution are presented in the documentary film *Portrait of Wally: The Face that Launched a Thousand Lawsuits* (P.O.W. Productions, 2012).

Kurtz, Michael J. 2006. *America and the Return of Nazi Contraband: The Recovery of Europe's Cultural Treasures*. Cambridge: Cambridge University Press.
Mueller, Christopher B., and Laird C. Kirkpatrick. 2012. *Evidence*. 5th ed. New York: Aspen.
O'Donnell, Thérèse. 2011. The Restitution of Holocaust Looted Art and Transitional Justice: the Perfect Storm or the Raft of the Medusa? *European Journal of International Law* 22: 49–80.
Piety, Tamara. 1991. Scorched Earth: How the Expansion of Civil Asset Forfeiture Doctrine Has Laid Waste to Due Process. *University of Miami Law Review* 45: 911–976.
Presidential Advisory Commission on Holocaust Assets in the United States. 2000. *Plunder and Restitution: The U.S. and Holocaust Victims' Assets*. Washington, DC: U.S. Government Printing Office.
Spiegler, Howard N. 2007. *Portrait of Wally*; The U.S. Government's Role in Recovering Holocaust Looted Art. In *Holocaust Restitution: The Litigation and Its Legacy*, ed. Michael J. Bazyler and Roger P. Alford, 280–287. New York: New York University Press.
van Woudenberg, Nout. 2012. *State Immunity and Cultural Objects on Loan*. Leiden: Martinus Nijhoff.

Cases

Banco Nacional de Cuba v. Sabbatino, 376 U.S. 398 (1964)
In re Maxwell Communications Corp., 93 F.3d 1036 (2d Cir. 1996)
In the Matter of the Grand Jury Subpoena Duces Tecum Served on the Museum of Modern Art, 93 N.Y.2d 729 (N.Y. 1999)
Oetjen v. Central Leather Co., 246 U.S. 297 (1918)
Regina v. Dolan, 29 Eng. Law & Eq. 533 (1855)
Regina v. Schmidt, L.R. 1 Cr. Cas. Res. 15 (1866)
Robins Island Pres. Fund, Inc. v. Southold Development Corp., 959 F.2d 409 (2d Cir. 1992)
Spatola v. United States, 925 F.2d 615 (2d Cir. 1991)
United States v. $2,500 in U.S. Currency, 689 F.2d 10 (2d Cir. 1982)
United States v. $250,000 in U.S. Currency, 808 F.2d 895 (1st Cir. 1987)
United States v. An Antique Platter of Gold, 991 F. Supp. 222 (S.D.N.Y. 1997)
United States v. Long Cove Seafood, Inc., 582 F.2d 159 (2d Cir. 1978)
United States v. Muzii, 676 F.2d 919 (2d Cir. 1982)
United States v. Parcel of Property, 337 F.3d 225 (2d Cir. 2003)
United States v. Portrait of Wally, a Painting by Egon Schiele, 105 F. Supp.2d 208 (S.D.N.Y. 2000); 2000 WL 1890403 (S.D.N.Y. 2000); 2002 WL 553532 (S.D.N.Y. 2002); 663 F. Supp.2d 232 (S.D.N.Y. 2009)
United States v. Reyes, 302 F.3d 48 (2d Cir. 2002)
United States v. Schultz, 333 F.3d 393 (2d Cir. 2003)
United States v. Smith, 686 F.2d 234 (5th Cir. 1982)
United States v. Turley, 352 U.S. 407 (1957)
W.S. Kirkpatrick & Co., Inc. v. Environmental Tectonics Corp., Int., 493 U.S. 400 (1990)

Chapter 3
Altmann v. Republic of Austria

3.1 Background

In 1903, Gustav Klimt was commissioned to paint a portrait of Adele Bloch-Bauer, a member of the Viennese social and intellectual elite famous for its patronage of modern art in the late nineteenth and early twentieth centuries.[1] The resulting work, *Adele Bloch-Bauer I* (1907), often nicknamed the Woman in Gold, is considered one of the great masterpieces of European modernism. Bloch-Bauer died in 1925, leaving a will in which she asked her husband Ferdinand Bloch to donate five Klimt paintings in their house, including *Adele Bloch-Bauer I*, to the Austrian Gallery Belvedere, the country's national museum. When her will was probated that year, however, the court determined that the paintings belonged to Ferdinand and were not part of Adele's estate. Ferdinand stated during the probate proceedings that he planned to write a will in accordance with Adele's wishes, but never acted on this intention. His last will, written shortly before his death in 1945, left everything to his nephew and two nieces.

Following the Anschluss in 1938, Ferdinand fled to Switzerland. Nazi officials aryanized his business and seized the extensive art collection at his home, selling off hundreds of items and taking several nineteenth-century paintings for Hitler and Göring's private collections. Erich Führer, the SS lawyer in charge of liquidating the estate, took possession of the six Klimts still belonging to Ferdinand, including the five mentioned in Adele's will. He traded two of these, including *Adele Bloch-Bauer I*, to the Belvedere in 1941, followed by a third in 1943; he sold a fourth to the Vienna City Museum, which later transferred it to the Gallery, and a fifth made its way into the hands of a private dealer, who eventually gave it to the Gallery. The sixth he kept in his home, where Ferdinand's nephew personally retrieved it after the Nazi government fell.[2] After the war, asked by Ferdinand's heirs to return the

[1]See generally Beller (1989) and Schorske (1979). On the Bloch-Bauer family, see Müller and Tatzkow (2010), pp. 156–172, and Krejci (2005).

[2]The wartime fate of the Klimts is detailed in Petropoulos (2005).

B.L. Hay, *Nazi-Looted Art and the Law*, DOI 10.1007/978-3-319-64967-2_3

Klimts in its possession, the Austrian Gallery refused, falsely claiming to have received them in a pre-war bequest from Adele and Ferdinand.[3] In 1948, at the urging of Belvedere director Karl Garzarolli, the Austrian government demanded that the heirs "donate" to the Belvedere the Klimt they had retrieved, and relinquish their rights to the ones already in the Gallery's possession, as a condition of obtaining export permits for other artworks in Ferdinand's collection that they had managed to recover.[4] Believing that recovery of the Klimts was hopeless, a lawyer acting on the heirs' behalf surrendered the one they had and signed documents acknowledging the Belvedere's purported ownership of the others.

In 1998, following the scandal caused by the seizure of Schiele's *Portrait of Wally* in New York, discussed in the previous chapter, the Austrian federal minister opened the Austrian Gallery's archives to allow research into the provenance of the national collections. Shortly afterward, investigative journalist Hubertus Czernin published a series of articles demonstrating that Austria's museums contained many artworks that the government had stolen or extorted from Jewish families during and after the war.[5] The articles revealed that *Adele Bloch-Bauer I*, which the Belvedere's catalogues reported as having been received as a gift from the Bloch-Bauer family in 1936, had in fact been traded to the Gallery by the SS lawyer in 1941, accompanied by a letter signed "Heil Hitler." In response to this and other revelations, Austria enacted a new restitution law calling for the return of artworks to individuals who had been coerced into surrendering them in exchange for export permits. A committee of government officials and art historians was created to administer the new law.

Maria Altmann, Ferdinand's niece and one of the heirs named in his will, had fled Austria in 1938 and eventually settled in Los Angeles. She had known Adele as a child, and had long believed that her aunt's famous portrait and the other Klimt paintings at the Belvedere had been donated to the state well before the war. Upon learning of the journalist's exposé, Altmann filed a claim with the restitution committee in Vienna, seeking to recover the six Klimt paintings and other artworks that had been taken from her uncle during the war. Her claim stirred up considerable political opposition because the paintings, particularly *Adele Bloch-Bauer I*, were widely regarded as national treasures. The restitution committee declined to return

---

[3]While telling the heirs that he had full documentation of the supposed gift, Gallery director Karl Garzarolli privately wrote to his predecessor that he was "in an extremely difficult position" because "there is no mention [of the gift] in the files of the Austrian Gallery," adding that "I cannot understand why even during the Nazi era an incontestable declaration of gift in favor of the state was never obtained from Ferdinand Bloch-Bauer." Stating that "the situation is growing into a sea snake," he encouraged his predecessor to "stick by me" in this "not exactly danger-free situation." (Quoted in *Altmann*, 142 F. Supp.2d at 1194 n. 8.)

[4]Garzarolli encouraged Otto Demus, the head of the Federal Monuments Office, to withhold export permits for Ferdinand's collection "for tactical reasons" until the heirs relinquished their claim to the Klimts. Demus acted accordingly (See *Altmann*, 142 F. Supp.2d at 1194–95).

[5]Some of the articles were collected in Czernin (1999). On other property seized from the Jews of Vienna during the war and never returned, see Decker (1984) and Walzer and Temple (2001).

the Klimt paintings, taking the position that the request in Adele's will had created a binding legal obligation for Ferdinand to bequeath the paintings to the Belvedere in his own will. One committee member resigned in protest and announced that she had been ordered by senior government officials to vote against the paintings' return. The Austrian government rejected Altmann's proposal to submit the matter to arbitration.

In 1999, Altmann filed suit in the Austrian courts seeking to recover the six paintings. Under Austrian law, she was required to post a bond equal to roughly one percent of the amount in controversy; because the value of the paintings was estimated at $150 million, the court informed her that her suit could not proceed unless she posted $1.6 million. Following her request for a waiver, the court reduced the bond to $135,000, which represented all of her liquid assets. The Austrian government appealed the reduction, arguing that Altmann should be ordered to sell her other property to post bond. At this point she abandoned the lawsuit in Austria and turned to the American courts.[6]

3.2 Proceedings

Altmann filed suit against the Republic of Austria and the Austrian Gallery Belvedere in 2000, bringing the action in federal court in Los Angeles.[7] In her complaint, Altmann sought a declaration that the six Klimts in the museum's possession rightfully belonged to Ferdinand's heirs under the 1998 Austrian restitution law, under the common law, and under international law; an order rescinding any agreement the heirs' lawyer made to surrender their claims to the paintings in 1948, on grounds of duress, mistake, and lack of authority; and recovery of the paintings along with damages and disgorgement of the profits earned from their wrongful retention. In support of her choice of the California forum, Altmann pointed to the following facts: Austria owned real property, maintained a consular office, and promoted Austrian filmmakers in Los Angeles; the Austrian Gallery advertised in the United States and attracted many American visitors; it published museum guidebooks that it had marketed in the United States, featuring *Adele Bloch-Bauer I* on the cover; and it had loaned that painting to American museums in the past.

Austria moved to dismiss the action on a variety of jurisdictional grounds. The strongest of these, and the one that consumed the most judicial attention because of its difficulty, was that the action was barred by sovereign immunity. On this issue, the district court made two rulings: first, the availability of sovereign immunity in

[6]For journalistic accounts of the events surrounding the case, see Bamsey (2006), Kun (2006), and O'Connor (2013). Cinematic treatments include *Stealing Klimt* (Films of Record 2007), *Adele's Wish* (Calendar Films 2008), and *The Woman in Gold* (BBC Films 2015).

[7]For convenience, we refer to the two defendants jointly as "Austria" in the discussion to follow.

the case was governed by the Foreign Sovereign Immunities Act of 1976, even though the government conduct complained of occurred in the 1940s, long before that statute was enacted; and second, Austria was stripped of immunity by FSIA's expropriation exception, which permits courts to hear lawsuits concerning property taken in violation of international law, if the foreign state defendant owns the property and engages in commerce in the United States.[8] Turning to the other grounds for dismissal raised by Austria, the court further ruled that it had the authority to adjudicate the case under the rules of personal jurisdiction supplied by the due process clause of the United States constitution, and also under applicable federal venue rules; that the doctrine of forum non conveniens did not warrant dismissal; and that the case could go forward even though Ferdinand's other heirs had not been made parties to the lawsuit.

Austria took an immediate appeal to the court of appeals for the Ninth Circuit, which upheld the lower court's rulings in full, though with certain differences in reasoning.[9] Austria then successfully petitioned for a writ of certiorari in the Supreme Court, which confined its review to a single issue that had been a point of contention among the federal courts in numerous cases: whether, and to what extent, the Foreign Sovereign Immunities Act of 1976 applies to claims of sovereign immunity for governmental conduct that preceded its enactment. In 2004, the Court ruled by a 6-3 vote that the statute governs all post-enactment assertions of immunity, regardless of when the underlying conduct took place.[10] The effect of the Court's decision was to let stand the court of appeals' ruling that Altmann's lawsuit could go forward. The case was accordingly remanded to the district court for further proceedings. A year later, the parties agreed to submit the dispute to binding arbitration.

3.3 Evolution of Foreign State Immunity

From a jurisprudential standpoint, the most significant issue engaged by the American courts in the Altmann litigation was the problem of determining the law applicable to Austria's assertion of sovereign immunity[11]—more precisely, determining whether the availability of immunity was governed by the Foreign Sovereign Immunities Act of 1976, which exposed foreign states to suit for expropriation claims, or was instead governed by the law prevalent in the 1940s, which generally

[8]Altmann v. Republic of Austria, 142 F.Supp.2d 1187 (C.D. Cal. 2001).

[9]Altmann v. Republic of Austria, 317 F.3d 954 (9th Cir. 2003). Though the denial of a motion to dismiss is generally not an appealable order, the court of appeals had jurisdiction under the collateral order doctrine, which allows an immediate appeal when a district court rejects a claim of sovereign immunity. See, for example, Gupta v. Thai Airways International, Ltd., 487 F.3d 759, 764 (9th Cir. 2007).

[10]Republic of Austria v. Altmann, 541 U.S. 699 (2004).

[11]The terms "state immunity" and "sovereign immunity" are used interchangeably.

accorded foreign states absolute immunity from suit in American courts. Deciding whether the Act's restrictive approach to immunity applied retrospectively to claims connected to the Second World War and its aftermath forced the Supreme Court to confront thorny questions concerning the retrospective application of legislation. The Court's conclusion that the statute governed such claims settled a matter that had long troubled American courts in international cases. To situate the problem we can begin, as did the Court, by briefly recapitulating the history of the judicial approach to foreign sovereign immunity in American law, which furnished the foundation for the Court's ruling.[12]

As the Court observed, the document generally viewed as the source of the American judiciary's foreign sovereign immunity jurisprudence is Chief Justice Marshall's opinion in the 1812 case *The Schooner Exchange v. McFaddon.*[13] In that admiralty case, American citizens sought to establish their ownership of a French naval ship that had dropped anchor in an American port. The Court ordered the claim dismissed on the basis of France's sovereign immunity, holding that it was "a principle of public law, that national ships of war, entering the port of a friendly power open for their reception, are to be considered as exempted by the consent of that power from its jurisdiction."[14] This principle, Marshall reasoned, flowed from the practice for reciprocal comity among nations. It was true, he stated, the United States had the power, if it chose, to subject the French ship to its jurisdiction, because the "jurisdiction of the nation within its own territory is necessarily exclusive and absolute" and "is susceptible of no limitation not imposed by itself."[15]

Nonetheless, the United States and other nations had made an unspoken agreement to waive jurisdiction over one another in certain cases. "The world being composed of distinct sovereignties," Marshall stated, "possessing equal rights and equal independence, whose mutual benefit is promoted by intercourse with each other, and by an interchange of those good offices which humanity dictates and its wants require, all sovereigns have consented to a relaxation in practice, in cases under certain peculiar circumstances, of that absolute and complete jurisdiction within their respective territories which sovereignty confers."[16] In particular, each sovereign, upon entering the territory of another, does so on the understanding that "the immunities belonging to his independent sovereign station, though not expressly stipulated, are reserved by implication, and will be extended to him."[17] Such was settled usage, according to Marshall; and a "nation would justly be considered as violating its faith, although that faith might not be expressly plighted"

---

[12]On the development of foreign state immunity in American law, see Giuttari (1970), Vandenberg (2006), and Whytock (2013). On the doctrine's development in international law more generally, see Badr (1984), Marasinghe (1991), and Sinclair (1980).

[13]11 U.S. (7 Cranch) 116 (1812).

[14]*Id.* at 145–46.

[15]*Id.* at 136.

[16]*Id.*

[17]*Id.* at 137.

if it were to "suddenly and without previous notice, exercise its territorial powers in a manner not consonant to the usages and received obligations of the civilized world."[18]

To be sure, continued Marshall, this immunity extended only to the property and personal representatives of foreign sovereigns, and not to parties acting in a private capacity. "When," his opinion declared, "private individuals of one nation spread themselves through another as business or caprice may direct, mingling indiscriminately with the inhabitants of that other, or when merchant vessels enter for the purposes of trade, it would be obviously inconvenient and dangerous to society, and would subject the laws to continual infraction, and the government to degradation, if such individuals or merchants did not owe temporary and local allegiance, and were not amenable to the jurisdiction of the country."[19] The foreign sovereign, he added, has no reason to seek immunity for such private individuals, because they "are not employed by him, nor are they engaged in national pursuits"; the "implied license, therefore, under which they enter can never be construed to grant such exemption."[20] In the case of a naval ship, in contrast, the implied license under which the ship enters friendly waters should be construed "as containing an exemption from the jurisdiction of the sovereign, within whose territory she claims the rites of hospitality."[21] The implied promise of immunity can be lifted by the host country, whose sovereign control over its territory is absolute, but the judiciary should not lightly assume that this power has been exercised. Until "such power be exerted in a manner not to be misunderstood, the sovereign cannot be considered as having imparted to the ordinary tribunals a jurisdiction, which it would be a breach of faith to exercise."[22] In Marshall's telling, then, foreign sovereign immunity was what in today's terminology we would call a default rule, for courts to follow unless they are explicitly advised otherwise by the appropriate authorities in government.

Marshall's opinion in *Schooner Exchange* furnished the template for the American judicial approach to foreign sovereign immunity, which was to view immunity as a matter of "grace and comity" in furtherance of sound foreign relations; and because the legislative and executive branches were responsible for the nation's foreign affairs, the judiciary's stance was one by which it "'consistently . . . deferred to the decisions of the political branches—in particular, those of the Executive Branch—on whether to take jurisdiction' over particular actions against foreign sovereigns and their instrumentalities."[23] For example, in *Ex parte Republic of Peru*,[24] an admiralty claim was brought against a ship owned by the Peruvian

[18] *Id.* at 137.

[19] *Id.* at 144.

[20] *Id.*

[21] *Id.*

[22] *Id.* at 146.

[23] *Altmann*, 541 U.S. at 689 (quoting Verlinden B.V. v. Central Bank of Nigeria, 461 U.S. 480, 486 (1983)).

[24] 318 U.S. 578 (1943).

government for breaching a contract to ship sugar. Seeking to resolve the dispute through diplomatic channels, the United States Department of State requested that the courts accord immunity to Peru. Viewing the case as sufficiently important to warrant its immediate intervention, the Supreme Court ordered dismissal of the case, invoking the "overriding principle" that "courts may not so exercise their jurisdiction, by the seizure and detention of the property of a friendly sovereign, as to embarrass the executive arm of the government in conducting foreign relations."[25] In particular, the Court stated, "the judicial seizure of the vessel of a friendly foreign state is so serious a challenge to its dignity, and may so affect our friendly relations with it, that courts are required to accept and follow the executive that the vessel is immune."[26] Similarly, in *Republic of Mexico v. Hoffmann*,[27] the Court stated that the courts must follow the State Department's determination that a given case involving a foreign state is barred by sovereign immunity, and that if no such determination has been made, the courts must attempt to establish whether the claim of immunity is consonant with the department's settled policy. Until the 1950s, this approach resulted in a rule of virtually absolute immunity for foreign states, because the State Department "followed a policy of requesting immunity in all actions against friendly sovereigns."[28]

In a 1952 document that has come to be known as the Tate Letter, the State Department announced that it was abandoning this policy in favor of one more in line with contemporary trends in international law. "A study of the law of sovereign immunity reveals the existence of two conflicting concepts of sovereign immunity," the Letter stated. "According to the classical or absolute theory of sovereign immunity, a sovereign cannot, without his consent, be made a respondent in the courts of another sovereign. According to the new or restrictive theory of sovereign immunity, the immunity of the sovereign is recognized with regard to sovereign or public acts (*jure imperii*) of a state, but not with respect to private acts (*jure gestionis*)."[29] Enumerating the many countries outside the Soviet bloc that in recent decades had embraced the restrictive theory, and expressing the view that "the widespread and increasing practice on the part of governments of engaging in commercial activities makes necessary a practice which will enable persons doing business with them to have their rights determined in the courts," the Letter stated that the State Department would henceforth "follow the restrictive theory of sovereign immunity in the consideration of requests of foreign government for a grant of sovereign immunity."[30]

---

[25]*Peru*, 318 U.S. at 588.

[26]*Id.*

[27]324 U.S. 30 (1945).

[28]*Altmann*, 541 U.S. at 689.

[29]Letter from Jack B. Tate, Acting Legal Adviser, U.S. Dept. of State, to Acting U.S. Attorney General Phillip B. Perlman, May 19, 1952, published in 26 Dept. of State Bulletin 984 (1952), reprinted in Alfred Dunhill of London, Inc. v. Republic of Cuba, 425 U.S. 682, 711–15 (1976). See generally Dobrovir (1968).

[30]Tate Letter, 26 Dept. of State Bulletin at 985.

However sound in theory, this 1952 change of policy proved difficult to implement in practice. Foreign nations exerted diplomatic pressure on the State Department to grant immunity even in cases not covered by the restrictive theory; and political considerations led to grants of such immunity for some countries, but not others. When the State Department did not receive an immunity request, the courts would have to rule on a claim of sovereign immunity on their own, with no clear guidance on the criteria to be applied. This process tended to "throw immunity determinations into some disarray," as the Supreme Court later observed, as "sovereign immunity determinations were made in two different branches, subject to a variety of factors, sometimes including diplomatic considerations. Not surprisingly, the governing standards were neither clear nor uniformly applied."[31] Concerns arose over disparate treatment of foreign states and also over justice toward litigants who, according to the regime's critics, were left to wonder whether their cases were being decided on legal rather than political grounds.[32]

To address these problems, Congress in 1976 enacted the Foreign Sovereign Immunities Act, whose passage "followed ten years of academic and legislative effort to establish a consistent framework for the determination of sovereign immunity when foreign nations are haled into our courts."[33] The statute's central purposes, its drafters explained, were to codify the restrictive theory of sovereign immunity and to transfer immunity determinations from the executive branch to the judiciary, bringing the United States into greater conformity both with the rule of law and with the practice of other countries in which sovereign immunity decisions "are made exclusively by the courts and not by a foreign affairs agency."[34] The Act accordingly creates a "set of legal standards governing claims of immunity in every civil action against a foreign state or its political subdivisions, agencies, or instrumentalities."[35]

For purposes of the Altmann litigation, the most important of these standards was the so-called expropriation exception, which provides that a foreign state does not enjoy sovereign immunity against a claim for property taken in violation of international law, provided that the state owns the property and conducts commercial activity in the United States.[36] Altmann contended that Austria's extortion of title to the Klimt paintings in 1948 fell within the terms of this exception. A threshold issue in the adjudication of her claim, however, was whether FSIA,

[31] *Verlinden*, 461 U.S. at 488, quoted in *Altmann*, 541 U.S. at 690–91.

[32] H.R. Rep. No. 94–1487 (1976), reprinted in 1976 U.S. Code Cong. & Admin. News 6604, 6606.

[33] *Altmann*, 541 U.S. at 716 (dissenting opinion).

[34] H.R. Rep. No. 94–1487, reprinted in 1976 U.S. Code Cong. & Admin. News at 6605–06. On institutional competence and foreign state immunity determinations, see Chilton and Whytock (2015).

[35] *Verlinden*, 461 U.S. at 488. On contemporary foreign state immunity doctrine in international law, see generally Cassese (2005), Fox and Webb (2013), and Shaw (1997).

[36] Foreign Sovereign Immunities Act, 28 U.S.C. §1605(a)(3).

including its expropriation exception, could be applied at all to events that had long preceded its enactment.

3.4 Temporal Reach of the Foreign Sovereign Immunities Act

By the time Altmann brought her lawsuit, the question of FSIA's application to pre-enactment occurrences had long vexed the federal judiciary, which had been confronted with numerous claims against foreign states for asserted wrongs committed many decades earlier. The courts could not agree on the matter. Some had taken the position that there was no temporal restriction on the statute's reach, for example in the case of a lawsuit that was allowed to go forward against Poland for the expropriation of property belonging to Jews during and immediately after the Second World War, and the case of a lawsuit allowed against Germany for damages sustained by a concentration camp inmate who had been forced into slave labor during the war.[37] Others had taken the position that FSIA applied only to lawsuits based on events occurring after 1952, when the restrictive theory of immunity it codified was first embraced by the Department of State; for lawsuits based on events before that, these courts held, the pre-1952 rule of absolute immunity for foreign sovereigns applied. Examples here include rulings that Mexico could not be sued for breach of contract in connection with the issuance of debt in 1922, that China could not be sued upon bonds issued by the Imperial Government in 1911, and that the Soviet Union could not be sued upon bonds issued by the Russian Imperial Government in 1916.[38] In seeking dismissal of Altmann's claims, Austria urged the courts hearing the case to align themselves with this latter set of decisions. All three courts in the case rejected Austria's argument, for distinctly different reasons that we will consider here.

3.4.1 The Lower Courts

The District Court The district court rested its decision on the distinction between jurisdictional statutes, which govern courts' authority to hear a case, and substantive statutes, which determine the lawfulness or unlawfulness of primary conduct and alter the rights, obligations, and liabilities of parties. Substantive statutes, the

[37] Haven v. Rzeczpospolita Polska (Republic of Poland), 68 F.Supp.2d 943 (N.D. Ill. 1999); Princz v. Federal Republic of Germany, 26 F.3d 1166 (D.C. Cir. 1994) (dictum).

[38] Slade v. United States of Mexico, 617 F. Supp. 351 (D.D.C. 1985); Jackson v. People's Republic of China, 794 F.2d 1490 (11th Cir. 1986); Carl Marks & Co. v. Union of Soviet Socialist Republics, 841 F.2d 26 (2d Cir. 1988).

court stated, are generally applied (unless they explicitly provide otherwise) only to conduct taking place after their enactment, in order to avoid the evident injustice of changing the legal character of "events that occurred prior to the enactment" and retroactively imposing on parties new legal duties that they have no chance of complying with.[39] In contrast, jurisdictional statutes are generally applied to all cases adjudicated after their enactment, without regard to when the underlying conduct occurred, because such statutes normally change no rights or duties concerning primary conduct, but simply affect the choice of tribunal for adjudicating the dispute. Put otherwise, courts generally apply the substantive statutes that were in effect at the time that the parties acted, and apply the jurisdictional statutes that are in effect at the time that the courts themselves act.

In support of its reasoning the district court relied primarily on the Supreme Court's earlier decision in *Landgraf v. USI Film Products, Inc.*[40] in which the Court observed that it had "regularly applied intervening statutes conferring or ousting jurisdiction, whether or not jurisdiction lay when the underlying conduct occurred," because "jurisdictional statutes 'speak to the power of the court rather than the rights or obligations of the parties.'"[41] In the district court's view, FSIA qualified as a jurisdictional statute for these purposes, because, in the words of its drafters, it "is not intended to affect the substantive law of liability."[42] The district court declined to follow the decisions holding FSIA inapplicable to pre-1952 conduct, because they had been rendered before *Landgraf* and, in the court's assessment, were less persuasive than later decisions holding that there was no restriction on FSIA's application to past events.

The Court of Appeals The court of appeals, in contrast, took a narrower approach to the problem, finding it unnecessary to "reach the broad conclusion of the district court that the FSIA may be generally applied to events predating the 1952 Tate Letter."[43] Unlike the district court, the court of appeals did not renounce altogether the rulings of the courts that had refused to apply the FSIA to pre-1952 events; instead, it found that the reasons adduced by those decisions were inapposite to Altmann's case. Those decisions, according to the court, had emphasized that applying FSIA to events predating the Tate letter would disrupt the settled expectations of foreign states because, in the words of one such decision, "only after 1952 was it reasonable for a foreign sovereign to anticipate being sued in the United States courts on commercial transactions."[44] But that was true, the court of appeals noted, only because the State Department's pre-1952 policy was to recognize

---

[39] *Altmann*, 142 F. Supp.2d at 1199.

[40] 511 U.S. 274 (1994).

[41] *Landgraf*, 511 U.S. at 274 (quoting Republic National Bank of Miami v. United States, 506 U.S. 80, 100 (1992) (concurring opinion)).

[42] H.R. Rep. No. 94–1487, reprinted in 1976 U.S. Code Cong. & Admin. News at 6610, quoted in *Altmann*, 142 F. Supp.2d at 1200.

[43] *Altmann*, 317 F.3d at 962.

[44] *Carl Marks*, 841 F.2d at 27, quoted in *Altmann*, 317 F.3d at 962.

immunity "in all actions against *friendly* foreign sovereigns,"[45] whereas the expropriation of Altmann's property was done by a government that had until recently been an enemy. Having officially repudiated all Nazi transactions in 1946, Austria could hardly have expected a free hand to compel Jews to ratify such transactions two years later.

Moreover, the court declared, the fact that "Austria and the United States were no longer on opposite sides of World War II at the time the Federal Monument Agency attempted to extort valid title to the Klimt paintings does not mean that Austria could reasonably expect the granting of immunity for an act so closely associated with the atrocities of the War."[46] The court pointed to a State Department announcement, issued only months after the coerced transfer of title to the Klimts, which stated that its policy was to undo forced transfers and return the property of the victims of Nazi persecution, and to "relieve American courts from any restraint upon the exercise of their jurisdiction to pass upon the validity of the acts of Nazi officials."[47] Under these circumstances, the court stated, "we are certain that the Austrians could not have had any expectation, much less a settled expectation, that the State Department would have recommended immunity as a matter of 'grace and comity' for the wrongful appropriation of Jewish property."[48]

3.4.2 *The Supreme Court*

Principal Opinion The Supreme Court found a more expansive ground of decision than did the court of appeals, in part presumably because it often seeks to establish general rules for the lower courts to follow, and in part because—as we will see—it thought the court of appeals' historically specific focus on hostilities with Austria was at odds with FSIA's purpose of depoliticizing immunity determinations. Rather than follow the court of appeals' approach of seeking a resolution tailored to the facts of Altmann's dispute with Austria, the Court instead addressed the larger issue of "FSIA's general applicability to conduct that occurred prior to the Act's 1976 enactment, and more specifically, prior to the State Department's 1952 adoption of the restrictive theory of sovereign immunity."[49] The opinion for the Court, written for a six-justice majority, was delivered by Justice John Paul Stevens.

---

[45] *Verlinden*, 461 U.S. at 486, quoted in *Altmann*, 317 F.3d at 964 (emphasis added by court of appeals).

[46] *Altmann*, 317 F.3d at 965.

[47] United States Department of State Press Release No. 296, "Jurisdiction of United States Courts Re Suits for Identifiable Property Involved in Nazi Forced Transfers," April 27, 1949, quoted in *Altmann*, 317 F.3d at 965.

[48] *Altmann*, 317 F.3d at 962.

[49] *Altmann*, 541 U.S. at 692.

To commence its analysis, the Court reviewed its earlier decision in the *Landgraf* case, which the district court had viewed as controlling the outcome of Altmann's case. *Landgraf* involved the temporal application of the Civil Rights Act of 1991, which augmented the remedies recoverable by victims of employment discrimination to include not just lost wages but also compensatory and punitive damages; the question (which the Court answered in the negative) was whether the amended statute applied to the claim of the plaintiff, whose case had already reached the appeals stage when the amendments were enacted into law. Noting "the axiom that 'retroactivity is not favored in the law,' and its interpretive corollary that 'congressional enactments and administrative rules will not be construed to have retroactive effect unless their language requires this result,'" the *Landgraf* Court read its earlier decisions as establishing a "presumption against retroactivity" in determining the temporal application of statutes—meaning that unless Congress indicates otherwise, a statute should not be read to establish the legal consequences of conduct that occurred before its enactment.[50] When Congress has not specified the temporal reach of a statute, then, a court should avoid applying it to past events if doing so "would impair rights a party possessed when he acted, increase a party's liability for past conduct, or impose new duties with respect to transactions already completed."[51] This presumption itself has a limited scope of application, however, and is generally inapposite to a statute affecting a court's procedures, or a jurisdictional statute that "takes away no substantive right but simply changes the tribunal that is to hear the case."[52]

Applied to Altmann's case the *Landgraf* analysis was, in the Supreme Court's view, informative but inconclusive. Here the Court disagreed with the district court, which in ruling in Altmann's favor had viewed FSIA as a purely jurisdictional statute that perforce could be applied to all cases pending after its enactment. This oversimplified the problem, the Supreme Court declared: tempting as it was to ask whether FSIA affected "substantive rights" or instead merely affected matters of jurisdiction and procedure, the fact is that "FSIA defies such categorization."[53] There is a sense in which it can be characterized as jurisdictional, in that it opens the courthouse doors to cases that otherwise must be pursued by other channels; yet it could be said with equal force that in stripping foreign states of absolute immunity, the statute dramatically increases the liability attaching to their conduct. A rule based on the distinction between substantive statutes and jurisdictional ones, then, "does not definitively resolve this case."[54] Nonetheless, the Court stated, there were

[50] *Landgraf*, 511 U.S. at 264–65 (quoting Bowen v. Georgetown University Hospital, 488 U.S. 204, 208 (1988)). As the Court noted, there are certain constitutional limits on Congress's power to enact retroactive legislation, such as the prohibition on ex post facto penal laws. These did not come up in the *Altmann* litigation and so are not discussed here.

[51] *Landgraf*, 511 U.S. at 280.

[52] *Id.* at 274.

[53] *Altmann*, 541 U.S. at 694.

[54] *Id.* at 696.

sound reasons for finding the *Landgraf* presumption largely inapplicable to FSIA, that is to say, for finding that the statute could be read to cover pre-1952 events without threatening the values that the presumption was meant to protect.

The aim of the presumption, the Court explained, "is to avoid unnecessary post hoc changes to legal rules on which parties relied in shaping their primary conduct."[55] But no one has ever supposed, according to the Court, that the purpose of foreign sovereign immunity was to protect such reliance, i.e., to enable states to conduct their activities based on the expectation that they will be shielded from future lawsuits in other countries. Instead, the purpose of immunity is to preserve amicable international relations that might be undermined if countries opened their courts to lawsuits against one another. Thus, for example, in the *Schooner Exchange* case, the reason for dismissing the case was not that France had seized the contested ship in the belief that it would face no legal consequences for doing so; rather, the reason was that adjudicating such a case in United States courts would imperil diplomatic relations with France. The *Landgraf* presumption's objective of protecting actors' past reliance on the law has little to do with the rationale for sovereign immunity, which "reflects current political realities and relationships, and aims to give foreign states and their instrumentalities some *present* 'protection from the inconvenience of suit as a gesture of comity.'"[56]

Further, the Court observed, in the area of foreign sovereign immunity the courts have always followed the practice of deferring to the decisions of the political branches in determining whether to allow cases against foreign states to go forward. The most recent such decision is Congress's enactment of FSIA itself, which put forth a set of criteria establishing whether a given case is barred by immunity. The historic practice of deference suggests, the Court stated, that courts should comply with that decision (that is, the text of the statute) as written, rather than "to presume that decision inapplicable merely because it postdates the conduct in question."[57] Nothing in the language of the statute, the Court stated, evinces any legislative intention of limiting its temporal reach. Moreover, the statute's twin objectives "of clarifying the rules that judges should apply in resolving sovereign immunity claims and eliminating political participation in the resolution of such claims" would be impaired if the courts were to create their own standards for deciding that some, but not other, countries would be accorded sovereign immunity based on the "reasonable expectations" they had at some point in the past. In this respect the Court distanced itself from the analysis offered by the court of appeals, which in the Court's view had "engaged in precisely the kind of detailed historical inquiry that the FSIA's clear guidelines were intended to obviate."[58] The Court nonetheless affirmed the court of appeals' judgment "because the Act, freed from *Landgraf*'s antiretroactivity presumption, clearly applies to conduct, like petitioners' alleged

---

[55] *Id.*

[56] *Id.* (quoting Dole Food Co. v. Patrickson, 538 U.S. 468, 479 (2003)).

[57] *Altmann*, 541 U.S. at 696.

[58] *Id.* at 700.

wrongdoing, that occurred prior to 1976 and, for that matter, prior to 1952 when the State Department adopted the restrictive theory of sovereign immunity."[59] The Court concluded by observing that the State Department, which had not weighed in on the Altmann case, remained free to advise courts of its views concerning the requirements of FSIA in other cases, and that the Court was leaving open the question of what deference, if any, courts should give the department on the issue.

Separate Opinions All six justices in the majority joined the Court's opinion in the Altmann case, but two filed concurring opinions. In one of these, Justice Antonin Scalia emphasized that as a jurisdictional statute, FSIA should be applied to all cases pending after its enactment. He noted the Court's "consistent practice of giving immediate effect to statutes that alter a court's jurisdiction," explaining that "'the purpose of provisions conferring or eliminating jurisdiction is to permit or forbid the exercise of judicial power' rather than to regulate primary conduct, so that the relevant time for purposes of retroactivity analysis is not when the underlying conduct occurred, but when judicial power was invoked."[60] This principle applies to FSIA, he contended, because the statute does not abridge or modify any substantive rights, which in Altmann's case were supplied by the common law, international law, and Austrian restitution legislation. The effect of FSIA is to alter the availability of the American court system as a forum in which claims may be brought, without affecting the possibility of pursuing litigation elsewhere. To be sure, he explained, "as to a claim that no foreign court would entertain, the FSIA can have the accidental effect of rendering enforceable what was previously unenforceable," but in this respect the statute "affects substantive rights only accidentally, and not as a necessary and intended consequence of the law."[61] Austria therefore could not object to the statute's application to Altmann's claims.

A concurring opinion was also filed by Justice Stephen Breyer, who pointed out that FSIA contained no explicit limitation on its temporal application, unlike some of its counterparts abroad that indicated they were only applicable to events that occurred before their enactment. This omission in FSIA was consistent with "the legal concept of sovereign immunity," which, "as traditionally applied, is about a defendant's status at the time of suit, not about a defendant's conduct before the suit"; so, in a French case, King Farouk's sovereign status permitted him to ignore fashion designer Christian Dior's demand of payment for "frocks and coats bought (while king) for his wife; but once the king lost his royal status, Christian Dior could sue and collect (for clothes sold before the abdication)."[62] And unlike immunity given to government officials for the conduct of their duties, foreign sovereign immunity "is not about 'chilling' or not chilling 'foreign states or their instrumentalities in the conduct of their business,'" but rather has the objective of protecting them "at the time of suit, 'from the inconvenience

[59]*Id.*

[60]*Id.* at 703 (concurring opinion) (quoting separate opinion in *Landgraf*, 511 U.S. at 292).

[61]*Altmann*, 541 U.S. at 704 (concurring opinion).

[62]*Id.* at 708 (concurring opinion) (quoting Ex–King Farouk of Egypt v. Christian Dior, 84 Clunet 717, 24 International Law Reports 228, 229 (Cour d'Appel Paris 1957)).

of suit as a gesture of comity.'"[63] This view, he argued, is reflected in the historic practice of the courts and also of the State Department, which, upon adopting the restrictive theory of sovereign immunity in 1952, immediately began applying it to events preceding its adoption. Given that practice, a "sovereign's reliance on future immunity here would have been unreasonable," because "a legally aware King Farouk or any of his counterparts would have or should have known that foreign sovereign immunity respects current status; it does not protect past conduct."[64] He added that invoking the idea of reliance in the present context was highly unrealistic. "What taking in violation of international norms is likely to have been influenced, not by politics or revolution, but by knowledge of, or speculation about, the likely future shape of America's law of foreign sovereign immunity? To suggest any such possibility," he remarked, "in respect to the expropriations carried out by the Nazi or Communist regimes, or any other such as I am aware, would approach the realm of fantasy"; and while "the matter is less clear in respect to less dramatic, more individualized takings, I still find any actual reliance difficult to imagine."[65] Austria therefore could not plausibly claim to have relied in the 1940s on the promise of future immunity when it took the paintings and extorted an acknowledgement of title from the rightful owners.

In a dissenting opinion joined by two other justices, Justice Anthony Kennedy argued that FSIA should fall within *Landgraf*'s presumption against retroactive application, because its effect was to "confer jurisdiction over a cause of action for which no jurisdiction existed when the sued-upon conduct occurred."[66] Taking issue with the Breyer concurrence, he contended that the Court should rest its decision on the "expectations" Austria had concerning sovereign immunity when it acted in the 1940s. That expectation, he said, was that a "baseline rule of sovereign immunity would apply, that the executive branch had the final word on immunity, and that foreign states could petition the executive branch to rule in their favor."[67] To honor those expectations, he stated, the Court should inquire into how the State Department would have decided the question of Austria's immunity; this approach would give foreign states a greater sense of certainty concerning future immunity rulings. In a brief reply in a footnote, the Court majority dismissed this suggestion, stating that "we fail to understand how our holding, which requires that courts apply the FSIA's sovereign immunity rules in all cases, somehow injects greater uncertainty into sovereign immunity law than the dissent's approach, which would require, for cases concerning pre–1976 conduct, case-by-case analysis of the status of that law at the time of the offending conduct—including analysis of the existence or nonexistence of any State Department statements on the subject."[68]

[63] *Altmann*, 541 U.S. at 709 (concurring opinion) (quoting Dole Food Co. v. Patrickson, 538 U.S. 468, 479 (2003)).

[64] *Altmann*, 541 U.S. at 711 (concurring opinion).

[65] *Id.*

[66] *Id.* at 722 (dissenting opinion).

[67] *Id.* at 724 (dissenting opinion).

[68] *Altmann*, 541 U.S. at 702 n. 23. On the *Altmann* ruling's significance for foreign sovereign immunity doctrine, see Vandenberg (2006).

3.5 Expropriation Exception to State Immunity

The Supreme Court confined itself to deciding that FSIA, rather than the predecessor legal regime, governed Austria's claim to sovereign immunity against Altmann's claims. It expressly declined to consider whether Altmann's claims were in fact barred by FSIA's grant of immunity, or instead fell within one of the statute's exceptions. The Court's decision thus had the effect of leaving intact the rulings of the court of appeals and the district court that the claims fell within the "expropriation" exception to immunity, to which we now turn. The exception reads, in relevant part, as follows:

> A foreign state shall not be immune from the jurisdiction of the courts of the United States or of the States in any case ... in which
> [1] rights in property taken in violation of international law are in issue and ...
> [2] that property or any property exchanged for such property is owned or operated by an agency or instrumentality of the foreign state and
> [3] that agency or instrumentality is engaged in a commercial activity in the United States.[69]

In their comments on this provision, the statute's drafters state that the "term 'taken in violation of international law' would include the nationalization or expropriation of property without payment of the prompt, adequate and effective compensation required by international law," and "would also include takings which are arbitrary or discriminatory in nature."[70] The reference to commercial activity reflects FSIA's purpose of confronting "a modern world where foreign state enterprises are every day participants in commercial activities"; the Act responds by enacting the restrictive theory of sovereign immunity, which denies immunity in "suits based on its commercial or private acts (*jure gestionis*)."[71]

The District Court In its analysis of the exception's application to Altmann's claims, the district court observed that the exception requires a claimant to establish three elements: (1) the foreign state defendant has taken the property at issue in violation of international law; (2) the foreign state owns or operates the property at issue, or property it was exchanged for; (3) the foreign state or its agency or instrumentality carries on commercial activity in the United States. As to the first element, the district court noted that in the early stages of litigation, when determining whether it has jurisdiction, a court need not conclusively decide whether the foreign state committed an expropriation in violation of international law; that may be one of the central issues for determination in a trial on the merits of the claim. Instead, to take jurisdiction over a case under the expropriation exception, it is enough for a court to find that there are "substantial and non-frivolous" grounds for the assertion that a taking in violation of international law has occurred.[72]

---

[69]Foreign Sovereign Immunities Act, 28 U.S.C. § 1605(a)(3).

[70]H.R. Rep. 94–1487, reprinted in 1976 U.S. Code Cong. & Admin. News at 6618.

[71]*Id.* at 6605. See generally American Law Institute (2016) § 455, and Yang (2012), pp. 298–316.

[72]*Altmann*, 142 F. Supp.2d at 1202.

In addition, the court noted that to satisfy the requirements of the expropriation exception, the foreign state against which the claim is made need not be the state that took the property in question, because the exception refers to cases in which "rights in property taken in violation of international law are in issue," rather than cases brought against states that have taken property in violation of international law.[73]

In an earlier case, *Siderman de Blake v. Republic of Argentina*,[74] the Ninth Circuit court of appeals—following the lead of the drafters' comments quoted above, as well as general principles of customary international law—had indicated that a state's taking of property from a noncitizen falls within FSIA's expropriation exception if it is not done for a public purpose; if it is arbitrary or discriminatory; or if it is not accompanied by just compensation. If a taking from a noncitizen "violates any one of the aforementioned proscriptions," the court of appeals declared, "it violates international law."[75] The *Siderman de Blake* case arose out of the atrocities committed by the Argentine military junta against a Jewish family in the 1970s. After overthrowing the civilian government in 1976, the military abducted and imprisoned one member of the family, torturing him with electric cattle prods while shouting antisemitic epithets at him. After a week he was released and ordered to leave the country with his relatives or face summary execution. Following their departure for the United States, the military junta seized the family's business, which included extensive real estate holdings and hotels, diverting the profits to the pockets of army officers. Sued by the family in federal court in California, the Argentine government moved to dismiss on grounds of sovereign immunity. Applying FSIA's expropriation exception, the court of appeals held that the claims of some members of the family failed because they were citizens of Argentina; the court explained, relying on previous decisions, that "expropriation by a sovereign state of the property of its own nationals does not implicate settled principles of international law."[76] One of the family members was not an Argentine national, however, and the court allowed her claims to proceed under the expropriation exception. Argentina's taking of her property violated international law, the court declared, because its government officials had acted "for their personal profit and not for any public purpose," had been motivated by the fact that "the Siderman family is Jewish—a discriminatory motivation based on ethnicity," and had not paid "*any* compensation for the seizure, let alone just compensation."[77]

Relying on *Siderman de Blake*, the district court found that Altmann's complaint set forth a substantial claim that a taking of property in violation of international

[73]*Id.*

[74]965 F.2d 699 (9th Cir. 1992).

[75]*Siderman de Blake*, 965 F.2d at 712.

[76]Chuidian v. Philippine National Bank, 912 F.2d 1095, 1105 (9th Cir. 1990), quoted in *Siderman de Blake*, 965 F.2d at 711.

[77]*Siderman de Blake*, 965 F.2d at 712.

law had taken place on two occasions. One of these was the Nazi seizure of Ferdinand's art collection after the German annexation of Austria. That taking, the court stated, "was not for a public purpose; instead some of the art was distributed to the collections of Hitler, Göring, and Dr. Führer. Other art was sold for the benefit of the Nazi party," which is "not recognized as a valid foreign sovereign in international law."[78] Further, the "aryanization of art collections was part of a larger scheme of the genocide of Europe's Jewish population," and was therefore discriminatory; and finally, "no payment of just compensation was made as a result of this taking."[79] The other taking in violation of international law, according to the district court, "occurred when the paintings were 'donated' to the Gallery in 1948 in order to secure export licenses for other works of art," because on this occasion as well the paintings were not taken for a public purpose; the Austrian policy of demanding "donations" from Jews in exchange for licenses to export artworks recovered from the Nazis was discriminatory; finally, no compensation was paid for the paintings when they were extorted, and the Austrian courts provided an "inadequate forum" for those presently seeking compensation.[80]

Having found that the first element of the expropriation exception—a taking in violation of international law—had been satisfied, the district court then turned to the remaining elements. There was no question, the court stated, that the second element (the foreign state's ownership of the property in issue) was satisfied, because despite having "privatized" the Gallery in 2000, Austria had retained title to the paintings.[81] With regard to the third element (the foreign state's involvement in commercial activity in the United States), the court noted that FSIA defines commercial activity as "either a regular course of conduct or a particular commercial transaction or act," and specifies that the "commercial character of an activity shall be determined by reference to the nature of the course of conduct or particular transaction or act, rather than by reference to its purpose."[82] Therefore, stated the court, in "determining whether a sovereign's acts are commercial, the focus of the inquiry is not whether the sovereign acts with a profit motive; 'rather, the issue is whether the particular actions that the foreign state performs (whatever the motive behind them) are the *type* of actions by which a private party engages in trade and traffic or commerce.'"[83] Austria's publication of museum catalogues available for sale in the United States, its advertising of tourist destinations, and its operation of the Gallery all qualified as commercial activity within this definition, the court concluded. It found the situation comparable to *Siderman de Blake*, in which Argentina's solicitation and hosting of American guests at the hotel it had

---

[78]*Altmann*, 142 F. Supp.2d at 1203 & n. 17.

[79]*Id.* at 1203.

[80]*Id.*

[81]*Id.*

[82]Foreign Sovereign Immunities Act, 28 U.S.C. § 1603(d).

[83]*Altmann*, 142 F. Supp.2d at 1204 (quoting Republic of Argentina v. Weltover, Inc., 504 U.S. 607, 614 (1992) (brackets omitted)).

expropriated had been deemed commercial activity in the United States. Altmann could accordingly proceed under the expropriation exception.

The Court of Appeals The court of appeals' analysis closely tracked that of the district court. The expropriation exception, the court remarked, "is based upon the general presumption that states abide by international law and, hence, violations of international law are not 'sovereign' acts."[84] To proceed under the exception, the court stated, echoing the district court, "we need not decide whether the taking actually violated international law; as long as a claim is substantial and non-frivolous, it provides a sufficient basis for the exercise of our jurisdiction."[85] The conventional sources of international law—court decisions, domestic law, the work of legal scholars, and the norms followed by other nations—establish that for a taking of property to be valid, three conditions must be satisfied: first, "valid expropriations must always serve a public purpose"; second, "aliens must not be discriminated against or singled out for regulation by the state"; and "an otherwise valid taking is illegal without the payment of just compensation."[86] The court further noted that to fall within the expropriation exception, the plaintiff cannot have been a citizen of the defendant state at the time the property was taken, because "settled principles of international law" do not prohibit countries from expropriating their own citizens.[87]

With these principles in mind, the court of appeals found that Altmann's complaint made out a claim under international law. "The Nazis did not even pretend to take the Klimt paintings for a public purpose," it stated, observing that the SS lawyer in charge of them "sold them for personal gain or exchanged them to supplement his private collection"; the taking was discriminatory, in that its victims were selected by the Nazis "because of their Jewish heritage"; and the Austrian state has not "justly compensated them for the value of the paintings."[88] The court further noted that the Altmanns were Czech, not Austrian, nationals, so that there was no occasion to apply the principle that international law permits states to expropriate property from their own citizens.

In addition, the court of appeals found that the remaining elements of the expropriation exception, namely the foreign state's ownership of the contested property and its participation in commercial activity, were both satisfied. The court emphasized Austria's publication of its English-language guidebook to the Gallery, sold in the United States, with a reproduction of *Adele Bloch-Bauer I* on its cover; its publication with the Yale University Press of a book entitled *Klimt's Women*, which was published in connection with a major exhibition at the Gallery

[84]West v. Multibanco Comermex, S.A., 807 F.2d 820, 826 (9th Cir. 1987), quoted in *Altmann*, 317 F.3d at 967.

[85]*Siderman de Blake*, 965 F.2d at 711, quoted in *Altmann*, 317 F.3d at 968 (internal quotation marks omitted).

[86]*West*, 807 F.2d at 831–32, quoted in *Altmann*, 317 F.3d at 968.

[87]*Altmann*, 317 F.3d at 968 (quoting *Siderman de Blake*, 965 F.2d at 711 (inner quotation marks omitted)).

[88]*Altmann*, 317 F.3d at 968.

featuring the art expropriated from Altmann's family; and its publication of English-language pamphlets in the United States advertising its cultural attractions, including a recent one on the subject of Austrian modernist painting, again with the celebrated *Adele* portrait on the cover. The publication and sale of these materials in the United States, and the American marketing campaigns for the Klimt exhibition and similar cultural events, not only "are commercial activities in and of themselves, but are also a means to attract American tourists to the Gallery,"[89] the court stated. "Given that the commercial activity is centered around the very paintings at issue in this action and far exceeds that which we found sufficient to justify applying [the expropriation exception] in *Siderman de Blake*," the court continued, "we must conclude that the Gallery is engaging in commercial activity sufficient to justify jurisdiction under the FSIA."[90]

3.6 Remaining Issues

The Supreme Court declined to rule on Austria's other proposed grounds for dismissing the case, which the lower courts dealt with at much less length than was devoted to the sovereign immunity question.

Personal Jurisdiction Invoking the line of cases stemming from the landmark *International Shoe* decision,[91] Austria argued that it lacked enough contact with the forum to support the district court's assertion of jurisdiction over it, so that the proceeding violated the constitutional command against the deprivation of property without due process of law. The district court rejected this argument on the ground that "foreign sovereigns are not 'persons' for purposes of the Due Process Clause," which "represents a restriction on judicial power not as a matter of sovereignty, but as a matter of individual liberty."[92] Various courts around the country had so ruled, the court observed, and the Supreme Court, while not addressing the precise issue, had previously stated that "in common usage, the term 'person' does not include the sovereign, and statutes employing the word are ordinarily construed to exclude it."[93]

The court of appeals rejected Austria's argument for a different reason. Unlike the district court, it left open the question whether foreign states qualified as "persons" entitled to the protection of the due process clause. Instead, it held that even assuming Austria was entitled to such protection, the requirements of due

---

[89] *Id.* at 969.

[90] *Id.*

[91] International Shoe Co. v. State of Washington, 326 U.S. 310 (1945). See generally American Law Institute (2016) § 302; see also Parrish (2006), Peterson (2010), and Rhodes and Robertson (2014).

[92] *Altmann*, 142 F. Supp.2d at 1207, 1208.

[93] Will v. Michigan Dept. of State Police, 491 U.S. 58, 64 (1989), quoted in *Altmann*, 142 F. Supp.2d at 1207.

process were satisfied in Altmann's case. A court's assertion of jurisdiction over a nonresident defendant satisfies the requirements of due process if, in the familiar formulation, the defendant has sufficient "minimum contacts" with the forum "such that maintenance of the suit does not offend traditional notions of fair play and substantial justice."[94] The matters to be considered in assessing the defendant's contacts, the court of appeals noted, "are whether the defendant makes sales, solicits or engages in business in the state, [or] serves the state's markets."[95] Moreover, for purposes of assessing a court's jurisdiction over a foreign sovereign, it stated, "the relevant area in delineating contacts is in the entire United States, not merely the forum state."[96] Under these standards, the court ruled, Austria's publishing and advertising ventures in the United States, "which capitalize on the very paintings at issue here," were enough to "support the reasonableness of the assertion of specific jurisdiction" over it.[97] (For the same reason, the court of appeals found that the district court could proceed under the applicable federal venue statute).[98]

Forum Non Conveniens Under the common law doctrine of forum non conveniens, a court "may decline to exercise its jurisdiction, even though the court has jurisdiction and venue, when it appears that the convenience of the parties and the court and the interests of justice indicate that the action should be tried in another forum."[99] The district court summarized the doctrine as providing that the party seeking dismissal "must demonstrate the existence of an adequate alternative forum and that the balance of relevant private and public interest factors favor dismissal"; for courts adjudicating a motion to dismiss under the doctrine, "the availability of an adequate alternative forum is a threshold issue, and dismissal is not appropriate if such a forum is unavailable."[100] Fleshing out the meaning of adequacy in this context, the court further noted that "though a court may dismiss on forum non conveniens grounds when the foreign forum does not provide the same range of remedies as are available in the home forum, the alternative forum must provide some potential avenue for redress. A foreign forum is inadequate when it offers no remedy at all."[101] Having set forth these standards, the district court found that the Austrian courts did not constitute an adequate alternative

---

[94] *International Shoe*, 326 U.S. at 316, quoted in *Altmann*, 317 F.3d at 970.

[95] Bancroft & Masters, Inc. v. Augusta National Inc., 223 F.3d 1082, 1086 (9th Cir. 2000), quoted in *Altmann*, 317 F.3d at 970.

[96] Richmark Corp. v. Timber Falling Consultants, Inc., 937 F.2d 1444, 1447 (9th Cir. 1991), quoted in *Altmann*, 317 F.3d at 970.

[97] *Altmann*, 317 F.3d at 971.

[98] The federal venue statute (28 U.S.C. § 1391(f)(3)) allows suit in any federal district in which a defendant is "doing business," a criterion that both the district court and the court of appeals found was met by Austria's book sales and advertising in Los Angeles.

[99] Piper Aircraft Co. v. Reyno, 454 U.S. 235, 250 (1981). See generally Brand (2013) and Samuels (2010).

[100] *Altmann*, 142 F. Supp.2d at 1209.

[101] *Id.* (citing Ceramic Corp. of America v. Inka Maritime Corp., 1 F.3d 947, 949 (9th Cir. 1993), and El–Fadl v. Central Bank of Jordan, 75 F.3d 668, 677–78 (D.C. Cir. 1996)).

forum, in two respects: the Austrian courts would probably hold Altmann's claims barred by Austria's thirty-year statute of limitations, depriving her of a remedy altogether, whereas the applicable California statute of limitations would permit her claims to go forward on the ground that she had only recently discovered their basis; and the bond Altman was required to post by the Austrian courts, amounting to at least $130,000, was "excessively burdensome" because it "would force an eighty-five-year-old woman to expend a great majority, if not all, of her liquid assets."[102]

The court of appeals ruled that the district court had not abused its discretion in refusing to dismiss under the *forum non conveniens* doctrine. It disagreed with the district court's suggestion that the exorbitant bond demanded of Altmann rendered the Austrian courts "unavailable" as a matter of law, noting that other civil law court systems also required plaintiffs to post bonds that were computed as a percentage of the value of the property in controversy; on numerous occasions, it observed, American courts had dismissed cases under *forum non conveniens*, even though the plaintiff's only alternative was to file suit in one of those court systems.[103] It also disagreed that the Austrian statute of limitations rendered that country's court system an inadequate forum. "Although Altmann is correct that a thirty-year statute of limitations generally applies to civil claims in Austria," the court stated, "under Austrian law, acts of fraudulent concealment toll the statute"; in addition, Austria's 1998 restitution legislation "authorizes the Minister of Finance to return artworks in special instances ... where claims could otherwise not be made."[104]

Notwithstanding these objections to the district court's reasoning, the court of appeals nonetheless sustained its decision because "Altmann's choice of forum should not be disturbed unless, when weighing the convenience of the parties and the interests of justice, 'the balance is strongly in favor of the defendant.'"[105] The documentary evidence and witnesses were located in Austria, a fact that supported conducting the litigation in the Austrian courts; but balanced against this was the fact that "Maria Altmann is an elderly United States citizen, who has resided in this country for over sixty years. The requisite foreign travel, coupled with the significant costs of litigating this case in Austria, weigh heavily in favor of retaining jurisdiction in the United States."[106] The considerations favoring an Austrian forum were not strong enough, the court concluded, to warrant dismissal of the case.

Missing Parties Austria's final proposed ground for dismissal was other heirs of Ferdinand, who were also potential claimants to the Klimt paintings, but had not been named as parties to the litigation. The basis for its argument was the Federal

[102] *Altmann*, 142 F. Supp.2d at 1210.

[103] *Altmann*, 317 F. 3d at 972–73 (citing Nai–Chao v. Boeing Co., 555 F. Supp. 9, 16 (N.D. Cal.1982) (one percent bond charged by courts in Taiwan), and Mercier v. Sheraton International, Inc., 981 F.2d 1345, 1353 (1st Cir. 1992) (fifteen percent bond charged by courts in Turkey)).

[104] *Altmann*, 317 F. 3d at 973 (internal quotation marks omitted).

[105] *Id.* (quoting Gulf Oil Corp. v. Gilbert, 330 U.S. 501, 508 (1947)).

[106] *Altmann*, 317 F. 3d at 973–74.

Rules of Civil Procedure, which require that persons be joined as parties if they claim an interest in the subject matter of the litigation, and their absence (1) would impair their ability to protect their own interests, or (2) would leave the defendant exposed to the possibility of multiple inconsistent liabilities or obligations. If such persons have not been joined as parties, the court should "determine whether, in equity and good conscience, the action should proceed among the existing parties or should be dismissed."[107] The court noted that the heirs agreed on their fractional claims on the paintings; three of the four other heirs had assigned their shares to Maria Altmann, giving her a 75 percent share, with the fourth heir, Maria's cousin, claiming the remaining 25 percent.

Under these circumstances, the district court held, the other heirs' participation in the litigation was unnecessary. On one hand, their interests would not be impaired by their absence, the court stated, because they "have chosen not to participate and their interest will be adequately represented by Plaintiff."[108] On the other hand, their absence would not subject Austria to the possibility of inconsistent liabilities, because "they have no disputes among themselves regarding the proportional interest of each" and their agreed-upon shares added up to 100 percent.[109] Nothing was to be gained, therefore, by insisting on their joinder as parties.

In a short passage, the court of appeals agreed. Joining a party to litigation, the court noted, is "contingent upon an initial requirement that the absent party *claim* a legally protected interest relating to the subject matter of the action."[110] Given that the other heirs "are aware of the litigation and have chosen not to claim an interest, joinder of these parties is unnecessary to this suit," the court concluded, and the proceeding could continue without them.[111]

3.7 Epilogue

Following the Supreme Court's ruling in June 2004 upholding Altmann's right to pursue her claims in federal court, the case was remanded to the district court for further pretrial proceedings. In May 2005, with a jury trial scheduled in the district court for the coming November, the parties agreed to submit the dispute to binding arbitration in Austria. Under the agreement, a panel of three arbitrators would apply Austrian law to determine ownership of the paintings, and their decision would be final. To Maria Altmann, who by then was eighty-nine years old, the arrangement was an

---

[107]Federal Rule of Civil Procedure 19(b).

[108]*Altmann*, 142 F. Supp.2d at 1213.

[109]*Altmann*, 142 F. Supp.2d at 1212.

[110]Northrop Corp. v. McDonnell Douglas Corp., 705 F.2d 1030, 1043 (9th Cir. 1983), quoted in *Altmann*, 317 F.3d at 971 (emphasis added by court of appeals).

[111]*Altmann*, 317 F.3d at 971.

expeditious alternative to further litigation in the courts, which would inevitably involve years of post-trial motions and appeals; to Austria, it offered a forum that, in all probability, would be more inclined to rule in its favor than would a jury in California. Hearings before the arbitration panel took place later that year, and the panel released its decision in January 2006.

To the surprise of many observers, the arbitration panel awarded victory in most respects to Altmann. The panel ruled that the paintings referred to in Adele Bloch-Bauer's will belonged to Ferdinand; that her testamentary request that he donate the paintings to the Austrian Gallery did not legally bind him to do so; that he had not in fact donated the paintings to the museum; and that the heirs' postwar acknowledgment of the purported donations had been unlawfully extorted and was invalid.[112] The panel ruled that five paintings, including *Adele Bloch-Bauer I*, therefore rightfully belonged to Maria Altmann and the others named in Ferdinand's last will.[113] A sixth, in the panel's view, had not been proved stolen and could therefore remain at the Gallery.[114] The panel's judgment brought the litigation to a close, and the five paintings were delivered to the heirs in March 2006.

Klimt's *Adele Bloch-Bauer I* now hangs in the Neue Galerie in New York.

References

American Law Institute. 2016. *Restatement (Fourth) of the Foreign Relations Law of the United States. Tentative Draft*. Philadelphia: American Law Institute.

Badr, Gamal Moursi. 1984. *State Immunity: An Analytical and Prognostic View*. The Hague: Martin Nijhoff.

Bamsey, Ben. 2006. The Golden Girl: A Portrait of Injustice. *ArtWorks*, Summer.

Beller, Steven. 1989. *Vienna and the Jews, 1867-1938: A Cultural History*. Cambridge: Cambridge University Press.

Brand, Ronald A. 2013. Challenges to Forum Non Conveniens. *New York University Journal of International Law and Politics* 45: 1003–1036.

Cassese, Antonio. 2005. *International Law*. 2nd ed. Oxford: Oxford University Press.

Chilton, Adam S., and Christopher A. Whytock. 2015. Foreign Sovereign Immunity and Comparative Institutional Competence. *University of Pennsylvania Law Review* 163: 411–486.

Czernin, Hubertus. 1999. *Die Fälschung. Der Fall Bloch-Bauer und das Werk Gustave Klimts*. Vienna: Czernin Verlag.

Decker, Andrew. 1984. Austria's Legacy of Shame. *ARTnews* 83 (10): 54–76.

---

[112]The panel's written judgment is available at http://www.bslaw.com/altmann/klimt.

[113]The paintings awarded to the heirs were *Adele Bloch-Bauer I (1907), Birkenwald/Buchenwald* (1903), *Adele Bloch-Bauer II* (1912), *Apfelbaum I* (1912), and *Häuser in Unterach am Attersee* (1916).

[114]The museum was allowed to keep *Amalie Zuckerkandl* (1918), which was removed from Ferdinand's collection by Erich Führer, the SS lawyer overseeing the liquidation of his estate. It was acquired in the 1940s by art dealer Vita Künstler, who eventually donated it to the Austrian Gallery in 1988. The panel concluded that Führer might have given it away with Ferdinand's permission; its ruling can be found http://www.bslaw.com/altmann/zuckerkandl. Altmann's lawyer has severely criticized the panel's ruling. See Schoenberg (2013).

Dobrovir, William. 1968. A Gloss on the Tate Letter's Restrictive Theory of Sovereign Immunity. *Virginia Law Review* 54: 1–19.
Fox, Hazel, and Philippa Webb. 2013. *The Law of State Immunity*. 3rd ed. Oxford: Oxford University Press.
Giuttari, Theodore R. 1970. *The American Law of Sovereign Immunity: An Analysis of Legal Interpretation*. New York: Praeger.
Krejci, Heinz. 2005. *Der Klimt-Streit*. Vienna: Verlag-Österreich.
Kun, Josh. 2006. The Art of Memory. *Los Angeles*, October.
Marasinghe, Lakshman. 1991. The Modern Law of Sovereign Immunity. *Modern Law Review* 54: 664–684.
Müller, Melissa, and Monika Tatzkow. 2010. *Lost Lives, Lost Art: Jewish Collectors, Nazi Art Theft*. London: Frontline.
O'Connor, Anne-Marie. 2013. *The Lady in Gold: The Extraordinary Tale of Gustav Klimt's Masterpiece, Portrait of Adele Bloch-Bauer I*. New York: Random House.
Parrish, Austen L. 2006. Sovereignty, Not Due Process: Personal Jurisdiction over Nonresident Aliens. *Wake Forest Law Review* 41: 1–60.
Peterson, Todd Davis. 2010. The Timing of Minimum Contacts. *George Washington Law Review* 79: 101–160.
Petropoulos, Jonathan. 2005. Report of Professor Jonathan Petropoulos, Department of History, Claremont McKenna College. Altmann v. Republic of Austria, No. 2:00-cv-08913 (C.D. Cal.). Accessed July 10, 2017. http://www.bslaw.com/altmann/Klimt/Petropoulos.pdf.
Rhodes, Charles W. "Rocky", and Cassandra B. Robertson. 2014. Toward a New Equilibrium in Personal Jurisdiction. *UC Davis Law Review* 48: 207-270.
Samuels, Joel H. 2010. When Is an Alternative Forum Available? Rethinking the Forum Non Conveniens Analysis. *Indiana Law Journal* 85: 1059–1112.
Schoenberg, E. Randol. 2013. London's National Gallery Hosts Klimt Portrait Seized by Nazis. *Al Jazeera America*, October 20.
Schorske, Carl. 1979. *Fin-de-siècle Vienna: Politics and Culture*. New York: Alfred Knopf.
Shaw, Malcolm. 1997. *International Law*. 4th ed. Cambridge: Cambridge University Press.
Sinclair, Ian. 1980. The Law of Sovereign Immunity: Recent Developments. *Receuil des Cours, Collected Courses of the Hague Academy of International Law* 167: 113–284.
Vandenberg, David P. 2006. In the Wake of *Republic of Austria v. Altmann*: The Current Status of Foreign Immunity in United States Courts. *University of Colorado Law Review* 77: 739–766.
Walzer, Tina, and Stephan Temple. 2001. *Unser Wien. Arisierung auf Österreichisch*. Berlin: Aufbau.
Whytock, Christopher A. 2013. Foreign State Immunity and the Right to Court Access. *Boston University Law Review* 93: 2033–2093.
Yang, Xiadong. 2012. *State Immunity in International Law*. Cambridge: Cambridge University Press.

Cases

Alfred Dunhill of London, Inc. v. Republic of Cuba, 425 U.S. 682 (1976)
Altmann v. Republic of Austria, 142 F.Supp.2d 1187 (C.D. Cal. 2001), aff'd, 317 F.3d 954 (9th Cir. 2003), aff'd, 541 U.S. 699 (2004)
Bancroft & Masters, Inc. v. Augusta National Inc., 223 F.3d 1082 (9th Cir. 2000)
Carl Marks & Co. v. Union of Soviet Socialist Republics, 841 F.2d 26 (2d Cir. 1988)
Ceramic Corp. of America v. Inka Maritime Corp., 1 F.3d 947, 949 (9th Cir. 1993)
Chuidian v. Philippine National Bank, 912 F.2d 1095 (9th Cir. 1990)
Dole Food Co. v. Patrickson, 538 U.S. 468 (2003)

El–Fadl v. Central Bank of Jordan, 75 F.3d 668 (D.C. Cir. 1996)
Ex parte Republic of Peru, 318 U.S. 578 (1943)
Ex–King Farouk of Egypt v. Christian Dior, 84 Clunet 717, 24 International Law Reports 228 (Cour d'Appel Paris 1957)
Haven v. Rzeczpospolita Polska (Republic of Poland), 68 F. Supp.2d 943 (N.D. Ill. 1999)
International Shoe Co. v. State of Washington, 326 U.S. 310 (1945)
Jackson v. People's Republic of China, 794 F.2d 1490 (11th Cir. 1986)
Landgraf v. USI Film Products, Inc., 511 U.S. 274 (1994)
Mercier v. Sheraton International, Inc., 981 F.2d 1345 (1st Cir. 1992)
Nai–Chao v. Boeing Co., 555 F. Supp. 9 (N.D. Cal. 1982)
Northrop Corp. v. McDonnell Douglas Corp., 705 F.2d 1030 (9th Cir. 1983)
Piper Aircraft Co. v. Reyno, 454 U.S. 235, 250 (1981)
Princz v. Federal Republic of Germany, 26 F.3d 1166 (D.C. Cir. 1994)
Republic of Argentina v. Weltover, Inc., 504 U.S. 607 (1992)
Republic of Mexico v. Hoffman, 324 U.S. 30 (1945)
Richmark Corp. v. Timber Falling Consultants, Inc., 937 F.2d 1444 (9th Cir. 1991)
Schooner Exchange v. McFaddon & Others, 11 U.S. (7 Cranch) 116 (1812)
Siderman de Blake v. Republic of Argentina, 965 F.2d 699 (9th Cir. 1992)
Slade v. United States of Mexico, 617 F. Supp. 351 (D.D.C. 1985)
Verlinden B.V. v. Central Bank of Nigeria, 461 U.S. 480 (1983)
West v. Multibanco Comermex, S.A., 807 F.2d 820 (9th Cir. 1987)
Will v. Michigan Dept. of State Police, 491 U.S. 58 (1989)

Chapter 4
Westfield v. Federal Republic of Germany

4.1 Background

Walter Westfeld (1889–1943) was a prominent art dealer and collector in Wuppertal-Elberfel, Germany, during the 1920s and 1930s.[1] In 1935, the Nazi government banned Jews from dealing in art, and in early 1936 the Reich Ministry of Fine Arts ordered Westfeld to close his gallery. Westfeld transferred his gallery's inventory to an approved Aryan dealer, and later secretly shipped portions of his remaining collection to business associates in Amsterdam and Paris, and sold some items to raise money to emigrate to the United States. His brother had settled years earlier in Nashville, Tennessee, and Westfeld planned to bring the best items of his collection with him and reestablish himself as an art dealer in the United States. The Gestapo was monitoring his activities, however, and arrested him before he was able to leave the country.

In late 1938, the Foreign Exchange Search Office confiscated all of Westfeld's assets, and the chief public prosecutor in Düsseldorf ordered that his art collection be auctioned off, with the proceeds paid to the government.

The collection was sold in late 1939 by the Kunsthaus Mathias Lempertz, an auction house in Köln, which advertised it as "non-Aryan" property. Convicted in 1940 of currency violations, Westfeld was imprisoned at the Remscheid penitentiary at Lüttringhausen, where the Gestapo brutally interrogated him over the whereabouts of art he was suspected of having hidden away, including an El Greco the Nazis had earmarked for inclusion in Hitler's private collection in Linz. At the end of his prison sentence, Westfeld was sent to Theresienstadt in late 1942 and then to his death at Auschwitz in early 1943. After the war, in 1952, his widow Emilie Scheulens successfully obtained an order from the Regional Court in Düsseldorf nullifying his conviction, and was able to recover four of the

[1]On Westfeld's life and milieu, see generally Müller and Tatzkow (2010), pp. 86–98; Reed (2015); Schmidt (2005), pp. 273–278.

B.L. Hay, *Nazi-Looted Art and the Law*, DOI 10.1007/978-3-319-64967-2_4

700 items sold at the 1939 auction. With a few exceptions, the locations of the remaining items are still unknown.

Westfeld's family members in Tennessee changed their names to Westfield. In 2004, Westfeld's nephew Fred Westfield learned that the Museum of Fine Arts in Boston, which was investigating the provenance of a Dutch painting in its collection, was looking for Westfeld's descendants. With the help of a curator at the museum, he and his family managed to find a copy of the catalogue of the Nazi government's 1939 auction of the Westfeld collection, despite the destruction of Kunsthaus Lempertz's records during the war. By order of a Tennessee state court in 2008, Westfield was designated administrator of Walter Westfeld's estate, giving him the right to sue on the estate's behalf over the lost art.[2]

4.2 Proceedings

Along with other family members, Fred Westfield filed suit against the Federal Republic of Germany in 2009, bringing the action in the state courts of Tennessee. The plaintiffs sought compensation for the art the Nazis had taken and sold, contending that, as successor in interest to the Third Reich, the Federal Republic was liable to the Westfeld estate under theories of unlawful conversion, constructive trust, and equitable accounting. Asserting that the Westfeld collection had included works by El Greco, van Dyck, and other European masters, the complaint requested damages for the value of the missing art, along with other monetary relief.

Germany removed the case to federal court, on the basis of federal subject matter jurisdiction over actions against foreign states.[3] It then filed a motion to dismiss the case, contending that the Westfields' action was barred by the doctrine of foreign state immunity under the Foreign Sovereign Immunities Act.[4] In opposition to the motion, the Westfields argued that their suit fell within the Act's so-called commercial activity exception, which lifts immunity for claims based on certain commercial activities undertaken by the foreign state.[5]

[2]The heirs of Emilie Scheulens, Walter Westfeld's widow, contended that they, rather than the Westfields, were the legitimate heirs to Westfeld's estate. The dispute became moot in view of the ultimate disposition of the case against Germany.

[3]The federal courts have non-exclusive jurisdiction over suits between American citizens and foreign states in which the amount in controversy exceeds $75,000. 28 U.S.C. § 1332. With exceptions not relevant here, if a plaintiff brings an action in state court that could have been brought in federal court, the defendant may remove the case to federal court. 28 U.S.C. § 1441.

[4]Germany also moved to dismiss on the ground that the action was time-barred. The courts ultimately found it unnecessary to rule on this issue.

[5]The commercial activity exception is codified at 28 U.S.C. § 1605(a)(2). For reasons that remain unclear, the Westfields did not invoke the expropriation exception to immunity (28 U.S.C. § 1605 (a)(3), encountered in the previous chapter).

The federal district court granted the motion to dismiss, agreeing with Germany that the Nazi government's seizure of the Westfeld collection did not constitute "commercial activity" as that term is used in FSIA.[6] For the definition of that statutory term, the court took as its principal authority a 1992 decision in which the Supreme Court stated that activities qualify as commercial under FSIA if they are "the type of actions by which a private party engages in 'trade and traffic or commerce,'"[7] as contrasted with activities that are characteristically undertaken only by public authorities. The district court concluded that the Nazis' seizure of Westfeld's art was not commercial activity under this formulation, and that "the subsequent disposition of the art collection on the private art market through privately-owned auction houses does not render the initial act of seizure a commercial activity."[8] The district court accordingly entered judgment for Germany.

The Westfields appealed to the United States Court of Appeals for the Sixth Circuit, which affirmed the judgment, though on grounds different from those relied on by the lower court.[9] The court of appeals ruled that the government's seizure of the collection, whether or not it qualified as commercial activity for purposes of FSIA, did not have a "direct effect in the United States," as the statute requires as a precondition of lifting immunity. Relying on the Supreme Court's definition of direct effect as "immediate consequence,"[10] and comparing the Westfields' claim to a line of decisions involving governments' nonpayment of debts, the court found that the seizure of the art produced only an indirect effect in the United States. To allow the case to go forward on the basis of Westfeld's own intention of transferring the art to the United States, the court reasoned, would expand federal jurisdiction over foreign governments beyond the limits set by Congress in FSIA.[11] The appeals court therefore upheld the lower court's judgment of dismissal, which brought an end to the case.

[6]Westfield v. Federal Republic of Germany, 2009 WL 2356554 (M.D. Tenn. 2009).

[7]Republic of Argentina v. Weltover, 504 U.S. 607, 614 (1992) (italics omitted).

[8]*Westfield*, 2009 WL 2356554, at *6.

[9]Westfield v. Federal Republic of Germany, 633 F.3d 409 (6th Cir. 2011).

[10]*Weltover*, 504 U.S. at 614.

[11]The plaintiffs also argued that even if the commercial activity exception did not apply, Germany could not claim sovereign immunity for the Nazi government's treatment of Westfeld, because his conviction was declared null and void after the war, and because American law generally accords no legal recognition to the acts of the Nazis. The court rejected this argument out of hand, stating only that the seizure and sale, "even though they constituted an abuse of police and prosecutorial powers by the German government at the time, were nonetheless the acts of a sovereign," and "Congress did not create an exception for lawless activities in the Act." 633 F.3d at 418. Because the argument was rejected without discussion, we do not address it further here. Our attention will be confined to the courts' adjudication of the commercial activity exception to FSIA.

4.3 Commercial Activity Exception to Foreign State Immunity

As we discussed briefly in the previous chapter, the Foreign Sovereign Immunities Act codifies what is generally known as the restrictive theory of sovereign immunity, which distinguishes between "public" and "private" actions of states, preserving their immunity from suit in cases involving the former while extinguishing it in cases involving the latter.[12] In the often-quoted Tate Letter of 1952, an advisory opinion from the United States Department of State which has guided much of American jurisprudence on the subject, the restrictive theory is described as providing that "the immunity of the sovereign is recognized with regard to sovereign or public acts (*jure impereii*) but not with respect to private acts (*jure gestionis*)."[13] This principle, commonly traced to Belgian and Italian judicial decisions of the nineteenth century, gained currency in the early twentieth century, as exemplified by a 1920 ruling in which a Romanian court distinguished for immunity purposes between a state's "public acts, acts of sovereignty, of government, *jure imperii*, generated by political needs" and its "private acts, acts of management, purchase and sale, all manner of transaction *jure privato* generated by the responsibilities and exigencies of the modern state, in which the state does not distinguish itself from other actors."[14] That general distinction has become widely accepted in international law in the decades since the Second World War. The American Law Institute summarizes it as follows: "Under international law, a state or state instrumentality is immune from the jurisdiction of the courts of another state, except with respect to claims arising out of activities of the kind that may be carried on by private persons."[15]

The principle finds expression in the commercial activity exception of FSIA, which lifts the immunity of foreign states in any lawsuit that is based—

> [1] upon a commercial activity carried on in the United States by the foreign state; or
>
> [2] upon an act performed in the United States in connection with a commercial activity of the foreign state elsewhere; or
>
> [3] upon an act outside the territory of the United States in connection with a commercial activity of the foreign state elsewhere and that act causes a direct effect in the United States.[16]

---

[12]See Section 4.3 above.

[13]Letter from Jack B. Tate, Acting Legal Adviser, U.S. Dept. of State, to Acting U.S. Attorney General Phillip B. Perlman, May 19, 1952, published in 26 Dept. of State Bulletin 984 (1952), reprinted in Alfred Dunhill of London, Inc. v. Republic of Cuba, 425 U.S. 682, 711–15 (1976).

[14]Banque roumaine de commerce et de crédit de Prague v. Etat polonais, 19 RDIP 581 (Romania, Tribunal de commerce d'Ilfov, 1920), quoted in van Alebeek (2008), p. 14 (author's translation).

[15]American Law Institute (1987), § 451.

[16]Foreign Sovereign Immunities Act, 28 U.S.C. § 1605(a)(2).

The statute defines "commercial activity" as follows:

> A "commercial activity" means either a regular course of commercial conduct or a particular commercial transaction. The commercial character of an activity shall be determined by reference to the nature of the course of conduct or particular transaction or act, rather than by reference to its purpose.[17]

Like its counterparts enacted abroad, such as the European Convention on State Immunity,[18] the commercial activity exception essentially rests on the idea that, in the words of an English court, "[o]nce the sovereign has descended from his throne and entered the marketplace, he has divested himself of his sovereign status and is therefore no longer immune to the domestic jurisdiction of the courts of other countries."[19]

At issue in the Westfield litigation was clause [3] of the exception just quoted, which suspends immunity when two conditions are satisfied: first, the lawsuit must rest upon an act done by the foreign state in connection with commercial activity; second, the act in question must have caused a direct effect in the United States. The district court ruled that the first condition was not satisfied, holding that the Nazi government's seizure and sale of Westfeld's art were not commercial in nature; the court of appeals, without ruling on the first condition, concluded that the second condition was not satisfied, because the seizure and sale did not cause a direct effect in the United States. These rulings are considered in the following two sections.

4.4 Nazi Confiscation as Commercial Activity

The problem confronted by the district court was whether the seizure and sale of Westfeld's collection, which the plaintiffs argued was part of a common Nazi practice to finance the war as well as to line the pockets of party officials, qualified as commercial activity. In ruling against the plaintiffs, the court relied in part on general principles set forth in two decisions of the Supreme Court, *Republic of Argentina v. Weltover* and *Saudi Arabia v. Nelson*, and also a decision of its own court of appeals, which attempted to define what qualifies as commercial activity. The court also relied on a series of cases from around the country applying these principles to property seizures. We will take up these components of the decision in turn and then look at the conclusion drawn by the district court.

[17]Foreign Sovereign Immunities Act, 28 U.S.C. § 1603(d).

[18]See European Convention on State Immunity art. 7 (state cannot claim immunity from jurisdiction of another state in which it "engages, in the same manner as a private person, in an industrial, commercial, or financial activity, and the proceedings relate to that activity").

[19]I Congreso Del Partido, House of Lords, 2 All Eng. Rep. 1064 ¶ 527 (House of Lords 1983). On the commercial activity exception in FSIA, see generally Dellapenna (2003), Donoghue (1992), and Foster (2014).

4.4.1 General Principles

The *Weltover* Decision The Supreme Court has on two occasions addressed the meaning of the term "commercial activity" in FSIA. In *Republic of Argentina v. Weltover*,[20] the Court took up this issue in the context of a government default on bond payments. Because of the instability of Argentine currency, Argentine businesses were finding it difficult to borrow money on the international market. In response, the Argentine government and its central bank adopted a foreign exchange insurance contract program, under which the government in essence agreed to take on the risk of currency depreciation in international transactions undertaken by Argentine borrowers. As the program unfolded, the government effectively assumed the Argentine borrowers' debts, issuing bonds to the creditors providing for payment in U.S. dollars. When the bonds came due, the government lacked sufficient funds to retire them, and therefore announced that it was unilaterally extending the time for payment. Several bondholders refused to accept the time extension and sued Argentina for breach of contract in New York federal court. Argentina raised the defense of sovereign immunity, and the case ultimately came before the Supreme Court, which had to decide whether the commercial activity exception applied to Argentina's conduct. The Court unanimously ruled that it did.

The definition of "commercial activity" in FSIA, the Court observed in its opinion, contains a gap at its center.[21] The definition indicates that the term encompasses both single acts and regular courses of conduct, and that commerciality is to be determined by the nature of the foreign state's conduct, rather than the purpose it pursues; but the critical term *commercial* itself remains undefined in the statute. The Court therefore turned to the meaning generally attributed to the term at the time of the statute's enactment, using as its principal source its own earlier decision in *Alfred Dunhill of London, Inc. v. Republic of Cuba*,[22] decided shortly before passage of FSIA. The *Dunhill* case presented a question concerning the commercial activity exception to sovereign immunity that was being applied, essentially as a judge-made rule, in the years after the Tate letter of 1952; in particular, the question was whether the same exception should also be applied to the act of state doctrine. The *Dunhill* Court could not reach consensus on that question, but (as the *Weltover* opinion noted) the different opinions in the case did not disagree on the definition of commercial activity for purposes of sovereign immunity. The *Dunhill* plurality opinion observed that the distinction between a state's sovereign acts and its private acts could be found in numerous decisions dating from the early nineteenth century; applied in the modern restrictive theory of international sovereign immunity, the distinction meant that a foreign state could not claim immunity in cases where it had participated in the marketplace in the

---

[20] 504 U.S. 607 (1992).

[21] *Weltover*, 504 U.S. at 612.

[22] 425 U.S. 682 (1976).

same manner as a private citizen or corporation.[23] "In their commercial capacities," the *Dunhill* plurality asserted, summarizing the extant understanding of the restrictive theory, "foreign governments do not exercise powers peculiar to sovereigns. Instead, they exercise only those powers that can also be exercised by private citizens."[24] Because the *Dunhill* decision was handed down only months before enactment of FSIA, the *Weltover* Court concluded that such language should be given great weight in construing the statute's commercial activity exception.

Building on that earlier case, the *Weltover* opinion therefore offered the following formulation of "commercial activity" for purposes of applying the statutory exception: "when a foreign government acts, not as a regulator of a market, but in the manner of a private player within it, the foreign sovereign's actions are 'commercial' within the meaning of FSIA."[25] In addition, because the statute specifies that it is the nature of the act, rather than its purpose, that determines whether it should be deemed commercial, "the question is not whether the foreign government is acting with a profit motive or instead with the aim of fulfilling uniquely sovereign aims," but is instead "whether the particular actions that the foreign state performs (whatever the motive behind them) are the type of actions by which a private party engages in 'trade and traffic or commerce.'"[26] Accordingly, a foreign government's promulgation of currency exchange regulations constitutes a sovereign, rather than commercial, activity, because no private party has the power to exercise such authority over the marketplace; but a contract entered into by the government to purchase military supplies qualifies as a commercial, rather than sovereign, activity, because private companies also enter into sales agreements.

With this formulation in hand, the Court decided that Argentina's issuance of bonds constituted commercial activity under the statute. The commercial character of the government's activity was underscored, in the Court's view, by its resemblance to the issuance of debt instruments by private corporations—instruments that, like the Argentine bonds, are typically negotiable, traded on international markets, and promise the holder payment in cash. There was nothing distinctively sovereign about Argentina's assumption of debt, with the exception of the purposes the government was pursuing; and FSIA makes clear that the government's objectives have no bearing on the commercial activity determination. In response to Argentina's argument that it had not used the bonds to raise money or finance purchases, the Court noted that their function had been to refinance debt, which is a common feature of privately-issued bonds, and for that reason was enough to bring them within the statutory exception. It was, the Court concluded, "irrelevant why Argentina participated in the bond market in the manner of a private actor; it matters only that it did so."[27]

---

[23]See *Weltover*, 504 U.S. at 613–14 (summarizing the plurality opinion in *Dunhill*, 425 U.S. at 698–75).

[24]*Dunhill*, 425 U.S. at 704 (plurality opinion), quoted in part in *Weltover*, 504 U.S. at 614.

[25]*Weltover*, 504 U.S. at 614.

[26]*Id.* (quoting Black's Law Dictionary 270 (6th ed. 1990)).

[27]*Weltover*, 504 U.S. at 617.

The *Nelson* Decision A year later, the Supreme Court again confronted the definition problem, this time in a case involving a foreign state's detention and torture of an American employee who had become a whistleblower against his employer. In *Saudi Arabia v. Nelson*,[28] the complaint alleged that Saudi Arabia had placed an advertisement in an American trade periodical seeking a systems engineer for a hospital owned and operated by the Saudi government in Riyadh. The plaintiff Nelson, a United States citizen, answered the advertisement and was eventually hired for the position. A few months after beginning work in Riyadh, Nelson began reporting serious safety problems at the hospital to managers and other government officials. Soon afterward, according to the complaint, the Saudi police arrested Nelson, held him incognito in prison, and used torture to interrogate him before finally releasing him after thirty-nine days of confinement. Nelson returned to the United States and, along with his wife, filed suit in federal court against the Saudi government, claiming damages for a variety of torts. Following proceedings in the lower courts the case arrived at the Supreme Court, which undertook to decide whether the plaintiff's lawsuit was "based upon a commercial activity" within the meaning of the statute.[29]

In an opinion delivered by Justice David Souter, the Court began its analysis by remarking that the term *based upon*, like the word *commercial*, goes undefined in the statute, making it necessary to look for conventional understandings of the term. In the term's most natural sense, according to the Court, a lawsuit is based upon those assertions of the claim that, if proven, would give the plaintiff the right to prevail in the case and receive the remedy sought after; thus, the term is essentially coextensive with the "elements" of a claim. The Court found support for this reading in the structure of the commercial activity exception, which, as quoted above, has three distinct clauses, each lifting immunity in different circumstances—the first applying to commercial activity carried on in the United States; the second applying to acts performed in the United States in connection with commercial activity conducted elsewhere; the third applying to commercial activity conducted elsewhere that causes a direct effect in the United States. Placed alongside one another, these clauses indicate a difference between a lawsuit based upon a commercial activity and a lawsuit based upon acts performed "in connection with" such activity, and imply that the former requires something more than just a connection with, or relation to, the foreign state's engagement in commercial activity.[30] Saudi Arabia's recruitment of Nelson in the United States undoubtedly constituted a commercial activity, the Court explained, but it was not the basis of the lawsuit, which arose out of injuries he sustained as a result of torts committed in Riyadh. Those torts, not the formation of the employment contract, were the basis of his claim.[31]

---

[28]507 U.S. 349 (1993).

[29]The plaintiff invoked the clause of the commercial activity exception that lifts immunity for an action "based upon a commercial activity carried on in the United States by the foreign State." Foreign Sovereign Immunities Act, U.S.C. § 1605(a)(2).

[30]*Nelson*, 507 U.S. at 357–58.

[31]The Court has more recently elaborated on FSIA's use of the term *based upon* in OBB Personenverkehr AG v. Sachs, 136 S. Ct. 390 (2015), which came after the conclusion of the Westfield litigation.

The Court then turned to the issue of characterizing the asserted torts. Though the statute leaves the key term commercial undefined, making its definition of "commercial activity" one that is "distinguished by its diffidence," Souter's opinion stated that the members of the Court cannot "throw up [their] hands," but must instead bear the "judicial responsibility to determine what a 'commercial activity' is for purposes of the Act."[32] One crucial concept for discharging this responsibility, the opinion noted, is the distinction made in international law between a state's exercise of "powers peculiar to sovereigns," and its exercise of "only those powers that can also be exercised by private citizens," with only the former being entitled to the protection of sovereign immunity.[33] Another crucial concept in the characterization of a state's activity as commercial or noncommercial is the distinction between the activity's "purpose (i.e., the reason why the foreign state engages in the activity)" and its "nature (i.e., the outward form of the conduct that the foreign state performs or agrees to perform)."[34] Applying these distinctions to Nelson's case, the Court determined that the intentional torts alleged by the plaintiffs to have been committed by Saudi Arabia—namely, wrongful arrest, false imprisonment, and torture—did not qualify as commercial activity on the government's part. The government's conduct essentially constituted an "abuse of the power of its police," and "however monstrous such abuse undoubtedly may be, a foreign state's exercise of the power of its police has long been understood for purposes of the restrictive theory [of sovereign immunity] as peculiarly sovereign in nature."[35]

Deployment of the police and the use of penal authority, the Court explained, are not activities by which a private party can engage in commerce. Rather, "such acts as legislation, or the expulsion of an alien, or a denial of justice, cannot be performed by an individual acting in his own name. They can be performed only by the state acting as such."[36] It was irrelevant that the Saudi government subjected Nelson to the alleged abuse in retaliation for his whistleblowing as a hospital employee, or that, as amicus curiae charged, the Saudi government made a practice of using unlawful detention and torture as means of resolving its commercial disputes. Such assertions concerned the purpose behind the government's action, which, in the Court's view, had no bearing on the question of its commercial character. "Whatever may have been the Saudi Government's motivation for its allegedly abusive treatment of Nelson," the Court stated, "it remains the case that the Nelsons' action is based upon a sovereign activity immune from the subject-matter jurisdiction of the United States courts under the Act."[37] The Court reached this conclusion both for the Nelsons' claims for intentional torts and for their claim of negligent failure to warn. The latter, the Court reasoned, amounted to a claim that

[32]*Nelson*, 507 U.S. at 359.

[33]*Weltover*, 504 U.S. at 614, quoted in *Nelson*, 507 U.S. at 360.

[34]*Nelson*, 507 U.S. at 361.

[35]*Id.*

[36]Lauterpacht (1952), p. 225, quoted in *Nelson*, 507 U.S. at 362.

[37]*Nelson*, 507 U.S. at 363.

the government had breached its obligation to warn of its own propensity for conducting its sovereign activities in a tortious manner. Allowing this claim to go forward would, according to Souter's opinion, virtually extinguish immunity for sovereign acts, because almost any claim based on such acts could, by creative drafting of a complaint, be recast in terms of failure to warn.[38]

The *O'Bryan* Decision Along with the Supreme Court's decisions in *Weltover* and *Nelson*, the district court in the Westfield litigation invoked a recent decision of its own court of appeals, the Sixth Circuit, setting forth standards for approaching the commercial activity exception. In *O'Bryan v. Holy See*,[39] the plaintiffs brought a class action against the Vatican over sexual abuse they had suffered at the hands of Roman Catholic priests in the United States. Pursuant to a 1962 policy document, the defendant had maintained a practice (according to the plaintiffs) of concealing its employees' molestation of children and refusing to cooperate with police, prosecutors, and child protection agencies. "The policies of the Holy See expressed in this and other documents," according to the plaintiffs' complaint, "require bishops in the United States to, among other things, refuse to report childhood sexual abuse committed by priests to criminal or civil authorities, even where such failure to report would itself be a criminal offense."[40] The plaintiffs sought compensatory and injunctive relief, asserting that the defendant was liable for a variety of torts as well as human rights violations under international law. The Vatican raised the defense of sovereign immunity, and the case came to the court of appeals presenting the question whether the plaintiffs' claims fell within FSIA's commercial activity exception.

The court of appeals posited two limitations on the exception's availability. First, the plaintiffs' claim must be based on activities that private individuals or organizations, and not just sovereign entities, characteristically engage in.[41] Second, courts must disregard the "artful pleadings" of plaintiffs, and must instead focus on the "core," or essential nature, of the governmental conduct complained of.[42] The court of appeals quoted with approval the opinion of another court that had recently adjudicated a comparable claim against the Vatican, which stated that judges must keep their eye on the "ultimate issue" in cases presenting the commercial activity exception, namely "whether the true essence of the complaint is commercial."[43] Claims arising out of sexual abuse by the clergy are not, according to that opinion, fundamentally commercial in character; they do not involve

[38]*Nelson*, 507 U.S. at 363.

[39]556 F.3d 361 (6th Cir. 2009), cert denied, 558 U.S. 819 (2009).

[40]*Id.* at 370.

[41]It is worth noting parenthetically that in earlier cases the Sixth Circuit, like other courts, had ruled that a defendant's behavior need not be lawful in order to qualify as commercial. Thus, an investment scam carried out by a government bank is commercial, even though it is illegal. See Keller v. Central Bank of Nigeria, 277 F.3d 811, 816 (6th Cir. 2002).

[42]*O'Bryan*, 556 F.3d at 380.

[43]Doe v. Holy See, 434 F.Supp.2d 925, 942 (D. Or. 2006), quoted in *O'Bryan*, 556 F.3d at 380.

"property damage, breach of contract for goods or services, product liability, copyright infringement, an indebtedness yet unpaid on a loan or other transaction, or any other theory whose true essence is commercial."[44] Embracing this language, the *O'Bryan* court declared that the same conclusion followed in the case before it. The Vatican's promulgation of the 1962 policy of secrecy and noncooperation with government officials was, in the court's view, sovereign rather than commercial in nature, despite whatever financial motivations lay behind it.[45]

4.4.2 Property Seizure Cases

The district court in the Westfield litigation also relied on a series of cases involving the application of the commercial activity exception to governmental expropriations of property, which the court viewed as comparable to the Nazi seizure of Westfeld's collection.

The *Garb* Decision In *Garb v. Republic of Poland*,[46] the plaintiffs sought compensation for the property taken by the Polish government from Jews in the years after World War II. Most of the three million Jews who lived in prewar Poland were exterminated by the Nazis and their Polish collaborators; those who avoided this fate often fled to the east, and at war's end about 230,000 Jewish refugees were returned to Poland from the Soviet Union. Upon their repatriation, these individuals were met with government-encouraged antisemitic persecution in which hundreds were murdered and many more lost their property; those who fled the violence saw their property nationalized by the government on the pretext that it had been abandoned. In 1999, a class action was filed by Garb against Poland in New York federal court on behalf of Jewish persons and their heirs who had lost property in the postwar period, either at the government's hands or at the hands of private individuals acting with government complicity. Poland successfully moved in the district court for a dismissal on sovereign immunity grounds, and the plaintiffs appealed to the Second Circuit court of appeals, which had to decide whether the case fell within the commercial activity exception.

The court of appeals commenced with the problem of determining the "basis" of the plaintiffs' claims. The plaintiffs called the court's attention to evidence that the confiscated property had been sold off by the government and its private accomplices in transactions that were unquestionably commercial in nature. Foreclosing this line of inquiry, the court of appeals ruled that the plaintiffs' claims were based on the seizure of their property, and not its subsequent disposition in the marketplace; that is to say, the gravamen of their complaint was "the manner in which the

[44] *Doe*, 434 F.Supp.2d at 942, quoted in *O'Bryan*, 556 F.3d at 380.
[45] *O'Bryan*, 556 F.3d at 380–81.
[46] 440 F.3d 579 (2d Cir. 2006).

property was obtained, not its subsequent management" by the government.[47] The post-seizure commercial treatment of the property was therefore irrelevant to the determination whether the commercial activity exception applied to the case. For that determination, the court of appeals ruled, the appropriate focus was on the confiscation.

As for the confiscation itself, the court held that it did not constitute commercial conduct. Governmental seizure of property, the court declared, quoting other courts to the same effect, is decidedly sovereign, rather than commercial, in character; the nationalization of property is a "quintessential government act."[48] Further, the court stated, the confiscation of the plaintiffs' property did not occur "in connection with" a commercial activity on the part of the Polish government. The statutory formulation "in connection with" in FSIA is a term of art that, in the court's view, must be construed narrowly. A governmental act is done in connection with a commercial activity only if there is "a 'substantive connection' or a 'causal link'" between the two.[49] The court cautioned against applying the commercial activity exception to cases in which a government's commercial conduct is only tangentially related to the acts being complained of, warning that if a merely "attenuated connection" to commercial conduct sufficed to trigger the exception, then the exception would potentially swallow the rule, exposing governments to lawsuits for acts that are essentially sovereign in nature.[50] The court acknowledged that the confiscation of the plaintiffs' property was causally related to the subsequent commercial treatment of the property or its proceeds, in the sense that if the Polish government had not taken the property, it would have not been in a position to manage or sell it. But the court declared that this connection was too remote to meet the statutory requirements, a conclusion it thought compelled by the purpose and design of FSIA. "Our reasoning," stated the court, "that subsequent commercial transactions involving expropriated property do not give rise to subject matter jurisdiction over claims arising from the original expropriation" accords with "Congress's intention to deny sovereign immunity only with respect to commercial, and not sovereign, acts."[51] The court of appeals therefore affirmed the judgment in favor of the Polish government.

---

[47] *Id.* at 586.

[48] Alberti v. Empresa Nicaragüense de la Carne, 705 F.2d 250, 254 (7th Cir. 1983), quoted in *Garb*, 440 F.3d at 587. Other formulations quoted by the court were Hunt v. Mobil Oil Corp., 550 F.2d 68, 73 (2d Cir. 1977) ("Expropriations [of property] within the boundaries of the sovereign state are traditionally considered to be public acts of the sovereign removed from judicial scrutiny"), cert. denied, 434 U.S. 984 (1977), and Haven v. Rzeczpospolita Polska, 68 F.Supp.2d 947, 954 (N.D. Ill. 1999) ("It is obvious that governmental expropriation of private property under government authority . . . is the classic type of activity" deemed sovereign rather than commercial in nature), aff'd, 215 F.3d 727 7th Cir. 2000), cert. denied, 531 U.S. 1014 (2000).

[49] *Garb*, 440 F.3d at 587.

[50] *Id.*

[51] *Id.*

The *Rong* Decision A similar result was reached in another case relied on by the district court in the Westfield litigation, this one involving a government's nationalization of a citizen's business. In *Rong v. Liaoning Province Government*,[52] a Chinese province was sued for seizing the plaintiff's controlling interest in an automobile manufacturing company. In the early 1990s Rong, a Hong Kong entrepreneur, and Shen Yang, a city in the Liaoning Province in northeast China, entered into a joint venture for the automobile production. A closely-held corporation was created with Rong as the principal shareholder and chief executive. As preparations were made to list the company on the New York stock exchange, Chinese officials informed Rong that the entity holding a controlling share should be based in the Liaoning Province rather than in Hong Kong. Rong then created a nongovernmental organization in the province and gave it a majority of shares in the company, on the understanding that the shares were held in trust for him and his Hong Kong company. Ten years later, the province declared that the nongovernmental organization and all of its assets, including its nominal ownership stake in the manufacturing company, were property of the state. The end result was that Rong was ousted from the company and lost his share of its stock, which the province soon sold off at a fraction of its value to a new company controlled by government officials who then arranged to acquire the remaining shares traded on the New York stock exchange. After unsuccessfully pursuing the matter in Chinese courts, Rong, his wife, and his Hong Kong company brought suit in federal court in Washington, D.C., seeking compensatory and relief for what he called the government's implementation of its scheme to seize their ownership stake in the company "and then to maintain control thereof for its own commercial benefit."[53] The district court dismissed the case on sovereign immunity grounds, and the plaintiffs appealed on the theory that their claims should be allowed to go forward under FSIA's commercial activity exception.

The court of appeals rejected the plaintiffs' position. The court acknowledged that in certain respects the province's takeover and subsequent operation of the company had counterparts in the private sector, such as its removal of Rong from the company's management and board of directors and replacing him with government officials. Yet these acts stemmed, in the court's view, from the province's declaration that the plaintiffs' holdings in the company were state assets, which was itself "an act that can be taken only by a sovereign."[54] The court distinguished a previous decision it had rendered in a case challenging Iran's nationalization of a dairy business, which the court had allowed to proceed under the commercial activity exception.[55] Rong's case was critically different from that earlier one, the court explained, because in the earlier one Iran had entered into a formal contract for a joint venture with the complainants, who alleged that Iran had in effect used its majority position in the business to freeze them out of management and deny them

---

[52]452 F.3d 883 (D.C. Cir. 2006).

[53]*Id.* at 887.

[54]*Id.* at 889.

[55]Foremost–McKesson, Inc. v. Islamic Republic of Iran, 905 F.2d 438 (D.C. Cir. 1990).

their contractual share of the profits. The Iran case was thus in essence a dispute among shareholders in a corporation, resting on claims of breach of contract and breach of fiduciary duty, no different from the typical corporate case except that the controlling bloc of shares was owned by the Iranian government instead of an ordinary private party. In Rong's case, by sharp contrast, there was no contract between the provincial government and Rong with respect to the automobile manufacturing company, and the government did not acquire a controlling stake in the company by buying up shares, as Iran had in the earlier case. Rather, the provincial government simply announced by fiat that the company was effectively its own property—an act that a private party in the marketplace could never have done. For this reason, the province's action "constituted a quintessentially sovereign act, not a corporate takeover."[56]

Moreover, the court stated, the province's formation of a new company and sale of the shares it had seized from Rong did not bring the case within the commercial activity exception. Those actions, the court pointed out, occurred after, and should be viewed as discrete from, the act of expropriation that formed the basis of the plaintiffs' claims. Like the Second Circuit court of appeals in *Garb*, the *Rong* court cautioned that acceptance of the plaintiffs' position would unacceptably expand the commercial activity exception. "If Rong's interpretation of commercial activity were correct," the court stated, "then almost any subsequent disposition of expropriated property could allow the sovereign to be haled into a federal court under FSIA."[57] Such a result, the court concluded, contravened earlier judicial decisions construing the statute and would frustrate Congress's purpose of creating only carefully-drawn, limited exceptions to the general rule that foreign governments enjoy sovereign immunity in the American courts.

The *Siderman de Blake* Decision Along with the *Garb* and *Rong* cases, the district court also took note of a contrary ruling by still another court of appeals: *Siderman de Blake v. Republic of Argentina*[58] arose out of the Argentine military junta's kidnapping and torture of a Jewish businessman, followed (after he and his family fled to the United States) by its seizure of his family's hotel and real estate business, which it kept in operation. In a lawsuit brought by the family against Argentina in federal court in California, one of the questions that the court of appeals had to decide was whether the plaintiffs' claims concerning their confiscated property could proceed under the commercial activity exception. The court decided that the claims could go forward, in part because the Argentine government's continued management of the confiscated business, and its receipt of profits from its operation, "were clearly activities 'of a kind in which a private party might engage.'"[59] It was

[56] *Rong*, 452 F.3d at 890.

[57] *Id.*

[58] 965 F.2d 699 (1992). This case was discussed in Chap. 3 in connection with FSIA's expropriation exception.

[59] *Id.* at 709 (quoting Joseph v. Office of Consulate General of Nigeria, 830 F.2d 1018 (9th Cir. 1988)).

equally clear, the court stated, that the government's original seizure of the business was an action "performed in connection with the commercial activity" of managing it and keeping the resulting profits.[60]

The district court in the Westfield case read this statement to mean that Argentina's confiscation of the plaintiff's property fell within the commercial activity exception because it was motivated by the prospect of reaping commercial profit. So read, according to the district court, the opinion no longer represented the state of the law. The language of the *Siderman de Blake* court conflicted (so the district court thought) with the Supreme Court's decision in *Republic of Argentina v. Weltover*, handed down several years later, which emphasized that it is the nature of the challenged government activity, and not its purpose or motive, that matters for purposes of the exception. The district court accordingly concluded that this portion of the *Siderman de Blake* decision had been implicitly overruled.[61]

4.4.3 The District Court Ruling

After surveying the foregoing authorities, the district court applied them to the Westfields' claims. In a few terse paragraphs, it explained that FSIA mandated dismissal of the case, however unjust this result might seem. "Although the treatment of Walter Westfield by the Nazi government was ineffably horrendous," the court wrote, "the Court concludes that the actions upon which Plaintiffs' Complaint is based were not taken in connection with a commercial activity of the Defendant."[62]

The seizure of the Westfeld collection could be viewed, the court explained, either as an expropriation of property or as a forfeiture to satisfy a criminal fine, because it had the qualities of each. If viewed as an expropriation, the court stated, then under the holdings of the property seizure rulings just canvassed, it was an action that must be judged sovereign in character. If viewed instead as the enforcement of a criminal fine, continued the court, it was an action that could only be taken by the state as sovereign through its police and judicial machinery, as were the arrest and torture inflicted on the plaintiff in the *Nelson* case. Under either view, therefore, the confiscation of Westfeld's collection was sovereign rather than private in nature. Furthermore, the court concluded, under the authorities canvassed above the "subsequent disposition of the art collection on the private art market through privately-owned auction houses does not render the initial act of seizure a commercial activity."[63]

---

[60] *Siderman de Blake*, 965 F.2d at 710.

[61] *Westfield*, 2009 WL 2356554, at *6.

[62] *Id.*

[63] *Id.*

The district court's opinion ended on a rueful philosophical note. The equities are with the plaintiffs, the court stated, and "call to mind the legal maxim that where there is a right, there ought to be a remedy."[64] But the principle of *Ubi jus, ibi remedium* could not, explained the court, displace positive law enacted by Congress. The law gave the court no jurisdiction over the defendant, "however monstrous the alleged conduct" that had occurred, and therefore the plaintiffs "must seek any remedy in a forum other than the Federal courts of the United States."[65] As if to underscore its misgivings about the justice of this result, the district court kept its opinion unpublished, preventing its appearance in the national case reports.

4.5 Direct and Indirect Effects

On appeal to the Sixth Circuit court of appeals, the plaintiffs mounted a vigorous challenge to the lower court's reasoning and conclusion. The plaintiffs' central argument was a textual one, calling the court's attention to the precise language of the statute: the third clause of the commercial activity exception suspends sovereign immunity for any lawsuit that is based "upon an act outside the territory of the United States in connection with a commercial activity of the foreign state elsewhere and that act causes a direct effect in the United States."[66] This language indicates, the plaintiffs argued, that they did not have to establish that the "act" upon which their claims were based was commercial in nature; all they needed to establish was that it was done in connection with a commercial activity. Even if the seizure of Walter Westfeld's collection was itself a sovereign act, they argued, it was part and parcel of the Nazis' ongoing participation in the art marketplace, in which they would routinely sell off the art they had taken from Jews. Therefore, they reasoned, the seizure should be considered an act done "in connection with" a commercial activity. They buttressed this textual argument with attempts to distinguish the facts of the cases that the district court had relied upon.

The court of appeals was impressed with the argument, remarking that "the Heirs quite persuasively navigate the morass of reported decisions and make a convincing argument that, based on Germany's sale of the collection at auction to raise capital, the seizure of Westfeld's artwork was sufficiently in connection with commercial activity to fall within this exception."[67] The court nonetheless found it unnecessary to decide the issue, concluding that there was a separate ground for dismissing the case, a ground that the court below (given its ruling that the threshold requirement of commercial activity was not met) had declined to address. "Even if Germany's actions were sufficiently in connection with commercial activity" to satisfy the

[64] *Id.* at *7.

[65] *Id.* (internal quotation marks omitted).

[66] Foreign Sovereign Immunities Act, 28 U.S.C. § 1605(a)(2) (emphasis added).

[67] *Westfield*, 633 F.3d at 414.

exception, the court of appeals stated, "Germany is nonetheless entitled to immunity because the Heirs have not established that those actions caused a direct effect in the United States."[68] Let us follow the appeals court's path to this judgment.

4.5.1 General Principles

The critical problem for courts in applying the "direct effect" requirement is that almost any commercial transaction in the world can be said to produce some effect, however remote or attenuated, in the United States. And yet, as the court of appeals observed, "Congress did not intend to provide jurisdiction whenever the ripples caused by an overseas transaction manage eventually to reach the shores of the United States."[69] The task for the courts has accordingly been to determine what sort of nexus must exist between a defendant's actions and the United States.[70]

The *Weltover* Decision The Supreme Court took this up in *Republic of Argentina v. Weltover*, which we examined earlier for its treatment of the distinction between commercial and noncommercial activity. In *Weltover*, having concluded that the Argentine government's issuance of bonds to support its currency and buttress the creditworthiness of domestic businesses constituted commercial activity, the Court confronted the question whether the issuer's failure to meet the payment schedule had caused a direct effect in the United States. The Court began by considering, and rejecting, Argentina's argument that for purposes of FSIA, an effect counted as "direct" only if it was "substantial" and "foreseeable." This argument rested on the legislative history of FSIA, which explained that the commercial activity exception "would embrace commercial conduct abroad having direct effects within the United States which would subject such conduct to the exercise of jurisdiction by the United States consistent with principles set forth in section 18, Restatement of the Law, Second, Foreign Relations Law of the United States (1965)."[71] That section of the Restatement provides in relevant part that a "state has jurisdiction to prescribe a rule of law attaching legal consequences to conduct that occurs outside its territory and causes an effect within its territory, if ... (i) the conduct and its effect are constituent elements of activity to which the rule applies; (ii) the effect within the territory is substantial; (iii) it occurs as a direct and foreseeable result of the conduct outside the territory; and (iv) the rule is not inconsistent with the principles of justice generally recognized by states that have reasonably developed legal

---

[68]*Id.*

[69]*Id.* (quoting Virtual Countries, Inc. v. Republic of South Africa, 300 F.3d 230, 236 (2d Cir. 2002)).

[70]See generally Nanda and Pansius (2011), § 3:12.

[71]House Judiciary Committee, Jurisdiction of the United States Courts in Suits Against Foreign States, H.R. Rep. No. 1487, 94th Cong., 2d Sess. 19, reprinted in 1976 U.S. Code Congressional & Administrative News 6604, 6618.

systems."[72] Drawing on this language, the majority of the courts of appeals had adopted a rule requiring that overseas conduct cause a "substantial and foreseeable effect" in order to satisfy the direct effect provision.

The Court nonetheless rejected this reasoning and abrogated that line of decisions. The Court refused to put any weight on the quoted passage of the legislative history, whose invocation of the Restatement provision (in the Court's words) "has been charitably described as 'a bit of a non sequitur,'" because the provision deals with legislative rather than adjudicative jurisdiction.[73] To be sure, the Court noted, FSIA leaves in place the general principle of *de minimis non curat lex*, so that purely trivial or speculative effects in the United States would not support jurisdiction under the statute. Apart from recognizing that conventional understanding, however, the Court rejected the position that the commercial activity exception "contains any unexpressed requirement of 'substantiality' or 'foreseeability,'" and instead adopted this concise definition: "an effect is 'direct' if it follows 'as an immediate consequence of the defendant's . . . activity.'"[74]

Applying that definition to the facts before it, the Court found "little difficulty" in reaching the conclusion that the Argentine government's unilateral extension of the maturity dates on its bonds had a direct effect in the United States.[75] The bondholders, which were Panamanian and Swiss corporations, had designated New York as the place of payment when purchasing the bonds, and the Argentine government had already paid some interest into those accounts before making its announcement that it was rescheduling the remaining payments. This was enough, in the Court's view, to make the case a straightforward instance of a direct effect in the United States. It made no difference that the bondholders were foreign corporations with no other connections to the United States. "Because New York was thus the place of performance for Argentina's ultimate contractual obligations, the rescheduling of those obligations necessarily had a 'direct effect' in the United States: Money that was supposed to have been delivered to a New York bank for deposit was not forthcoming."[76]

The *Keller* Decision In addition to taking note of the rule set forth in *Weltover*, the court of appeals in the Westfield litigation adverted to one of its own earlier decisions addressing the meaning of the direct effect requirement. In *Keller v. Central Bank of Nigeria*,[77] the plaintiff was a seller of medical devices in the state of Michigan who fell for a scam run by employees of a government-owned

---

[72] American Law Institute, Restatement of the Law, Second, Foreign Relations Law of the United States § 18 (1965).

[73] *Weltover*, 504 U.S. at 618 (quoting Texas Trading & Milling Corp. v. Federal Republic of Nigeria, 647 F.2d 300, 311 (2d Cir. 1981)).

[74] *Weltover*, 504 U.S. at 618 (quoting *Weltover v. Republic of Argentina*, 941 F.2d 145, 152 (2d Cir. 1991)).

[75] *Weltover*, 504 U.S. at 618.

[76] *Id.* at 504.

[77] 277 F.3d 811 (6th Cir. 2002).

bank in Nigeria, who tricked him into sending them thousands of dollars in order to participate in a promised arrangement in which he would supply them with medical devices to sell to government hospitals, and would receive millions of dollars in kickbacks. Sued for racketeering by the plaintiff in federal court, the bank, as a government entity, invoked sovereign immunity; following an unsuccessful motion to dismiss in the district court, the defendant sought relief in the court of appeals.[78] The court determined that the defendant's alleged actions were undertaken in connection with commercial activity, and then turned to the question of whether there had been a direct effect in the United States. On this issue, the defendant called the court's attention to rulings from the courts of appeals in other circuits holding that to establish a direct effect in the United States, a plaintiff must show that a "legally significant act" occurred in the United States.[79] For example, in one case, a foreign government unlawfully detained the aircraft of an American airline, causing the airline significant losses in the United States. The Second Circuit court of appeals held that the claim must be dismissed because all of the legally significant actions had occurred abroad, adding that "the fact that an American individual or firm suffers some financial loss from a foreign tort cannot, standing alone, suffice to trigger the [commercial activity] exception."[80]

The court in *Keller* declined to follow the lead of the circuits that had embraced this "legally significant act" requirement. As it observed, the Supreme Court's Weltover decision, in rejecting the proposed requirement of a "substantial and foreseeable effect" in the United States, had admonished courts against importing unexpressed elements into the statute. That admonishment, in the *Keller* court's view, applied with equal force to the proposed requirement of a legally significant act in the United States. Accordingly, the court reasoned, the commercial activity exception of FSIA is satisfied if an act taken in connection with a commercial activity abroad causes a direct effect in the United States, even if all of the legally significant acts occur abroad. The court therefore concluded that the Nigerian government could be sued in the United States because it had promised to pay funds into his bank account in Cleveland. The breach of that promise, the court concluded, produced a direct effect in the United States. The losses allegedly sustained by the plaintiff in the United States were, to use the definition set forth

[78]As the court noted, the denial of a motion to dismiss on sovereign immunity grounds is considered a collateral order that may be immediately appealed. See *id.* at 815. As an aside, it is worth noting that the district court dismissed the plaintiff's fraud and misrepresentation claims "because it concluded that plaintiff, by entering into a scheme 'that was certainly questionable, and most probably illegal,' had 'unclean hands' and was barred from asserting these claims in equity." *Id.* at 815 (quoting district court judgment). However, it allowed the federal racketeering claims to go forward.

[79]There was a sharp division among the circuits on this issue. Some circuits took the position that a legally significant act in the United States was required; others said such an act was relevant but not required; and others said it was irrelevant. See American Telecom Co., L.L.C. v. Republic of Lebanon, 501 F.3d 534, 540 (6th Cir. 2007) (collecting cases).

[80]Antares Aircraft, L.P. v. Federal Republic of Nigeria, 999 F.2d 33, 37 (2d Cir. 1993).

in *Weltover*, an immediate consequence of the defendant's commercial activities abroad. The *Keller* court accordingly remanded the case to the district court for further proceedings on the merits of the claim.

4.5.2 Points of Comparison

Having surveyed the Supreme Court's ruling that "an effect need not be substantial or foreseeable" to qualify as a direct effect, and its own prior ruling that no "legally significant act" need take place in the United States, the court of appeals was compelled to admit that courts had struggled for the most part unsuccessfully to provide "objective standards [or] clear rules for determining what does and does not qualify as a direct effect in the United States," because "'direct effect' is hard to define."[81] Aside from the Supreme Court's rather parsimonious definition equating direct effect with "immediate consequence," the only general rule the court of appeals found available was the principle that the judiciary should be "wary of applying this requirement too loosely such that our courts become a haven for airing the world's disputes."[82] Beyond that, the court stated, the only guideposts available to it were previous cases applying FSIA to concrete factual situations. "Without objective standards to guide us, much of our analysis is drawn from comparison to other decisions addressing the scope of the direct effect requirement," as the court put it.[83]

The court focused on cases involving foreign governments' contractual debt obligations, giving primary attention to the Supreme Court's decision in *Weltover* and its own decision in *Keller*. The decisions established, the court stated, that the direct effect requirement was satisfied when a foreign government breached a promise to wire money to the United States. In *Weltover*, the promise in question was a bond covenant to pay the balance due to a New York bank; in *Keller*, it was an agreement to pay the proceeds of government equipment acquisitions into the plaintiff's bank account in Cleveland. The key feature of these cases, the court of appeals explained, was not just (in the Supreme Court's words) that money "that was supposed to have been delivered to [an American] bank for deposit was not forthcoming"[84]; it was that the money was to have been delivered by the defendant foreign government. That element sufficed to fulfill the direct effect requirement. For when a foreign sovereign complied with its contractual obligation to send money to the United States, it was obvious enough that this produced an immediate consequence there; by the same token, if it failed to comply with that obligation, it would produce a consequence of the same financial magnitude, albeit with a negative rather than a positive numerical value. By way of further illustration, the court of appeals referred to its earlier decision

[81] *Westfield*, 633 F.3d at 414, 417.
[82] *Id.* at 414.
[83] *Id.* at 414–15.
[84] *Weltover*, 504 U.S. at 619.

in a case involving Venezuela's issuance of bonds that placed no restrictions on where the holder could demand payment. Because "the holder could demand payment anywhere," the court said of that case, "when the holder demanded payment in Ohio, the failure to pay caused a direct effect in the United States."[85]

In sharp contrast, the court asserted, are situations in which a debtor's default prevents a creditor from moving funds to the United States. According to the court, the DRFP case would have been decided very differently if Venezuela's debt had been payable only somewhere outside the United States, and the holder had intended to transfer the payment proceeds to the United States. In such a situation, if Venezuela had made payment and then the holder had moved the money to the United States, its arrival in the United States would have been only an indirect effect of Venezuela's payment. And by the same token, if Venezuela had failed to make payment, then the non-arrival of money in the United States would have been only an indirect effect of its breach. The "dispositive issue," therefore, "was whether the terms of the bonds called for Venezuela to make payment in the United States"; if they had not done so, the direct effect requirement would not have been met.[86] The court generalized the point: "When funds are due abroad and not paid, the direct effects occur abroad," and although the creditor "might ultimately feel the financial injury at home in the United States, we have held that those reverberations are too attenuated to qualify as direct effects."[87] Such a conclusion was necessary, the court intimated, to keep the commercial activity exception with suitable bounds, for if financial losses in the United States caused by a tort or breach of contract abroad sufficed to extinguish a foreign sovereign's immunity, foreign states' exposure to suit in this country would expand dramatically.

The court of appeals also pointed to its decision in *American Telecom Co., L.L.C. v. Republic of Lebanon*,[88] which involved the application of the commercial activity exception to the breach of a contract concerning provision of cellular telephone services in Lebanon. American Telecom paid $30,000 to participate in the bidding for a contract to manage wireless telephone networks, and was assured by government officials that its submission would be treated fairly and in good faith. It then spent $500,000 preparing its bid in compliance with government guidelines. Its final bid was the lowest submitted by any carrier. It was disqualified, however, on the ground that portions of the bid had been sent by email, in reliance on a government employee's verbal approval. After the contract was awarded to another carrier, American Telecom filed suit in federal court, alleging breach of contract and misrepresentation. On appeal from a dismissal of the lawsuit under FSIA, the court of appeals had to address whether Lebanon's admittedly commercial actions had caused a direct effect in the United States.

---

[85] *Westfield*, 633 F.3d at 415 (describing *DRFP L.L.C. v. Republica Bolivarian de Venezuela*, 622 F.3d 513 (6th Cir. 2010)).

[86] *Westfield*, 633 F.3d at 415.

[87] *Id.* at 416.

[88] 501 F.3d 534 (6th Cir. 2007).

The court held it did not, deeming this "perhaps the rare case in which the Supreme Court's holding in *Weltover* requires no elaboration: 'an effect is direct if it follows as an immediate consequence of the defendant's activity.'"[89] The only immediate consequence of Lebanon's action, the court ruled, was the removal of the plaintiff's bid from the auction; everything else, including the losses of the millions that the plaintiff would have earned if awarded the contract, qualified only as indirect consequences. Its earlier decision in *Keller* was distinguishable, the court stated, because in that case Nigeria had promised to send money to the plaintiff in the United States; here Lebanon had indicated that contract payments to the winning bidder would be paid into a Lebanese bank. The court expressed the view that if the plaintiff's claim for lost profits were accepted, then virtually any government contract bidding process in the world involving an American company would expose foreign governments to jurisdiction in the United States. Indeed, the court worried that under the plaintiff's theory, a "foreign country's failure even to conduct a bidding process would have a direct effect in the United States because no money would flow to a U.S. company that would presumably have won the bid and brought money back to the U.S."[90]

4.5.3 *The Court of Appeals Ruling*

Applying the logic of these cases to the Westfields' claims, the court of appeals ruled that the Nazi expropriation of Walter Westfeld's art collection caused no direct effect in the United States. Though Westfeld had planned to take the art to America, its non-arrival in that country was only an indirect effect of the Nazis' action, because they had not undertaken to send it there. The cases just surveyed, in which the foreign government had breached a "pre-existing duty" created by contract to send assets to the United States, were inapplicable: "here, the Heirs have not alleged that Germany ever promised to deliver Westfeld's art collection to the United States."[91] This was the critical missing element in the claim. "Because Germany had not obligated itself to do anything in the United States," the court concluded, "we cannot say that its actions caused a direct effect in the United States."[92] The plaintiffs "cannot establish that Germany's actions had direct effects in the United States based on allegations that its expropriation of the artwork prohibited Westfeld from sending his collection to Nashville," because such a transfer of the art would have required his intervening action.[93] "Consistent with the *Weltover* line of cases, because Germany was under no obligation to send the

[89] *American Telecom*, 501 F.3d at 540 (quoting *Weltover*, 504 U.S. at 618 (emphasis added)).
[90] *American Telecom*, 501 F.3d at 541.
[91] *Westfield*, 633 F.3d at 415.
[92] *Id.*
[93] *Id.*

collection to the United States," the expropriation had no immediate effect in the United States.[94]

The court acknowledged that the seizure of the collection produced very real consequences in America. It was undisputed, the court stated, that Westfeld sought to send his art collection to the United States, that the seizure interrupted those plans, and that this had a profound impact on his family. That impact, however, was only an indirect effect. To be sure, "the action that prevented the transfer was in this case an illegal seizure and not a failure to pay" a contractual debt, the court stated, but "that does not distinguish the cases cited above, which recognize that a foreign country's actions do not cause direct effects in the United States merely because the entity to which it owed money planned to move the funds to the United States."[95] While the court had every reason to believe that Westfeld "genuinely wished to transfer his artwork to Nashville, finding a direct effect based on plans to send property to the United States would largely eliminate the protections of sovereign immunity."[96] To rule in the plaintiffs' favor, the court asserted, would "effectively read the 'direct' requirement out of the statute and greatly expand the jurisdiction of our courts," frustrating "Congress's goals in enacting the Foreign Sovereign Immunities Act."[97]

As had the district court, the court of appeals ended its opinion on an apologetic note. The Nazis' seizure of Westfeld's art collection was "abhorrent," and no doubt had caused a profound and lasting impact on his family in America.[98] "We are deeply sympathetic to the loss the Heirs suffered as a result of Germany's unspeakable acts," the court declared. "However, our jurisdiction is limited by both Article III of the Constitution and the statutes Congress enacts," and courts "must operate within those restrictions."[99] Judgment was entered for Germany.

4.6 Epilogue

In May 2011, a few months after the court of appeals issued its ruling, the Museum of Fine Arts in Boston announced that it had reached a settlement with the Westfield family over the painting whose questionable provenance had caused the museum to search for Walter Westfeld's relatives, which in turn had led them to bring suit against Germany. The painting, *Portrait of a Man and Woman in an Interior* (c. 1665) by Dutch artist Eglon van der Neer (1634–1703), once belonged to Westfeld, but was not among the catalogued items in the 1939 Nazi-ordered auction

---

[94]*Id.*at 416.

[95]*Id.*

[96]*Id.*

[97]*Id.* at 417.

[98]*Id.* at 418.

[99]*Id.*

for which the heirs sought damages in the case against Germany. It was purchased by the Museum of Fine Arts in 1941 from a dealer who claimed to have purchased it from a refugee. The museum's research indicated that Westfeld had probably parted with the painting a year or two before the 1939 auction, either selling it in Germany or entrusting it to people in France or the Netherlands.[100] "Based on these scenarios," the museum stated in announcing its settlement with the Westfields, "it is unlikely that Westfeld gave or sold the painting voluntarily, but rather, as a Jewish art dealer living in Nazi Germany, disposed of it due to persecution," adding that "it is difficult to imagine a scenario by which he sold the painting voluntarily in Nazi Germany, receiving proceeds over which he had free disposal."[101] Under the terms of the settlement, the painting remains at the museum.

References

American Law Institute. 1987. *Restatement (Third) of the Foreign Relations Law of the United States*. St. Paul, MN: American Law Institute.

Dellapenna, Joseph W. 2003. *Suing Foreign Governments and Their Corporations*. 2nd ed. Ardsley, NY: Transnational Publishers.

Donoghue, Joan E. 1992. Taking the "Sovereign" Out of the Foreign Sovereign Immunities Act: A Functional Approach to the Commercial Activity Exception. *Yale Journal of International Law* 17: 489–538.

Foster, George K. 2014. When Commercial Meets Sovereign: A New Paradigm for Applying the Foreign Sovereign Immunities Act in Crossover Cases. *Houston Law Review* 52: 361–414.

Lauterpacht, Hersch. 1952. The Problem of Jurisdictional Immunities of Foreign States. *British Yearbook of International Law* 28: 220–272.

Müller, Melissa, and Monika Tatzkow. 2010. *Lost Lives, Lost Art: Jewish Collectors, Nazi Art Theft*. London: Frontline.

Museum of Fine Arts, Boston. 2011. Provenance Outreach Conducted by Museum of Fine Arts, Boston, Results in Agreement to Retain Ownership of van der Neer's *Portrait of a Man and Woman in an Interior*. Press release, June 26. Reprinted at http://www.mfa.org/collections/provenance/nazi-era-provenance-research (visited June 5, 2017).

Nanda, Ved P., and David K. Pansius. 2011. *Litigation of International Disputes in U.S. Courts*. 2nd ed. St. Paul, MN: Thomson/West.

Reed, Victoria. 2015. Walter Westfeld and the van der Neer Portrait in Boston: The Case Study of a Jewish Art Dealer in Düsseldorf. In *Alfred Flechtheim: Raubkunst und Restitution*, ed. Andrea Bambi and Axel Drecol, 179–186. Berlin: De Gruyter Oldenbourg.

Schmidt, Herbert. 2005. *Der Elendsweg der Düsseldorfer Juden, Chronologie des Schrecken, 1933-1945*. Düsseldorf: Droste.

van Alebeek, Rosanne. 2008. *The Immunity of States and Their Officials in International Criminal Law and International Human Rights Law*. Oxford: Oxford University Press.

[100]On the possible trajectories the painting might have followed out of Germany, see Reed (2015).

[101]Museum of Fine Arts, Boston (2011).

Cases

Alberti v. Empresa Nicaragüense de la Carne, 705 F.2d 250 (7th Cir. 1983)
Alfred Dunhill of London, Inc. v. Republic of Cuba, 425 U.S. 682 (1976)
American Telecom Co., L.L.C. v. Republic of Lebanon, 501 F.3d 534 (6th Cir. 2007)
Antares Aircraft, L.P. v. Federal Republic of Nigeria, 999 F.2d 33 (2d Cir. 1993)
Banque Roumaine de Commerce et de Crédit de Prague v. Etat polonais, 19 RDIP 581 (Romania, Tribunal de commerce d'Ilfov, 1920)
Doe v. Holy See, 434 F.Supp.2d 925 (D. Or. 2006)
DRFP L.L.C. v. Republica Bolivarian de Venezuela, 622 F.3d 513 (6th Cir. 2010)
Foremost–McKesson, Inc. v. Islamic Republic of Iran, 905 F.2d 438 (D.C. Cir. 1990)
Garb v. Republic of Poland, 440 F.3d 579 (2d Cir. 2006)
Haven v. Rzeczpospolita Polska (Republic of Poland), 68 F.Supp.2d 947 (N.D. Ill. 1999), aff'd, 215 F.3d 727 (7th Cir. 2000), cert. denied, 531 U.S. 1014 (2000)
Hunt v. Mobil Oil Corp., 550 F.2d 68 (2d Cir. 1977), cert. denied, 434 U.S. 984 (1977)
I Congreso Del Partido, House of Lords, 2 All Eng. Rep. 1064 ¶ 527 (House of Lords 1983)
Joseph v. Office of Consulate General of Nigeria, 830 F.2d 1018 (9th Cir. 1988), cert. denied, 405 U.S. 905 (1988)
Keller v. Central Bank of Nigeria, 277 F.3d 811 (6th Cir. 2002)
O'Bryan v. Holy See, 556 F.3d 361 (6th Cir. 2009), cert denied, 558 U.S. 819 (2009)
Republic of Argentina v. Weltover, 504 U.S. 607 (1992)
Rong v. Liaoning Province Government, 452 F.3d 883 (D.C. Cir. 2006)
Saudi Arabia v. Nelson, 507 U.S. 349 (1993)
Siderman de Blake v. Republic of Argentina, 965 F.2d 699 (1992)
Texas Trading & Milling Corp. v. Federal Republic of Nigeria, 647 F.2d 300 (2d Cir. 1981)
Virtual Countries, Inc. v. Republic of South Africa, 300 F.3d 230 (2d Cir. 2002)
Westfield v. Federal Republic of Germany, 2009 WL 2356554 (M.D. Tenn. 2009), aff'd, 633 F.3d 409 (6th Cir. 2011)

Chapter 5
Orkin v. Taylor

5.1 Background

Margarete Mauthner (1863–1947) was a prominent arts patron and participant in the intellectual life of Berlin, known for her support of contemporary writers and artists. An early enthusiast of the recently deceased Vincent van Gogh, she published a collection of his letters that went through numerous editions, and began collecting his paintings at a time when most viewers still considered them an affront to serious art.[1] One of the works she acquired was van Gogh's *Vue de l'Asile et de la Chapelle de Saint-Rémy*, painted near the town of Auvers during the summer or fall of 1889, in the final year of the artist's life. Mauthner purchased it from the Cassirer gallery in Berlin in 1907.

Mauthner, who was Jewish, fled Nazi Germany with her family in 1939. She settled in South Africa, where she died a few years after the end of the war. The immediate fate of *Vue de l'Asile*, which she left behind in Germany, remains unclear. The 1939 edition of the *catalogue raisonné* of van Gogh's work lists Mauthner as the painting's current owner; the 1970 edition lists the next owner as Alfred Wolf, a Jewish businessman who fled Germany for Switzerland in 1934.[2] It is not known how, when, or from whom Wolf came to acquire the painting.[3] In 1963, Wolf's estate commissioned Sotheby's in London to sell the work at auction. The winning bidder was Francis Taylor, an art dealer and the father of the film star Elizabeth Taylor, who purchased the work for £92,000, adding it to the family's collection of impressionist and post-impressionist paintings. Elizabeth Taylor placed *Vue de l'Asile* up for auction at Christie's in London in 1990, but it did not sell, and the work remained at her Los Angeles home.

[1] See her posthumously published memoir, Mauthner (2004).

[2] See de La Faille (1939, 1970).

[3] A 1990 auction catalogue issued by Christie's listed Frankfurt art dealer Marcel Goldschmidt as an intermediate owner between Mauthner and Wolf.

B.L. Hay, *Nazi-Looted Art and the Law*, DOI 10.1007/978-3-319-64967-2_5

In 2003, a lawyer representing Mauthner's great-grandchildren Sarah-Rose Adler, Andrew Orkin, and Mark Orkin contacted Taylor, informing her of their belief that *Vue de l'Asile* rightfully belonged to Mauthner's estate. The 1939 *catalogue raisonné* established, in their view, that the painting belonged to Mauthner at the time that she fled Germany. Though they did not know what had become of the painting at that time, they knew she did not bring it with her into exile in South Africa. Either she sold it in desperation before leaving Germany, they contended, or it was taken away from her in some other way. In either case, according to the heirs, she parted with the painting involuntarily as a result of Nazi persecution, and neither Wolf nor Taylor after him could have acquired good title to the work. Following unsuccessful settlement negotiations, lawyers for Taylor stated that she held valid title to the painting, and would not return it.

The matter attracted considerable attention from the press because of Taylor's fame. Asked why they had waited so long to seek the painting's return, the heirs stated that they hadn't known that Mauthner once owned the painting. "I knew that the family had owned works of art that hadn't come to South Africa. But we didn't talk about it. Our way of dealing with the Holocaust was total silence," Andrew Orkin explained.[4] After the passage in the late 1990s of American restitution legislation, the heirs had asked a lawyer to conduct a search of works once owned by Mauthner. When rumors surfaced on the internet in 2002 that Taylor was interested in selling *Vue de l'Asile*, they learned that the painting had once been part of Mauthner's collection.

5.2 Proceedings

In October 2004, the Mauthner heirs filed suit against Taylor in federal district court in Los Angeles, invoking both diversity of citizenship and federal question jurisdiction.[5] In their complaint, the plaintiffs asserted that Mauthner had lost *Vue de l'Asile* as a result of Nazi persecution, and that when purchasing the painting the Taylor family had not properly investigated its provenance, and had ignored warning signs that it had been stolen or sold under duress. The heirs sought recovery of the painting on theories of replevin, conversion, constructive trust, and unjust enrichment, basing their claims on the common law and legislation of the state of California, and also on federal Holocaust restitution legislation that, they contended, contained an implied private right of action independent of state law.

The district court granted Taylor's motion to dismiss the case.[6] The common law claims, it ruled, were barred by California's three-year statute of limitations.

[4]Quoted in Berlins (2004).

[5]Several months earlier, Taylor had filed suit against the heirs in the same court, seeking a declaration that they had no valid claims to the painting. The two lawsuits were consolidated.

[6]Adler v. Taylor, 2005 WL 4658511 (C.D. Cal. 2005).

California law was unclear, in the district court's view, as to whether the heirs' claims had accrued when Taylor acquired the painting, or instead had accrued at some later date when the heirs knew or should have known that they had claims against her. The question made no difference in the present case, the court ruled, because reasonable diligence on the heirs' part would have revealed the existence of their claims after Taylor's highly publicized purchase of the painting. The statute of limitations on the common law claims had thus expired three years after the 1963 purchase. Regarding the claims based on state and federal legislation, the court ruled that the statutes invoked by the plaintiffs did not create any independent private right of action for property claimants.

The court of appeals for the Ninth Circuit affirmed the judgment against the heirs.[7] Agreeing with the lower court, the court ruled that they had failed to state any valid claims under federal law, because the federal statute on which they relied in their complaint did not create any independent rights of action. The statute, the Holocaust Victims Redress Act of 1998, was purely "precatory," the court stated; in it, Congress expressed its view that governments should facilitate restitution of Nazi-looted property, but did not "create individual rights or, for that matter, any enforceable law."[8] As for the heirs' state law claims, the court agreed with the district court that they were time-barred. As had the district court, the court of appeals found California law unclear as to whether the heirs' claims had accrued at the time of Taylor's purchase or at the time they knew or should have known of their claims. Even granting them the benefit of the latter possibility, the court stated, the heirs should have discovered the existence of their claim by 1990 at the latest, when Taylor advertised it for sale at an internationally-known auction house. The statute of limitations had accordingly expired long before they filed suit.

The United States Supreme Court declined to hear the case.

5.3 Rights of Action Under Federal Law

In their complaint, the Mauthner heirs contended that their right to recover the painting was guaranteed not only by state law, but also by the federal Holocaust Victims Redress Act of 1998. Their strategy in urging this federal right to recovery, presumably, was to avoid the potential time bar that might be imposed on their state law claims. The federal cause of action they proposed contained no remedies not already provided by state law theories, such as replevin and conversion, but unlike them was unconstrained by state time limitations periods. "[A] primary purpose of the acts was to enable Holocaust victims—as 'rightful owners'—to locate Nazi confiscated artworks and other assets and secure their return," they argued; and "due to the enormity of the crime committed against the Jewish people, Congress

---

[7]Orkin v. Taylor, 487 F.3d 734 (9th Cir.), cert. denied, 552 U.S. 990 (2007).

[8]*Id.* at 739.

rejected any notion that a 'statute of limitations' defense be used to bar the claims of Nazi victims for the return of their property."[9] Because the Holocaust Victims Redress Act does not contain any explicit provision concerning lawsuits, the question for the courts was whether, as the heirs contended, it implicitly created a private right of action to effectuate its objectives. Resolution of the issue required a detour through the Supreme Court's jurisprudence on the subject of implied rights of action under federal statutes.

5.3.1 *The Jurisprudence of Implied Rights of Action*

The court of appeals relied on the framework set forth in *Cort v. Ash*,[10] the leading modern decision on the subject. *Cort* concerned a federal election statute that prohibited corporations from making contributions or expenditures in connection with American presidential campaigns, which authorized criminal penalties for violators but contained no explicit provisions for civil enforcement. A shareholder of Bethlehem Steel filed a civil suit under the statute against the company's managers after they used the company's name in published advertisements that criticized a 1972 presidential candidate; the complaint sought damages to compensate the corporation for the unlawful use of its assets. Following a decision by the court of appeals allowing the claim to go forward, the Supreme Court undertook to decide whether the federal election statute implicitly authorized a civil damage remedy available to private plaintiffs.

Reviewing its cases going back many years, the Court identified four criteria relevant to determining whether a federal statute should be read to contain a private right of action when it did not provide for one on its face. The first concerns the position of the plaintiff: "is the plaintiff 'one of the class for whose especial benefit the statute was enacted'—that is, does the statute create a federal right in favor of the plaintiff?"[11] Here the Court cited an old case, *Texas Pacific Railway Co. v. Rigsby*,[12] in which a freight railroad employee, injured by falling from a car equipped with a defective ladder, filed suit under a federal statute that required ladders on the type of car in question. Rejecting the railroad's contention that the plaintiff could not recover damages under the statute because it contained no express provision for private suits, the Court reasoned that "[t]here can be no question that a box car having a hand brake operated from the roof requires also a secure ladder to enable the employee to safely ascend and descend, and that the provision quoted was intended for the especial protection of employees engaged in

---

[9]Brief of Appellants, Orkin v. Taylor, No. 09-1922 (9th Cir. Aug. 8, 2005), at 46.

[10]422 U.S. 66 (1975). On private rights of action under federal statutes, see generally Marcantel (2013), Stabile (1996), and Ziegler (2001).

[11]*Id.* at 78.

[12]241 U.S. 33 (1916).

duties such as that which the plaintiff was performing."[13] The railroad's "disregard of the command of the statute is a wrongful act, and where it results in damage to one of the class for whose especial benefit the statute was enacted, the right to recover the damages from the party in default is implied, according to a doctrine of the common law . . . [that] 'in every case, where a statute enacts or prohibits a thing for the benefit of a person, he shall have remedy upon the same statute for the thing enacted for his advantage, or for the recompense of a wrong done to him contrary to the said law.' This is but an application of the maxim, *Ubi jus ibi remedium*."[14]

The second criterion, according to *Cort*, is the available evidence in the legislative history concerning the intention of Congress: "is there any indication of legislative intent, explicit or implicit, either to create such a remedy or to deny one?"[15] The Court pointed to *National Railroad Passenger Corp. v. National Association of Railroad Passengers*,[16] in which a passenger association sued to enjoin a railway from discontinuing service along certain lines. The plaintiffs invoked the Amtrak Act of 1970, a section of which, for cases in which a railroad "neglects to discharge is duties and responsibilities under this chapter," gave the courts jurisdiction to issue injunctive relief "upon the petition of the Attorney General of the United States or, in a case involving a labor agreement, upon petition of any employee affected thereby."[17] Though by its terms the section "purports only to confer jurisdiction not to create a cause of action," the Court stated, the "legislative history, however, makes clear that the congressional purpose was to authorize certain types of suits for the enforcement of the Act's provisions."[18] But the legislative history also indicated that the only private enforcement in court contemplated by Congress was litigation brought by railroad employees to redress violations of labor agreements; other privately-initiated complaints, including those concerning discontinued service, were expected to be brought in comparatively expeditious administrative proceedings rather than in court. The Court concluded that the passenger association had no private right of action under the statute.

The third *Cort* criterion is whether an implied right of action would further the overall objectives and design of the statute: "is it consistent with the underlying purposes of the legislative scheme to imply such a remedy for the plaintiff?"[19] The Court again cited the Amtrak case, which had held that permitting a private right of action to challenge service discontinuances would not only be at odds with the available evidence of legislative intent, but would frustrate the smooth operation of the statutory scheme, because the slow process of court litigation "would force Amtrak to continue the train's operation and to incur the resulting deficits and

[13] *Id.* at 37.

[14] *Id.* at 39 (citation omitted).

[15] *Cort*, 422 U.S. at 78.

[16] 414 U.S. 522 (1974).

[17] Quoted in *id.* at 456.

[18] *Id.* at 457.

[19] *Cort*, 422 U.S. at 78.

dislocations within its entire system while the court considered the propriety of the proposed discontinuance."[20] To similar effect the Court also cited *Calhoon v. Harvey*,[21] in which it denied a private right of action under federal labor law to mount a judicial challenge to the results of a union election, reasoning that the statute relegated such complaints to administrative proceedings, and that permitting a private litigant to sue would not be "in harmony with the general congressional policy to allow unions great latitude in resolving their own internal controversies and, where that fails, to utilize the agencies of Government most familiar with union problems to aid in bringing about a settlement through discussion before resort to the courts."[22]

Finally, the fourth *Cort* criterion is considerations of federalism: "is the cause of action one traditionally relegated to state law, in an area basically the concern of the States, so that it would be inappropriate to infer a cause of action based solely on federal law?"[23] Here the Court referred to its decision in *Wheeldin v. Wheeler*,[24] involving a suit brought against a federal investigator who, without authorization, had publicly ordered the plaintiff to appear before the House Un-American Activities Committee, causing harm to his reputation. The plaintiff sued for damages, asserting a claim not under tort law but under the federal statute providing for the issuance of subpoenas by the Committee. Rejecting the claim, the Court stated that "it is difficult for us to see how the present statute, which only grants power to issue subpoenas, implies a cause of action for the abuse of that power."[25] According to the Court, "[w]hen it comes to suits for damages for abuse of power, federal officials are usually governed by local law"; it was true that "[o]ver the years Congress has considered the problem of state civil and criminal sanctions against federal officials many times," but "no general statute making federal officers liable for acts committed 'under color,' but in violation, of their federal authority has been passed."[26] If state law was to be displaced, the Court ruled, it should be up to Congress to make that decision; "it is not for us to fill any hiatus Congress has left in this area."[27] By way of contrast, the *Cort* opinion cited the decision in *J.I. Case Co. v. Borak*,[28] which, in a suit arising out of a corporate merger involving deceptive proxy statements, recognized an implied right of action for damages under the disclosure provisions of the federal Securities Exchange Act of 1934. The federal statute's intervention in securities markets went well beyond traditional doctrines of state tort and contract law, the Court reasoned, and would lose much of

[20] *Id.* at 463.

[21] 379 U.S. 139 (1964).

[22] *Id.* at 140.

[23] *Cort*, 422 U.S. at 78.

[24] 373 U.S. 647 (1963).

[25] *Id.* at 651.

[26] *Id.* at 652.

[27] *Id.*

[28] 377 U.S. 426 (1964).

its effectiveness if a damage remedy were unavailable for violations. For then "victims of deceptive proxy statements would be obliged to go into state courts for remedial relief," the Court stated, and "if the law of the State happened to attach no responsibility to the use of misleading proxy statements, the whole purpose of the section might be frustrated."[29] There was accordingly no federalism rationale for denying a private right of action to enforce the statute in question.

Having gleaned these criteria from the case law, the Court turned in its *Cort* opinion to applying them to the federal statutory prohibition on corporate participation in presidential election campaigns. First, with respect to whether the plaintiff was part of a class of people the statute was specially designed to benefit, the Court concluded that preventing political corruption was the main object of the statute, and that "the protection of ordinary stockholders was at best a secondary concern."[30] Originally enacted in 1907 in response to progressive-era concerns about corporate control of politics, the statute was designed, in the Court's words, "to assure that federal elections are 'free from the power of money,' to eliminate 'the apparent hold on political parties which business interests ... seek and sometimes obtain by reason of liberal campaign contributions.'"[31] The statute, in the Court's view, was thus "primarily concerned with corporations as a source of aggregated wealth and therefore of possible corrupting influence, and not directly with the internal relations between the corporations and their stockholders."[32] Though not conclusive, this counseled against finding a private right of action, because "in those situations in which we have inferred a federal private right of action not expressly provided, there has generally been a clearly articulated federal right in the plaintiff, or a pervasive legislative scheme governing the relationship between the plaintiff class and the defendant class in a particular regard."[33]

Second, examining extrinsic evidence of Congress's intentions, the Court could find no support for the private right of action claimed by the plaintiff. There is "no indication whatever in the legislative history," the Court declared, "which suggests a congressional intention to vest in corporate shareholders a federal right to damages for violations" of the statute.[34] The Court emphasized that the existence of such evidence was not essential, and that in suitable cases a private right of action might be inferred with no indicia drawn from the legislative history. In "situations in which it is clear that federal law has granted a class of persons certain rights, it is not necessary to show an intention to create a private cause of action" in the legislative history, the Court explained; but "where, as here, it is at least dubious whether Congress intended to vest in the plaintiff class rights broader than those

---

[29] *Id.* at 434–35.

[30] *Cort*, 422 U.S. at 82.

[31] *Id.* at 82 (quoting United States v. Auto Workers, 352 U.S. 567, 576–77 (1957) (citations and internal quotation marks omitted)).

[32] *Cort*, 422 U.S. at 82.

[33] *Id.*

[34] *Id.* at 82.

provided by state regulation of corporations, the fact that there is no suggestion that [a violation of the statute] may give rise to a suit for damages or, indeed, to any civil cause of action, reinforces the conclusion that the expectation, if any, was that the relationship between corporations and their stockholders would continue to be entrusted entirely to state law."[35]

Third, with regard to effectuating the purpose and design of the statute, the Court saw relatively little to recommend the plaintiff's claim to recover misspent funds from corporate management on behalf of the corporation. The "remedy sought would not aid the primary congressional goal" of curbing corruption or undue corporate influence on elections, the Court suggested.[36] "Recovery of derivative damages by the corporation for violation of [the statute] would not cure the influence which the use of corporate funds in the first instance may have had on a federal election," it observed.[37] "Rather, such a remedy would only permit directors in effect to 'borrow' corporate funds for a time," according to the Court; "the later compelled repayment might well not deter the initial violation and would certainly not decrease the impact of the use of such funds upon an election already past."[38] A private right of action would therefore add little or nothing to the remedy Congress had chosen, which was criminal enforcement by public authorities.

Finally, with respect to federalism considerations, the Court believed the dispute to be one properly left to state law. It was "entirely appropriate in this instance to relegate [the plaintiff shareholder] and others in his situation to whatever remedy is created by state law," the Court declared, noting that common law doctrines of *ultra vires* action and breach of fiduciary duty might or might not be triggered by management's misuse of corporate funds in violation of federal law.[39] "Corporations are creatures of state law," the Court observed, "and investors commit their funds to corporate directors on the understanding that, except where federal law expressly requires certain responsibilities of directors with respect to stockholders, state law will govern the internal affairs of the corporation."[40] Federal courts should be reluctant to intrude on state law regulation of corporate governance without explicit congressional authorization, the Court stated; unlike in the *Borak* case, which involved a statute that "was clearly an intrusion of federal law into the internal affairs of corporations," the statute at issue in the present case had nothing to say about the duties of corporate officers toward shareholders.[41] To recognize an implied right of action would therefore "intrude into an area traditionally committed to state law without aiding the main purpose" of the statute, concluded the Court.[42]

[35] *Id.* at 83.

[36] *Id.* at 84.

[37] *Id.*

[38] *Id.*

[39] *Id.*

[40] *Id.*

[41] *Id.* at 85.

[42] *Id.*

5.3.2 *The Holocaust Victims Redress Act*

With the *Cort* framework in mind, the court of appeals in the Orkin litigation took up the question whether the Holocaust Victims Redress Act created a private right of action. The passage relied on by the plaintiffs, entitled "Sense of the Congress Regarding Restitution of Private Property, Such as Works of Art," reads as follows:

> It is the sense of Congress that consistent with the 1907 Hague Convention, all governments should undertake good faith efforts to facilitate the return of private and public property, such as works of art, to the rightful owners in cases where assets were confiscated from the claimant during the period of Nazi rule and there is reasonable proof that the claimant is the rightful owner.[43]

The central problem for the plaintiffs, in the court of appeals' view, was that the provision created no legal obligations. "'Sense of the Congress' provisions are precatory provisions," the Court declared, "which do not in themselves create individual rights or, for that matter, any enforceable law."[44] Such provisions may be useful in determining whether other provisions, mandatory in nature, create implied private rights of action, according to the court. But here, "the Orkins can point to no provision of the Act or any of its companion legislation that can fairly be characterized as mandatory," the court stated.[45] "There is simply no 'right- or duty-creating language' anywhere in the statutory scheme, and [the statute's] announcement of a 'sense of the Congress cannot, of its own force, imply a private right of action."[46]

None of the *Cort* criteria supported the plaintiffs, in the court's view. "With respect to the first *Cort* factor, although there is no doubt that the Act was focused on Holocaust victims and (in a colloquial sense) intended to benefit them, Holocaust victims do not constitute a 'beneficiary class' within the meaning of the *Cort* test," according to the court.[47] "The provision's focus is on 'governments' rather than individuals, urging those governments 'to facilitate' enforcement of preexisting property rights," it continued.[48] "The statute, thus, does not 'explicitly confer a benefit on' Holocaust victims; it merely expresses Congress's sense that Holocaust survivors and heirs should benefit fully from preexisting protections."[49] This was not enough to make victims and their heirs a beneficiary class. As for the second criterion, evidence in the legislative history, this too was no help to the plaintiffs. "[T]he Act's legislative history indicates that even its most ardent supporter did not intend for the bill to create a private right of action"; rather,

---

[43] Pub.L. No. 105-158, § 202, 112 Stat 17–18 (1998).

[44] *Orkin*, 487 F.3d at 739.

[45] *Id.*

[46] *Id.* (quoting Cannon v. University of Chicago, 441 U.S. 677, 690 n. 13 (1979)).

[47] *Orkin*, 487 F.3d at 740.

[48] *Id.*

[49] *Id.*

"the legislative intent was to encourage state and foreign governments to enforce existing rights for the protection of Holocaust victims."[50] The principal sponsor of the legislation, according to the court, indicated his belief that "existing law would suffice to restitute Nazi-stolen artworks to the Nazi-era owners."[51]

As for the third *Cort* criterion, the statute's "overarching purpose was not to provide for private litigation," in the court's view.[52] "Rather, the general purpose of the statutory scheme was to fund research efforts and to declassify records, while simultaneously encouraging foreign governments, as well as public and private institutions, to do likewise."[53] The "motivating concern," in other words, "was not access to courts; it was access to information."[54] Indeed, during the hearings preceding the statute's enactment, some participants viewed court litigation as a relatively poor method of handling restitution claims, and that alternatives such as mediation and arbitration were preferable avenues. "Finally, with respect to the fourth *Cort* factor, there can be no doubt—as this case amply demonstrates—that state law provides causes of action for restitution of stolen artworks," and that "the torts asserted here are undoubtedly causes of action that are traditionally relegated to state law."[55] The "[i]mplication of a federal remedy in this case, therefore, would be inappropriate," particularly given the indications that "Congress did not intend to supersede traditional state-law remedies when it passed the Act."[56] In sum, given "the absence of congressional intent to create a private right of action, the Orkins' assertion of a federal right of action must fail," concluded the court.[57]

5.4 The Statute of Limitations

The remaining question for the courts was whether the claims rooted in state law were barred by the California statute of limitations.[58] The question had two parts: establishing the rule for determining the point in time at which a claim accrues under state law; and deciding when, under that rule, the Orkin plaintiffs' claim against Taylor accrued.

[50] *Id.* at 739.

[51] *Id.*

[52] *Id.* at 740.

[53] *Id.*

[54] *Id.*

[55] *Id.*

[56] *Id.*

[57] *Id.* at 741.

[58] Here the courts were following the rule established in the *Guaranty Trust* decision, which generally establishes that in adjudicating state law claims, the federal courts must apply the corresponding state statute of limitations. See Guaranty Trust Co. of New York v. York, 326 U.S. 99 (1945).

5.4.1 *The California Discovery Rule*

Accrual in Stolen Property Cases In *Naftzger v. American Numismatic Society*,[59] the California court of appeals took up the problem of determining the time of accrual for claims to recover stolen property. The facts were as follows. The American Numismatic Society, a coin museum in New York, received a donation of valuable antique coins in 1937. Sometime in the ensuing decades, a visitor stole the coins from the museum, substituting inferior duplicates to conceal the theft. The museum did not learn of the theft until 1990, when an expert examined its collection and announced that the coins in its possession were not the same as the ones that had been donated. Shortly afterward, the museum learned that the stolen coins were in the possession of Naftzger in California, who had purchased them from the suspected thief. Naftzger refused the museum's request to return the coins and filed suit in California state court, seeking a declaration that he had enjoyed good title to the coins since 1973. The museum filed a counterclaim to recover the coins. The trial court ruled in Naftzger's favor, holding that the museum's rights to the coins had been extinguished by the statute of limitations, which provides that claims "for taking detaining, or injuring goods or chattels, including actions for the specific recovery of personal property" must be brought "within three years."[60] In the trial court's view, the museum's claim had accrued when the coins were stolen several decades earlier, and had expired three years afterward.

On appeal, the court of appeals reversed, holding that a claim to recover stolen property accrues not when the theft occurs, but rather when the owner discovers the identity of the property's possessor. The court began by observing that the applicable statute of limitations was silent on the timing of accrual; in enacting the statute, "the Legislature left unanswered the general question of whether the cause of action accrues when the theft occurs, or when the owner discovers: (a) the theft, (b) the identity of the thief, or (c) the identity of the person in possession of the stolen property."[61] A 1983 amendment to the statute, the court noted, provided a "partial answer" to the question, by specifying that a claim "does not accrue until the owner, the owner's agent, or the investigating law enforcement agency discovers the whereabouts of the stolen articles, provided that the articles possess historical, interpretive, scientific, or artistic significance."[62] This 1983 amendment did not, however, indicate its own temporal scope of application, leaving open the question of which, if any, pre-1983 events it might be applied to. The court nonetheless found it unnecessary to address that question. Instead, it effectively ruled that the amendment simply clarified what was already implicitly provided for

[59] 49 Cal.Rptr.2d 784 (App. 1996). On California statute of limitations law, see generally Ochoa and Wistrich (1997).

[60] Cal. Civ. Proc. Code § 338(c).

[61] *Naftzger*, 49 Cal.Rptr.2d at 786.

[62] Cal. Civ. Proc. Code § 338(c).

in the statute: "we hold, as a matter of law, that there was a discovery rule of accrual implicit in the prior version of [the statute] for the return of stolen property."[63]

This conclusion represented the extension of a principle the California courts had been developing for some years. In a series of tort cases not involving stolen property, the courts had relaxed the traditional common law rule "that 'an action accrues on the date of injury,'"[64] that is, "upon the occurrence of the last element essential to the cause of action."[65] The traditional rule had proved too onerous, in the courts' view, for cases in which there was a temporal lag between the time of injury and the time of its discovery by the plaintiff, for example when the wrong involves latent defects in a construction project; in such cases, the traditional rule meant that the plaintiff's claim might expire before she knew she had been harmed or by whom. To ease its rigors, the courts had replaced the traditional rule with the so-called discovery rule, "which provides that the accrual date may be 'delayed until the plaintiff is aware of her injury and its negligent cause.'"[66] The discovery rule, as the courts have explained, has the objective of giving the plaintiff a reasonable opportunity to bring her claim within the statutory limitations period, and of safeguarding claims in cases "where it is manifestly unjust to deprive plaintiffs of a cause of action before they are aware that they have been injured."[67] By providing for "delayed accrual until a plaintiff knew or should have known of the wrongful conduct at issue," the discovery rule "protects those who are ignorant of their cause of action through no fault of their own."[68]

Some earlier decisions, the *Nafzger* court observed, might be read to hold the discovery rule inapplicable to claims for the recovery of wrongfully converted property. For example, in one 1943 decision, a borrower defaulted on a loan financing the purchase of construction equipment, and unbeknownst to the bank later sold the equipment to a third party. When, more than three years later, the bank attempted to recover the property from the third party, the court held the claim time-barred, ruling that the claim had accrued when the borrower had wrongfully converted the property, albeit without the bank's knowledge.[69] In the *Nafzger* court's view, however, such rulings were limited to situations in which the plaintiff, like the bank, were victims of conversion at the hands of someone to whom it had entrusted the property in question. At least part of their rationale, the court explained, was that the plaintiff, by entrusting the property, had in effect cloaked

[63]*Naftzger*, 49 Cal.Rptr.2d at 786. On the discovery rule in stolen art cases, see generally Phelan (2000).

[64]*Id.* at 788 (quoting Jolly v. Eli Lilly & Co., 751 P.2d 923, 926 (Cal. 1988)).

[65]*Naftzger*, 49 Cal.Rptr.2d at 788 (quoting Neel v. Magana, Olney, Levy, Cathcart & Gelfand, 98 Cal.Rptr. 837, 842 (1971)).

[66]*Naftzger*, 49 Cal.Rptr.2d at 788 (quoting *Jolly*, 751 P.2d at 926–27).

[67]Leaf v. City of San Mateo, 163 Cal.Rptr. 711, 715 (App. 1980).

[68]*Naftzger*, 49 Cal.Rptr.2d at 788 (quoting April Enterprises, Inc. v. KKTV, 195 Cal.Rptr. 421, 437 (App. 1983)).

[69]First National Bank v. Thompson, 140 P.2d 75 (Cal. App. 1943).

the wrongdoer with apparent authority to sell the property to the innocent third party. But that rationale had no application, the court explained, to cases of stolen property; in such cases, the plaintiff has not given possession of the property to the wrongdoer, cannot monitor his activities, and may have no idea who or where he is. Moreover, the court noted, the criminal laws, though not applicable to the civil case at hand, provide support for the idea that in a suit to recover stolen property from an innocent purchaser, the claim does not accrue until the plaintiff discovers the purchaser's identity. "Stolen property remains stolen property, no matter how many years have transpired from the date of the theft," and the criminal laws provide that "an innocent purchaser cannot withhold or sell the stolen property after learning of the theft."[70]

The court accordingly concluded that "common sense dictates that the civil cause of action for recovering stolen property under [the statute of limitations] does not necessarily accrue when the theft occurs, or even when the owner discovers the theft. For until the owner discovers the *identity* of the thief of or the person in possession of the stolen property, the owner is powerless to institute an action under [the statute] for the return of the property."[71] The court rejected Naftzger's argument that the 1983 amendment to the statute, which explicitly provided a discovery rule for accrual, implicitly established that no such rule was in existence before then. The discovery rule, the court explained, was largely a judicial creation, and had been applied in many other contexts without overt legislative authorization; there was no reason to treat stolen property cases any differently. The court therefore remanded the case to the trial court for further proceedings, because the museum had filed suit within three years of discovering that Naftzger was in possession of the stolen coins.

Contours of the Discovery Rule The discovery rule, as the California supreme court has formulated it in *Jolly v. Eli Lilly & Co.*,[72] provides that a claim accrues when the plaintiff becomes "aware" of its factual basis.[73] For this purpose, according to the *Jolly* court, the word *aware* refers not only to what the plaintiff realizes, but also to what, under the circumstances, she ought to realize. That is, under the discovery rule, the "plaintiff is held to her actual knowledge as well as knowledge that could reasonably be discovered through investigation of sources open to her," so that "the statute of limitations begins to run when the plaintiff suspects or should suspect that her injury was caused by wrongdoing, that someone has done something wrong to her."[74] Elaborating on this idea, the *Jolly* court explained that "the limitations period begins to run once the plaintiff 'has notice or information of circumstances to put a reasonable person on inquiry,'" and "[s]o

[70]*Naftzger*, 49 Cal.Rptr.2d at 791.

[71]*Id.*

[72]751 P.2d 923 (1988).

[73]*Id.* at 927.

[74]*Id.*

long as a suspicion exists, it is clear that the plaintiff must go find the facts; she cannot wait for the facts to find her."[75]

The plaintiff in *Jolly* was the daughter of a woman who had taken the anti-miscarriage drug DES during pregnancy in the early 1950s. In 1972, the plaintiff learned that DES daughters were at heightened risk of contracting cancer, and began undergoing medical monitoring; she was treated for cancer in 1976 and 1978. During this period, the plaintiff attempted to discover which of the numerous manufacturers of DES had produced the drug ingested by her mother. Her efforts were unsuccessful, as her mother's pharmacist and medical providers had lost or destroyed the relevant records. In 1980, the California supreme court handed down its decision in *Sindell v. Abbott Laboratories*,[76] which held that a DES victim who was unable to identify the particular manufacturer of the drug that had harmed her could nonetheless recover for her injuries, collecting on a pro rata basis from those manufacturers that had enjoyed a significant share of the market in which the drug had been purchased. Following this ruling, in 1981, the *Jolly* plaintiff brought suit against multiple DES manufacturers. After dismissal by the trial court and reinstatement by the court of appeals, the case reached the state supreme court, presenting the question whether the action was barred by the statute of limitations, which provides that a suit "for injury . . . caused by the wrongful act or neglect of another" must be brought within one year.[77]

The supreme court ruled that the action was untimely. It rejected the reasoning of the court of appeals, which had held that the statute of limitations had not elapsed because the plaintiff was unable to determine the identity of her injurer. In the supreme court's view, the statute of limitations had begun to run when the plaintiff suspected that she was the victim of a tort. "A plaintiff need not be aware of the specific 'facts' necessary to establish the claim; that is a process contemplated by pretrial discovery," the court explained; "[o]nce the plaintiff has a suspicion of wrongdoing, and therefore an incentive to sue, she must decide whether to file suit or sit on her rights."[78] The court compared the case to an earlier decision, *Miller v. Bechtel Corp.*,[79] in which a woman filed suit for fraud after discovering evidence that her former husband had concealed from her the true value of his stock holdings during the course of divorce proceedings. Though the plaintiff had suspected the concealment at the time of the divorce, she and her lawyer did not investigate the matter, and the suspicions were confirmed only years later when the husband sold the stock for an amount far in excess of the value he had claimed it had during the proceedings. The court held that the action was time-barred because the plaintiff's early suspicions put her on notice of potential wrongdoing, which would have been

[75]*Id.* at 927–28 (quoting Gutierrez v. Mofid, 218 Cal.Rptr. 313, 315 (1985) (internal quotation marks and italics omitted)).

[76]163 Cal.Rptr. 132 (1980).

[77]Cal. Civ. Proc. Code § 340(3).

[78]*Jolly*, 751 P.2d at 928.

[79]191 Cal.Rptr. 619 (1983).

verified upon further investigation; this was enough to start the clock running under the discovery rule. "Her failure timely to investigate," as the *Jolly* court summarized the decision, "barred the action."[80] The result in *Miller* and similar cases, it explained, effectuates the central purposes of statutes of limitations, which are, first, "to give defendants reasonable repose, that is, to protect parties from defending stale claims," and, second, "to require plaintiffs to diligently pursue their claims."[81] Hence the structure of the discovery rule. "Because a plaintiff is under a duty to reasonably investigate and because a suspicion of wrongdoing, coupled with a knowledge of the harm and its cause, will commence the limitations period, suits are not likely to be unreasonably delayed, and those failing to act with reasonable dispatch will be barred," while "plaintiffs who file suit as soon as they have reason to believe that they are entitled to recourse will not be precluded."[82]

This rationale, in the court's view, supported the conclusion that the *Jolly* plaintiff, filing suit in 1981, had waited too long to bring her claim. By 1978, according to her statements, she had wanted to bring a claim for her injuries, believing that DES was a defective product and that she was entitled to compensation. This was enough to start the clock running in 1978, and the court's 1980 *Sindell* decision, which changed the law governing claims such as hers, did not start the clock running anew. It is "the discovery of facts, not their legal significance, that starts the statute," the court observed, and "[a]ll of the facts set out in *Sindell* that are relevant to plaintiff's case were either already known by her in 1978 or could have been discovered through a reasonable investigation"; indeed, the plaintiff "learned of no new facts between 1978 and 1980."[83] The *Sindell* decision, by changing the proof requirements for DES plaintiffs, did not "create a new tort with an independent starting date for purposes of the statute of limitations"; rather, it "demonstrated the legal significance of facts already known to [the] plaintiff."[84] And while it was true that under the law as it stood before *Sindell* the plaintiff would surely have lost any lawsuit because she could not identify the manufacturer whose conduct had injured her, this fact did not entitle her to sue after the law was made more favorable to her claim, because "a change in the law, either by statute or by case law, does not revive claims otherwise barred by the statute of limitations," and "to hold otherwise would allow virtually unlimited litigation every time precedent changed."[85] Under the discovery rule, then, the statute of limitations had commenced running no later than 1978.

---

[80]*Jolly*, 751 P.2d at 928.

[81]*Id.*

[82]*Id.* (italics omitted).

[83]*Id.* at 929.

[84]*Id.* at 931.

[85]*Id.* at 931, 932.

5.4.2 The Court of Appeals Ruling

Construing State Law Invoking the principles associated with *Erie Railroad Co. v. Tompkins*[86] and the jurisprudence built around it, the court of appeals in the Orkin litigation sought to follow the lead of the California courts in construing that state's statute of limitations. "The task of a federal court in a diversity action," the court stated, "is to approximate state law as closely as possible in order to make sure that the vindication of the state right is without discrimination because of the federal forum."[87] Further, the court noted, "if the state's highest appellate court has not decided the question presented, then we must predict how the state's highest court would decide the question."[88]

The problem in the case, as the court saw things, lay in the application of the discovery rule to claims that had arisen before the 1983 amendment to the statute of limitations applicable to theft and conversion claims. That amendment, as we saw above, specified that a claim to recover stolen or converted property "does not accrue until the owner, the owner's agent, or the investigating law enforcement agency discovers the whereabouts of the stolen articles, provided that the articles possess historical, interpretive, scientific, or artistic significance."[89] Pointing to the *Naftzger* decision, the Orkin plaintiffs argued that the 1983 amendment only made explicit what was already implicit in the statute of limitations, namely that a claim does not accrue before the plaintiff's discovery of the location of the property she seeks to recover. The court of appeals was bound to follow *Naftzger*, the plaintiffs argued; and under that decision their claim was timely, they contended, because they had sued Taylor within three years of their 2002 discovery that she was in possession of *Vue de l'Asile et de la Chapelle de Saint-Rémy*.[90] The defense, for its part, took the position that the court of appeals was not obliged to follow *Naftzger*, because that decision had been rendered only by an intermediate state appellate court and conflicted with the views expressed by another intermediate court of the state.[91]

The court of appeals found it unnecessary to decide whether *Naftzger* accurately represented the law of California. For even if *Naftzger* was correct in holding the discovery rule applicable to claims that materialized before the 1983 amendment to the statute of limitations, the court reasoned, that discovery rule was subject to the precepts set forth in *Jolly*. "The California Supreme Court has never confronted the

---

[86] 304 U.S. 64 (1938). The *Erie* decision is generally understood to require the federal courts to defer to state courts on matters of state law. On the decisions and its ramifications, see generally Green (2008), Sherry (2016), and Steinman (2008).

[87] *Orkin*, 487 F.3d at 741.

[88] *Id.* On the prediction approach, see Erbsen (2013).

[89] Cal. Civ. Proc. Code § 338(c).

[90] Brief of Appellants (filed Aug. 8, 2005), Orkin v. Taylor, No. 09-cv-1922 (9th Cir.), at 60–72.

[91] Brief of Appellees (filed Aug. 31, 2005), Orkin v. Taylor, No. 09-cv-1922 (9th Cir.), at 20–24. In Society of California Pioneers v. Baker, 50 Cal.Rptr.2d 865 (App. 1991), an intermediate court stated, in dictum, that the discovery rule was inapplicable to pre-1983 theft and conversion claims.

question of what rule governs accrual of pre-1983 causes of action for theft and conversion," the court explained; the state's high court "has, however, specifically held that the discovery rule, whenever it applies, incorporates the principle of constructive notice," meaning that "a plaintiff is held to her actual knowledge as well as knowledge that could reasonably be discovered through investigation of sources open to her."[92] That is to say, as the *Jolly* court ruled, "under the discovery rule, a cause of action accrues when the plaintiff discovered *or reasonably could have discovered* her claim to and the whereabouts of her property."[93] Though the state's court had not recently spoken to the issue, court elaborated, "we conclude that it is highly unlikely the California Supreme Court would abandon the *Jolly* rule, much less adopt a new rule that eschewed the concept of constructive notice."[94]

The Claims' Timeliness The court of appeals agreed with the district court that the Orkin plaintiffs should have known of their claim against Taylor long before they brought suit. "Under *Jolly*," the court stated, "the latest possible accrual date of the Orkins' cause of action was the date on which they first reasonably could have discovered, through investigation of sources open to them, their claim to and the whereabouts of the van Gogh painting," which in its view was much more than three years before the claim was filed in 2003.[95] The court was unpersuaded by the plaintiffs' argument that their claim accrued only in 2002, when they learned that the painting was being put on the market. "From the face of the Orkins' complaint," the court declared, "it is apparent that Taylor's acquisition of the painting was certainly discoverable at least by 1990, when she held it out for sale in an international auction, and most probably as early as 1963, when she acquired the painting in a highly publicized international auction."[96] Taylor was also listed as the painting's owner in the 1970 *catalogue raisonné* of van Gogh's works, the court observed. "Had the Orkins investigated any of those publicly-available sources, they could have discovered their claim to the painting and the painting's whereabouts long before the 2002 internet rumor [that Taylor was interested in selling the painting] was posted," according to the court.[97] "Even under the most generous possible rule for accrual of the causes of action," the court declared, "the claims expired in or before 1993—three years after the last public announcement of Taylor's ownership."[98] The plaintiffs' state law claims having been brought too late, the district court had properly dismissed the entire action, concluded the appeals court.

---

[92]*Orkin*, 487 F.3d at 741 (quoting *Jolly*, 751 P.2d at 927) (brackets omitted)).

[93]*Orkin*, 487 F.3d at 741 (italics in original).

[94]*Id.*

[95]*Id.*

[96]*Id.* at 741–42.

[97]*Id.* at 742.

[98]*Id.*

5.5 Epilogue

In a separate case, one of the Orkin plaintiffs also sued the government of Switzerland in New York federal court, seeking return of a van Gogh drawing Margarete Mauthner had sold in 1933 to a private collector, Oskar Reinhart, who later donated it to a Swiss museum. The courts dismissed the case on grounds of sovereign immunity, writing only brief opinions.[99]

Van Gogh's *Vue de l'Asile de la Chapelle de Saint-Rémy* was sold to an anonymous buyer at a London auction in 2012.[100]

References

Berlins, Marcel. 2004. Hanging in the Balance. *The Guardian*, December 7.

Erbsen, Allan. 2013. Erie's Four Functions: Reframing Choice of Law in Federal Courts. *Notre Dame Law Review* 89: 579–659.

de La Faille, Jacob Baart. 1939. *Vincent van Gogh*. Paris: Hypérion.

———. 1970. *The Works of Vincent van Gogh: His Paintings and Drawings*. New York: Reynal.

Green, Craig. 2008. Repressing *Erie*'s Myth. *California Law Review* 96: 595–660.

Marcantel, Jonathan A. 2013. Abolishing Private Rights of Action Pursuant to Federal Statutes. *Journal of Legislation* 39: 251–294.

Mauthner, Margerete. 2004. *Das Verzauberte Haus*. Berlin: Transit Buchverlag.

Ochoa, Tyler T., and Andrew J. Wistrich. 1997. The Puzzling Purposes of Statutes of Limitation. *Pacific Law Journal* 28: 453–513.

Phelan, Marilyn E. 2000. Scope of Due Diligence Investigation in Obtaining Title to Valuable Artwork. *Seattle University Law Review* 23: 631–733.

Reyburn, Scott. 2012. Elizabeth Taylor's Painting Collection Sells for $21.9 Million. *Bloomberg News*, February 7.

Sherry, Suzanna. 2016. Normalizing *Erie*. *Vanderbilt Law Review* 69: 1161–1229.

Stabile, Susan J. 1996. The Role of Congressional Intent in Determining the Existence of Implied Rights of Action. *Notre Dame Law Review* 71: 861–912.

Steinman, Adam A. 2008. What Is the *Erie* Doctrine? *Notre Dame Law Review* 84: 245–331.

Ziegler, Donald J. 2001. Rights, Rights of Action, and Remedies. *Washington Law Review* 76: 67–147.

---

[99]Orkin v. Swiss Confederation, 770 F. Supp.2d 612 (S.D.N.Y. 2011), aff'd, 444 Fed.Appx. 469 (2d Cir. 2011). The courts ruled that the expropriation exception to sovereign immunity did not apply, because Mauthner had transferred the work to a private party rather than to a sovereign entity; there was no allegation that Reinhart, the purchaser, was acting on behalf of any government when he purchased it from her.

[100]See Reyburn (2012).

Cases

Adler v. Taylor, 2005 WL 4658511 (C.D. Cal. 2005), aff'd sub nom. Orkin v. Taylor, 487 F.3d 734 (9th Cir.), cert. denied, 552 U.S. 990 (2007)
April Enterprises, Inc. v. KKTV, 195 Cal.Rptr. 421 (App. 1983)
Calhoon v. Harvey, 379 U.S. 139 (1964)
Cort v. Ash, 422 U.S. 66 (1975)
Erie Railroad Co. v. Tompkins, 304 U.S. 64 (1938)
First National Bank v. Thompson, 140 P.2d 75 (Cal. App. 1943)
Gutierrez v. Mofid, 218 Cal.Rptr. 313 (1985)
J.I. Case Co. v. Borak, 377 U.S. 426 (1964)
Jolly v. Eli Lilly & Co., 751 P.2d 923 (Cal. 1988)
Leaf v. City of San Mateo, 163 Cal.Rptr. 711 (App. 1980)
Miller v. Bechtel Corp., 191 Cal.Rptr. 619 (1983)
Naftzger v. American Numismatic Society, 49 Cal.Rptr.2d 784 (App. 1996)
National Railroad Passenger Corp. v. National Association of Railroad Passengers, 414 U.S. 522 (1974)
Neel v. Magana, Olney, Levy, Cathcart & Gelfand, 98 Cal.Rptr. 837 (1971)
Orkin v. Swiss Confederation, 444 Fed.Appx. 469 (2d Cir. 2011)
Sindell v. Abbott Laboratories, 163 Cal.Rptr. 132 (1980)
Texas Pacific Railway Co. v. Rigsby, 241 U.S. 33 (1916)
United States v. Auto Workers, 352 U.S. 567 (1957)
Wheeldin v. Wheeler, 373 U.S. 647 (1963)

Chapter 6
Von Saher v. Norton Simon Museum of Art

6.1 Background

Jacques Goudstikker (1897–1940) was a Jewish art dealer in Amsterdam, specializing in the works of European old masters.[1] Following the Nazi invasion of the Netherlands in May 1940, he and his family fled the country, leaving all of their possessions behind. Goudstikker died in a shipboard accident, but his wife Desirée and their infant son Eduard made it safely to New York with a handwritten notebook listing the works in the family's collection. Immediately after their escape, Hermann Göring visited their gallery and took away over a thousand artworks, papering over the theft with documents in which he purported to purchase the works. After the war, Allied forces repatriated several hundred of the looted works to the Netherlands, whose government refused to return them to the Goudstikker family, claiming they had been legally sold to Göring and were now part of the Dutch national collection. Desirée Goudstikker, having remarried and taken the last name von Saher, was able to buy back a few of the stolen works in the 1950s; the government auctioned off numerous items, and kept the rest in national museums. Following an exposé by a Dutch journalist in 1997 and a protracted legal conflict, the government agreed in 2006 to return about 200 works in its possession to the family.[2]

One work that escaped this restitution process was *Adam and Eve*, an oil-on-wood diptych painted in about 1530 by the German artist Lucas Cranach the Elder (1472–1553), which Jacques Goudstikker purchased from the Soviet government at a Berlin auction in 1931. The two paintings in the diptych were among the works taken by Göring for his personal collection and then returned to the Netherlands after the war. In 1961, an American descendant of the Stroganoff family in Russia

[1]On the Goudstikker family, see Müller and Tatzkow (2010), pp. 216–232, and Sutton (2008).

[2]These events are detailed in Gennochio (2008), Riding (2006a, b), and Rickman (2007). The journalist's investigative work appears in den Hollander (1998). The Dutch Restitution Committee report leading to the return of the artwork is contained in Restitutiecommissie (2005).

B.L. Hay, *Nazi-Looted Art and the Law*, DOI 10.1007/978-3-319-64967-2_6

filed a claim for the two paintings with the Dutch government, contending that the Soviet Union had unlawfully seized them from the Stroganoffs during the 1920s. The Dutch government settled the matter by selling the diptych in 1966 to the claimant, George Stroganoff, who sold it to California business magnate Norton Simon in 1971. The two paintings eventually became part of the Norton Simon Museum in Pasadena, California.

Marei von Saher, widow and heir of Desirée von Saher's son Eduard and a resident of Connecticut, learned of the diptych's whereabouts in 2000 and contacted the museum to request the work's return. There followed six years of discussion and negotiation, at the conclusion of which the museum ultimately refused von Saher's request, contending that it had rightful title to the paintings. The museum did not dispute the fact that the Nazis had stolen the diptych from the Goudstikker gallery in 1940. It took the position, however, that the work had never rightfully belonged to the Goudstikkers in the first place. Because the Soviets had unlawfully seized the work from the Stroganoffs in the 1920s, the museum contended, the diptych was already stolen property when Jacques Goudstikker purchased it in 1931. In buying it from the Dutch government in 1966, according to the museum, George Stroganoff had merely taken back what had rightfully belonged to his family all along. The subsequent sale thus transferred valid title to Norton Simon.

For her part, von Saher took the position that the Stroganoff family in fact had never owned the diptych. The 1931 auction at which Jacques Goudstikker had purchased the work was advertised as a sale of "The Stroganoff Collection." Nonetheless, von Saher noted, the Soviets had indiscriminately included at the auction many works they had taken from other places. The diptych had hung in the Church of the Holy Trinity in Kiev before its seizure by the Soviets in 1927; it was, she asserted, never part of the Stroganoff collection. The Dutch government therefore had no right to transfer the work to the Stroganoff family in 1966, she argued, and title to the work remained with the Goudstikker heirs. The Norton Simon Museum rejected this account of the diptych's provenance, and adhered to its position that it was the rightful owner of the paintings.

6.2 Proceedings

In May 2007, Marei von Saher filed suit against the Norton Simon Museum in federal district court in Los Angeles, invoking jurisdiction based on diversity of citizenship. The complaint asserted state law claims of replevin and conversion, and sought a judicial declaration giving title to the Cranach work to von Saher, along with restitution of the work and an award of damages for the delay in its return. The museum filed an answer in which it denied the claim on the merits, and also filed a motion to dismiss on the ground that the action was time-barred. In opposition to the motion to dismiss, von Saher called the court's attention to a 2002 statute enacted by the California legislature that extended the state limitations period for Holocaust-era art claims against museums and galleries, giving claimants until the end of 2010 to bring suit.

The district court granted the motion to dismiss in October 2007.[3] The court held that von Saher's claim was untimely under California's general statute of limitations for claims to recover personal property, which requires suit to be filed within three years of a claim's accrual. According to the court, von Saher's claim had accrued when the museum obtained the artwork in 1971, and had long since expired. The court further held that the state's 2002 extension of the limitations period for Holocaust-era claims was invalid, on the ground that it unconstitutionally infringed the federal government's exclusive authority over foreign relations. The Ninth Circuit court of appeals upheld the district court's ruling on the statute's unconstitutionality in January 2010, but remanded the case for further proceedings.[4]

A few months after the appeals court decision, the California legislature amended the 2002 statute in an effort to cure the constitutional defect identified by the courts. The 2010 amendment extended the statute of limitations from three to six years for all claims to recover fine art from a museum or gallery (without regard to whether a claim was Holocaust-related), and provided that the limitations period did not begin to run until a claimant had actual notice of an artwork's whereabouts. In light of the 2010 amendment, the district court held that von Saher's claims were no longer barred by the statute of limitations.[5]

In 2011, the museum again moved to dismiss the action, contending that even if von Saher's claims were timely, they were nonetheless barred by the doctrine of foreign affairs preemption. At the war's end, the museum argued, the Allies had adopted a policy of repatriating looted art to the countries of origin, leaving each country's government responsible for processing individual restitution claims. To permit California law to second-guess the Dutch government's rejection of von Saher's claims in the 1950s, the museum argued, conflicted with that allied policy and therefore infringed on the federal government's authority over foreign relations. The district court accepted this argument and granted the motion to dismiss in March 2012.[6] The court of appeals reversed that judgment in June 2014, holding that von Saher's claims did not conflict with federal policy, and again remanded the case to the district court for further proceedings.[7]

---

[3]Von Saher v. Norton Simon Museum of Art, 2007 WL 4302726 (C.D. Cal. 2007).

[4]Von Saher v. Norton Simon Museum of Art, 592 F.3d 954 (9th Cir. 2010), cert. denied, 564 U.S. 1037 (2011). The court of appeals reasoned that, depending on when it had accrued, von Saher's claim might satisfy the original three-year statute of limitations, even though the legislature's extension of the limitation period was invalid. In remanding, the court of appeals instructed the district court to consider that possibility (We will refer to the 2010 appeals court decision as "*Von Saher I*").

[5]Order Denying Defendants' Motion to Dismiss, Von Saher v. Norton Simon Museum of Art, No. CV 07-2866-JFW (C.D. Cal. Apr. 2, 2015). The court reasoned that the 2007 claims were timely because they had accrued in 2000, when von Saher learned of the artwork's whereabouts, and the museum had agreed in 2003 to toll any further running of the statute of limitations.

[6]Von Saher v. Norton Simon Museum of Art, 862 F. Supp.2d 1044 (C.D. Cal. 2012).

[7]Von Saher v. Norton Simon Museum of Art, 754 F.3d 712 (9th Cir. 2014), cert. denied, 135 S.Ct. 1158 (2015). We will refer to the 2014 appeals court decision as "*Von Saher II*."

Following pretrial discovery, both parties filed motions for summary judgment. In August 2016, the district court entered summary judgment for the museum, holding that it held title to the Cranach work.[8] In its opinion, the court noted that after the war, Desirée von Saher had refrained from filing a claim with Dutch restitution officials for return of the works Göring had "purchased" from her family in 1940. Under Dutch law the works therefore belonged to Göring, the court reasoned, and when repatriated at the war's end they constituted "enemy property" subject to confiscation by the government of the Netherlands. The Cranach work became the property of the Dutch government in 1951, according to the court, and then became the property of George Stroganoff when he purchased it from the government in 1966. Norton Simon obtained good title to the painting when he purchased it from Stroganoff in 1971, the court concluded.

The district court's 2016 judgment is currently on appeal.

6.3 Constitutionality of State Time Extensions

The initial question taken up by the courts, in the 2007 judgment of dismissal and the ensuing appeal decided in 2010, concerned the constitutionality of the California legislature's extension of the statute of limitations for Holocaust-era art recovery lawsuits. The court of appeals' resolution of the issue turned primarily on two previous decisions addressing other California legislation concerning non-art-related Holocaust-era litigation. After a brief review of the state's art claims legislation, we will consider these earlier decisions and then the court of appeals' application of them to the von Saher litigation.

6.3.1 The 2002 California Legislation

In 1999, the California legislature enacted laws to facilitate two types of Holocaust-related litigation, namely, claims to recover the proceeds of unpaid Nazi-era insurance policies and claims to compensate victims of Nazi slave labor. Among other things, the legislation extended the statute of limitations for such claims.[9] In 2002, the

---

[8]Order Granting Defendants' Motion to for Summary Judgment and Denying Plaintiff's Motion for Summary Judgment, Von Saher v. Norton Simon Museum of Art, No. 07-cv-2866 (C.D. Cal. Aug. 9, 2016).

[9]Cal. Civ. Proc. Code § 354.5 (insurance claims), § 354.6 (slave labor claims). Both provisions extended the statute of limitations until 2010. Like other California legislation from the period that singled out Holocaust-related claims, the enactments were struck down by the courts as infringing the federal government's authority over foreign affairs. See Deutsch v. Turner Corp., 324 F.3d 692 (9th Cir. 2003) (invalidating § 354.6); Steinberg v. International Commission on Holocaust Era Insurance Claims, 34 Cal.Rptr.3d 944 (App.Div. 2005) (invalidating § 354.5).

legislature enacted a parallel provision for certain Holocaust-era art restitution claims, granting the same extension of time as it had for the other types of claims.[10] The preamble to the 2002 enactment set forth the legislature's purposes:

> The Legislature finds and declares the following:
>
> (a) During World War II, untold millions of lives and property were destroyed.
> (b) In addition to the many atrocities that befell the victims of the Nazi regime, treasured pieces of artwork were wrongfully taken.
> (c) Thousands of victims of Nazi persecution, and the heirs of victims of Nazi persecution, are residents of the State of California. Many of these victims and descendants are investigating the whereabouts of artwork that rightfully belonged to their families.
> (d) California has a moral and public policy interest in assuring that its residents and citizens are given a reasonable opportunity to commence an action in court for those pieces of artwork now located in the museums and galleries of the State of California.[11]

The rationale for extending the ordinary three-year statute of limitations, the preamble continued, was as follows:

> (e) Currently, an individual has three years, after discovering the whereabouts of the artwork, to commence an action in court.
> (f) However, due to the unique historical nature of Holocaust-era artwork, commencement of an action requires detailed investigation in several countries, involving numerous historical documents and the input of experts.
> (g) In order to obtain all necessary data, investigating a prospective action may take several years.
> (h) The current three-year statute of limitation, after discovery of the whereabouts of the artwork, is an insufficient amount of time to finance, investigate, and commence an action.[12]

The enactment gave Holocaust victims and their heirs until the end of 2010 to bring suit against any museum or gallery to recover art lost as a result of Nazi persecution. The extension applied retroactively to claims that had already expired under the preexisting statute of limitations.[13]

6.3.2 *Principles of Foreign Affairs Preemption*

The Norton Simon Museum's constitutional challenge to the California legislation rested primarily on two earlier decisions that invalidated the state's statutes concerning Holocaust-era insurance and slave labor claims under the doctrine of foreign affairs preemption.[14] In one, *American Insurance Association*

---

[10]Cal. Civ. Proc. Code § 354.3. On statutes of limitations in Nazi-looted art litigation, see Kreder (2012) and Demarsin (2010).

[11]2002 Cal. Legis. Serv. Ch. 332 (A.B.1758).

[12]*Id.*

[13]*Id.* The statute was inapplicable in *Orkin v. Taylor*, discussed in the previous chapter, because that case did not involve a claim against a museum or gallery.

[14]For overviews and analyses of the doctrine, see Henkin (1996) and Schaefer (2011).

v. Garamendi,[15] the Supreme Court held that parts of the legislation concerning Holocaust-era insurance claims conflicted with, and were therefore preempted by, some international accords entered into by the federal government. In the other, *Deutsch v. Turner Corp.*,[16] the court of appeals for the Ninth Circuit struck down California's slave labor claims legislation.

The *Garamendi* Decision In the 1990s, a number of class action lawsuits were filed in American courts against insurance companies that had sold life insurance policies to Jews in Germany during the Nazi period. After Hitler came to power, some of the plaintiffs had been robbed of their policies, or forced to cash them in and turn over the proceeds, by the Nazi government; others had kept their policies but were unable to collect on them after the war, either because premiums had not been paid or because the Nazis did not issue death certificates for those they murdered in the camps. "Responsibility as between the [Nazi] government and insurance companies is disputed," the Supreme Court later noted in its opinion, "but at the end of the day, the fact is that the value or proceeds of many insurance policies issued to Jews before and during the war were paid to the Reich or never paid at all."[17] After the war, the London Debt Agreement of 1953 prevented many victims living in the United States from pursuing their claims in court; decades later, this obstacle was lifted by new diplomatic accords following the reunification of Germany, and the victims turned to the American courts, filing class actions to recover the unpaid insurance proceeds from the insurers.

This litigation led to negotiations between the German and American governments to establish a system for processing the claims out of court. Under the resulting accord, entered into by the two governments in 2000, Germany established a compensation fund jointly financed by both the government and the insurance companies.[18] The fund was to be administered in cooperation with the International Commission on Holocaust Era Insurance Claims, an organization created a few years earlier by insurance companies working with the State of Israel and Holocaust survivor associations. "The willingness of the Germans to create a voluntary compensation fund was conditioned on some expectation of security from lawsuits in United States courts, and after extended dickering President Clinton put his weight behind two specific measures toward that end," the Court explained.[19] These measures took the form of trying to curb, though not to ban outright, resort to the court system. First, the administration agreed to take the position in court that the German compensation fund should be "the exclusive forum and remedy for the resolution of all asserted claims against German [insurance] companies arising from their involvement in the National Socialist era and

[15]539 U.S. 396 (2003).

[16]324 F.3d 692 (9th Cir. 2003), cert. denied, 540 U.S. 820 (2003).

[17]*Garamendi*, 539 U.S. at 402–3.

[18]See generally Bazyler (2005), Eizenstat (2003), Hennig (2007), and Kill and Gerstel (2007).

[19]*Garamendi*, 539 U.S. at 405–6.

World War II."[20] Second, the administration "promised to use its 'best efforts, in a manner it considers appropriate,' to get state and local governments to respect the [fund] as the exclusive mechanism."[21] As a result of the agreement, observed the Court, the German government had identified several hundred thousand Holocaust victims whose families were entitled to life insurance proceeds. After entering into the agreement with Germany, the Clinton administration signed similar accords with France and Austria.[22]

"While these international efforts were underway," the Court continued, "California's Department of Insurance began its own enquiry into the issue of unpaid claims under Nazi-era insurance policies, prompting state legislation designed to force payment by defaulting insurers."[23] The resulting state statute required all insurers doing business in California to disclose the details of any insurance issued in Europe between 1920 and 1945, in order to "ensure that any involvement that they or their related companies may have had with insurance policies of holocaust victims [is] disclosed to the state," and to "ensure that Holocaust victims or their heirs can take direct action on their own behalf with regard to insurance policies and claims."[24] Pursuant to the new law, California officials issued administrative subpoenas to several European insurance companies that were participating in the German, Austrian, and French compensation programs, a move that led the United States Department of State to object that California's actions were undercutting the federal government's diplomatic efforts and "damaging the one effective means now at hand to process quickly and completely unpaid insurance claims from the Holocaust period."[25] The California insurance commissioner turned aside these criticisms, announcing that the new statute would be enforced "to its fullest, requiring the affected insurers to make the disclosures, leave the State voluntarily, or lose their licenses."[26] The insurance industry then filed suit in federal court, seeking an injunction against enforcement of the statute, and the case arrived at the Supreme Court two years later.

The question for the Court was whether, as the insurance companies argued, the California law unconstitutionally interfered with the "foreign policy of the Executive Branch, as expressed principally in the executive agreements with Germany, Austria, and France."[27] The argument's "major premises," as the Court called them, were uncontroversial. First, state laws must sometimes give way to the federal government's control over foreign affairs. There is "no question that at some point

[20] *Id.* at 406 (quoting agreement).

[21] *Id.* (quoting agreement).

[22] The agreements did not have the status of formal treaties and were not submitted to the Senate for ratification as such.

[23] *Garamendi*, 539 U.S. at 408.

[24] *Id.* at 410 (quoting statute and legislative committee report).

[25] Quoted in *id.*

[26] *Id.* at 411.

[27] *Id.* at 413.

an exercise of state power that touches on foreign relations must yield to the National Government's policy, given the 'concern for uniformity in this country's dealings with foreign nations' that animated the Constitution's allocation of the foreign relations power to the National Government in the first place."[28] A long line of cases, the Court noted, established that the federal government could take the steps necessary to ensure that the nation speaks with "one voice" in its dealings with foreign powers.[29] "The peace of the WHOLE ought not to be left at the disposal of a PART," in the words of the Federalist.[30]

Second, though the Constitution is famously reticent on the distribution within the federal government of power over foreign affairs, it has become settled that the executive branch has a "vast share of responsibility for the conduct of our foreign relations."[31] In particular, the Court noted, "our cases have recognized that the President has authority to make 'executive agreements' with other countries, requiring no ratification by the Senate or approval by Congress, this power having been exercised since the early years of the Republic."[32] Indeed, "[m]aking executive agreements to settle claims of American nationals against foreign governments is a particularly longstanding practice, the first example being as early as 1799, when the Adams administration settled demands against the Dutch Government by American citizens who lost their cargo when Dutch privateers overtook the schooner *Wilmington Packet*."[33] Such executive agreements may address claims not only against foreign governments but also against corporations, because "untangling government policy from private initiative during wartime is often so hard that diplomatic action settling claims against private parties may well be just as essential in the aftermath of hostilities as diplomacy to settle claims against foreign governments."[34]

Third, even if they do not expressly preempt state law, executive agreements can preempt state laws that cause an "interference with the foreign policy those agreements embody."[35] Here the Court emphasized its decision in *Zschernig v. Miller*,[36] involving a 1951 anti-communist Oregon statute that restricted the inheritance rights of foreigners whose home nations confiscated inherited property. Like its counterparts in other states, the Oregon statute was "providing occasions

[28] *Id.*

[29] Japan Line, Ltd. v. County of Los Angeles, 441 U.S. 434, 449 (1979), quoted in *Garamendi*, 539 U.S. at 414.

[30] The Federalist No. 80 (Alexander Hamilton), in Cooke (1961), pp. 535–36, quoted in Crosby v. National Foreign Trade Council, 530 U.S. 363, 381–82 n. 16 (2000), in turn quoted in *Garamendi*, 539 U.S. at 414 (brackets omitted).

[31] Youngstown Sheet & Tube Co. v. Sawyer, 343 U.S. 579, 610–11 (1952) (Frankfurter, J., concurring), quoted in *Garamendi*, 539 U.S. at 414.

[32] *Id.* at 415.

[33] *Id.* at 417.

[34] *Id.* at 416.

[35] *Id.* at 417.

[36] 389 U.S. 429 (1968).

for state judges to disparage certain foreign regimes, employing the language of the anti-Communism prevalent here at the height of the Cold War."[37] State courts' "notorious" practice of denying inheritances to heirs residing in communist countries, the Court stated, "has a direct impact upon foreign relations and may well adversely affect the power of the central government to deal with [international] problems."[38] Declaring that the "Oregon law does, indeed, illustrate the dangers which are involved if each State, speaking through its probate courts, is permitted to establish its own foreign policy," the Court struck down the statute on the ground that state laws, even in areas of traditional state competence such as estate regulation, "must give way if they impair the effective exercise of the Nation's foreign policy."[39] This was true even though, as the Court later observed, the state law did not conflict with any federal law on the subject of property inheritance; the ruling stood for the proposition that state action impairing federal foreign policy must be set aside "even absent any affirmative federal activity in the subject area of the state law."[40] The "likelihood that state legislation will produce something more than incidental effect in conflict with express foreign policy of the National Government" is enough to warrant preemption.[41]

Given these premises, the *Garamendi* Court ruled, the California insurance statute had to be struck down. The problem of "resolving Holocaust-era insurance claims that may be held by residents of this country is a matter well within the Executive's responsibility for foreign affairs," the Court stated; and because "claims remaining in the aftermath of hostilities may be 'sources of friction' acting as an 'impediment to resumption of friendly relations' between the countries involved," the problem is one "in which national, not state, interests are overriding."[42] In approaching the problem, "the consistent Presidential foreign policy has been to encourage European governments and companies to volunteer settlement funds in preference to litigation or coercive sanctions," and to "encourage European insurers to work with [the International Commission on Holocaust Era Insurance Claims] to develop acceptable claim procedures, including procedures governing disclosure of policy information."[43] Central to this executive branch strategy, the Court continued, has been the position that these negotiated procedures "should be considered the exclusive remedy for resolving insurance claims from the World War II era," and that an insurance company's voluntary participation in the compensation program "should give it 'safe haven' from sanctions, subpoenas, and hearings relative to the Holocaust period."[44] In this way, stated the Court, the

[37] *Garamendi*, 539 U.S. at 417.

[38] *Zschernig*, 389 U.S. at 440–41.

[39] *Id.*

[40] *Garamendi*, 539 U.S. at 418 (describing *Zschernig* ruling).

[41] *Id.* at 420.

[42] *Id.* at 420–21 (quoting United States v. Pink, 315 U.S. 203, 225 (1942)).

[43] *Garamendi*, 539 U.S. at 421.

[44] *Id.* at 422 (quoting State Department).

executive agreements in question had struck a balance among several competing concerns, including "the national interest in maintaining amicable relationships with current European allies," and "survivors' interests in a 'fair and prompt' but nonadversarial resolution of their claims so as to 'bring some measure of justice in their lifetimes.'"[45]

The California legislature, in the Court's view, had taken a much more adversarial approach than the federal executive branch, following the "different tack of providing regulatory sanctions to compel disclosure and payment [by insurance companies], supplemented by a new cause of action for Holocaust survivors if the other sanctions should fail."[46] The resulting "economic compulsion to make public disclosure," the Court stated, "undercuts the President's diplomatic discretion and the choice he has made exercising it"; by "making exclusion from a large sector of the American insurance market the automatic sanction for noncompliance with the State's own policies on disclosure," the California law produces a situation in which "the President has less to offer and less economic and diplomatic leverage as a consequence."[47] While it was true that the California law's objective of facilitating compensation for Holocaust victims was shared by the federal executive agreements, "the fact of a common end hardly neutralizes conflicting means," and here the state law created "an obstacle to the success of the National Government's chosen 'calibration of force' in dealing with the Europeans using a voluntary approach."[48] The Court found that the state's interest in its legislation was comparatively weak: resolving international claims was not a "traditional state legislative subject matter," and though its objective of helping the Holocaust survivors in the state was "powerful," the "very same objective dignifies the interest of the National Government in devising its chosen mechanism for voluntary settlements, there being about 100,000 survivors in the country, only a small fraction of them in California."[49] The Court concluded that "[a]s against the responsibility of the United States of America, the humanity underlying the state statute" was insufficient to save it given "the conflict with national policy."[50]

The *Deutsch* Decision Josef Deutsch, a Hungarian Jew, was deported in 1944 to Auschwitz, where he was forced to work as a slave laborer for Hochtief AG, a German construction company. He survived the war and settled in California. In 2000, he filed suit in California against Hochtief and its American subsidiary, seeking compensation for his labor and also for the suffering he had endured. His

---

[45]*Id.* at 422–23 (quoting executive agreement with Germany).

[46]*Id.* at 423.

[47]*Id.* at 423–24 (quoting Crosby v. National Foreign Trade Council, 530 U.S. 363, 377 (2000). Here the Court drew a comparison to a Massachusetts statute that indirectly imposed economic sanctions on Burma, in a manner at variance with the policy toward that country pursued by the federal government; that statute was struck down in the *Crosby* case.

[48]*Garamendi*, 539 U.S. at 425 (quoting *Crosby*, 530 U.S. at 379, 380).

[49]*Garamendi*, 539 U.S. at 426.

[50]*Id.* at 426–27.

suit was consolidated in federal district court with numerous lawsuits brought by victims of wartime Japanese slave labor, seeking compensation from Japanese corporations and their American affiliates. The lawsuits were all based on the 1999 California legislation that created a cause of action for injuries sustained by individuals forced into slave labor by the Nazis and other Axis powers during the Second World War era, giving them until the end of 2010 to file suit.[51] The district court dismissed all of the suits on the ground that the California legislation was unconstitutional. The court of appeals for the Ninth Circuit affirmed the lower court's judgment. Though there was not, in the court's view, a conflict between state law and federal policy of the sort found in *Garamendi*, the court of appeals nonetheless ruled that the California legislation, having "created—or at least resurrected—a special class of tort actions, with the aim of rectifying wartime wrongs committed by our enemies," was invalid because it "exceeds California's power to engage in foreign affairs."[52]

The court began its analysis by observing that the Constitution expressly grants certain powers over foreign relations, such as the making of treaties, to the federal government, and expressly denies them to the states. In addition to those express provisions is the long-recognized "generally applicable principle that power over foreign affairs is reserved to the federal government," meaning that "'even in the absence of a treaty' or federal statute, a state may violate the Constitution by 'establishing its own foreign policy.'"[53] The court gave the example of *Zschernig v. Miller*,[54] discussed above, in which the Supreme Court struck down an Oregon statute that allowed foreign nationals to inherit property in the state only if their countries gave Americans a reciprocal right of inheritance. The statute, as the court put it, was an invalid "intrusion by the State into the field of foreign affairs which the Constitution entrusts to the President and the Congress."[55]

Though previous judicial decisions, observed the court of appeals, have not "defined the precise scope of the foreign relations power that is denied to the states," it was nonetheless "clear that matters concerning war are part of the inner core of this power."[56] Most of the Constitution's explicit references to the federal government's foreign affairs powers, and to the states' lack thereof, concern international conflict; and even those provisions that do not expressly address it have the implicit purpose of preventing such conflict. The framers made clear, the court continued, that their overarching concern was that "disunity in international affairs risked unnecessary war."[57] Indeed, the inheritance provision struck down in *Zschernig*, "although superficially unrelated to war, was seen by a Court operating

[51]Cal. Civ. Proc. Code § 354.6.

[52]Deutsch v. Turner Corp., 324 F.3d 692, 708 (9th Cir. 2003).

[53]*Id.* (quoting Zschernig v. Miller, 389 U.S. 429, 441 (1968) (brackets omitted)).

[54]389 U.S. 429 (1968).

[55]*Id.* at 432, quoted in *Deutsch*, 324 F.3d at 710.

[56]*Deutsch*, 324 F.3d at 711.

[57]*Id.*

at the height of the Cold War as a potential provocation to foreign powers," raising the concern of conflict among nations arising from "real or imagined wrongs to another's subjects inflicted, or permitted, by a government."[58]

The constitutional defect of California's slave labor compensation law, in the court's view, was that it "intrudes on the federal government's exclusive power to make and resolve war, including the procedure for resolving war claims."[59] By its terms, the court explained, the statute "seeks to redress wrongs committed in the course of the Second World War," affording the right to compensation for those who were enslaved by "the Nazi regime, its allies and sympathizers, or enterprises transacting business in any of the areas occupied by or under control of the Nazi regime or its allies or sympathizers."[60] Plainly, the court stated, "California has sought to create its own resolution to a major issue arising out of the war—a remedy for wartime acts that California's legislature believed had never been fairly resolved."[61] The United States federal government had entered into numerous treaties and international agreements to end the war and establish arrangements for postwar debt settlements and reparations, including some compensation payments to victims of forced labor.[62] These federal agreements, the court remarked, did not include a private right of action of the sort California proposed to create, imposing liability on corporations that had exploited forced labor. California, "dissatisfied with how the federal government chose to address the wartime injuries suffered by victims of the Nazis and their allies," had enacted its own system for compensating "victims of Nazi persecution [who] have been deprived of their entitlement to compensation for their labor and injuries sustained while performing that labor."[63]

The court acknowledged that the California law did not directly conflict with federal policy, inasmuch as the various federal treaties and international agreements with both Germany and Japan did not explicitly foreclose a private right of action against corporations. That lack of direct conflict, however, was not enough to save the state's statute, which was unconstitutional simply by virtue of having intruded on a domain reserved for the federal government. Because "the issue is the lack of state power, it is immaterial whether the federal government enacted a prohibition" on litigation against corporations for wartime slave labor.[64] "The federal government, acting under its foreign affairs authority, provided its own resolution to the war," the court declared, and "California has no power to modify that resolution."[65] For this reason, the California legislature's creation of a special cause of action for

---

[58] *Id.* (quoting *Zschernig*, 389 U.S. at 441 (internal quotation omitted)).

[59] *Deutsch*, 324 F.3d at 712.

[60] *Id.* (quoting Cal. Civ. Proc. Code § 354.6).

[61] *Deutsch*, 324 F.3d at 712.

[62] *Id.* at 712–15. On the German compensation fund for slave laborers established in 2000, see Kent (2007), Lambsdorff (2007), and Sturman (2007).

[63] *Deutsch*, 324 F.3d at 715 (quoting Cal. Civ. Proc. Code § 354.6).

[64] *Id.* at 715.

[65] *Id.*

wartime slave labor was invalid. In addition, to the extent that the plaintiffs had preexisting slave labor tort claims arising out of general tort law, the legislature's extension of the statute of limitations for such claims was also invalid. "Because California lacks the power to create a right of action—or, alternatively, to resurrect time-barred claims—in order to provide its own remedy for war-related injuries inflicted by our former enemies and those who operated in their territories," the entire statute was preempted, the court concluded.[66]

6.3.3 Preemption of the California Legislation

In evaluating the constitutionality of California's Holocaust-era art claims legislation, the court of appeals in the von Saher litigation observed that there are two categories of potential federal foreign affairs preemption of state law. First, as in the case of the insurance legislation at issue in *Garamendi*, state legislation may be preempted because it conflicts with federal foreign policy; this is the category known as "conflict" preemption. Second, even if there is no such conflict, state legislation may be preempted because, as in the case of the *Deutsch* case, it addresses a subject within the exclusive power of the federal government; this is the category known as "field" preemption.[67] The Norton Museum argued that California's 2002 extension of the statute of limitations for Holocaust-era art claims was invalid under both types of preemption.

Conflict Preemption The museum contended that the California legislation conflicted with the federal government's policy of external restitution, as set forth in documents during the war and at its conclusion. In the London Declaration of January 1943, the Allies condemned the expropriations being committed by the Nazis, and reserved the right to invalidate wartime property transfers, "whether such transfers or dealings have taken the form of open looting or plunder, or of transactions apparently legal in form, even when they purport to be voluntarily effected."[68] At the Potsdam Conference in July 1945, following the Allied recovery of large troves of Nazi-looted art hidden in castles, banks, mines, and caves in Germany, U.S. authorities approved a policy of external restitution, by which plundered works would be given "proper care and study" and returned to the countries of origin, leaving the governments of those newly-liberated countries responsible for restitution to individual owners.[69] The California legislation, argued the museum, contradicted these federal measures.

---

[66] *Id.* at 716.

[67] For explanation of the two categories, see Chiang (2003) and Spiro (1999), along with the sources in note 14 above.

[68] Inter-Allied Declaration against Acts of Dispossession Committed in Territories under Enemy Occupation and Control (January 5, 1943), quoted in *Von Saher v. Norton Simon Museum of Art*, 592 F.3d 954, 962 (9th Cir. 2010).

[69] Report on Art Objects in U.S. Zone (July 29, 1945), quoted in *Von Saher I*, 592 F.3d at 962.

The court of appeals disagreed. If California had enacted such an art-restitution law in the immediate aftermath of the war, stated the court, its law might well have conflicted with the federal external restitution policy. But the California law was not enacted until 2002. Federal external restitution, in contrast, ended in September 1948, when the U.S. authorities, having returned some three million items of cultural property to a dozen different countries, announced that it would no longer handle property restitution claims. California's 2002 law "cannot conflict with or stand as an obstacle to a policy that is no longer in effect," declared the court, and it does not "conflict with any current foreign policy espoused by the Executive Branch."[70]

Field Preemption On the question of field preemption, the court of appeals began by observing that the California legislation ventured beyond areas of "traditional state responsibility," a common criterion for determining whether state legislation is preempted. While providing a forum for the return of stolen property is a core state function, the Holocaust-era art claims law "cannot be fairly categorized as a garden variety property regulation," the court stated; though it "purports to regulate property, an area traditionally left to the states," its "real purpose is to provide relief to Holocaust victims and their heirs."[71] That "entirely sympathetic" legislative goal was also present in the insurance and slave labor claims legislation that was struck down in the *Deutsch* and *Garamendi* decisions.[72] Moreover, the California law was not even confined to property in the state, but rather applied to actions against any museum or gallery wherever located, the court pointed out, which "belies any purported state interest in regulating stolen property or museums or galleries within the State."[73] With this statute, "California has created a world-wide forum for the resolution of Holocaust restitution claims," and laudable as this objective is, "it is not an area of 'traditional state responsibility.'"[74]

The court then turned to whether the statute encroached on a domain reserved to the federal government. Relying on the analysis set forth in its *Deutsch* opinion, the court observed that, like the slave labor law, the art restitution law "seeks to redress wrongs committed in the course of the Second World War," which generally is "for the federal government alone to address."[75] In the area of Holocaust-era art restitution, the court stated, there is a "documented history of federal action addressing the subject," notably the postwar external restitution policy, and the ongoing problem of returning Nazi-looted art is an international issue entrusted to the federal government.[76] Observing that there had been calls for an international commission to settle outstanding restitution claims, the court declared that "[o]nly

---

[70]*Von Saher I*, 592 F.3d at 963.

[71]*Id.* at 964.

[72]*Id.* (quoting *Garamendi*, 539 U.S. at 426).

[73]*Von Saher I*, 592 F.3d at 965.

[74]*Id.*

[75]*Id.* at 966 (quoting *Deutsch*, 324 F.3d at 712).

[76]*Von Saher I*, 592 F.3d at 967.

the federal government possess the power to negotiate and establish these or other remedies with the international community."[77] That no such commission had yet been established "did not," according to the court, "justify California's intrusion into a field occupied exclusively by the federal government."[78] The extension of time for Holocaust-art claims was invalid, the court concluded, because "California may not improve upon or add to the resolution of the war."[79]

6.4 Federal Preemption of State Substantive Law

Von Saher's case ultimately survived the court of appeals ruling, because in response to the ruling the California legislature amended its law to create a new statute of limitations for all art restitution claims brought against museums and galleries, without singling out Holocaust-era claims.[80] On remand from the court of appeals, the district court eventually ruled that von Saher's claims were timely under the amended statute.[81] The next question for the courts then was whether, as the Norton Simon Museum contended, von Saher's claims were nonetheless foreclosed by current federal restitution policy.

6.4.1 Current Federal Policy

The museum called attention to several aspects of contemporary federal restitution policy that, it argued, would be undermined if the court awarded the Cranach work to von Saher. First, it pointed to a brief filed by the United States urging the Supreme Court to let stand the court of appeals decision striking down the 2002 California extension of the statute of limitations for Holocaust-era art claims.[82]

[77]*Id.*

[78]*Id.* at 968.

[79]*Id.* For criticism of the court's ruling, see Conway (2010) and Demarsin (2010). A similar California law extending the statute of limitations for insurance claims of Armenian genocide victims was struck down in Movsesian v. Victoria Versicherung AG, 670 F.3d 1067 (9th Cir. 2012)(en banc).

[80]2010 Cal. Legis. Serv. Ch. 691 (A.B. 2765), codified at Cal. Code Civ Proc. § 338(c)(3). On the 2010 legislation, see Shah (2017).

[81]Order Denying Defendants' Motion to Dismiss, Von Saher v. Norton Simon Museum of Art, No. CV 07-2866-JFW (C.D. Cal. Apr. 2, 2015). As previously noted, the amended statute allowed an art restitution lawsuit against a museum or gallery to be brought within six years of the plaintiff's actual discovery of the facts supporting her claim. The district court concluded that von Saher had met this deadline.

[82]Brief of the United States as Amicus Curiae, Von Saher v. Norton Simon Museum of Art at Pasadena, No. 09-1254 (U.S. May 27, 2011).

In that brief, the solicitor general's office argued that the federal government had an ongoing interest in ensuring that the results of its external restitution policy, whereby other countries' governments adjudicated individual claims to artworks returned to them by the Allies, were not disrupted. The federal government, according to the brief, had sought to "achieve finality in the wartime restitution process," and has a "continuing interest in that finality when appropriate actions have been taken by a foreign government concerning the internal restitution of art."[83]

Second, the museum called attention to the Washington Conference Principles on Nazi Confiscated Art and the Terezín Declaration on Holocaust Era Assets, to which both the United States and the Netherlands, among numerous other countries, were signatories. In the Washington Conference Principles, issued following the Washington Conference on Holocaust-Era Art Assets in 1998, signatories agreed that Nazi-looted art should be identified and their owners encouraged to come forward, that "steps should be taken expeditiously to achieve a just and fair solution," and that signatories should "develop national processes to implement these principles."[84] In the Terezín Declaration, issued following the Prague Holocaust Era Assets Conference in 2009, signatories reaffirmed their support of the Washington Principles and undertook "to make certain that claims to recover such art are resolved expeditiously and based on the facts and merits of the claims."[85]

6.4.2 Compatibility with State Law Claims

The district court agreed with the museum that von Saher's state law restitution claims conflicted with these federal policies, and again dismissed the action.[86] On appeal from that judgment, the appeals court disagreed, for two reasons.

In the first place, the court stated, the California lawsuit was compatible with federal policy because the Cranach was "never subject to postwar internal restitution proceedings in the Netherlands."[87] Desirée von Saher "could have brought a claim [in the Netherlands] for restitution as to all of the artworks Göring looted in the immediate postwar period," the court remarked, "but she understandably chose not to do so" because she was, in her words, "'met with hostility by the postwar Dutch Government,' and 'confronted a restitution regime that made it difficult for Jews like her to recover their property.'"[88] Following the journalistic exposés of the

[83] *Von Saher II*, 754 F.3d at 720 (quoting brief).

[84] U.S. Dept. of State, The Washington Conference on Holocaust Era Assets, Washington Principles on Nazi-Confiscated Art (Dec. 3, 1998), quoted in *Von Saher II*, 754 F.3d at 721.

[85] Prague Holocaust Era Assets Conference, Terezín Declaration (June 30, 2009), quoted in *Von Saher II*, 754 F.3d at 721.

[86] *Von Saher*, 862 F. Supp.2d at 1052.

[87] *Von Saher II*, 754 F.3d at 721.

[88] *Id.* at 722 (quoting Desirée von Saher).

late 1990s, even the "Dutch government later admitted as much" when it "described the immediate postwar restitution process as legalistic, bureaucratic, cold and often even callous."[89] Given that the postwar Dutch authorities took the "astonishing position" that "the transaction between Göring and the Goudstikker Gallery was voluntary," it was not surprising, stated the court, that "Desi decided that she could not achieve a successful result in a sham restitution proceeding to recover the artworks Göring had looted."[90]

Because there had been no restitution proceeding in the Netherlands, the federal government's concern for giving effect to such proceedings had no application to the von Saher litigation. "Though we recognize that the United States has a continuing interest in respecting the finality of 'appropriate actions' taken in a foreign nation to restitute Nazi-confiscated art," the court declared, the Dutch government itself had effectively acknowledged that no such appropriate action had taken place in the case of the Cranach work. Indeed, acknowledging the inadequacy of its postwar internal restitution system, the Dutch government "eventually ordered the return of all the Göring-looted artworks possessed by the Netherlands," though by then it was too late to return the Cranach diptych, which had left the country in the 1960s.[91] These subsequent events "raise serious questions," the court stated, "about whether the initial postwar internal restitution process constitutes an appropriate action" within the meaning of the Washington Principles and other federal policy documents.[92] It was however unnecessary to decide that question about the general adequacy of Dutch restitution procedures, the court explained; for in its view, no proceeding had ever been conducted in connection with the Cranach work. Therefore, it reasoned, "allowing von Saher's claim to go forward would not disturb the finality of any internal restitution proceedings—appropriate or not—in the Netherlands."[93] Concerns about the finality of external and internal restitution proceedings, such as those expressed in the solicitor general's brief to the Supreme Court earlier in the litigation, were unwarranted.[94]

In the second place, the court continued, allowing von Saher's claims to go forward would actually advance current federal policies. "Von Saher is just the sort of heir that the Washington Principles and Terezín Declaration encouraged to come forward to make claims," according to the court, "because the Cranachs were never subject to internal restitution proceedings."[95] Further, the court continued,

---

[89] *Id.*

[90] *Id.*

[91] *Id.* at 723. The court acknowledged that the Dutch government's transfer of the painting in 1966 might constitute an "act of state" immune to judicial challenge, but concluded that the record in the case was insufficiently developed to decide the question at that stage of the litigation. *Id.* at 725–26.

[92] *Id.* at 723.

[93] *Id.*

[94] *Id.* at 724.

[95] *Id.* at 723.

"allowing her lawsuit to proceed would encourage the Museum, a private entity, to follow the Washington Principles, as the Terezín Declaration urged."[96] And "most importantly, this litigation may provide von Saher an opportunity to achieve a just and fair outcome to rectify the consequences of the forced transaction with Göring during the war, even if such a result is no longer capable of being expeditiously obtained."[97] The appeals court therefore concluded that the lawsuit was not preempted by the federal foreign affairs power, and again remanded to the district court for further proceedings.

6.5 Title to the Artwork

The case then proceeded to pretrial discovery, at the end of which the Norton Simon Museum moved for summary judgment, arguing that it held valid title to the artwork. The district court granted the motion in 2016, ruling that under Dutch law, the Netherlands had acquired valid title to the work and had passed it on to the museum.

6.5.1 Choice of Law

Because the parties did not dispute the question of which nation's law controlled, the district court held, without discussion, "under California's conflict of law rules, that Dutch law governs whether the Dutch government acquired ownership of the Cranachs while the Cranachs were in the Netherlands."[98]

6.5.2 Ownership Under Dutch Law

Based on the submissions of foreign law experts, the district court outlined the applicable Dutch laws as follows. While in exile following the Nazi invasion of 1940, the Dutch government issued Royal Decree A6, which prohibited trading with the enemy without the permission of the *Commissie Rechtsverkeer in Oorlogstidt*, the wartime trade commission, and declared all unapproved transactions void unless special circumstances were present. Following the war, this

[96]*Id.*

[97]*Id.*

[98]Order Granting Defendants' Motion to for Summary Judgment and Denying Plaintiff's Motion for Summary Judgment, Von Saher v. Norton Simon Museum of Art, No. CV 07-2866-JFW (C.D. Cal. Aug. 9, 2016), at 10 n. 5.

commission announced that transactions involving goods "recuperated" from enemy territory were presumptively lawful.[99]

In late 1944, the government issued Royal Decree E100, creating a Council for the Restoration of Rights that had authority to review all wartime transactions, to order restitution of property, and to "modify any legal relations that originated or were modified during enemy occupation."[100] It established administrative and judicial divisions of the Council to process restitution claims. The decree generally required claimants to return any money received from the Nazis in order to recover their property, and established a deadline of July 1951 for filing restitution claims.

Also in late 1944, the government issued Royal Decree E133, which was designed for reparations to the nation rather than restitution to private parties. It ordered the expropriation of enemy assets in order to compensate the Netherlands for the losses sustained during the Nazi occupation. The decree announced that "all enemy property within the jurisdiction of the Netherlands automatically passed in ownership to the State on an ongoing basis."[101]

On the district court's reading of these materials, the Netherlands had acquired valid title to the Cranach work and had passed it on to the museum. It reasoned as follows. First, the Dutch wartime trade commission had determined in 1947 that transactions involving recuperated goods, such as the artworks Göring had taken in the forced sale from the Goudstikker gallery, were presumptively valid. "Accordingly," the court stated, "the Göring transaction, as a transaction that occurred 'under coercion, threat or improper influencing by or on behalf of the enemy,' was subject to being declared void (i.e., voidable) and was not automatically void."[102]

Second, in order to have the Göring transaction invalidated, Desirée von Saher was required to apply to the restitution commission established under Royal Decree E100. The deadline for filing a claim was July 1951. Acting on advice from lawyers, von Saher decided against filing a claim for restitution of the artworks taken by Göring, in part because of the costs involved.[103] The artworks therefore remained Göring's property.

Third, because they belonged to Göring, the artworks constituted enemy property and, under Royal Decree E133, became the property of the Dutch state upon their repatriation by the Allies. The Netherlands therefore had title to the Cranach work, which passed to George Stroganoff when he acquired it from the government in 1966, and then passed to Norton Simon when he purchased it from Stroganoff a few years later.

In support of its conclusion, the district court pointed to a ruling of the Dutch restitution commission concerning a work stolen by the Nazis from the Kohn family

---

[99]*Id.* at 3.

[100]Quoted in *id.* at 4.

[101]*Id.*

[102]*Id.* at 11 n. 6 (quoting Royal Decree E100).

[103]Von Saher did obtain restitution of other property, including her residence and the Goudstikker gallery space, that had been taken in a forced sale to Göring's associate Aloïs Riedl.

in the Netherlands in 1940. After the war, the Kohns recovered the painting without going through the restitution procedures specified by Royal Decree E100. The Rebholz family, which had purchased it from the Nazis, then filed a claim for the painting with the restitution commission. The commission ruled that (1) because the Kohns had not filed a proper restitution claim by the 1951 deadline, the Rebholzs were the rightful owners of the stolen painting, and (2) because the Rebholzs were "enemies" within the meaning of Royal Decree E133, the Dutch state now owned the painting. In the district court's view, the Dutch ruling in the Kohn case reinforced the conclusion (in the von Saher litigation) "that, because the Göring transaction was never annulled under Royal Decree E100 (and because Göring never filed a petition for de-enemization, which certainly would have been denied), the Dutch State owned the Cranachs pursuant to Royal Decree E133."[104]

The district court acknowledged that the Dutch government eventually decided to return the von Saher artworks in its possession to the family in 2006. But that decision, in the court's view, had no bearing on ownership of the Cranach diptych, which was sold to a third party decades ago. Explaining its 2006 decision, the Dutch government had stated that it was departing "'from a purely legal approach to the restitution issue' in favor of 'a more policy-oriented approach . . . in which priority is given to moral rather than strictly legal arguments.'"[105] That policy, the district court declared, "is inapplicable to artworks, such as the Cranachs, that have been transferred to a third party," and "[u]nlike the Dutch government and Restitution Committee, this court is required to apply a 'strictly legal' approach, as opposed to one that is based on policy or moral principles."[106] A strictly legal approach "compels the conclusion," the court declared, "that the Dutch State acquired ownership of the Cranachs, which necessarily resolves this action as a matter of law in favor of Norton Simon."[107]

6.6 Epilogue

Marie von Saher appealed the judgment to the court of appeals, arguing that the district court had misconstrued Dutch law. Under a proper reading, she contended, the Netherlands became the custodian, not the owner, of the works stolen by Göring when they were repatriated. The government therefore lacked authority to sell the Cranach, and the Norton Simon Museum accordingly never acquired good title to the work. The appeal is still pending.

---

[104] *Id.* at 15.

[105] *Id.* at 17 (quoting Dutch authorities).

[106] *Id.*

[107] *Id.*

References

Bazyler, Michael J. 2005. *Holocaust Justice: The Battle for Restitution in America's Courts*. New York: New York University Press.

Chiang, Emily. 2003. Think Locally, Act Globally? Dormant Federal Common Law Preemption of State and Local Activities Affecting Foreign Affairs. *Syracuse Law Review* 53: 923–994.

Conway, Mikka Gee. 2010. Foreign Affairs Preemption and *von Saher v. Norton Simon Museum*: Complicating the "Just and Fair Solution" to Holocaust-Era Art Claims. *Law & Inequality* 28: 373–406.

Cooke, Jacob E., ed. 1961. *The Federalist*. Middletown, CT: Wesleyan University Press.

Demarsin, Bert. 2010. The Third Time Is Not Always a Charm: The Troublesome Legacy of a Dutch Art Dealer. *Cardozo Journal of Arts and Entertainment Law* 28: 255–316.

den Hollander, Pieter. 1998. *De Zaak Houdstikker*. Amsterdam: Meulenhoff.

Eizenstat, Stuart. 2003. *Imperfect Justice: Looted Assets, Slave Labor, and the Unfinished Business of World War II*. New York: Public Affairs Press.

Gennochio, Benjamin. 2008. Seized, Reclaimed, and now on View. *New York Times*, April 27.

Henkin, Louis. 1996. *Foreign Affairs and the United States Constitution*. 2nd ed. New York: Oxford University Press.

Hennig, Kai. 2007. The Road to Compensation of Life Insurance Policies: The Foundation Law and ICHEIC. In *Holocaust Restitution: The Litigation and Its Legacy*, ed. Michael J. Bazyler and Roger P. Alford, 251–259. New York: New York University Press.

Kent, Roman. 2007. It's Not About the Money: A Survivor's Perspective on the German Foundation Initiative. In *Holocaust Restitution: The Litigation and Its Legacy*, ed. Michael J. Bazyler and Roger P. Alford, 205–214. New York: New York University Press.

Kill, Lawrence, and Linda Gerstel. 2007. Holocaust-Era Insurance Claims: Legislative, Judicial, and Executive Remedies. In *Holocaust Restitution: The Litigation and Its Legacy*, ed. Michael J. Bazyler and Roger P. Alford, 239–251. New York: New York University Press.

Kreder, Jennifer Anglim. 2012. Fighting Corruption of the Historical Record: Nazi-Looted Art Litigation. *Kansas Law Review* 61: 75–137.

Lambsdorff, Otto Graf. 2007. The Negotiations on Compensation for Nazi Forced Laborers. In *Holocaust Restitution: The Litigation and Its Legacy*, ed. Michael J. Bazyler and Roger P. Alford, 170–181. New York: New York University Press.

Müller, Melissa, and Monika Tatzkow. 2010. *Lost Lives, Lost Art: Jewish Collectors, Nazi Art Theft*. London: Frontline.

Restitutiecommissie. 2005. Recommendation Regarding Application by Amsterdamse Negotiatie Compagnie NV in Liquidation for the Restitution of 267 Works of Art From the Dutch National Art Collection. Accessed July 1, 2017. http://www.restitutiecommissie.nl/en/recommendations/recommendation_115.html.

Rickman, Gregg J. 2007. *Conquest and Redemption: A History of Jewish Assets from the Holocaust*. New Brunswick, NJ: Transaction Publishers.

Riding, Alan. 2006a. Dutch to Return Art Seized by Nazis. *New York Times*, February 7.

———. 2006b. Göring, Rembrandt, and the Little Black Book. *New York Times*, March 26.

Schaefer, Matthew. 2011. Constraints on State-Level Foreign Policy: (Re)justifying, Refining and Distinguishing the Dormant Foreign Affairs Doctrine. *Seton Hall Law Review* 41: 201–318.

Shah, Rajika L. 2017. The Making of California's Art Recovery Statute: The Long Road to Section 338(c)(3). *Chapman Law Review* 20: 77–118.

Spiro, Peter J. 1999. Foreign Relations Federalism. *University of Colorado Law Review* 70: 1223–1277.

Sturman, Deborah. 2007. Germany's Reexamination of Its Past Through the Lens of the Holocaust Litigation. In *Holocaust Restitution: The Litigation and Its Legacy*, ed. Michael J. Bazyler and Roger P. Alford, 215–225. New York: New York University Press.

Sutton, Peter C. 2008. *Reclaimed: Paintings from the Collection of Jacques Goudstikker*. New Haven, CT: Yale University Press.

Cases

American Insurance Association v. Garamendi, 539 U.S. 396 (2003)
Crosby v. National Foreign Trade Council, 530 U.S. 363 (2000)
Deutsch v. Turner Corp., 324 F.3d 692 (9th Cir. 2003), cert. denied, 540 U.S. 820 (2003)
Japan Line, Ltd. v. County of Los Angeles, 441 U.S. 434 (1979)
Movsesian v. Victoria Versicherung AG, 670 F.3d 1067 (9th Cir. 2012)(en banc)
United States v. Pink, 315 U.S. 203, 225 (1942)
Von Saher v. Norton Simon Museum of Art, 2007 WL 4302726 (C.D. Cal. 2007), aff'd in part and rev'd part, 592 F.3d 954 (9th Cir. 2010), cert. denied, 564 U.S. 1037 (2011), on remand, 862 F. Supp.2d 1044 (C.D. Cal. 2012), rev'd, 754 F.3d 712 (9th Cir. 2014), cert. denied, 135 S. Ct. 1158 (2015), on further remand, Order Denying Defendants' Motion to Dismiss, No. 07-cv-2866 (C.D. Cal. Apr. 2, 2015) (unpublished), and Order Granting Defendants' Motion to for Summary Judgment and Denying Plaintiff's Motion for Summary Judgment, No. 07-cv-2866 (Aug. 9, 2016) (unpublished), appeal docketed, No. 16-56308 (9th Cir. Sep. 9, 2016)
Youngstown Sheet & Tube Co. v. Sawyer, 343 U.S. 579 (1952)
Zschernig v. Miller, 389 U.S. 429 (1968)

Chapter 7
Cassirer v. Kingdom of Spain and Thyssen-Bornemisza Collection Foundation

7.1 Background

Julius Cassirer (1841–1924) was a Jewish industrialist who, with his sons Paul and Bruno, owned a Berlin art gallery and publishing house that would become well known in the early twentieth century for championing the works of the French impressionists.[1] In 1900, he acquired Camille Pissarro's painting *Rue Saint-Honoré, après-midi, effet de pluie* (1897) from Pissarro's dealer in Paris. After his death, the painting was inherited by Lilly Cassirer (1876–1962), his daughter-in-law.[2] Lilly, who was also Jewish, emigrated from Germany with her second husband in 1939. In order to obtain a German exit visa, she was forced to surrender the Pissarro painting to a Munich art dealer appointed by the Nazis to appraise the family's belongings.

The painting then followed a tortuous path. The Nazi-appointed dealer who seized it, Jakob Scheiderwimmer, traded it to another dealer who took it to the Netherlands. After the Nazi invasion of that country, it was returned to Germany and sold to an anonymous buyer at an auction in 1943. Smuggled to the United States in 1951 by a California gallery, it was sold by a New York gallery the following year to a Missouri collector, and then sold once again by a New York gallery in 1976 to a Swiss collector. The Swiss collector, Hans Heinrich Thyssen-Bornemisza, sold the painting in 1993 to the government of Spain, which purchased his collection on behalf of a newly-created museum named in his honor. On its verso side, the painting still bears a partially removed ownership label indicating the Cassirers' Berlin address.

After the war, Lilly Cassirer returned to Germany and filed a claim for restitution against the German government and against Scheiderwimmer, the Nazi functionary who had seized and sold the painting. Unable to discover the whereabouts of the

---

[1]On the Cassirer family, see Müller and Tatzkow (2010), pp. 10–28. They were also the source of the van Gogh at issue in *Orkin v. Taylor*, discussed in Chap. 5.

[2]Lilly was the widow of Julius's son Fritz Cassirer (1871–1926).

B.L. Hay, *Nazi-Looted Art and the Law*, DOI 10.1007/978-3-319-64967-2_7

painting, she settled her claim in 1958, receiving a payment of compensation from the government. She died in 1962. Four decades later, in 2000, her grandson and heir Claude Cassirer (1921–2010), who had escaped an internment camp in Europe and emigrated to the United States during the war, learned from friends that the Pissarro was on display at the Thyssen-Bornemisza Museum in Madrid. Distressed to find "the painting is being displayed in a museum named after the family that bankrolled Hitler,"[3] Claude asked Spain's culture minister, who sat on the museum's board, to arrange for the painting's return. That request was refused, as were subsequent requests made on Cassirer's behalf by several members of the U.S. Congress and American diplomats. Cassirer, living in retirement in California, then took the matter to court.

7.2 Proceedings

In May 2010, Claude Cassirer filed suit in federal court in Los Angeles, naming as defendants both the Kingdom of Spain and the Thyssen-Bornemisza Collection Foundation, which operates the eponymous museum in Madrid. The complaint asserted that the court could assert jurisdiction over the defendants based on their commercial activities in the United States, which included advertisements for the museum and marketing materials featuring the Pissarro painting. The plaintiff sought restitution of the painting and damages under common-law theories of replevin and conversion, along with a declaration awarding the artwork to Cassirer. The defendants filed motions to dismiss on various procedural and jurisdictional grounds, including foreign state immunity, as well as contesting the claims on the merits.

The district court denied the motions to dismiss, and certified the case for interlocutory review.[4] On appeal, the court of appeals for the Ninth Circuit upheld the district court's ruling that neither Spain nor the museum enjoyed immunity against the suit.[5] The court agreed with the district court that the suit was authorized by the Foreign Sovereign Immunities Act,[6] which lifts immunity for specified types of litigation against foreign states, including certain claims to recover property expropriated in violation of international law.[7] The court of appeals accordingly remanded to the lower court for further proceedings.

---

[3]Soto (2005). Hans Thyssen-Bornemisza's uncle Fritz, a German industrialist, was an early supporter of the Nazi regime, which later turned against him because of his Catholicism.

[4]Cassirer v. Kingdom of Spain and Thyssen-Bornemisza Foundation, 461 F. Supp.2d 1157 (C.D. Cal. 2006).

[5]The appeal was initially decided by a three-judge panel, and then reheard *en banc* by an eleven-judge panel.

[6]28 U.S.C. § 1601 (1976).

[7]Cassirer v. Kingdom of Spain and Thyssen-Bornemisza Foundation, 616 F.3d 1019 (9th Cir. 2010)(en banc), cert. denied, 564 U.S. 1037 (2011). (We will refer to this 2010 court of appeals decision as "*Cassirer I*.") The court of appeals dismissed the appeal with respect to the defendants' objections to personal jurisdiction, justiciability, and venue, holding that these issues were beyond its jurisdiction on interlocutory review.

Claude Cassirer died in 2010, leaving his children to take over the case. In an agreement reached with the defendants, the Cassirer heirs dropped the Kingdom of Spain from the case, leaving the Thyssen-Bornemisza Foundation as the lone defendant.[8]

In May 2012, the district court dismissed the case as time-barred, holding that under California's three-year statute of limitations, Cassirer's claim had been filed two years too late.[9] The court further held that the California legislature's 2010 law extending the statute of limitations,[10] which lengthened the period to six years for art claims against museums and galleries, was unconstitutional under the doctrine of foreign affairs preemption. The court of appeals reversed the district court's decision in 2013, ruling that the 2010 legislation statute was not preempted, and rejecting the Thyssen-Bornemisza museum's other constitutional challenges to it.[11] The case was again remanded for further proceedings.

Following pretrial discovery, in June 2015 the district court entered summary judgment for the museum, holding that it was the rightful owner of the painting.[12] The court ruled, first, that under applicable choice-of-law principles, the law of Spain governed the question of the painting's ownership. It held, second, that under the Spanish law of adverse possession, the museum had acquired good title to the painting because it had publicly claimed ownership to it since 1993. That judgment is now on appeal.

7.3 Jurisdiction of the American Courts

Spain and the Thyssen-Bornemisza Foundation contended that Cassirer's case could not be brought in the American courts, because both were shielded by sovereign immunity.[13] They also challenged the courts' personal jurisdiction over the museum and the justiciability of the claims. Let us consider these issues in turn.

---

[8]In return, the Thyssen-Bornemisza Foundation dropped its remaining jurisdictional defenses.

[9]Cassirer v. Thyssen-Bornemisza Foundation, 2012 WL 1285771 (C.D. Cal. 2012). The court reasoned that the claim had accrued in 2000, when Cassirer learned of the painting's location, and had expired in 2003, two years before the complaint had been filed.

[10]Cal. Civ. Proc. Code § 338(c)(3) (2010).

[11]Cassirer v. Thyssen-Bornemisza Foundation, 737 F.3d 613 (9th Cir. 2013). We will refer to this 2013 court of appeals decision as "*Cassirer II*."

[12]Cassirer v. Thyssen-Bornemisza Foundation, 153 F. Supp.3d 1148 (C.D. Cal. 2015).

[13]The Thyssen-Bornemisza Foundation sought immunity on the theory that the museum, while privately held, was nonetheless an "instrumentality" of the state.

7.3.1 Foreign State Immunity

The question for the courts was whether the case fell into one of the categories for which the Foreign Sovereign Immunities Act of 1976 allows suits against foreign states and their instrumentalities. As we have seen in earlier chapters, the Act codifies the so-called restrictive theory of immunity, which generally bars suits arising out of *acta jure impereii*, a state's "public" acts, while allowing suits based on *jure gestionis*, its "private" acts.[14] One of its categories, encountered in our discussion of the *Altmann* case in Chap. 3, is the provision allowing certain lawsuits to recover expropriated property. The Act's expropriation (or "takings") exception, as it is known, reads in relevant part as follows:

> A foreign state shall not be immune from the jurisdiction of the courts of the United States or of the States in any case … in which
>
> [1] rights in property taken in violation of international law are in issue and …
>
> [2] that property or any property exchanged for such property is owned or operated by an agency or instrumentality of the foreign state and
>
> [3] that agency or instrumentality is engaged in a commercial activity in the United States.[15]

There was little dispute that the Thyssen-Bornemisza Foundation is an "instrumentality" of the Kingdom of Spain, in view of that state's role in creating and paying for the museum and its power to appoint and remove directors.[16] There were nonetheless several contested issues concerning application of the expropriation provision to the Cassirers' claims.

Taking in Violation of International Law The defendants argued that the Nazis' seizure of the Pissarro painting from Lilly Cassirer did not violate international law, pointing to cases holding that international law generally does not govern a state's taking of property from its own citizens. The district court rejected the argument. It recognized, as the court of appeals had observed in the *Altmann* decision, that "[t]o fall into [the expropriation exception of the Act], the plaintiff cannot be a citizen of the defendant country at the time of expropriation, because expropriation by a sovereign state of its own nationals does not implicate settled principles of international law."[17] That principle did not apply to the confiscation of Lilly Cassirer's painting, however, because the plaintiffs had furnished "compelling evidence that Ms. Cassirer was not a German citizen at the time of Nazi Germany's taking of the Painting since, according to the Nazis' citizenship laws at that time, '[a] Jew cannot be a citizen of the Reich.'"[18]

[14] See Sections 3.3 and 4.3 above. On the American law of foreign state immunity, see American Law Institute (2016) §§ 455–63; Vandenberg (2006); Whytock (2013). For comparative perspectives, see Cassese (2005), Fox and Webb (2013), and Shaw (1997).

[15] Foreign Sovereign Immunities Act, 28 U.S.C. § 1605(a)(3).

[16] See *Cassirer*, 461 F. Supp.2d at 1164.

[17] Altmann v. Republic of Austria, 317 F.3d 954, 968 (9th Cir. 2002), quoted in *Cassirer*, 461 F. Supp.2d at 1165.

[18] *Cassirer*, 461 F. Supp.2d at 1165 (quoting Nazi citizenship laws).

The court concluded that "since Germany itself did not consider Ms. Cassirer to be a citizen, Ms. Cassirer's alleged German 'citizenship' at the time of the taking does not preclude the application of the expropriation exception in this case."[19]

Application to Non-expropriating State Pointing out that it was the government of Germany that had seized the painting from Lilly Cassirer, the defendants argued that the Cassirers could not invoke the expropriation exception against Spain, which had acquired the painting long afterward and played no part in the seizure. The defendants' argument was that the expropriation exception creates jurisdiction only for suits against "the foreign state that expropriated the property," and not for suits against "some later purchaser who was not complicit in the taking."[20] This line of argument had not been addressed by the courts before, raising another question of first impression produced by the long interval of time that had elapsed since the Nazi era. By the time Lilly Cassirer's painting was acquired by Spain for the museum, more than fifty years had gone by since the Nazis had taken it from her, and it had passed through the hands of a half-dozen purchasers.

The question thus presented—whether the Act's expropriation exception is confined to suits against the state that committed the unlawful taking, or instead may also be invoked against other states that have come into later possession of the property—was decided in the Cassirers' favor. The court of appeals, agreeing with the district court, ruled that "the plain language of the statute" is expansive enough to allow suits against states other than the one that committed the wrongful expropriation.[21] The language contains no requirement, the court explained, "that the foreign state against whom the claim is made be the entity which took the property in violation of international law."[22] By its terms, the expropriation exception "simply excepts from immunity 'a foreign state' in any case 'in which rights *in property taken in violation of law* are in issue"; Congress wrote this text "in the passive voice, which 'focuses on an event that occurs without respect to a specific actor.'"[23] The "text already connotes '*any* foreign state,'" and "would have to be rewritten in order to carry the meaning the Foundation ascribes to it," according to the court.[24] Nor could the court find anything in the legislative history to support the museum's contention that only the expropriating state was susceptible to suit under the statutory provision. "We understand that Congress meant for jurisdiction to exist over claims against a foreign state," the court concluded, "whenever property that its instrumentality ends up claiming to own had been taken in violation of international law, so long as the instrumentality engages in a commercial activity in the United States."[25]

---

[19] *Id.* at 1165–66. The defendants did not dispute this conclusion on appeal.

[20] *Cassirer I*, 616 F.3d at 1028.

[21] *Id.*

[22] *Id.*

[23] *Id.* (quoting 28 U.S.C. § 1605(a)(3) and Dean v. United States, 556 U.S. 568, 572 (2009)) (emphasis in original).

[24] *Cassirer I*, 616 F.3d at 1028.

[25] *Id.* at 1028.

Commercial Nexus The defendants unsuccessfully argued that the museum, being a nonprofit cultural institution, was not engaged in commercial activity in the United States. In ruling against them, the courts emphasized the Act's proviso that the "commercial character of an activity shall be determined by reference to the nature of the course of conduct or particular transaction or act, rather than by reference to its purpose."[26] The museum, the courts found, sold merchandise in the United States, hired writers and speakers there, and advertised in American periodicals—all of which, in the courts' view, constituted commercial activities as contemplated by the Act. It "does not matter," the court of appeals stated, "that the Foundation's activities are undertaken on behalf of a non-profit museum to further its cultural mission"; the "important thing is that the actions are 'the *type* of actions by which a private party engages in trade and traffic or commerce.'"[27] Citing its own previous decision in the *Altmann* case, the court concluded that the museum's transactions in the United States, designed in part to "encourage Americans to visit the museum where the Pissarro is featured," easily satisfied the statutory requirement.[28]

Exhaustion of Remedies The courts also rejected the defense argument that the Cassirers were required to seek judicial relief in Germany or Spain before suing in the American courts. Relying again on the "plain language" of the statute, the court of appeals held that the Act contains no exhaustion requirement for claims concerning expropriated property.[29] "The expropriation exception says nothing at all about exhaustion of remedies," the court declared.[30] "It does not, for example, condition immunity on a claimant's having first presented his claim to the courts of the country being sued, or to the courts of the country that did the taking, or to any international tribunal."[31] Noting that in the legislative history Congress had indicated that the Act "sets for the sole and exclusive standards to be used in resolving questions of sovereign immunity raised by foreign states,"[32] the court was of the view that its "objectives would be undercut were courts to read requirements into the statute that Congress itself has not clearly prescribed."[33] The court acknowledged that the availability of foreign remedies may bear on the ultimate determination whether, on the merits, a claimant has suffered a wrongful taking of property

[26] Foreign Sovereign Immunities Act, 28 U.S.C. § 1603(d).

[27] *Cassirer I*, 616 F.3d at 1032 (quoting Republic of Argentina v. Weltover, Inc., 504 U.S. 607, 614 (1992)).

[28] *Cassirer I*, 616 F.3d at 1033–34, citing *Altmann*, 317 F.3d at 969.

[29] *Id.* at 1034.

[30] *Id.*

[31] *Id.*

[32] H.R.Rep. No. 94–1487 (1976), reprinted in 1976 U.S. Code Cong. & Admin. News 6604, 6610, quoted in *Cassirer I*, 616 F.3d at 1035.

[33] *Cassirer I*, 616 F.3d at 1035. The court pointed to the Supreme Court's repeated emphasis on the comprehensiveness of the Act's criteria. See Republic of Austria v. Altmann, 541 U.S. 677, 699 (2004); Republic of Argentina v. Weltover, Inc., 504 U.S. 607, 610 (1992); Verlinden B.V. v. Central Bank of Nigeria, 461 U.S. 480, 488 (1983).

without just compensation. But the existence of such remedies did not, it held, deprive a court of jurisdiction to hear a case brought under the Act.[34]

7.3.2 *Personal Jurisdiction*

Contending that it lacked the contacts with California necessary to support personal jurisdiction over it, the museum argued that the proceeding violated the constitutional prohibition on depriving persons of their property without due process of law. Here it relied on the familiar line of cases tracing to the *International Shoe* decision, which announced that due process generally prohibits a court from asserting jurisdiction over a nonresident party unless the party has sufficient "minimum contacts" with the forum to render the proceeding consistent with conventional standards of "fair play and substantial justice."[35] The district court rejected this argument for the same reason that it had in its *Altmann* decision, ruling that foreign states and their instrumentalities are not "persons" within the meaning of the Due Process Clause, which is a protection of "individual liberty" rather than of foreign sovereignty.[36] Congress had effectively decreed that the American courts could assert jurisdiction over foreign states in any case satisfying the criteria of the Foreign Sovereign Immunities Act, the court explained, and a defendant could not insist on any requirement of a territorial connection to the United States beyond those set forth in the Act itself. Because the Cassirers' claim against the museum fell within the Act's expropriation exception, the court reasoned, there was no need for further inquiry into the degree of contacts between the museum and the United States.[37]

7.3.3 *Justiciability*

Spain, for its part, contended that there was no justiciable "case or controversy" as required by Article III for the exercise of federal judicial power. Its argument was

[34]*Cassirer I*, 616 F.3d at 1036–37.

[35]International Shoe Co. v. State of Washington, 326 U.S. 310 (1945). See generally Parrish (2006), Peterson (2010), and Rhodes and Robertson (2014); see also American Law Institute (2016) § 302.

[36]*Cassirer*, 461 F. Supp.2d at 1168 (quoting Altmann v. Republic of Austria, 142 F. Supp.2d 1187, (C.D. Cal. 2001)).

[37]The court also concluded that California was an appropriate venue under the Act, which authorizes suit "in any judicial district in which the [foreign state] agency or instrumentality is . . . doing business." 28 U.S.C. § 1391(f). The court found that the museum's documented sales of merchandise to residents of the district was enough to constitute "doing business." *Cassirer*, 461 F. Supp.2d at 1177. The museum dropped its objections to personal jurisdiction and venue before the court of appeals could rule on them.

that the Cassirers had not suffered any injury that was, in the parlance of the Supreme Court's jurisprudence on party standing, "fairly traceable" to Spain, and that a judgment in their favor would not redress any injury to them.[38] The district court rejected this argument, noting that it "begs the question whether this Court may properly entertain an action to force Spain to disgorge the painting even though Spain was not involved in the illegal expropriation."[39] That was ultimately a question for disposition on the merits, as were several subsidiary questions, including "whether or not Cassirer can ultimately establish an interest in the Painting, whether he can establish that his interest is superior to that of Spain and the Foundation, and whether he can establish a legal basis for vindicating that interest."[40] The "fact that such issues must be resolved," the court stated, "tends to prove, rather than disprove, the existence of a case or controversy in the present circumstances."[41] That Spain disclaimed liability was, the court concluded, hardly a basis for dismissing the case given that its liability was one of the central issues raised by the complaint.[42]

7.4 Constitutionality of State Art Restitution Law

Following the interlocutory court of appeals ruling on foreign state immunity, the Cassirers agreed to release Spain from the litigation, in return for which the Thyssen-Bornemisza Foundation agreed to drop its remaining objections to the court's jurisdiction. At that point, attention shifted to whether the claims against the museum were timely under the applicable California statute of limitations. Filed five years after Claude Cassirer's discovery in 2000 of the painting's whereabouts, the plaintiffs' claims ordinarily would have been time-barred under the state's three-year statute of limitations for claims to recover personal property.[43] In 2010, however, the California legislature extended the statute of limitations applicable to the claims, retroactively granting them six years from the time of discovery to bring suit. The question for the courts in the Cassirer litigation was whether that enactment was constitutional.

[38] Allen v. Wright, 468 U.S. 737, 750 (1984), quoted in *Cassirer*, 461 F. Supp.2d at 1163.

[39] *Cassirer*, 461 F. Supp.2d at 1168.

[40] *Id.*

[41] *Id.*

[42] As with personal jurisdiction and venue, the museum dropped its justiciability objection before it could be ruled on by the court of appeals.

[43] Cal. Code Civ. Proc. §338(c)(1). See Section 5.4 above.

7.4.1 *The 2010 California Legislation*

In 2002, declaring that "[i]n addition to the many atrocities that befell the victims of the Nazi regime, treasured pieces of artwork were wrongfully taken," and "California has a moral and public policy interest in assuring that its residents and citizens are given a reasonable opportunity to commence an action in court for those pieces of artwork," the California legislature amended the statute of limitations to provide a time extension for Nazi-era art claims against galleries and museums, reviving claims that would otherwise be barred by the three-year limitations period.[44] As we saw in the preceding chapter, the Ninth Circuit court of appeals struck down that statute in the von Saher litigation, ruling that the state legislature's effort "to redress wrongs committed in the course of the Second World War" unconstitutionally encroached upon the federal government's authority over foreign affairs.[45]

In response, the California legislature in 2010 again amended the statute of limitations for property recovery lawsuits, this time directing its efforts not specifically at Holocaust art restitution, but at all claims to recover lost art from galleries and museums. The new amendments, covering all claims against galleries and museums for art lost to "unlawful taking or theft," allowed claimants to sue within six years of their "actual discovery" of the art's whereabouts.[46] The amendment specified that a claim accrues only when a claimant has actual knowledge of the lost art's location; galleries and museums could not invoke the rule of constructive discovery, according to which a claim may be time-barred if the claimant should have known, or failed to learn, the work's whereabouts.[47] The amendments were made retroactively applicable to all pending and future actions commenced before 2017, provided that the missing art had been taken within the past hundred years.[48]

In the preamble to the 2010 amendments, the legislature stated that its objectives included easing the burdens facing claimants to missing art as a result of limitations periods. "Because objects of fine art often circulate in the private marketplace for many years before entering the collections of museums or galleries," the preamble stated, "existing statutes of limitation, which are solely the creatures of the Legislature, often present an inequitable procedural obstacle to recovery of these objects by parties that claim to be their rightful owner."[49] The preamble announced the additional purpose of encouraging responsible behavior on the part of museums and

---

[44]2002 Cal. Legis. Serv. Ch. 332 (A.B. 1758).

[45]Von Saher v. Norton Simon Museum of Art, 592 F.3d 954 (9th Cir. 2010) (quoting Deutsch v. Turner Corp., 324 F.3d 692, 712 (9th Cir. 2003)), cert. denied, 564 U.S. 1037 (2011). See Section 6.3 above.

[46]Cal. Code Civ Proc. § 338(c)(3)(A). On the 2010 legislation, see Shah (2017).

[47]"Actual discovery," the statute states, "does not include any constructive knowledge imputed by law." Cal. Code Civ Proc. § 338(c)(3)(B)(i). On constructive discovery, see Section 5.4 above.

[48]Cal. Code Civ Proc. § 338(c)(3)(B).

[49]2010 Cal. Legis. Serv. Ch. 691 (A.B. 2765).

galleries, which play "an important role in making information about their collections, exhibitions and acquisitions publicly available," and making their "resources more accessible to individuals and organizations seeking information about the location and history of particular art objects, thereby assisting the rightful owners of works of fine art who may have a claim for the recovery of these works"; by making the accrual of claims turn on an owner's "actual discovery" of a work's location, the amended statute would, according to the preamble, "provide incentives for research and publication of provenance about these art works, in order to encourage the prompt and fair resolution of claims."[50]

7.4.2 Foreign Affairs Preemption

The Thyssen-Bornemisza Foundation contended that the 2010 amendments were invalid under the doctrine of foreign affairs preemption. Its position was accepted by the district court, which thought the case was controlled by the court of appeals decision overturning the 2002 Nazi-era art claims legislation in *Von Saher v. Norton Simon Museum*.[51] In that decision, as we have seen, the court of appeals declared that Holocaust restitution policy was "for the federal government alone to address," that federal authorities had negotiated numerous international accords on the subject in the postwar period, and that "California may not improve upon or add to the resolution of the war."[52] Though the 2002 legislation "purports to regulate property, an area traditionally left to the states," the *Von Saher* court stated, its "real purpose is to provide relief to Holocaust victims and their heirs," which, however praiseworthy, "is not an area of 'traditional state responsibility.'"[53]

The 2010 amendments, according to the district court, were not meaningfully different. "Although the statute on its face does not mention Holocaust-era thefts," the district court stated, "the amendments were enacted shortly after the Ninth Circuit overturned a functionally equivalent statute expressly enacted to allow recovery of Holocaust-era artwork."[54] The 2010 amendments represented an attempt by the California legislature to "do an end run around *Von Saher* by enacting legislation which, though worded differently in an attempt to appear of general applicability, has the identical purpose" as the invalidated 2002 enactment.[55] "The language of the amended statute bears numerous similarities to the overturned statute," the court observed, and the circumstances of its passage indicate that it was "primarily intended to provide relief to the same class of

---

[50]*Id.*

[51]592 F.3d 954 (9th Cir. 2010), cert. denied, 564 U.S. 1037 (2011).

[52]*Von Saher*, 592 F.3d at 966, 968 (quoting *Deutsch*, 324 F.3d at 712).

[53]*Von Saher*, 592 F.3d at 964, 965.

[54]Cassirer v. Thyssen-Bornemisza Foundation, 2012 WL 1285771, *2 (C.D. Cal. 2012).

[55]*Id.*

plaintiffs as those targeted by [the 2002 legislation]," despite "eliminating references to the Holocaust and nominally sweeping within its scope a broader temporal and substantive range of claims."[56] Even the legislative history of the 2010 amendments "references *Von Saher*," noted the court, "and indicates that a purpose of the legislation was 'to provide protection for victims that the Legislature has already intended to protect' and would 'provide the necessary remedy for these victims.'"[57] Accordingly, like the 2002 statute, the 2010 enactment "impermissibly intrudes on foreign affairs because its aim is to provide a remedy for wartime wrongs through California courts that would otherwise not exist."[58]

The court of appeals disagreed. The 2010 enactment "does not create a remedy for wartime injuries," according to the court of appeals, but rather addresses "preexisting claims concerning a class of artwork that is unrelated to foreign affairs on its face."[59] The legislation "does not require that those claims arise out of wartime injuries, or from any other specific source that might implicate the federal government's foreign affairs power."[60] Nor was the district court correct, in the appeals court's view, that the 2010 amendments were "functionally equivalent" to the invalidated 2002 law, because they cover art claims unrelated to Holocaust restitution, and in fact "since its enactment, non-Holocaust era artwork cases have invoked" them, including claims to recover manuscripts stolen in Armenia in 1915 and photographs stolen in Los Angeles in the 1970s.[61] Stating that the "district court erred in concluding that [the 2010 legislation] intrudes on foreign affairs," the court of appeals ruled that the law was not preempted by the federal foreign affairs power.[62]

7.4.3 Other Constitutional Issues

Due Process of Law The museum also moved to dismiss on the ground that the 2010 statute's revival of the Cassirers' claims, which otherwise would have been time-barred by the three-year statute of limitations, deprived it of its property without due process of law in violation of the Fourteenth Amendment. The court of appeals, agreeing with the district court, held that the case could not be dismissed on this ground, because it was an open question whether the Pissarro was in fact the

---

[56]*Id.* *2, *18.

[57]*Id.* at *2 (quoting legislative history).

[58]*Id.* at *18.

[59]*Cassirer II*, 737 F.3d at 617–18.

[60]*Id.* at 618.

[61]*Id.* (citing Western Prelacy of the Armenian Apostolic Church v. J. Paul Getty Museum, No. BC438824 (L.A. Co. Super. Ct. Aug. 1, 2011), and Rafaelli v. Getty Images, Inc., No. 2:12–cv–00563–CAS–PJW (C.D. Cal. Jan. 20, 2012)).

[62]*Cassirer II*, 737 F.3d at 619.

museum's property. The court noted an earlier decision in which it had held that "[w]here a lapse of time has not invested a party with title to real or personal property, a state legislature may extend a lapsed statute of limitations without violating the fourteenth amendment, regardless of whether the effect is seen as creating or reviving a barred claim."[63] Whether "a lapse of time invested the Foundation with title to the Painting," the court of appeals stated, was a question whose resolution would require inquiry into a number of "factual disputes" between the parties concerning the museum's acquisition and possession of the artwork.[64] The museum was therefore not entitled to dismissal on the pleadings.[65]

Freedom of Expression The museum also argued that the 2010 amendments violated the First Amendment's guarantee of free speech and expression by singling out for unfavorable treatment institutions that specialize in the exhibition of art. Citing the *Minneapolis Star* decision,[66] in which the Supreme Court invalidated a selective tax on newspapers, the museum argued that in targeting galleries and museums, the statute effectively penalizes "those who regularly engage in the public display and distribution of fine art—a form of protected expression," in that it "subjects them to civil liability and possible forfeiture of their artwork for claims that are otherwise stale," while "entities or individuals who keep their artwork in a private collection and thus do not engage in expressive conduct are not subject to this penalty."[67] The court of appeals, following the district court, rejected this argument, stating that the 2010 legislation singled out galleries and museums "not on the basis of any protected speech," but because the legislature had deemed them "sophisticated" players in the art market, having "access to methods of tracing title to their artifacts" and being well aware "that often 'lost artifacts have a break in the chain of title.'"[68] The court concluded that the Thyssen-Bornemisza Foundation had "failed to demonstrate that [the 2010 legislation] burdens its right to free speech."[69]

---

[63]Starks v. S.E. Rykoff Co., 673 F.2d 1106, 1109 (9th Cir. 1982), quoted in *Cassirer II*, 737 F.3d at 620.

[64]*Cassirer II*, 737 F.3d at 620. On remand.

[65]Following remand, as discussed below in Section 7.6, the district court found that the museum was the rightful owner of the painting under the Spanish law of adverse possession. In dictum, it opined that if the 2010 California statute were employed to strip the museum of ownership, due process of law would be violated. See its 2015 opinion in *Cassirer*, 153 F. Supp.3d at 1167–68.

[66]Minneapolis Star and Tribune Co. v. Minnesota Commissioner of Revenue, 460 U.S. 575 (1983).

[67]Quoted by the district court in *Cassirer*, 2012 WL 1285771, *22.

[68]*Cassirer II*, 737 F.3d at 621.

[69]*Id.*

7.5 Conflicts of Law

At the close of pretrial discovery in 2015, the Thyssen-Bornemisza Foundation moved for summary judgment, arguing that under the law of Spain, the museum had acquired valid title to the painting by adverse possession. The Cassirers filed an opposing motion, requesting a ruling that the substantive law of California, not Spain, governed the question whether the museum had acquired title. The problem for the courts was to determine which place—Spain or California—should supply the applicable substantive law governing the museum's claim of ownership.[70]

7.5.1 Choice of Law in Actions Against Foreign States

The Foreign Sovereign Immunities Act gives the courts jurisdiction to hear actions against foreign states, but does not create any substantive duties or liabilities, and contains no choice-of-law provision specifying what substantive law to apply, indicating only that a non-immune foreign state "shall be liable in the same manner and to the same extent as a private individual under like circumstances."[71] In a series of cases, the Ninth Circuit court of appeals has held that, "lacking statutory guidance" for the selection of the applicable substantive law, federal courts should follow their own "federal common law" choice-of-law rules for suits against foreign states.[72] This represents a departure from the familiar *Klaxon* principle (which the Supreme Court based on the *Erie* decision) that, in cases where federal jurisdiction is based on diversity of citizenship, the federal court follows the forum state's choice-of-law rules.[73]

Thus, for example, consider *Harris v. Polskie Linie Lotnicze*,[74] involving a suit brought in federal court in California against the Polish national airline for a plane crash that killed a California resident. One question in the case was whether damages should be computed according to the tort law of Poland or according to

[70]The museum also argued that it had acquired title by adverse possession under Swiss law. The district court found it unnecessary to address this argument because it ruled in the museum's favor on the application of Spanish law.

[71]Foreign Sovereign Immunities Act, 28 U.S.C. § 1606. The Act does modify the substantive law in some cases by specifying that compensatory, but not punitive, damages are available against foreign states. *Id.*

[72]Harris v. Polskie Linie Lotnicze, 820 F.2d 1000, 1003–4 (9th Cir. 1987). See also Liu v. Republic of China, 892 F.2d 1419, 1425 (9th Cir. 1989), cert. dismissed, 497 U.S. 1058 (1990); Schoenberg v. Exportadora de Sal, S.A. de C.V., 930 F.2d 777, 782 (9th Cir. 1991).

[73]Klaxon Co. v. Stentor Electric Manufacturing Co., 313 U.S. 487, 496 (1941); Erie Railroad Co. v. Tompkins, 304 U.S. 64 (1938). The *Erie* decision held that diversity cases are generally governed by state law; the *Klaxon* decision held that in selecting the applicable law, the federal court should follow the forum state's choice-of-law rules.

[74]820 F.2d 1000 (9th Cir. 1987).

the tort law of California, the latter allowing for a more generous recovery. Under the *Klaxon* principle, the federal court hearing the case would have followed California's choice-of-law rule to determine which of those substantive laws should govern the case; that is, it would have applied the same law that a California state court would have applied in the case. The Ninth Circuit ruled, however, that the federal court was not bound by California's choice-of-law rule, and should instead make its own selection of the applicable substantive law.[75] Its decision was based on the premise that "[t]he use of federal common law in specialized areas where jurisdiction is not based on diversity has been sanctioned by the Supreme Court since the day *Erie* was decided."[76]

The courts of appeals in other circuits have disagreed with this approach. Unlike the Ninth Circuit, these courts take the position that in determining the applicable substantive law in cases against foreign states brought under the Act, the federal courts should not devise their own choice-of-law rules. They should instead follow the *Klaxon* principle and apply the forum state's choice-of-law rule.[77] "[A]pplying the forum state's choice-of-law principles, rather than constructing a set of common law principles, better effectuates Congress' intent that foreign states be 'liable in the same manner and to the same extent as a private individual under like circumstances,'" as one court has put it.[78] The reasoning here is that if immunity is lifted in a given case, the litigation should proceed as if the plaintiff had brought suit against a private party; and as *Klaxon* would require application of the forum state's choice-of-law rule in a case against a private party, the same should be applied against the foreign state.

In ruling on the choice-of-law problem in the Cassirer litigation, the district court was unsure which of these approaches to follow. It noted the series of Ninth Circuit cases calling for application of a federal common law choice-of-law rule, and observed that these cases had not been overruled. Perhaps in recognition of the other circuits' disagreement with that approach, however, it read a more recent Ninth Circuit decision as having "called its holding into question" and as "stating that it may be permissible to apply the forum state's choice-of-law rules" in cases brought under the Act.[79] The district court therefore decided, "out of an abundance of caution," to "conduct a choice-of-law analysis under both federal common law and California law."[80]

---

[75] *Harris*, 820 F.2d at 1003–4.

[76] Corporacion Venezolana de Fomento v. Vinteror Sales Corp., 629 F.2d 786, 795 (2d Cir. 1980), quoted in *Harris*, 820 F.2d at 1003.

[77] See, for example, Oveissi v. Islamic Republic of Iran, 573 F.3d 835, 841–42 (D.C. Cir. 2009); O'Bryan v. Holy See, 556 F.3d 361, 381 n. 8 (6th Cir. 2009), cert denied, 558 U.S. 819 (2009); Barkanic v. General Administrator of Civil Aviation of the People's Republic of China, 923 F.2d 957, 959–60 (2d Cir. 1991).

[78] *Oveissi*, 573 F.3d at 841 (quoting 28 U.S.C. § 1606).

[79] *Cassirer*, 153 F. Supp.3d at 1154. The court was referring to Sachs v. Republic of Austria, 737 F.3d 584, 600 n. 14 (9th Cir. 2013), rev'd on other grounds, 136 S. Ct. 390 (2015).

[80] *Cassirer*, 153 F. Supp.3d at 1154.

7.5.2 Federal Choice-of-Law Principles

In fashioning federal common law rules of choice of law, the Ninth Circuit has said, the courts should follow the precepts of the Second Restatement of Conflicts, developed by the American Law Institute in the late 1960s.[81] That work, the court of appeals stated in its 1987 *Harris* decision, "is a source of general choice-of-law principles and an appropriate starting point for applying federal common law in this area."[82] This position crystallized in subsequent cases, to the point that the court's later opinions essentially equate federal common law in this domain with the precepts of the Restatement.[83] The district court in the Cassirer litigation, observing that "[f]ederal common law follows the approach of the Restatement (Second) of Conflict of Laws," therefore based its analysis of the case on that source.[84]

The Restatement generally calls upon courts to use an interest-balancing approach to choice-of-law problems. In cases involving disputed claims to a piece of property, it urges courts to apply the law of the state with the "most significant relationship to the thing and the parties"—a determination to be made in light of the interests of the affected states, the justified expectations of the parties, the needs of the interstate system, and the policies of the particular field of law, among other considerations.[85] More particularly, in cases involving a question of adverse possession or prescriptive ownership of property, the Restatement provides as follows:

> Whether there has been a transfer of an interest in a chattel by adverse possession or by prescription and the nature of the interest transferred are determined by the local law of the state where the chattel was at the time the transfer is claimed to have taken place.[86]

In support of this rule, the Restatement's authors expressed the view that the "[t]he state where a chattel is situated has the dominant interest in determining the circumstances under which an interest in the chattel will be transferred by adverse possession or by prescription."[87]

The district court in the Cassirer case found that rule to be controlling for purposes of federal common law. "The Court finds no reason to depart from the rule," it declared, "that the 'local law of the state where the chattel was at the time the transfer is claimed to have taken place' should apply."[88] In keeping with that

[81]See American Law Institute (1971). In this discussion we will refer to this work simply as the Restatement.

[82]*Harris*, 820 F.2d at 1003.

[83]See *Liu*, 892 F.2d at 1426; *Schoenberg*, 930 F.2d at 782; see also *Sachs*, 600 n. 14.

[84]*Cassirer*, 153 F. Supp.3d at 1154. On American choice-of-law doctrines, see generally Weintraub (2005) and Symeonides (2006).

[85]American Law Institute (1971) §§ 6, 222, quoted in *Cassirer*, 153 F. Supp.3d at 1154.

[86]American Law Institute (1971) § 246, quoted in *Cassirer*, 153 F. Supp.3d at 1155.

[87]American Law Institute (1971) § 246 comment, quoted in *Cassirer*, 153 F. Supp.3d at 1155.

[88]*Cassirer*, 153 F. Supp.3d at 1155.

rule, "Spain has the dominant interest in determining the circumstances under which ownership of the Painting may be acquired by adverse possession or prescription," the court declared, adding that applying that rule lends needed certainty and predictability to the field of property law, and protects the justified expectations of owners.[89] Moreover, the painting had been located at the museum in Madrid for more than twenty years, and was only in California for a short time in the 1950s; California's connection to the case lay primarily in the Cassirer family's personal ties to the state, and "[a]lthough Plaintiffs' relationship to California is significant, the Painting's relationship to California is not."[90] The court accordingly concluded that "Spain has the most significant relationship to the Painting and the parties," and therefore "under federal common law, the law of Spain governs the Foundation's claim of ownership by adverse possession."[91]

7.5.3 State Choice-of-Law Principles

The California state courts also apply an interest-balancing approach to choice of law, similar to but formulated in terms slightly different from that of the Restatement. As outlined by the California supreme court, the approach calls for courts to ask three questions in any case presenting the problem of choosing among the laws of more than one state on a given issue. First, do the laws of the affected states concerning the issue differ from one another in material respects? Second, if their laws do differ, does each state have an interest in having its own law applied to the case? And third, if they do each have an interest, which state would suffer the greater impairment of its interest if another state's policy were given priority over its own? Having answered these questions, the court "ultimately applies the law of the state whose interest would be more impaired if its law were not applied."[92]

Following these steps, the district court in the Cassirer litigation observed, first, that the laws of Spain and California differ with respect to the acquisition of ownership by adverse possession, in that "California has not extended the doctrine of adverse possession to personal property," whereas Spain allows possessors of "movable property" to acquire ownership by adverse possession after a specified period of years.[93]

Second, the court found that both states had a strong interest in seeing their respective laws applied to the dispute. On one hand, in extending the law of adverse possession to items of movable property as well as real estate, Spain had concluded

---

[89]*Id.*

[90]*Id.*

[91]*Id.*

[92]Kearney v. Salomon Smith Barney, Inc., 45 Cal.Rptr.3d 730, 740 (2006); Bernhard v. Harrah's Club, 128 Cal.Rptr. 215, 219 (1976).

[93]*Cassirer*, 153 F. Supp.3d at 1156.

that allowing adverse possession of personal property served the goals of "certainty of title, protecting defendants from stale claims, and encouraging plaintiffs not to sleep on their rights."[94] Spain "unquestionably has an interest in serving these policy goals and applying its law of adverse possession to the Foundation's claim of ownership," the court declared, "especially given that the Foundation is an instrumentality of the Kingdom of Spain and the Painting has been located within its borders for over twenty years."[95] On the other hand, the interests of California were at stake as well: "California's decision not to extend the doctrine of adverse possession to personal property recognizes the difficulties faced by owners in discovering the whereabouts of personal property even when held openly and notoriously," and "serves to encourage subsequent purchasers to determine the true owner of property before purchasing that property."[96] California, the court observed, had a "legitimate interest in applying its laws governing personal property to 'rightful owners' who reside within its borders," as the Cassirers did.[97]

Third, the court ruled that Spain's interests would suffer the greater impairment if its law were not applied. The court emphasized that in addressing the question of comparative impairment, it was refraining—as the California supreme court had said it must—from passing judgment on which of the two states' interests were more important, or which had the "'better' or the 'worthier' social policy on the specific issue."[98] To apply California law to the dispute, the court stated, would introduce unpredictability into Spain's property laws, and "would significantly undermine Spain's interest in certainty of title."[99] In contrast, to apply Spanish law would cause "significantly less" impairment of California's interests: although California "has an interest in protecting its residents claiming to be rightful owners of stolen art, that interest is far less significant where the original victim did not reside in California, where the unlawful taking did not occur within its borders, and where the defendant and the entity from which the defendant purchased the property were not located in California."[100]

The court therefore concluded that under California's choice-of-law rule, like under the federal common law rule, "Spanish law governs the Foundation's claim of ownership by adverse possession."[101]

---

[94]*Id.* at 1157.

[95]*Id.*

[96]*Id.*

[97]*Id.* at 1157–58.

[98]McCann v. Foster Wheeler LLC, 105 Cal.Rptr.3d 378, 399 (2010), quoted in *Cassirer*, 153 F. Supp.3d at 1158.

[99]*Cassirer*, 153 F. Supp.3d at 1159.

[100]*Id.*

[101]*Id.* at 1160.

7.6 Title to the Artwork

Having decided to apply the law of Spain, the district court turned to the question whether the museum had acquired ownership of the painting under that country's doctrine of prescriptive acquisition, the civil law analogue to the common law doctrine of adverse possession. To answer the question, the court relied on academic publications and the written submissions of experts in Spanish law.

7.6.1 The Law of Acquisitive Prescription

The court began by noting that the law of *usucapio* or acquisitive prescription, as set forth in the Spanish Civil Code, allows a possessor to acquire ownership of property if three conditions are met. First, the possessor must "possess the property for the statutory period, i.e. three years if in 'good faith' ('ordinary adverse possession') or six years if in 'bad faith' ('extraordinary adverse possession')."[102]

Second, the possessor must hold the property as owner, meaning that the possessor "projects an external image of being the owner."[103] This requirement "does not relate to the internal intention of the subject, but external behavior consistent with the character of being the actual owner."[104] The "person may believe that he is the owner or know that he is not (this is a question of good faith or bad faith)," stated an expert the district court relied on, "but, even if a person knows that he is not the owner of what he bought (precisely because he bought it from someone who was not the owner either), a person who performs acts relating to the asset which those that witness them will see as typical of ownership possesses said asset as the owner."[105]

Third, the possessor must hold the property "publicly, peacefully, and without interruption."[106] The possessor "must show by means of ostensible acts that he possesses the asset: without supreme effort but with reasonable and ongoing publicity, said reasonableness being considered based on the nature of use of the asset in question."[107] The purpose of this requirement is to ensure that "the real owner has the possibility of defending his or her right against [the possessor's] acts."[108] At the same time, "it is not necessary for the person claiming to be 'the real owner' to have full knowledge of third party possession," but only that such knowledge be available to the owner "using average diligence."[109]

[102] *Id.*, citing Spanish Civil Code Article 1955.

[103] *Id.*

[104] Pacanowska and Soto (2011), p. 646, quoted in *Cassirer*, 153 F. Supp.3d at 1161.

[105] Declaration of Prof. Alfonso-Luis Calvo Caravaca, quoted in *Cassirer*, 153 F. Supp.3d at 1161.

[106] *Cassirer*, 153 F. Supp.3d at 1161.

[107] Declaration of Prof. Alfonso-Luis Calvo Caravaca, quoted in *id.* at 1161.

[108] Pacanowska and Soto (2011), p. 647, quoted in *Cassirer*, 153 F. Supp.3d at 1161.

[109] Declaration of Prof. Alfonso-Luis Calvo Caravaca, quoted in *Cassirer*, 153 F. Supp.3d at 1161.

7.6.2 *Ownership Under Spanish Law*

The district court found that the museum's possession of the painting met all three requirements for prescriptive acquisition under Spanish law. First, the museum had held the painting since 1993, easily satisfying the six-year prescription period for bad-faith possessors. It was unnecessary to decide whether the museum was a good-faith possessor, the court declared, because its possession satisfied the prescription period even if it was not.[110]

Second, the museum had consistently held the painting as its owner, in that "it has projected an external image of ownership" since acquiring it.[111] "Indeed," stated the court, "the Foundation has publicly displayed the Painting in its Museum without any contrary indication of ownership, and loaned the Painting to others for public exhibition consistent with its claim of ownership." In addition, the court noted, the Thyssen-Bornemisza Foundation had identified itself as the owner in several books it had published.[112]

Third, the museum's possession had been "peaceful, public, and uninterrupted," in the court's view, having been on display on the premises since its acquisition, with the exception of two brief loans to outside exhibitions.[113] Under Spanish law, the court noted, possession would be deemed interrupted for this purpose if possession ceased for more than a year; if there was a judicial summons to the possessor; if there was an "act of conciliation" between the possessor and the owner; or if there was an "express or implied recognition by the possessor of the owner's right."[114] None of these conditions had been met to defeat the claim of prescriptive acquisition, the court ruled.[115]

7.7 Epilogue

In its 2015 order declaring that the museum was the painting's owner under Spanish law, the district court expressed discomfort with the result and urged the Thyssen-Bornemisza Foundation to offer the Cassirers a fair settlement. "Although the

[110] *Id.* at 1163.

[111] *Cassirer*, 153 F. Supp.3d at 1161.

[112] *Id.*

[113] *Id.*

[114] Spanish Civil Code Article 1948, quoted in *Cassirer*, 153 F. Supp.3d at 1162.

[115] *Cassirer*, 153 F. Supp.3d at 1162. The district court rejected the Cassirers' argument that the museum's claim of ownership was defeated by a provision of Spanish law denying adverse possession rights to thieves and their accessories. The museum, the court ruled, was not an accessory to the Nazis who stole the painting in 1939. *Id.* at 1163. The district court also rejected the Cassirers' contention that Spain's law of adverse possession violated the European Convention on Human Rights, ruling that the law served the "legitimate interests of certainty of title, protecting defendants from stale claims, and encouraging plaintiffs not to sleep on their rights." *Id.* at 1167.

Foundation has now prevailed in this prolonged and bitterly contested litigation," it wrote, "the Court recommends that, before the next phase of litigation commences in the Ninth Circuit, the Foundation pause, reflect, and consider whether it would be appropriate to work towards a mutually-agreeable resolution of this action."[116] The court encouraged the museum to consider its next step "in light of Spain's acceptance of the Washington Conference and the Terezín Declaration, and, specifically, its commitment to achieve 'just and fair solutions' for victims of Nazi persecution."[117] No settlement has been reached in the time since then, and the Cassirers' appeal is pending.

References

American Law Institute. 1971. *Restatement (Second) of Conflicts of Law*. Philadelphia, PA: American Law Institute.

———. 2016. *Restatement (Fourth) of the Foreign Relations Law of the United States. Tentative Draft*. Philadelphia, PA: American Law Institute.

Cassese, Antonio. 2005. *International Law*. 2nd ed. Oxford: Oxford University Press.

Fox, Hazel, and Philippa Webb. 2013. *The Law of State Immunity*. 3rd ed. Oxford: Oxford University Press.

Müller, Melissa, and Monika Tatzkow. 2010. *Lost Lives, Lost Art: Jewish Collectors, Nazi Art Theft*. London: Frontline.

Pacanowska, Isabel V. González, and Carlos Manuel Díez Soto. 2011. National Report on the Transfer of Movables in Spain. In *National Report on the Transfer of Movables in Europe*, ed. Wolfgang Faber and Brigitta Lurger, vol. 5, 393–656. Munich: Sellier.

Parrish, Austen L. 2006. Sovereignty, Not Due Process: Personal Jurisdiction over Nonresident Aliens. *Wake Forest Law Review* 41: 1–60.

Peterson, Todd Davis. 2010. The Timing of Minimum Contacts. *George Washington Law Review* 79: 101–160.

Rhodes, Charles W. "Rocky", and Cassandra B. Robertson. 2014. Toward a New Equilibrium in Personal Jurisdiction. *UC Davis Law Review* 48: 207–270.

Shah, Rajika L. 2017. The Making of California's Art Recovery Statute: The Long Road to Section 338(c)(3). *Chapman Law Review* 20: 77–118.

Shaw, Malcolm. 1997. *International Law*. 4th ed. Cambridge: Cambridge University Press.

Soto, Onell R. 2005. Holocaust Survivor Wants Art Returned. *San Diego Tribune*, May 11.

Symeonides, Symeon C. 2006. *The American Choice-of-Law Revolution in the Courts: Past, Present and Future*. Leiden: Martinus Nijhoff.

Vandenberg, David P. 2006. In the Wake of *Republic of Austria v. Altmann*: The Current Status of Foreign Immunity in United States Courts. *University of Colorado Law Review* 77: 739–766.

Weintraub, Russell J. 2005. *Commentary on the Conflict of Laws*. 5th ed. New York: Foundation Press.

Whytock, Christopher A. 2013. Foreign State Immunity and the Right to Court Access. *Boston University Law Review* 93: 2033–2093.

[116] *Id.* at 1168.

[117] *Id.*

Cases

Allen v. Wright, 468 U.S. 737 (1984)
Altmann v. Republic of Austria, 142 F. Supp.2d 1187 (C.D. Cal. 2001), aff'd, 317 F.3d 954 (9th Cir. 2003), aff'd, 541 U.S. 699 (2004)
Barkanic v. General Administrator of Civil Aviation of the People's Republic of China, 923 F.2d 957 (2d Cir. 1991)
Bernhard v. Harrah's Club, 128 Cal.Rptr. 215 (1976)
Cassirer v. Kingdom of Spain and Thyssen-Bornemisza Foundation, 461 F. Supp.2d 1157 (C.D. Cal. 2006), aff'd in part and appeal dismissed in part, 616 F.3d 1019 (9th Cir. 2010) (en banc), cert. denied, 564 U.S. 1037 (2011), on remand, 2012 WL 1285771 (C.D. Cal. 2012), aff'd in part and rev'd in part, 737 F.3d 613 (9th Cir. 2013), on remand, 153 F. Supp.3d 1148 (C.D. Cal. 2015), appeal docketed, No. 15-55977 (9th Cir. June 24, 2015)
Corporacion Venezolana de Fomento v. Vinteror Sales Corp., 629 F.2d 786 (2d Cir. 1980), cert. denied, 449 U.S. 1080 (1981)
Deutsch v. Turner Corp., 324 F.3d 692 (9th Cir. 2003), cert. denied, 540 U.S. 820 (2003)
Erie Erie Railroad Co. v. Tompkins, 304 U.S. 64 (1938)
Harris v. Polskie Linie Lotnicze, 820 F.2d 1000 (9th Cir. 1987)
International Shoe Co. v. State of Washington, 326 U.S. 310 (1945)
Kearney v. Salomon Smith Barney, Inc., 45 Cal.Rptr.3d 730 (2006)
Klaxon Co. v. Stentor Electric Manufacturing Co., 313 U.S. 487 (1941)
Liu v. Republic of China, 892 F.2d 1419 (9th Cir. 1989), cert. dismissed, 497 U.S. 1058 (1990)
McCann v. Foster Wheeler LLC, 105 Cal.Rptr.3d 378 (2010)
Minneapolis Star and Tribune Co. v. Minnesota Commissioner of Revenue, 460 U.S. 575 (1983)
O'Bryan v. Holy See, 556 F.3d 361 (6th Cir. 2009), cert denied, 558 U.S. 819 (2009)
Oveissi v. Islamic Republic of Iran, 573 F.3d 835 (D.C. Cir. 2009)
Rafaelli v. Getty Images, Inc., No. 2:12–cv–00563–CAS–PJW (C.D. Cal. Jan. 20, 2012)
Republic of Argentina v. Weltover, Inc., 504 U.S. 607 (1992)
Sachs v. Republic of Austria, 737 F.3d 584 (9th Cir. 2013), rev'd, 136 S. Ct. 390 (2015)
Schoenberg v. Exportadora de Sal, S.A. de C.V., 930 F.2d 777 (9th Cir. 1991)
Starks v. S.E. Rykoff Co., 673 F.2d 1106 (9th Cir. 1982)
Verlinden B.V. v. Central Bank of Nigeria, 461 U.S. 480, 488 (1983)
Von Saher v. Norton Simon Museum of Art, 592 F.3d 954 (9th Cir. 2010), cert. denied, 564 U.S. 1037 (2011)
Western Prelacy of the Armenian Apostolic Church v. J. Paul Getty Museum, No. BC438824 (L.A. Co. Super. Ct. Aug. 1, 2011)

Chapter 8
Grosz v. Museum of Modern Art

8.1 Background

The German artist George Grosz (1893–1959) was a leader of the Dada and New Objectivity movements in Berlin, famous for his political caricatures and satirical depictions of life during the Weimar period.[1] He was a staunch critic of the Nazis, who after taking over denounced him as an enemy of the state and prohibited the sale or display of his art, and burned his work in their periodic bonfires of "degenerate" art. Unsafe in Germany after Hitler came to power, Grosz emigrated to the United States with his family in early 1933, settling in New York to take a teaching position. He left many of his paintings and drawings with Alfred Flechtheim, a prominent Berlin art dealer with whom he had maintained an exclusive consignment arrangement since the mid-1920s.

Flechtheim, who was Jewish, also fled Germany in 1933 and settled in London. He was able to bring some of his inventory with him when he emigrated; the rest remained in Germany, where his business was liquidated to pay off creditors. After Flechtheim's death in 1937, an Amsterdam art dealer to whom he had entrusted his inventory auctioned off a number of works, including two paintings by Grosz. One of these, *Self-Portrait with Model* (1928), was purchased by a third party and later sold to a collector in Canada. The other, *Republican Automatons* (1920), was purchased by the auctioneer himself and resold to an American collector. Meanwhile, a third Grosz painting, *The Poet Max Hermanne-Neisse with Cognac* (1927), which Flechtheim had left in Berlin, was taken by a German art historian at some point during the dissolution of Flechtheim's business.

The three paintings quickly found their way into the collection of the Museum of Modern Art in New York, whose management was alert to the buying opportunities Hitler had created.[2] The museum bought *Republican Automata* from the Canadian

---

[1]See generally Hess (1985), Lewis (1991), and Jentsch et al. (2008).

[2]In 1935, Flechtheim had written to MoMA director Alfred Barr, announcing that he was penniless and wanted to sell a sculpture he had taken with him into exile. Upon receiving the letter, Barr

B.L. Hay, *Nazi-Looted Art and the Law*, DOI 10.1007/978-3-319-64967-2_8

collector in 1946 and received *Self-Portrait with Model* as a gift from its American purchaser in 1954. As for *The Poet Max Hermanne-Neisse with Cognac*, its German acquirer brought it to New York, claiming to have inherited it from Flechtheim.[3] Hoping to sell it to the museum, she enlisted the help of Curt Valentin, a onetime assistant to Flechtheim who had helped the museum acquire "degenerate" artworks auctioned off by the Nazis.[4] Valentin brokered the sale of the painting to the museum in 1952.

Grosz learned of the museum's acquisition of *Hermanne-Nesse with Cognac* a short time later. Upon hearing that the painting was hanging in the museum in January 1953, Grosz wrote to his brother-in-law that it had been stolen, but expressed the belief that there was nothing he could do about it. "Modern Museum exhibited a painting that was stolen from me (I am powerless against that) they bought it from someone, who stole it." In a letter to a friend, he wrote: "Modern Museum bought a painting that was stolen from me . . . (one cannot do anything) old affair."[5] He returned to Germany in 1959 and died shortly afterward, without ever having sought restitution from the museum. There the matter rested for the next four decades.[6]

In November 2003, the director of the George Grosz Estate contacted the museum about the three paintings, announcing that his research for the Grosz *catalogue raisonné* persuaded him that they had been stolen from the artist. There followed a series of exchanges between the museum and the estate over the next few years. In a July 2005 letter, museum director Glenn Lowry asserted that the available evidence supported the museum's title to all three paintings, but that the

---

wrote to a museum trustee that "Alfred Flechtehim, the unfortunate refugee owner of Lembruck *Standing Man*" was in "dire straits" and would perhaps "take as little as $2,000 for this really great modern figure. We might offer him even less." Letter to Mrs. Stanley Resor, October 24, 1935, Exhibit 9 to First Amended Complaint, Grosz v. Museum of Modern Art, No. 09-CV-3706 (S.D.N.Y. May 25, 2009). A benefactor bought the item for the museum shortly afterward. On this and other Nazi-era acquisitions by the museum, see Cohan (2011) and Vincent (2012).

[3]In a separate incident, the acquirer of *Max Hermanne-Nesse* was accused of wrongfully keeping a trove of art entrusted to her by collector Paul Westheim in the 1930s, and selling it off after the war. Litigation is now pending against her estate. See Frenk v. Solomon, 998 N.Y.S.2d 42 (App. Div. 2014). The underlying events are detailed in Müller and Tatzkow (2010), pp. 30–43.

[4]The museum employed Valentin as a bidder at the Galerie Fischer auction in Lucerne in June 1939, at which the Nazis sold off a number of prominent modern works they had purged from German museums. (See generally Nicholas 1994, pp. 4–5; Petropoulos 1996, pp. 81–82.) Museum director Alfred Barr wrote to an employee that he was "just as glad not to have the museum's name or my own associated with the auction," adding that it was "very important" that the museum's press release state that it had purchased the works from Valentin's gallery in New York (Quoted in Marquis 1989, p. 178).

[5]Letters of January 8 and 9, 1953, quoted in First Amended Complaint, Grosz v. Museum of Modern Art, No. 09-CV-3706 (S.D.N.Y. May 25, 2009), at 22.

[6]In 1961 the German government compensated Grosz's family for the harm to his health and career resulting from Nazi persecution, and in 1971 compensated them for the paintings that had been burned in bonfires.

museum was willing to continue discussing the matter. The letter also suggested a compromise in which the museum and the estate would share ownership of *Hermanne-Nesse with Cognac*, an offer the estate rejected. The exchanges came to an end with an April 2006 letter in which Lowry announced that the board of trustees had voted to deny the estate's claims, on the basis of a report it had commissioned on the matter from a former United States attorney general. The report, which emphasized the lack of evidence concerning how the paintings had changed hands in the 1930s, did not reach a firm conclusion on whether the paintings were stolen. The report nonetheless recommended against returning the paintings, because of Grosz's failure to seek restitution in the 1950s. Had he raised the matter then, the report argued, the museum would have been in a much better position to ascertain the works' rightful ownership and, perhaps, to have reached a settlement with Grosz. The heirs' demand that it return the paintings after a delay of fifty years was, the report concluded, unreasonable.[7]

For their part, the heirs maintained that George Grosz had never wavered in his belief that the paintings were rightfully his, but he was unwilling to make trouble in the country that had saved him from the Nazis. This, they contended, was the reason he kept his silence about the matter. "He was very reluctant to in any way assail or complain about the treatment he got from anybody in the United States," according to his son Martin, who added that his father had this reply for other refugees who had complaints about America: "You should kiss the ground you are walking on because they let you in."[8]

8.2 Proceedings

In April 2009, Grosz's son Martin, joined by the widow of Grosz's son Peter, filed suit against the Museum of Modern Art in federal district court in New York. In their complaint, the heirs alleged that *The Poet Max Hermanne-Nesse* was stolen by the Berlin collector who later claimed to have inherited it. They further alleged that *Republican Automatons* and *Self-Portrait with Model* were stolen by the Amsterdam dealer to whom Flechtheim had entrusted his inventory and that the paintings' unauthorized sale after Flechtheim's death, they alleged, was a sham transaction designed to launder title to the paintings. The heirs requested a declaration that the paintings belonged to them, and sought recovery of the paintings and monetary damages on common-law theories of conversion, replevin, and constructive trust.

The museum moved to dismiss the complaint, contending that the action was time-barred. It made two arguments to this effect. First, relying on various

[7]Nicholas deb. Katzenbach, *Report to the Trustees of the Museum of Modern Art with Respect to Two Paintings of George Grosz* (March 22, 2006), Exhibit F to Defendant's Motion to Dismiss First Amended Complaint, Grosz v. Museum of Modern Art, No. 09-CV-3706 (S.D.N.Y. June 4, 2009).
[8]Cohen (2013).

provisions of Dutch and German law, it argued that the action was untimely because Grosz himself had done nothing in the 1950s, after the museum had acquired the paintings. Second, relying on the New York statute of limitations, the museum argued that the heirs had waited too long to sue after the museum denied their 2003 request for the paintings' return. The museum (it argued) had made clear to the heirs in its July 2005 letter that it believed it had legitimate title to the paintings; under the state statute of limitations, the heirs' claim expired three years after they received that letter.

Following limited discovery the district court granted the motion to dismiss, accepting the latter of the museum's arguments.[9] The applicable New York statute of limitations, the court explained, requires a property claim to be brought within three years of its accrual. In disputes over allegedly stolen property obtained by a good-faith buyer, a "demand and refusal" rule applies, meaning that the claim accrues when the buyer refuses the owner's demand to return the property. In the present case, reasoned the court, the museum's July 2005 correspondence constituted such a refusal, and the statute of limitations accordingly had run out in July 2008. The court also rejected the heirs' argument that the statute of limitations should be "equitably tolled," or suspended, for the period of negotiations that occurred between July 2005 and the museum's final letter of April 2006.

In a short, unpublished opinion, the Second Circuit court of appeals affirmed the judgment of dismissal.[10] Agreeing with the lower court's analysis, the appeals court ruled that the museum's refusal had taken place more than three years before suit was filed, and that the statute of limitations should not be tolled for the period of negotiations.

The Supreme Court denied review in 2011.

8.3 Equities and Technicalities

The Grosz case was nominally decided on the basis of a "technicality," namely the fact that, in the courts' view, the complaint was filed nine months too late under the New York statute of limitations. We will presently be looking at the courts' reasoning in this regard. Before doing so we should observe, however, that the courts' application of this technicality was rather overtly influenced by their perception of the equities in the case. Indeed, the language of the district court's opinion, apparently approved by the court of appeals, makes it tempting to view the dismissal as a kind of shortcut to what the courts saw as the just result, avoiding protracted litigation of a case they thought the museum should win.

---

[9]Grosz v. Museum of Modern Art, 772 F. Supp.2d 473 (S.D.N.Y.2010).

[10]Grosz v. Museum of Modern Art, 403 Fed. Appx. 575 (2d Cir. 2010), cert. denied, 565 U.S. 819 (2011).

Here it is important to understand the tenor of the museum's argument for dismissal, which stressed two themes. First, the heirs' assertion that the paintings were stolen was unconvincing. "This is not a 'looted art' case," the museum declared; "[t]he Paintings were not stolen from Grosz by the Nazis or anyone else."[11] Grosz had consigned the paintings to his dealer Flechtheim, who "had no connection to the Nazis"; two of them were "sold by auction in Holland two years *before* it came under Nazi domination"; as for the third, Grosz was aware that it was at the museum and said nothing, suggesting that he himself knew it was not stolen.[12] The museum's own investigation, it asserted, had "confirmed the total lack of merit" in the plaintiffs' claims.[13] Rather than pointing to evidence of theft, the museum argued, the plaintiffs' complaint relied on "general, conclusory innuendo—and on headline-catching accusations whose only purpose is to invoke the powerful but wholly irrelevant specter of the Holocaust."[14]

The second theme of the museum's argument concerned the fifty-year delay in the claims' filing. The long delay, the museum contended, had placed essential evidence beyond reach. "Grosz and Flechtheim, the two individuals most likely to know the true facts, are long dead," the museum pointed out, "as are several other important individuals who would have had direct and personal knowledge about the disposition or transfers of one or more of the Paintings and of the accusations made in the complaint," including the museum's director at the time it acquired the paintings and the people from whom it acquired them.[15] "Critical documentary proof is also long since destroyed," the museum added.[16] The plaintiffs' delay in bringing their claims, the museum suggested, was unjustifiable, had deprived the court of the evidence necessary to adjudicate the case, and had made it impossible for the museum to defend itself.

Both of these themes were prominently echoed in the district court's opinion. At several points, the court indicated its skepticism toward the plaintiffs' theory that the paintings had been stolen from Grosz. The artist may not even have owned the paintings in question, the court noted, since there was some evidence that they had been given to Flechtheim as security for a debt[17]; the plaintiffs' conjecture that Flechtheim lost the paintings as a "result of Nazi coercion" was "contradicted by certain documents they have attached to their Complaint" that suggest he was suffering "acute financial troubles, going back as far as 1931, before the Nazis came to power"[18]; the plaintiffs employed "rank hearsay" to suggest the acquirer of

---

[11]Defendant's Memorandum of Law in Support of its Motion to Dismiss First Amended Complaint, Grosz v. Museum of Modern Art, No. 09-CV-3706 (S.D.N.Y. June 4, 2009), at 1.

[12]*Id.* at 1–2.

[13]*Id.* at 4.

[14]*Id.* at 3.

[15]*Id.* at 6.

[16]*Id.*

[17]*Grosz*, 772 F. Supp.2d at 478.

[18]*Id.*

The Poet Max Hermanne-Nesse was a Nazi spy[19]; they made "circumstantial allegations" that the museum should have realized that the painting was stolen.[20] More generally, the court's opinion expressed incredulity toward what it plainly viewed as hyperbolic, unsubstantiated assertions about the "cunning Dutch art dealer" who conducted a "sham auction" to "launder artworks stolen by the Nazis," and the art critic who was really an "international art thief and/or Nazi agent" and was "busy embezzling the third of the three Paintings."[21] In addition, the court was evidently troubled by the Grosz family's long delay in seeking the paintings' return. "It is undisputed," the court observed, "that Grosz knew where at least one of the works—*Poet*—was a half century before plaintiffs demanded its return," and yet never raised the issue with the museum.[22]

Neither of these themes, it bears noting, was strictly relevant to the ultimate disposition of the case, which in theory turned entirely on the length of time that had elapsed *after* the museum refused the heirs' 2003 demand. Nonetheless, their emphatic presence in the opinion indicates where the sympathies of both the district court and the court of appeals lay in the case. Rightly or wrongly, they clearly believed that the equities favored the museum. This may help explain their willingness to dismiss the complaint on the basis of a "technical" issue that, as we will see, might easily have been resolved in either party's favor.

8.4 The Statute of Limitations

We begin with the courts' interpretation of the New York statute of limitations. We then turn, in Section 5, to their analysis of whether the statute was subject to equitable tolling.

8.4.1 The "Demand and Refusal" Rule

The *Menzel* Decision As the district court and the court of appeals both noted, the leading New York state case concerning the application of the statute of limitations to stolen art claims is *Menzel v. List*,[23] a precursor to the later generation of Holocaust-era restitution cases. In *Menzel*, the Jewish plaintiffs had fled their Brussels home in 1941, leaving behind a Chagall painting among other artworks. The Nazis seized their apartment and confiscated the painting along with the rest of

[19] *Id.*

[20] *Id.* at 480.

[21] *Id.*

[22] *Id.* at 482.

[23] 267 N.Y.S.2d 804 (Sup. 1966).

their collection, leaving a receipt indicating they had been put in "safekeeping." In 1955, the Chagall resurfaced in the Galerie Art Moderne in Paris. It was acquired there by the Perls Gallery of New York, which sold it to List, a New York collector.

The Menzels, meanwhile, had settled in the United States. According to the court, they had diligently searched for their lost painting since the end of the war, but were unable to find it until 1962, when they discovered it was in List's possession. Following List's refusal to return it, the plaintiffs filed suit in New York state court. List brought the Perls Gallery into the case as a third-party defendant. Both defendants denied knowing that the painting was stolen, having relied on the Paris gallery's representation of good title. A jury returned a verdict in the Menzels' favor. On a motion to set aside the verdict, the court took up the defendants' contention that the Menzels' action was barred by the statute of limitations, which requires that an action to recover stolen or converted property be brought within three years after the claim has accrued.[24]

The critical question for the court was when the plaintiffs' claim had accrued. The defendants argued that it had accrued in 1941, when the painting was stolen. The court rejected this argument, observing that an innocent possessor of property does not commit conversion until learning that the property belongs to another. Here it referred to an old case holding that "demand and refusal" were "necessary to show a conversion," refusing to follow decisions from other jurisdictions suggesting that an innocent purchaser could be "held liable on account of his purchase from one who had no title, without a demand and refusal" by the aggrieved owner.[25] According to this old decision, the "rule is a reasonable and just one, that an innocent purchaser of personal property from a wrong-doer shall first be informed of the defect in his title, and have an opportunity to deliver the property to the true owner, before he shall be made liable as a tort feasor for a wrongful conversion."[26] Following this logic, the *Menzel* court reasoned that a claim "against a person who lawfully comes by a chattel arises, not upon the stealing or the taking, but upon the defendant's refusal to convey the chattel upon demand."[27] Thus, the Menzels' claim against List accrued, and the statute of limitations clock began running, only when List refused their demand for the return of the painting.

The *Elicofon* Decision What came to be called the "demand and refusal" rule of the *Menzel* decision was given elaboration in another decision relied upon by the district court in the Grosz litigation. The case, *Kunstsammlungen Zu Weimar v. Elicofon*,[28] concerned two Dürer paintings stolen at the end of the Second World War. The paintings had belonged to a series of successive Grand Dukes of

[24]The statute of limitations is codified at N.Y. CPLR 214[3].

[25]Gillet v. Roberts, 57 N.Y. 28, 33 (1874).

[26]*Id.* at 34 (italics omitted).

[27]*Menzel*, 267 N.Y.S.2d at 304.

[28]678 F.2d 1150 (2d Cir. 1982).

Saxony-Weimar, and beginning in the early twentieth century were displayed in the public art museum of Weimar. In 1943, to protect them from anticipated allied bombardment, museum officials stored the paintings along with other artworks in a nearby castle, the Schloss Schwarzburg. In 1945, the castle was occupied by American troops. The paintings disappeared sometime in the summer of that year as the castle was abandoned by American forces and turned over to the Russian Army. The director of the museum noticed the paintings missing shortly afterward, and launched an intensive, unsuccessful search for them.

Elicofon, a Brooklyn resident, bought the paintings in 1946 from an American serviceman who claimed to have purchased them in Germany. Not realizing what they were, he framed the unsigned paintings and put them on his wall. Some twenty years later, a friend of his recognized the paintings from a book about artworks that had been missing since the war. The discovery made international headlines, and Elicofon soon received demands for the paintings' return from the Weimar museum and the Federal Republic of Germany,[29] as well as from the Grand Duchess of Saxony-Weimar, who claimed the paintings were her family's private property. Elicofon refused the demands, and in the lengthy litigation that followed the trial court entered summary judgment for the museum, ruling that it was the rightful owner of the artworks. The case then went to the court of appeals, which had to decide, among other things, whether the museum's claim was barred by the three-year statute of limitations.

It was undisputed that the claim had been filed within three years of Elicofon's refusal of the museum's 1966 demand. Elicofon argued, however, that the museum's claim had accrued in 1946, when he purchased the paintings. Rejecting this argument, the court began with the general rule under New York law that "an innocent purchaser of stolen goods becomes a wrongdoer only after refusing the owner's demand for their return," and until refusing "is considered to be in lawful possession."[30] The *Menzel* decision, the court noted, had applied "these principles to a case involving a *bona fide* purchaser of stolen art works, holding that the cause of action accrues only after demand and refusal."[31] The court disagreed with Elicofon's attempts to distinguish the *Menzel* decision, as well as his contention that subsequent decisions of the New York state courts had called it into question. It also rejected his position that "the *Menzel* rule should be abandoned because it favors a thief as against a *bona fide* purchaser."[32] According to this position, "for a thief the statute begins to run immediately upon the theft," whereas "a *bona fide* purchaser must wait, possibly indefinitely, for a demand from the owner"; this

[29]Because the United States did not recognize the Soviet-era German Democratic Republic (GDR) at the time the dispute arose, the Federal Republic of Germany (FRG) undertook to act on the Weimar museum's behalf. Midway through the ensuing litigation, the United States formally recognized the GDR government, enabling it to take over the matter from the FRG.

[30]*Elicofon*, 678 F.2d at 1161.

[31]*Id.*

[32]*Id.* at 1163.

"anomalous" state of affairs should be ended, Elicofon argued, because public policy should advantage, not disadvantage, the innocent purchaser in comparison to the thief or the knowing purchaser of stolen property.[33]

The problem with this line of reasoning, the appeals court stated, was its assumption that courts will unconditionally permit thieves and knowing purchasers of stolen goods to take advantage of the statute of limitations. On the contrary, the New York courts had made clear in other decisions "that familiar principles of equitable estoppel will prevent a wrongdoer from asserting the statute of limitations defense and thereby 'take refuge behind the shield of his own wrong.'"[34] Given these constraints on the invocation of statutes of limitations by deliberate wrong-doers, the court declared, in actual application "the *Menzel* rule does not prefer the thief or bad faith purchaser over the *bona fide* purchaser."[35] Moreover, the court stated, it is in any event not for the federal courts to cure the anomalies, if that is what they are, of the system of time limits the state has put in place; "we are charged only with applying New York law, not with remaking or improving it."[36] In choosing "between the policy, urged by Elicofon, of allowing the statute of limitations to run against an owner regardless of his ignorance, and tolling it indefinitely against a good faith purchaser until a demand is made, we are satisfied that New York has chosen the latter course."[37] The claim had thus accrued only upon Elicofon's refusal of the museum's demand, and the museum's lawsuit was timely.

8.4.2 The Problem of Delayed Demands

The central question presented in the Grosz case was what significance, if any, attaches to the amount of time that precedes a claimant's delay. In essence, the issue was whether the "demand and refusal" rule is qualified by a rule proscribing the owner from unreasonably delaying a demand, as the Museum of Modern Art asserted that the Grosz heirs had done. The district court ruled against the museum on this question; though it openly disapproved of the Grosz heirs' decision to bring a claim so long after the operative events had occurred, it concluded that the delay was not a proper basis for dismissal.[38] Reaching this conclusion required a detour through the New York case law.

---

[33]*Id.*

[34]*Id.* (quoting General Stencils, Inc. v. Chiappa, 18 N.Y.2d 125, 127 (1966)).

[35]*Id.*

[36]*Id.*

[37]*Id.* at 1163–64.

[38]The court of appeals did not rule on the issue, apparently considering it unnecessary in light of the ultimate disposition of the case.

8.4.2.1 The New York Cases

8.4.2.1.1 Unknown Possessors: *DeWeerth* and *Lubell*

In two much-discussed cases, the federal and state courts of New York have grappled with the issue of an owner's delay in demanding the return of stolen art. Both cases involved situations in which the current possessor of the stolen work was unknown to the owner, but could perhaps have been discovered if the owner had exerted greater effort to discover the work's whereabouts.

The *DeWeerth* Decision In *DeWeerth v. Baldinger*,[39] the plaintiff was a German national who owned a Monet painting that she kept at her home in Wuppertal-Elberfeld beginning in the 1920s. In 1943, she sent the painting and other valuables for safekeeping to a castle belonging to her sister in southern Germany. In 1945, the castle was occupied by American soldiers, and after their departure the sister noticed that the painting was missing. DeWeerth reported the painting stolen with the military government after the war, and made various failed efforts to locate it in the ensuing decade.

Meanwhile, the painting made its way into the hands of a Swiss art dealer, who consigned it in 1956 to the Wildenstein Gallery in New York for sale. It was purchased shortly afterward by Baldinger, a collector who kept the painting at her home in New York, occasionally displaying it at public exhibitions. In 1981, DeWeerth's nephew was told that she had lost a Monet during the war, and set about researching the matter. He located the painting in a *catalogue raisonné* of the artist's works, which indicated that it had been sold by the Wildenstein Gallery in 1957 and exhibited there in 1970. At that point, DeWeerth hired a lawyer in New York, who contacted the Wildenstein Gallery and learned that Baldinger had purchased the painting. Following a rejected demand for the painting's return, DeWeerth sued Baldinger in New York federal court. The trial court ruled that the painting was stolen and ordered it restored to the plaintiff.

On appeal to the Second Circuit court of appeals, the defendant successfully argued that the lawsuit was barred because of the time lag between the painting's theft and the plaintiff's demand for its return. Because the case was governed by state law, the court observed that its role was "to sit as another court of the state."[40] Surveying previous decisions, the court discerned the following principle: "Under New York law, even though the three-year limitations period begins to run only once a demand for return of the property is refused, a plaintiff may not delay the action simply by postponing his demand. Where demand and refusal are necessary to start a limitations period, the demand may not be unreasonably delayed."[41]

---

[39]836 F.2d 103 (2d Cir. 1987).

[40]*Id.* at 108.

[41]*Id.* at 107.

The court elaborated upon the rule in two respects. First, it emphasized that the rule was more expansive than the doctrine of laches, which provides that a court may take a party's unreasonable delay into account when it is asked to award "equitable" relief such as the return of property. According to the court, though the "proscription against unreasonable delay has been referred to as 'laches,' the New York courts have explained that the doctrine refers solely to an unexcused lapse of time and not to the equitable principle of laches, which requires prejudice to the defendant as well as delay."[42] In other words, the unreasonable delay rule was an implicit part of the New York statute of limitations. Second, the court observed that the New York courts had already applied the rule to claimants who knew the identity of the possessor of stolen property; in all likelihood, the court opined, they would also apply it to claimants who did not know, but through ordinary diligence could have discovered, the possessor's identity. "In light of New York's policy of favoring the good faith purchaser and discouraging stale claims," the court therefore held, "an owner's obligation to make a demand without unreasonable delay includes an obligation to use due diligence to locate stolen property."[43]

Turning to the facts of the case before it, the *DeWeerth* court ruled in the defendant's favor. Though the claimant took some steps to find the missing Monet in the decade after it was stolen, "[c]onspicuously absent from her attempts to locate the painting is any effort to take advantage of several mechanisms specifically set up to locate art lost during World War II," including contacting relevant government agencies and advertising the loss in publications.[44] "Most indicative of DeWeerth's lack of diligence," however, was "her failure to conduct any search for twenty-four years from 1957 until 1981," during which time she could easily have found references to the painting in exhibition catalogues as well as in the *catalogue raisonné* in which her nephew quickly found it when he began looking.[45] Moreover, being a "wealthy and sophisticated art collector," Deweerth "could easily have hired someone to conduct the search for her."[46] Finally, the policy against "prosecution of stale claims" supported a ruling against the claim: witnesses were dead, documents were missing, "DeWeerth's claim of superior title is supported largely by hearsay testimony of questionable value," and "[m]emories have faded."[47] To force "a good-faith purchaser who has owned a painting for thirty years to defend under these circumstances would be unjust," the court declared, and "New York law avoids this injustice by requiring a property owner to use reasonable diligence in locating his property," which DeWeerth had failed to do.[48]

---

[42]*Id.*

[43]*Id.* at 109–10.

[44]*Id.* at 111.

[45]*Id.* at 112.

[46]*Id.*

[47]*Id.*

[48]*Id.*

The *Lubell* Decision The *Deweerth* court's incorporation of a "reasonable diligence" rule into the New York statute of limitations was effectively overruled a few years later by the state's highest court. In *Guggenheim Foundation v. Lubell*,[49] a mailroom employee stole a Chagall watercolor from New York's Guggenheim museum in the mid-1960s. The museum discovered the painting was missing a few years later and immediately suspected the employee, but refrained from reporting the theft out of fear that publicity would drive the painting further underground and make its recovery more difficult. The thief sold the painting to a New York gallery, which in turn sold it in 1967 to Lubell, who kept it in her home for the next twenty years without realizing it was stolen. When she looked into selling the painting in 1985, an auction house employee recognized it as having once belonged to the Guggenheim and contacted the museum, which asked Lubell to return it. Upon her refusal, the museum filed suit in New York state court.

The trial court granted summary judgment to Lubell under the statute of limitations, holding that the museum's demand had been unreasonably delayed by its failure to seek the location of the stolen painting. The painting had been publicly exhibited in 1973; though the museum did not know that, it (the court reasoned) could have been alerted to that fact if it had notified others that the painting had been stolen. Accordingly, the court concluded, the museum's claim had accrued in 1973, and expired three years later. Adopting the reasoning of the *DeWeerth* decision, the trial court ruled that the statute of limitations implicitly contained a requirement of ordinary diligence on the part of property owners.

On appeal, the state's high court disagreed. The *DeWeerth* court, it ruled, "should not have imposed a duty of reasonable diligence on the owners of stolen art work for purposes of the Statute of Limitations."[50] By design, the New York statute of limitations is "the rule that affords the most protection to the true owners of stolen property," as it does not begin to run until after an owner's demand for the property has been refused.[51] Other states have embraced rules less generous to the owner, for example by starting the clock when the owner discovered, or reasonably should have discovered, the location of the stolen property. However, such a "discovery rule" had recently been considered, and rejected, in the New York legislative process; in vetoing a bill that would have adopted it, the governor expressed concern that accelerating the cutoff for bringing suit would nurture the market for stolen art in New York by shielding from recovery some stolen works that were recoverable under current law.[52] These considerations "convince us that [the demand and refusal] rule remains the law in New York and that there is no

---

[49] 569 N.E.2d 426 (N.Y. 1991).

[50] *Id.* at 430.

[51] *Id.*

[52] Impetus for the proposed legislation came from New York's Metropolitan Museum of Art, which faced potential claims for its holdings of looted antiquities imported from abroad. See Rose and Acar (1995), p. 46.

reason to obscure its straightforward protection of true owners by creating a duty of reasonable diligence."[53]

The court acknowledged that its own "case law already recognizes that the true owner, having discovered the location of its lost property, cannot unreasonably delay making demand upon the person in possession of that property."[54] However, the court stated, "it would not be prudent to extend that case law and impose the additional duty of diligence before the true owner has reason to know where its missing chattel is to be found."[55] This was so in part because the *Menzel* decision had established that "the demand and refusal is a substantive and not a procedural element of the cause of action," meaning that before the refusal the good-faith possessor is not a wrongdoer and there is no claim to be brought.[56] Further, the court suggested, creating a reasonable-diligence component to the statute of limitations would have troubling policy implications. It would scarcely be easy to establish what measures an owner must take to satisfy the requirement, given that "some members of the art community believe that publicizing a theft exposes gaps in security and can lead to more thefts," and also "pushes a missing painting underground"; because "members of the art community have apparently not reached a consensus on the best way to retrieve stolen art," it would be "particularly inappropriate for this Court to spell out arbitrary rules of conduct that all true owners of stolen art work would have to follow to the letter."[57] Moreover, to "place the burden of locating stolen artwork on the true owner and to foreclose the rights of that owner to recover its property if the burden is not met would, we believe, encourage trafficking in stolen art"; in the court's view, "the better rule gives the owner the relatively greater protection and places the burden of investigating the provenance of a work of art on the potential purchaser."[58]

To be sure, the court observed, its holding concerned only the interpretation of the statute of limitations. The possibility remained that an owner's unjustified delay in making a demand could be made the basis of an argument "directed at the conscience of the court and its ability to bring equitable considerations to bear in the ultimate disposition of the painting."[59] In particular, "although [Lubell's] Statute of Limitations argument fails, her contention that the museum did not exercise reasonable diligence in locating the painting will be considered by the Trial Judge in the context of her laches defense."[60] In the adjudication of the laches defense, the conduct of both parties will be considered, and "prejudice will also need to be shown," meaning that Lubell would have to show that she was harmed by

[53]*Lubell*, 569 N.E.2d at 430.

[54]*Id.*

[55]*Id.*

[56]*Id.*

[57]*Id.* at 431.

[58]*Id.*

[59]*Id.*

[60]*Id.*

the museum's delay.[61] The court accordingly ordered the case remanded to the trial court for further proceedings on, among other things, the question of laches.[62]

8.4.2.1.2 Known Possessors: *Republic of Turkey*

While the *Lubell* case was pending before New York's high court, the federal district court in New York confronted the problem presented by an owner who is slow to make a demand after discovering the whereabouts of stolen art. In *Republic of Turkey v. Metropolitan Museum of Art*,[63] Turkey sought to recover what was known as the Lydian Hoard, a collection of several hundred gold and silver antiquities from the sixth century B.C.E., which had been looted from burial mounds in the Manisa and Usak regions of Turkey and illegally exported in 1966. The Metropolitan Museum acquired the collection a few years afterward from dealers in New York and Switzerland, making no public announcement of the acquisition. Amid newspaper rumors that the museum had acquired a Lydian treasure, the Turkish contacted the museum in 1970 and 1973 requesting information, but received no reply. In 1984, the museum for the first time put a substantial part of the collection on display, enabling Turkish authorities to see its similarity to objects recovered from the thieves, who had been caught and prosecuted in the intervening period.[64]

In 1986, the Turkish ambassador made a written demand for the collection's return, which the museum refused. Turkey immediately filed suit in federal court, claiming title to the collection and seeking its restitution. The Museum moved for summary judgment under the statute of limitations, relying on the principle that "an owner of stolen property may not unreasonably delay making the requisite demand" for the property's return from an innocent purchaser.[65] The museum invoked the Second Circuit's pronouncement in *DeWeerth* that, in addition to having a "duty of reasonable diligence in locating stolen property," an owner has a "duty to make a demand for return within a reasonable time after the current possessor is identified."[66] Because Turkey had known of the museum's possession of the disputed objects since the early 1970s, the museum argued, the statute of limitations had long since elapsed.

The district court rejected the museum's argument, relying on the ruling of New York's intermediate appellate court in *Lubell*, which anticipated the ruling the high court would issue in that case the following year.[67] According to the

---

[61] *Id.*

[62] The case settled two years later, after the first day of trial. See Perez-Pena (1993).

[63] 762 F. Supp. 44 (S.D.N.Y. 1990).

[64] See Rose and Acar (1995), p. 46.

[65] *Republic of Turkey*, 762 F. Supp. at 45.

[66] *Id.*

[67] Solomon R. Guggenheim Foundation v. Lubell, 550 N.Y.S.2d 618 (App. Div. 1990).

intermediate court, *DeWeerth* had erred in holding that the statute of limitations bars an otherwise-timely action if the plaintiff unreasonably delayed making a demand upon the innocent purchaser of stolen property; such a delay is relevant to the equitable defense of laches, but not to the application of the statute of limitations, which focuses exclusively on the time lag between the rejection of the demand and the filing of suit. When the plaintiff is responsible for "inexcusable delay in [making a demand], or in acquainting himself with the facts that would enable him to perform such an act, an appeal can be made to the conscience of the court to dismiss the action as untimely notwithstanding that it was commenced within the statutory period," the intermediate court announced, as would the high court the next year.[68]

The Metropolitan Museum argued that *Lubell* was distinguishable from its own case, in that the Republic of Turkey knew the location of the collection for many years before making its demand. *Lubell*, the museum argued, stood only for the proposition that the statute of limitations imposes no "reasonable diligence" requirement on a claimant to search out the possessor of stolen property in order to make a demand. The case did not, according to the museum, stand for the very different proposition that the statute of limitations allows a claimant who *knows* the possessor's identity to wait an indefinitely long period before making a demand. In other words, the *Lubell* holding was limited, in the museum's view, to cases in which "a plaintiff has no knowledge of the whereabouts of his stolen property, but would have discovered its whereabouts had he exercised reasonable diligence."[69] For cases in which the plaintiff discovers the property's whereabouts but does nothing, *Lubell* left intact the implicit rule of earlier decisions that the claim accrues, and the statute of limitations begins running, at the time of the plaintiff's discovery.

The district court found this argument unpersuasive, and ruled in Turkey's favor. The principles underlying the intermediate court's decision in *Lubell*, the court reasoned, allowed no meaningful distinction between, on one hand, cases in which the plaintiff failed to take steps necessary to ascertain the information necessary to make a demand, and on the other hand, "cases like this one, where the Republic of Turkey allegedly had actual knowledge of the facts needed to make a demand."[70] Assertions of unreasonable delay in the making of a demand, whether in one or the other type of case, were properly dealt with by means of the equitable doctrine of laches, which requires "a showing of prejudice," that is, a demonstration that the defendant was adversely affected by the delay.[71] Because "there are genuine issues of material fact as to whether defendant was prejudiced by the alleged delay," the court denied the Metropolitan Museum's motion for summary judgment.[72]

---

[68]*Id.* at 621.

[69]Quoted in *Republic of Turkey*, 762 F. Supp. at 46.

[70]*Id.*

[71]*Id.*

[72]*Id.* at 47. The case settled before trial, with the Metropolitan Museum agreeing to return the Lydian Hoard to Turkey. See Rose and Acar (1995), p. 47.

8.4.2.2 The District Court's Ruling

Canvassing these cases, the district court in the Grosz litigation considered it "an open question" whether, under New York law, the statute of limitations could be set in motion by a claimant's unreasonable delay in making a demand.[73] "Under the demand-and-refusal rule as set forth in *Menzel*," the court observed, "it appears that a person who knows where a missing item is could delay the accrual of an action against a good faith purchaser indefinitely simply by failing to make a demand."[74] *Lubell* cast doubt on that idea, referring with approval to older cases holding that "the true owner, having discovered the location of its lost property, cannot unreasonably delay making demand upon the person in possession of that property."[75] At the same time, however, *Lubell* left it unclear whether those older cases had survived the *Menzel* decision. *Lubell*'s ambiguity on the issue apparently convinced the district court that the matter remained an open question.

Given this uncertainty, the district court in the Grosz litigation opted to follow the lead of the *Republic of Turkey* decision, which, as we saw before, preceded the high court's pronouncements in *Lubell*. The *Republic of Turkey* decision held (in the district court's words) that "the reasonableness of the plaintiff's delay in filing suit did not bear on the statute of limitations but was properly raised only in the context of laches."[76] The district court followed suit: "This court agrees with the reasoning of *Republic of Turkey*, and holds that the issue of unreasonable delay is relevant only to the defense of laches—even where, as here, it is undisputed that a potential plaintiff (Grosz) had actual knowledge of the whereabouts of at least one of the missing art works (*Poet*) a half century before anyone tried to replevy the piece."[77] The court could not, however, rule on the laches defense in the context of a motion to dismiss, because the defense requires a weighing of the equities as well as actual proof that the defendant was prejudiced by the delay. "In light of the fact-sensitive nature of a laches inquiry, it would be premature to resolve the question now," the court declared.[78] Troubling as the Grosz heirs' delay was to the court, it did not warrant immediate dismissal.

8.4.3 Accrual of the Claims

The problem was thus reduced to that of determining how much time had elapsed between the museum's refusal of the plaintiffs' demand and the filing of suit in April 2009. Here the central question was at what point, in the exchanges of

[73] *Grosz*, 772 F. Supp.2d at 482.
[74] *Id.*
[75] *Lubell*, 569 N.E.2d at 430.
[76] *Grosz*, 772 F. Supp.2d at 483.
[77] *Id.*
[78] *Id.*

communication following the Grosz heirs' November 2003 letter claiming ownership of the paintings, the museum had "refused" their demand. "All parties agree," the district court noted, "that MoMA has in fact rejected plaintiffs' demand and refused to return the paintings. They differ only on the date rejection occurred."[79] The plaintiffs contended that the refusal did not occur until the April 2006 letter, written just under three years before suit was filed, in which the museum director informed them that the board had voted to reject their claim. The museum contended that the refusal occurred nine months earlier, in the July 2005 letter in which the museum director indicated his own belief that the available evidence did not support the claim.

As the district court noted, there is little New York decisional law defining what constitutes a "refusal" such that a claim for stolen property accrues and the statute of limitations clock begins ticking. In *Feld v. Feld*,[80] the plaintiff lived with his parents, as an adult, until he moved out in 1967, leaving behind a collection of antiques and art objects. In a series of letters in the early 1970s, the plaintiff wrote to his parents asserting ownership of the items and requesting their return via another person. In 1974, his father wrote in reply that the items would not be returned until the plaintiff resolved an unrelated claim his parents had against him, concerning the operation of his antiques business. There was no further communication between the plaintiff and his parents, who both died in 1995. Following their death, the plaintiff filed suit against his brother, both individually and as executor of the parents' estate, seeking to recover the contested items and also monetary damages on theories of replevin, conversion, and fraud. The trial court granted summary judgment in the defendant's favor on the fraud claim, holding it time-barred on the ground that the statute of limitations for such claims expires two years after the fraud is, or could have been, discovered by the plaintiff; the court ruled that the plaintiff could have discovered the alleged fraud decades before bringing suit. As to the replevin and conversion claims to recover the collection, however, the court rejected the defendant's motion for summary judgment under the statute of limitations; such claims to recover stolen property are governed by the demand-and-refusal rule, the court reasoned, and in its view the plaintiff's parents had made no "clear refusal" to return the disputed property.[81]

The appellate court reversed, holding that the replevin and conversion claims were barred by the statute of limitations. The trial court, it ruled, had of course been correct that these claims to recover the contested property were governed by the three-year statute of limitations, and that accrual occurred when a demand for the property was refused. However, the appellate court held, the trial court had erred by concluding that the plaintiff's parents had not refused his demand for the property back in the 1970s. The trial court, it ruled, had mistakenly taken the position that to qualify as a "refusal," a property holder's response to a request for the return of

[79] *Id.*

[80] 720 N.Y.S.2d 35 (App. Div. 2001).

[81] *Id.* at 37.

property must contain specific wording to that effect. The law did not require such formality or explicitness. "A demand need not use the specific word 'demand' so long as it clearly conveys the exclusive claim of ownership," the court stated.[82] "A demand consists," according to the court, "of an assertion that one is the owner of the property and that the one upon whom the demand is made has no rights in it other than allowed by the demander."[83] The same was true of refusals. "By the same reasoning, a refusal need not use the specific word 'refuse' so long as it *clearly conveys an intent to interfere with the demander's possession or use of his property*," the court ruled.[84] In the present case, the letters exchanged in the 1970s satisfied the requirements of both demand and refusal. "Since plaintiff's 1971 and 1974 letters clearly stated his claim of ownership to the disputed property and succinctly directed that the parents make such property available to a third party, the demand requirement was met. The father's 1974 letter just as clearly constituted a refusal as it conditioned return of the disputed property on resolution of other disputes, which was inconsistent with plaintiff's claim of ownership."[85] Accordingly, because "a demand and a refusal had been made by 1974, plaintiff's causes of action in replevin and conversion were time barred long before he commenced this action."[86]

A federal court encountered the problem of identifying New York law's timing of a possessor's refusal to return contested property in *Borumand v. Assar*.[87] Miriam Borumand sued Assar, her former brother-in-law, seeking to recover stock in a corporation. She alleged that in 1994 she entrusted Assar with $13,400 on the understanding that he would use it to purchase stock for her in Helix Technologies, the company that employed him. She alleged that he purchased Helix stock with money, which by the time suit was filed in 2001 she alleged had appreciated in value to $85,500, and had wrongfully withheld the stock from her when she requested that he turn it over to her. The defendant moved to dismiss under the New York statute of limitations, which the court postponed ruling on because there were factual disputes concerning the sequence of communications between the parties in the period before the lawsuit was commenced.

At trial, the plaintiff testified that she repeatedly asked the defendant to turn over the stock over a period of six years beginning in 1995, and that he assured her that he would give it to her in the future. Assar, however, "failed to turn over the shares, and ignored her repeated requests for documentation of the purchases."[88] Moreover, in 1995 Assar was caught embezzling from his employer, and shortly afterward was sent to prison for bank fraud. In the court's view, Assar's behavior

---

[82] *Id.*

[83] *Id.*

[84] *Id.* (emphasis added).

[85] *Id.*

[86] *Id.*

[87] 2005 WL 741786 (W.D.N.Y. 2005).

[88] *Id.* at *12.

constituted a refusal that, while it could not be pinpointed to a certain date, occurred at least five years before the plaintiff finally filed suit. "A refusal," the court noted, "need not be unequivocally stated in words; rather, actions may be sufficient to constitute a refusal if they amount to 'an overt and positive act of conversion.'"[89] In the present case, the plaintiff's own testimony established that her claim was untimely, the court ruled. She claimed that "she demanded possession of the shares in 1995 and 'all the time' thereafter," the court noted, and "[w]hile, according to Borumand, Assar never explicitly informed her that he would not relinquish possession, he never in fact turned over the shares and continually maintained that he would do so at some future time."[90] In the court's view, "by the time Borumand discovered that during the same time period that Assar had been accepting funds from her, he had also been embezzling from Helix, she should have reasonably concluded that his failure to turn over the requested shares, let alone any written verification of the purchases, amounted to a refusal."[91] At the latest, the court opined, the plaintiff should have drawn this conclusion by 1996, meaning that the statute of limitations had expired in 1999.[92]

These cases were the foundation for the district court's analysis of the timing question in the Grosz litigation. "In line with *Feld* and *Borumand*," the court declared, "a court must analyze the actions as well as his [sic] words of a person who receives a demand before deciding whether and when it was refused. If either the recipient's words or actions evinces [sic] 'an intent to interfere with the demander's possession or use of his property'—which is an 'overt and positive act of conversion'—then the demand has been refused and the cause of action accrues, even if the words 'I refuse your demand' were not explicitly used."[93] This formulation "comports with the purpose behind the demand-and-refusal rule," the court stated, "which is to give an innocent purchaser the opportunity to turn over chattel in his possession after learning that it had been stolen from someone else"; nothing "in the rule's history or purpose suggests that a party who receives a demand, and who thereafter acts in a manner that is inconsistent with the demander's claim of ownership, should be held not to have 'refused' the demand simply because he failed to recite some magic words of rejection. Actions, as we all know, can sometimes speak louder than words."[94]

Under these standards, the court agreed with the museum that it had "refused" the Grosz heirs' November 2003 demand by the time of, if not before, the museum director's letter of July 2005. While not as definitive as the April 2006 letter

---

[89] *Id.* at *14 (quoting Hefferan v. Marine-Midland Bank, N.A., 727 N.Y.S.2d 60 (App. Div. 2001)).

[90] *Borumand*, 2005 WL 741786, at *14.

[91] *Id.*

[92] *Id.* The court also concluded that the plaintiff's claim failed on the merits because of inconsistencies in her account of what had happened.

[93] *Grosz*, 772 F. Supp.2d at 484 (quoting *Feld*, 720 N.Y.S.2d at 37, and *Borumand*, 2005 WL 741786 at *14).

[94] *Grosz*, 772 F. Supp.2d at 484.

announcing the museum board's decision, the director's letter "constituted the sort of refusal contemplated by the demand and refusal rule," in the court's view.[95] "If MoMA's failure to return the Paintings for more than a year and a half did not constitute a refusal as a matter of law (and this Court thinks it did), then the July 20, 2005 letter—in which the defendant clearly communicated its intent to keep all three works despite plaintiffs' demand—was an act utterly inconsistent with plaintiffs' claim of right."[96] The museum director's letter to the director of the Grosz estate read in pertinent part:

> We have, as you know, a fiduciary obligation to our collection. Before we remove a work from the Museum's collection, we need to establish convincing and conclusive evidence that another party—in this instance the Estate of George Grosz—has ownership rights superior to the Museum's. Anyone seeking to challenge MoMA's ownership rights must prove his claim, not the other way around....
>
> [W]e appreciate the collegial manner in which we have worked with you and remain committed to continuing that process. I think it is fair to say that we have now reached a point where it appears that no more information currently available for us to consider, a point on which I sense, we both agree. We have, however, reached somewhat different conclusions about the results of our extensive study of the provenance of *Portrait of the Poet Max Herrmann Neisse*: we believe that the available evidence does not lead to any definitive conclusion that challenges the Museum's ownership of the picture....
>
> In a spirit of friendship and recognition of the limitations of the present state of our knowledge about the provenance of this work, I suggested the possibility of shared ownership of *Max Herrmann Neisse* at our May 31 meeting. I did this not out of a conviction that the picture was tainted in some way, but because shared ownership would be a gracious, amicable means of addressing the fact that we may never be able to fully understand the work's history in the decades before the Museum purchased it in 1952 ....
>
> I think our greatest difference of opinion, however, concerns *Self-Portrait with a Model*. Though we are aware of the restitution of a painting with a similar provenance, based on material that you have shared with us, and on our own extensive research—much of which we have done in collaboration with Yale University—we cannot reach the conclusion that restitution either of this picture, or of the drawing, *Republican Automaton*, would be appropriate at this time.
>
> Our goal, like yours, is to do what is right and to do so in a manner that best serves the needs of George Grosz. To this end, I think the best course of action would be for us to meet together with Peter Grosz and his brother, if he is available, to review the facts and determine an appropriate course of action.[97]

In the court's reading, with this letter "MoMA rejected plaintiffs' assertion that they had an immediate right to possession of the three Grosz works," and indicated that it "intended to keep all three paintings."[98] The letter, "coupled with the museum's

---

[95] *Id.* at 485.

[96] *Id.*

[97] Letter of Glenn D. Lowry to Ralph Jentsch (July 20, 2005), Exhibit A to Defendant's Motion to Dismiss First Amended Complaint, Grosz v. Museum of Modern Art, No. 09-CV-3706 (S.D.N.Y. June 4, 2009).

[98] *Grosz*, 772 F. Supp.2d at 486.

continued retention of the works after it was sent, indicates its continuing intent to interfere with the rights asserted by plaintiffs in their demand."[99] This, the court ruled, "is all the 'refusal' the law could possibly require before plaintiffs' causes of action for conversion and replevin (as well as the corresponding equitable claims) accrued."[100]

The court acknowledged that the letter contained "temporizing language" indicating the museum's willingness to continue investigating and negotiating the matter. Somewhat unconvincingly, however, the court reasoned that this language in no way "tempered" the museum's "flat-out rejection" of the plaintiffs' claims.[101] "The museum's suggestions about 'shared ownership' of *Poet* pending 'further research,' and future meetings to 'review the facts,' suggest that perhaps MoMA might one day be open to giving plaintiffs one or more of the works—but that is no different from the *Feld* defendant's assertion that he would return the stolen property if the parties could resolve their other disputes."[102]

One surmises that if the district court had believed the equities favored the plaintiffs, it would have placed a good deal more weight on that "temporizing language" and been more reluctant to conclude that the 2005 letter constituted an unambiguous rejection of the heirs' claims. That is to say, if the court had not credited (as it obviously did) the museum's assertions that the heirs had waited far too long before bringing their 2003 demand, and that the available evidence did not support their claims, the court would probably have found that the museum's refusal did not occur until the April 2006 letter in which the director announced that the board had rejected the claims. In both tone and content, the 2005 letter hardly seems to be the "flat-out rejection" the district court portrayed it as; at least that is not the only reading to which it is susceptible. The court's rather dogmatic treatment of this debatable question likely indicates that the decision actually rests on other, unstated grounds.

In any event, the district court's ruling on this issue was upheld in a brief paragraph by the court of appeals, which stated that "[a]s the District Court explained in its thoughtful and comprehensive opinion, the record indicates that refusal took place, at the latest, in a letter from the Director of MoMA to the Grosz heirs' agent on July 20, 2005."[103]

---

[99] *Id.*

[100] *Id.*

[101] *Id.* at 487.

[102] *Id.*

[103] *Grosz*, 403 Fed. Appx. at 577.

8.5 Equitable Tolling

The Grosz heirs also argued that the running of the statute of limitations should be tolled, or suspended, on equitable grounds. Their argument was that for the nine months between the July 2005 letter just discussed and the April 2006 letter announcing the museum board's decision to reject the claims, the museum behaved as though it was actively considering the return of the paintings. The plaintiffs placed particular emphasis on a letter of January 2006 from the museum director in which he indicated that he had referred the matter to the board, which had engaged a former attorney general to investigate. This letter, argued the plaintiffs, led them to believe their demand was still being considered and that suit was therefore premature; having encouraged them in that belief, the museum should not be permitted to insist that the claims accrued in July 2005. The argument was based on the idea of equitable estoppel: the statute of limitations was tolled, the plaintiffs contended, because they had reasonably relied on the museum's representations that their demand had not yet been refused.[104]

The district court rejected this argument as "utterly unpersuasive."[105] While the federal courts do have the power to toll the statute of limitations on equitable grounds, stated the court, "equitable tolling 'applies only in the rare and exceptional circumstance,' and is appropriately invoked only where a plaintiff has 'acted with reasonable diligence throughout the period he seeks to toll.'"[106] The Grosz heirs' case, the court declared, "does not present one of the 'rare and exceptional circumstances' in which any tolling of the limitations period would be equitable."[107] The January 2006 letter to which the plaintiffs referred, in the court's view, "did not disavow MoMA's determination to keep the Grosz works in its collection in derogation of plaintiffs' purported rights."[108] The letter stated that the museum had sought the assistance of the former attorney general "not out of any sense of uncertainty about our conclusions, or any wavering in our resolve, but rather to obtain an intelligent, candid, independent assessment of the situation."[109] This language made clear, the court opined, that the museum was adhering to its earlier "conclusion that plaintiffs' claims were unfounded."[110] Moreover, nothing in the January 2006 letter "prevented the plaintiffs from bringing suit during the period when [the former attorney general] was reviewing the matter or at any time thereafter"; indeed, the court declared, by the time of that letter "litigation was

[104]On equitable estoppel of statutes of limitations defenses, see Malveaux (2005) and Richardson (1997).

[105]*Grosz*, 772 F. Supp.2d at 489.

[106]*Id.* at 488 (quoting Smith v. McGinnis, 208 F.3d 13, 17 (2d Cir. 2000) (internal quotation marks omitted).

[107]*Grosz*, 772 F. Supp.2d at 488.

[108]*Id.* at 489.

[109]Quoted in *id.*

[110]*Id.*

clearly warranted—more than two years had passed since plaintiffs had made their original demand, MoMA still had not returned the Paintings, and it had repeatedly indicated that it would not do so."[111]

In its short unpublished opinion, the court of appeals agreed. "Under New York law," the court declared, "'the doctrine of equitable estoppel applies where it would be unjust to allow a defendant to assert a statute of limitations defense'—specifically, 'where plaintiff was induced by fraud, misrepresentations or deception from filing a timely action.'"[112] The fact that settlement discussions are ongoing, the court stated, is not enough to warrant equitable tolling of the statute of limitations: "Indeed, where 'there was never any settlement agreement; continued difficulties in trying to settle the matter; no fraud or misrepresentation by defendants; and no agreement or promise by defendants upon which plaintiffs relied in failing to commence their lawsuit within the requirement period,' equitable estoppel does not apply."[113] In the present case, the court ruled, the "record indicates no fraud or misrepresentation on the part of MoMA, nor does it indicate evidence of reasonable reliance by plaintiffs on any alleged misrepresentations by MoMA."[114]

8.6 Epilogue

After the final judgment in the museum's favor, a dispute arose concerning the documents the museum had disclosed to the heirs concerning the provenance of the disputed works. Upon learning that the heirs planned to donate the documents to the United States Holocaust Museum and to the Yad Vashem Memorial in Israel to assist scholars studying the fate of Holocaust-era artworks, the museum sought a judicial order compelling the heirs to "return or destroy" the documents. The district court granted the order in 2011 on confidentiality grounds.[115]

The three Grosz works remain in the collection of the Museum of Modern Art. *The Poet Max Herrmann-Neisse with Cognac* is part of the museum's permanent display. *Republican Automatons* and *Self-Portrait with Model* are kept in storage.

[111] *Id.* at 490. In denying the plaintiffs' motion for reconsideration, the court stated that its conclusion was also supported by the deposition testimony of the Grosz estate's director. *Id.* at 498–99.

[112] *Grosz*, 403 Fed. Appx. at 577 (brackets omitted).

[113] *Id.* (brackets omitted).

[114] *Id.* For criticism of the court's ruling, see Kreder (2012), pp. 118–125.

[115] Order, Grosz v. Museum of Modern Art, No. 09-CV-3706 (S.D.N.Y. Nov. 29, 2011).

References

Cohan, William D. 2011. MoMA's Problematic Provenances. *ARTnews*, November 17.

Cohen, Patricia. 2013. Museums Faulted on Restitution of Nazi-Looted Art. *New York Times*, June 30.

Hess, Hans. 1985. *George Grosz*. New Haven, CT: Yale University Press.

Jentsch, Ralph, Enrico Crispolti, and Philippe Degan. 2008. *George Grosz: Berlin-New York*. Milan: Skira.

Kreder, Jennifer Anglim. 2012. Fighting Corruption of the Historical Record: Nazi-Looted Art Litigation. *Kansas Law Review* 61: 75–137.

Lewis, Beth Irwin. 1991. *George Grosz: Art and Politics in the Weimar Republic*. Princeton, NJ: Princeton University Press.

Malveaux, Suzette M. 2005. Statutes of Limitations: A Policy Analysis in the Context of Reparations Litigation. *George Washington Law Review* 74: 68–122.

Marquis, Alice Goldfarb. 1989. *Alfred H. Barr: Missionary for the Modern*. New York: Contemporary Books.

Müller, Melissa, and Monika Tatzkow. 2010. *Lost Lives, Lost Art: Jewish Collectors, Nazi Art Theft*. London: Frontline.

Nicholas, Lynn. 1994. *The Rape of Europa: The Fate of Europe's Treasures in the Third Reich and the Second World War*. New York: Knopf.

Perez-Pena, Richard. 1993. Suit over Chagall Watercolor Is Settled Day After Trial Starts. *New York Times*, December 29.

Petropoulos, Jonathan. 1996. *Art as Politics in the Third Reich*. Chapel Hill, NC: University of North Carolina Press.

Richardson, Eli J. 1997. Eliminating the Limitations of Limitations Law. *Arizona State Law Journal* 29: 1015–1074.

Rose, Mark, and Özgen Acar. 1995. Turkey's War on the Illicit Antiquities Trade. *Archeology* 48 (2): 44–56.

Vincent, Isabel. 2012. New York Museums Have Not Returned Nazi-Seized Art. *New York Post*, October 7.

Cases

Borumand v. Assar, 2005 WL 741786 (W.D.N.Y. 2005)

DeWeerth v. Baldinger, 836 F.2d 103 (2d Cir. 1987)

Frenk v. Solomon, 998 N.Y.S.2d 42 (App. Div. 2014)

General Stencils, Inc. v. Chiappa, 18 N.Y.2d 125, 127 (1966)

Gillet v. Roberts, 57 N.Y. 28, 33 (1874)

Grosz v. Museum of Modern Art, 772 F. Supp.2d 473 (S.D.N.Y.), aff'd, 403 Fed. Appx. 575 (2d Cir. 2010), cert. denied, 565 U.S. 819 (2011)

Hefferan v. Marine-Midland Bank, N.A., 727 N.Y.S.2d 60 (App. Div. 2001)

Kunstsammlungen Zu Weimar v. Elicofon, 678 F.2d 1150 (2d Cir. 1982)

Menzel v. List, 267 N.Y.S.2d 804 (Sup. 1966)

Republic of Turkey v. Metropolitan Museum of Art, 762 F. Supp. 44 (S.D.N.Y. 1990)

Smith v. McGinnis, 208 F.3d 13, 17 (2d Cir. 2000)

Solomon R. Guggenheim Foundation v. Lubell, 550 N.Y.S.2d 618 (App. Div. 1990), aff'd, 569 N.E.2d 426 (N.Y. 1991)

Chapter 9
Bakalar v. Vavra

9.1 Background

Franz (Fritz) Grünbaum (1880–1941) was a cabaret performer, film actor, writer, and director in Vienna whose satirical sketches mocking the Austrian Nazis were very popular in the mid-1930s.[1] The son of an art dealer, he compiled an extensive collection of Austrian modernist art that included many works by Egon Schiele. As a prominent and outspoken Jew he was a top target of the Nazis, and was arrested within days of the Anschluss. His wife Elisabeth (Lily) Grünbaum (1898–1942), also a Jew, was evicted from their apartment by Nazi authorities, who appointed an art historian to take an inventory of all the art in their possession. Shortly afterward, Lily applied for an export permit for the art and entrusted the art to a Viennese shipping company. Her prolonged efforts to win Fritz's release were unsuccessful, and he died at Dachau in 1941. Lily was arrested in 1942 and murdered later that year at the Maly Trostinec camp near Minsk.

There are no records of what became of the art collection after the Grünbaums' arrests. Parts of the collection surfaced in Switzerland in the mid-1950s and were displayed as part of a Schiele exhibition at the Galerie Gutekunst in Bern in 1956. That year, the Galerie Gutekunst sold twenty of these works to a New York gallery, including an untitled Schiele drawing generally referred to as *Seated Woman with Bent Left Leg (Torso)* (1917). David Bakalar, a private collector, purchased the drawing from the New York gallery in 1963.

When Bakalar listed the drawing with Sotheby's for sale in 2005, heirs of Fritz Grünbaum wrote to the auction house claiming that the Nazis had stolen the work along with the rest of the collection and that whoever sold it to the gallery in Switzerland in the 1950s had no authority to do so. Sotheby's conducted an investigation, from which it concluded that the collection had never been taken by the Nazis but rather had remained with the Grünbaum family all along. The

[1]See generally Arnbom and Wagner-Trenkwitz (2005).

B.L. Hay, *Nazi-Looted Art and the Law*, DOI 10.1007/978-3-319-64967-2_9

auction house further concluded that the Galerie Gutekunst had purchased the drawing, along with numerous other items from the collection, from Elisabeth Grünbaum's sister Mathilde Lukacs, who had survived the war in Belgium.

9.2 Proceedings

In March 2005, Bakalar brought an action in federal district court in New York, basing jurisdiction on diversity of citizenship and naming as defendants Milos Vavra and Leon Fischer, the Grünbaum heirs who had approached Sotheby's claiming title to the Schiele drawing.[2] In his complaint, Bakalar sought a declaration that he was the rightful owner of the drawing, and that in any event the heirs' claims to the work were time-barred. The heirs filed an answer with counterclaims, contending that Bakalar had not obtained good title and that their action was timely. In a pretrial ruling, the district court held that the question of the drawing's ownership would be determined according to Swiss law, and that questions concerning the timeliness of the heirs' claims would be decided under New York law.[3]

Following a bench trial in July 2008, the district court entered judgment for Bakalar.[4] In its written opinion, the court set forth its findings, based on various documentary and testimonial evidence, that the drawing had been part of Fritz Grünbaum's collection; that it had come into Mathilde Lukacs' possession through an unknown course of events sometime during or after the war; and that Lukacs had sold it to the Galerie Gutekunst in Bern in 1956. The court went on to rule that the gallery had purchased the drawing in "good faith," with no reason to doubt Lukacs's authority to sell it, and therefore had acquired title to the drawing under Swiss law. As a downstream purchaser from the Bern gallery, Bakalar had also acquired good title to the drawing, the court concluded.

The Second Circuit court of appeals overturned the judgment in September 2010, holding that the district court had erred in applying Swiss law to the case.[5] In the court of appeals' view, the relevant choice-of-law rule mandated the application of the substantive law of New York, because that state had a stronger

---

[2]Vavra and Fischer were designated legal heirs to Fritz Grünbaum's estate by an Austrian court.

[3]Bakalar v. Vavra, 550 F. Supp.2d 548 (S.D.N.Y. 2008). In a separate pretrial ruling the court declined to award Bakalar summary judgment on the basis of his laches defense, holding that further development of the evidence was needed. Bakalar v. Vavra, 2006 WL 2311113 (S.D.N.Y. 2006). The court also denied the heirs' motion to certify a class action against dealers and galleries possessing works from the Grünbaum collection, as well as against the German shipping company to which Elisabeth Grünbaum entrusted the collection in 1939. Bakalar v. Vavra, 237 F.R.D. 59 (S.D.N.Y. 2006).

[4]Bakalar v. Vavra, 2008 WL 4067335 (S.D.N.Y. 2008).

[5]Bakalar v. Vavra, 691 F.3d 136 (2d Cir. 2010). We will refer to this court of appeals decision as "*Bakalar I.*"

connection to the parties and the dispute than did Switzerland. The court also indicated that under the substantive law of New York, a purchaser could not acquire title to a stolen artwork, even if acting in good faith, and that the purchaser bore the burden of proving that the work was not stolen. The court remanded for further proceedings.

On remand, in August 2011, the district court withdrew its earlier ruling that Bakalar was the rightful owner of the drawing.[6] While there was no proof that the Nazis had stolen the Grünbaum collection, the court stated, there was also no proof that Mathilde Lukacs had lawfully inherited the collection or had authority to sell it. Under New York law, the court ruled, Bakalar had therefore failed to discharge his burden of demonstrating good title to the work. However, the court also ruled that the Grünbaum family had unreasonably delayed bringing a claim for the drawing, which Bakalar had purchased nearly fifty years earlier, and which the family could have located long ago if they had tried. The court therefore ruled that the heirs' claim was barred by New York's common law doctrine of laches, and again entered judgment for Bakalar.

The court of appeals affirmed the judgment in an unpublished opinion in October 2012.[7] The United States Supreme Court denied review the following spring.

9.3 Conflicts of Law

There were two choice-of-law problems in the case: to determine which state's substantive law governed ownership of the drawing; and to determine which state's law governed the timeliness of the heirs' claims. We will consider these in turn.

9.3.1 Property Ownership

The first, more contentious issue was that of resolving the conflict among laws concerning ownership of possibly stolen property. The relevant jurisdictions' laws differed with respect to whether a purchaser of stolen art can acquire title, and also differed with respect to which party bears the burden of proof when the evidence is unclear.

---

[6]Bakalar v. Vavra, 819 F. Supp.2d 293 (S.D.N.Y. 2011).

[7]Bakalar v. Vavra, 500 Fed. Appx. 6 (2d Cir. 2012), cert. denied, 133 S. Ct. 2038 (2013). We will refer to this court of appeals decision as "*Bakalar II*."

9.3.1.1 Austria, Switzerland, and New York

Several states were plausible candidates for supplying the applicable law: Austria, where the work was allegedly stolen; Switzerland, where title was purportedly transferred after the war; and New York, where the possessor ultimately purchased it. In its 2010 decision, the court of appeals canvassed the laws of all three, finding that the law of Switzerland bore a "significant difference" from the laws of both New York and Austria in the treatment of Holocaust-era art restitution.[8]

Switzerland The critical feature of Swiss law, stated the court of appeals, echoing the district court, lay in the generous protection it accords to buyers of stolen property.[9] First, the court noted, under Article 934 of the Swiss Civil Code, a person "who acquires and takes possession of an object in good faith becomes the owner, even if the seller was not entitled or authorized to transfer ownership," subject to the proviso that if the object was stolen, "the owner who previously lost the object retains the right to reclaim the object for five years."[10] After the five-year period, "a previous owner of a stolen object is no longer entitled to request the return of the stolen object from a good-faith possessor."[11]

Second, the court noted, Swiss law "presumes that a purchaser acts in good faith, and a plaintiff seeking to reclaim stolen property has the burden of establishing that a purchaser did not act in good faith."[12] This presumption fully applies to the case of Holocaust-era claims, the court observed, quoting an expert witness in the litigation. "There has never been a legal presumption," according to that witness, "that art works with a potential relationship to Germany during World War II (i.e. emanating from a German collection or created by artists deemed "degenerate" by the Nazis) would in general and *per se* be tainted, and that a dealer accepting such art works would automatically be subject to a heightened standard of diligence in the 1950s. Such a presumption did not in the 1950s and does not today exist in Swiss law."[13] As a result, the court of appeals remarked, Swiss law "places significant hurdles to the recovery of stolen art, and almost 'insurmountable' obstacles to the recovery of artwork stolen by Nazis from Jews and others during World War II and the years preceding it."[14]

New York In sharp contrast, according to the court of appeals, was the law of New York, whose position toward purchasers of stolen art could be summed up as

---

[8]*Bakalar I*, 619 F.3d at 139.

[9]The court of appeals agreed with, and incorporated by reference, the district court's description of Swiss law. See *Bakalar I*, 619 F.3d at 140.

[10]*Id.* (quoting district court).

[11]*Id.* at 140 (quoting expert witness).

[12]*Id.*

[13]Quoted in *id.*

[14]*Id.* (quoting In re Holocaust Victims Assets Litigation, 105 F. Supp.2d 139, 159 (E.D.N.Y. 2000), aff'd, 413 F.3d 183 (2d Cir. 2005)).

caveat emptor. The court emphasized two differences from Swiss law. First, "[u]nlike Switzerland, in New York, a thief cannot pass good title," which means that "absent other considerations an artwork stolen during World War II still belongs to the original owner, even if there have been several subsequent buyers and even if each of those buyers was completely unaware that she was buying stolen goods."[15] The protection accorded to the original owner, explained the court, "reflects an overarching concern that New York not become a marketplace for stolen goods and, in particular, for stolen artwork."[16] The court pointed to the well-known *Lubell* case, in which the state's high court observed of the New York City art market that "masterpieces command extraordinary prices at auction and illicit dealing in stolen merchandise is an industry all its own," for which reason "New York case law has long protected the right of the owner whose property has been stolen to recover that property, even if it is in the possession of a good-faith purchaser for value."[17] To discourage "trafficking in stolen art," according to the *Lubell* decision, "the better rule gives the owner the relatively greater protection," and puts responsibility for "investigating the provenance of a work of art on the potential purchaser."[18]*Lubell* therefore sought "the rule that affords the most protection to true owners of stolen property," and "rejected any suggestion that less protective measures should be adopted."[19]

The second difference between the laws of New York and Switzerland concerned allocation of the burden of proof among the parties in cases of alleged theft. According to the court of appeals, if there is a factual question as to whether an artwork was stolen from the original owner, the current possessor bears the burden of proving that it was not stolen. This also came from the *Lubell* case, which involved a museum's attempt to recover a gouache that, it contended, had been stolen and sold by an employee. Because "an issue of fact exists as to whether the gouache was stolen," ruled the state's appellate division in *Lubell*, "the burden of proof with respect to this issue is on the defendant," meaning the current possessor.[20] "While the appellate division recognized that the burden it was placing on the good-faith possessor was an 'onerous one,'" the court observed, "it held that 'it well serves to give effect to the principle that persons deal with the property in chattels or exercise acts of ownership over them at their peril.'"[21]

[15]*Bakalar I*, 619 F.3d at 141 (quoting Turner 1999, p. 1534). New York is typical of common law jurisdictions in this respect.

[16]*Bakalar I*, 619 F.3d at 141.

[17]Solomon R. Guggenheim Foundation v. Lubell, 569 N.E.2d 426, 427, 429 (N.Y. 1991), quoted in *Bakalar I*, 619 F.3d at 141. On the *Lubell* case, see Section 8.4.2.1 above.

[18]*Lubell*, 569 N.E.2d at 430.

[19]*Bakalar I*, 619 F.3d at 141 (quoting *Lubell*, 569 N.E.2d at 430).

[20]Solomon R. Guggenheim Foundation v. Lubell, 550 N.Y.S.2d 618, 624 (A.D. 1990), quoted in *Bakalar I*, 619 F.3d at 142. The state's high court adopted the reasoning of the appellate division. *Lubell*, 569 N.E.2d at 431.

[21]*Bakalar I*, 619 F.3d at 142 (quoting *Lubell*, 550 N.Y.S.2d at 624).

Austria The law of Austria, the court found, did not significantly conflict with that of New York on the subject of Holocaust-era claims. The court pointed to the postwar Austrian Nullification Act, which provided: "Any paid and unpaid legal transactions and other legal business which occurred during the German occupation of Austria will be considered null and void if they were contracted as a consequence of any political or economic influence exercised by the German Reich in order to deprive individuals or entities of property assets owned by or due them as of March 13, 1938."[22] Though implementing legislation had expired, noted the court of appeals, the Austrian supreme court had declared that the restitution of property stolen during the Nazi era was "in accordance with the immutable principles of our General Civil Code" and "an integral part of Austrian law."[23] From this the court of appeals concluded that the laws of New York and Austria were largely compatible with respect to the Grünbaum heirs' claims. "Although it is unclear whether a cause of action comparable to [the heir's claims] against Bakalar could be successfully brought in Austria," the court declared, "allowing the claims to go forward under New York law is consistent with the principles underlying the decision of the Supreme Court of Austria."[24]

9.3.1.2 Resolving the Conflict

Because the case did not arise under federal law, the courts were required to apply the forum state's conflicts rules in order to select the applicable law.[25] At this juncture the district court and the court of appeals parted ways: though they agreed that New York's choice-of-law rules controlled, they disagreed on what those rules called for in the case at hand. Let us look at their reasoning.

The District Court In its brief opinion, the district court concluded that New York's conflicts rules unambiguously required the application of Swiss law, because that was the location of the challenged sale. "Under New York's choice of law rules," it declared, quoting earlier decisions, "questions relating to the validity of a transfer of personal property are governed by the law of the state where the property is located at the time of the alleged transfer."[26] Here it relied on another district court decision,

[22]NichtigkeitsG 106/1946, § 1, quoted in *Bakalar I*, 619 F.3d at 146. See generally Schnabel and Tatzkow (2007), pp. 127–128.

[23]Oberster Gerichtshof, Apr. 1, 2008, Docket No. 5 Ob 272/07x, quoted in *Bakalar I*, 619 F.3d at 146.

[24]*Bakalar I*, 619 F.3d at 146.

[25]This is the principle of the *Klaxon* decision, which held that in cases in which jurisdiction is based on diversity of citizenship, the federal courts must generally apply the same substantive law that the forum state courts would apply. See Klaxon Co. v. Stentor Electric Manufacturing Co., 313 U.S. 487 (1941).

[26]*Bakalar*, 550 F. Supp.2d at 550 (internal quotation marks omitted). The court drew this language from Greek Orthodox Patriarchate of Jerusalem v. Christie's, Inc., 1999 WL 673347, *4–5

Greek Orthodox Patriarchate of Jerusalem v. Christie's, Inc., involving a medieval manuscript that was taken from a Jerusalem monastery, acquired by a French purchaser in the 1920s, and auctioned in New York by Christie's in the 1990s. Adjudicating the monastery's suit to recover the manuscript, the federal district court in New York held that French law governed the case, because the entire case turned on whether title had validly been transferred in France.[27] By the same token, reasoned the district court in the Bakalar litigation, Swiss law should determine whether the Bern gallery acquired valid title when it purchased the Schiele drawing in Switzerland. Because the Grünbaum family's "'title passed, if at all,' in Switzerland when [the gallery] acquired the drawing, Swiss law applies."[28]

The court also considered, and rejected, the possibility that the New York courts would decline to enforce Swiss law on grounds of public policy. "If the choice of law analysis leads to the application of foreign law," the court declared, describing the New York judiciary's approach to conflicts, "a court may refuse to apply that law only if its application would be violative of fundamental notions of justice or prevailing concepts of good morals."[29] Swiss law, the court stated, did not run afoul of that standard. Though "the application of Swiss law would arguably provide less protection to the original owner of property than New York law," Swiss law could not be described as so fundamentally unjust that the New York courts would decline to enforce it when their choice-of-law rules called for its application.[30]

The Court of Appeals The court of appeals disagreed, holding that New York's choice-of-law rules required the application of New York law rather than Swiss law. To begin, the court took issue with the district court's assertion that disputes over the validity of a transfer of personal property are automatically governed by the law of the state where the transfer occurred. Such a "situs rule," which focuses exclusively on the location of the property at a given point in time, "no longer accurately reflects the current choice of law rule in New York."[31] Rather, declared

---

(S.D.N.Y. 1999), which in turn took it from Kunstsammlungen Zu Weimar v. Elicofon, 536 F. Supp. 829, 845–46 (E.D.N.Y. 1981).

[27] *Greek Orthodox Patriarchate*, 1999 WL 673347, at *5.

[28] *Bakalar*, 550 F. Supp.2d at 550 (quoting *Greek Orthodox Patriarchate*, 1999 WL 673347, at *5).

[29] *Bakalar*, 550 F. Supp.2d at 550 (internal quotation marks omitted). The court took this language from Curley v. AMR Corp., 153 F.3d 5, 12 (2d Cir. 1998).

[30] *Bakalar*, 550 F. Supp.2d at 550–51. The court pointed to an unpublished opinion in which a New York state trial court held that a claim to recover some manuscripts, allegedly stolen by the Nazis in France and returned to that country after the war, was time-barred under the French law of adverse possession. The New York choice-of-law rule called for the application of French law, the court ruled, and "[t]his court can ignore otherwise applicable foreign law only when the foreign law violates 'some fundamental principle of justice, some prevalent conception of good morals, some deep-rooted tradition of the common weal.'" Warin v. Wildenstein & Co., Inc., 2001 WL 1117493, *5 (N.Y. Sup. 2001), aff'd, 746 N.Y.S.2d 282 (A.D. 2002). Though the French law differed from New York's, it was "not offensive to the State's public policy" because it provided "reasonable commercial protection" to owners seeking to recover stolen art. 2001 WL 1117493, *6.

[31] *Bakalar I*, 619 F.3d at 143.

the court, the New York judiciary had decreed that the interests of affected jurisdictions, and not the location of specific events, are the proper focus in the analysis of choice-of-law problems. The district court, like the court in *Greek Orthodox Patriarchate* on which it relied, had therefore been in error to apply the situs rule. For the state's judiciary (in the words of the federal court of appeals) had "explicitly rejected the 'traditional situs rule' in favor of interest analysis," and had instead held that in property disputes "the law of the jurisdiction having the greatest interest in the litigation will be applied."[32]

It was New York, continued the court of appeals, that had the strongest interest in the litigation over the Schiele drawing. Quite simply, New York's interest was "to prevent the state from becoming a marketplace for stolen goods," in the words of an earlier decision.[33] "[I]f the claim of Vavra and Fischer is credited," the court explained, "a stolen piece of artwork was delivered in New York to a New York art gallery," making "New York a 'marketplace for stolen goods' and, more particularly, for stolen artwork."[34] Therefore, in the court's view, "[h]owever the Drawing came into the possession of the Swiss art gallery, New York has a compelling interest in the application of its law."[35]

In contrast, the interests of Switzerland in the litigation were relatively slight. The "resolution of an ownership dispute in the Drawing between parties who otherwise have no connection to Switzerland does not implicate any Swiss interest simply because the Drawing passed through there," declared the court.[36] It was true, the court of appeals acknowledged, that the application of New York law would compromise, to some extent, Switzerland's ability to act as a conduit for artwork of questionable provenance. New York purchasers will "take greater care in assuring themselves of the legitimate provenance of their purchase," which, "in turn, may adversely affect the extraterritorial sale of artwork by Swiss galleries."[37] Nonetheless, declared the court, the interest of Swiss galleries in reaching the New York market "must yield to the significantly greater interest of New York" in "preventing the state from becoming a marketplace for stolen goods."[38]

Nor, according to the court, were the interests of Austria harmed by the application of New York law to the dispute. As we saw above, the court read Austrian law to be largely in harmony with New York law with respect to ownership of art

---

[32]Karaha Bodas Co., LLC v. Perusahaan Pertambangan Dan Gas Bumi Negara, 313 F.3d 70, 85 n. 15 (2d Cir. 2002) (quoting Istim, Inc. v. Chemical Bank, 581 N.E.2d 1042, 1044 (N.Y. 1991)), cert denied, 539 U.S. 904 (2003), quoted in *Bakalar I*, 619 F.3d at 143. On the adoption of interest analysis in New York, see the state high court's discussion in Schultz v. Boy Scouts of America, Inc., 480 N.E.2d 679, 683–85 (N.Y. 1985).

[33]Kunstsammlungen Zu Weimar v. Elicofon, 536 F. Supp. 829, 846 (E.D.N.Y. 1981), quoted in *Bakalar I*, 619 F.3d at 144.

[34]*Bakalar I*, 619 F.3d at 144.

[35]*Id.*

[36]*Id.*

[37]*Id.* at 145.

[38]*Id.* at 145.

alleged to have been taken by the Nazis.[39] Because "allowing the claims to go forward under New York law is consistent with the principles underlying the decision of the Supreme Court of Austria," declared the court, "we conclude that Austria has no competing interest" in having its own law applied.[40]

9.3.2 Time Limitations

In addition to contending that he had valid title to the drawing, Bakalar asserted a defense of laches, an equitable doctrine that bars recovery to claimants who are guilty of unreasonable delay in bringing their claims. The choice-of-law problem for the courts was to determine which jurisdiction supplied the applicable doctrine of laches. This they found easy to answer. In cases brought under the diversity jurisdiction, the federal court applies the same time limits, including equitable doctrines such as laches, that would be applied by the courts of the forum state.[41] The question therefore was which jurisdiction's laches doctrine the New York state judiciary would apply to the case.

The courts considered the answer clear: regardless of what state's substantive law applies, "the local law of the forum determines whether an action is barred by laches."[42] This was an instance, the district court explained, of the "well-settled conflict-of-laws rule that the forum [may] apply the foreign substantive law, but will follow its own rules of procedure."[43] Accordingly, declared the district court, "this Court must apply New York's law concerning laches to [the heirs'] counterclaims, regardless of the foreign substantive law applied."[44] The court of appeals agreed that this point was uncontroversial, stating without discussion that the defense of laches would be determined under New York law.[45]

---

[39] *Id.* at 146.

[40] *Bakalar I*, 619 F.3d at 146.

[41] See Guaranty Trust Co. of New York v. York, 326 U.S. 99 (1945).

[42] American Law Institute (1971), § 142 comment d, quoted in *Bakalar*, 550 F. Supp.2d at 551.

[43] Bournias v. Atlantic Maritime Co., 220 F.2d 152, 154 (2d Cir. 1955), quoted in *Bakalar*, 550 F. Supp.2d at 551.

[44] *Bakalar*, 550 F. Supp.2d at 551.

[45] *Bakalar I*, 619 F.3d at 147.

9.4 Title to the Artwork

The district court twice adjudicated the merits of the ownership dispute: first applying Swiss law, which resulted in a ruling for Bakalar; second (after that judgment was overturned on appeal) applying New York law, which resulted in a ruling for the Grünbaum heirs. Let us look at the two rulings in turn.

9.4.1 Factual Findings

"Although the turmoil of World War II and the loss of evidence in the intervening years have obscured the Drawing's provenance, this Court previously made certain findings of fact," the district court stated, referring to the opinion it rendered after the 2008 trial.[46] It will be helpful for us to begin with a summary of its findings of fact from the trial, which was conducted without a jury.

The Grünbaum Family Fritz Grünbaum was arrested in March 1938, eight days after the Anschluss. In July 1938 his art collection was appraised by Franz Kieslinger, a Nazi functionary, who counted 449 items in the collection, including 81 Schieles. In September 1938, Lily Grünbaum, who had obtained a power of attorney from her imprisoned husband, entrusted 417 unidentified artworks to Schenker & Co., a shipping and storage company, which obtained an export permit. There is no record of whether, or when, the property left Austria in this period.

Following Fritz's death at Dachau in June 1941, Lily signed his death certificate, identifying herself as his heir and writing that "there is no estate" and "in the absence of an estate, there are no estate-related proceedings."[47] Lily was arrested, deported and murdered by the Nazis the following year.

Two of Lily's sisters, Mathilde Lukacs and Anna Reis, successfully emigrated from Austria to Belgium and survived the war. Her sister Mathilde, together with her husband Sigmund, left in August 1938, shipping about thirty artworks through the Schenker firm. Anna, together with her husband Berthold, left in early 1939, shipping about twenty artworks. Unlike the export permit prepared by Elisabeth Grünbaum, the export permits obtained by Lily's sisters indicated that the items in question passed through Austrian customs.

Sale in Switzerland In the early 1950s, Mathilde Lukacs contacted the Galerie Gutekunst in Bern, seeking to sell some Dutch and French artworks, which the gallery auctioned for her in 1953. She informed Eberhard Kornfeld, the gallery owner, that she was selling the art to finance a planned retirement in Switzerland. A few years later she sold a total of fifty-four Schiele works to the gallery, which displayed them in a 1956 exhibition. Kornfeld did not ask her for any

[46] *Bakalar*, 819 F. Supp.2d at 295.

[47] Quoted in *Bakalar*, 2008 WL 4067335, *4.

documentation of the Schieles' provenance. In his 2007 deposition testimony in the case, he recalled that "[w]hen he asked Lukacs where she acquired the Schieles, she told him they were 'an old Viennese family possession,' and he did not inquire further."[48]

Events Leading to the Claim After the 1956 exhibition, the Galerie St. Etienne in New York bought twenty of the Schieles from the Bern gallery, including *Seated Woman with Bent Left Leg (Torso)*, which it then sold to David Bakalar in 1963. Matters rested there until 1998, when an ownership dispute arose concerning another of the twenty Schieles—a painting called *Dead City III*—which carried a label naming Fritz Grünbaum as the owner. When a Grünbaum heir came forward to claim the painting, New York authorities seized it from the Museum of Modern Art, where it was on loan from an Austrian museum.[49] In the ensuing controversy, Austrian newspapers reported a Viennese archivist's discovery of the familial connection between Mathilde Lukacs and Fritz Grünbaum. At that point Jane Kallir, the owner of the Galerie St. Etienne, obtained the catalog of the 1956 Bern exhibition and compared it to a 1925 Schiele catalog that listed Grünbaum as the owner of several works. From this and other evidence, Kallir concluded that all of the Schieles in the 1956 exhibition had come from Fritz Grünbaum's collection.

When Bakalar decided to sell the drawing through Sotheby's in 2004, the auction house contacted Kallir, who shared her findings. From further research, Sotheby's concluded that Mathilde Lukacs had indeed sold the drawing along with the other Schieles to the Galerie Gutekunst, and that there was no evidence that the Nazis had stolen them.[50] Sotheby's also contacted representatives of another possible Grünbaum heir, who stated that she did not plan to challenge Bakalar's title to the drawing. "Sotheby's was satisfied that the Drawing had remained in the Grünbaum family without having been looted by the Nazis," the district court remarked, "and proceeded to auction it in February 2005," at which point Vavra and Fischer came forward to claim it.[51]

---

[48]*Id.*, at *3. The court found Kornfeld's testimony about his dealings with Lukacs credible because it was consistent with the available documents. See *id.* at *2.

[49]Austrian collector Rudolf Leopold had purchased *Dead City III* from Galerie St. Etienne and later placed it in his eponymous museum in Vienna. In early 1998, during an exhibition of the Leopold Museum's Schiele collection put on by the Museum of Modern Art, the New York district attorney's office issued a subpoena for the painting, along with *Portrait of Wally*, upon receiving reports that they were stolen. New York state's high court quashed the subpoena under state law, at which point federal authorities seized *Portrait of Wally* under the federal forfeiture laws, leading to the protracted proceeding discussed in Chap. 2. Federal authorities did not seize *Dead City III*, and it was returned to the Leopold Gallery in 1999. See generally van Woudenberg (2012), pp. 184–190.

[50]For a contrary view, see Bergman (2015), written by the daughter of another purchaser of Schieles from the Grünbaum collection. On the Swiss market for Nazi-looted art, see Feliciano (1997), pp. 155–164; Smale (2013); and Petropoulos (2014).

[51]*Bakalar*, 2008 WL 4067335, *6.

9.4.2 Title Under Swiss Law

"Under Swiss law, a person who acquires and takes possession of an object in good faith becomes the owner, even if the seller was not entitled or authorized to transfer ownership," the district court observed.[52] Drawing on expert testimony offered in the case, the court noted several contours of the good faith requirement. First, "a purchaser acts in good faith if he sincerely believes that the seller was authorized to transfer ownership, and the purchaser may presume from the seller's possession of the object that the seller has the authority to sell it."[53] Second, "the purchaser's good faith is presumed, and a claimant to the object bears the burden of establishing otherwise by proving either (1) the purchaser's actual knowledge that the seller lacked authority to sell the object, or (2) that the purchaser failed to exercise due diligence before purchasing the object."[54] Third, "[e]ven if the purchaser fails to exercise due diligence, the burden remains on the claimant to show that the required investigation would likely have revealed the seller's lack of authority to sell the object."[55]

Given these principles, the court had no trouble concluding that the Galerie Gutekunst acquired valid title when it purchased the drawing from Mathilde Lukacs in 1956. "Under Swiss due diligence standards," according to the court, "a purchaser of an object has no general duty to inquire about a seller's authority to sell the object, unless suspicious circumstances exist," such as eagerness on the seller's part to sell quickly for cash, or at an unusually low price; if "the seller gives a plausible explanation for these, no further investigation is required."[56] When Kornfeld, the Swiss gallery owner, bought the drawing and the other Schieles from Lukacs in 1956, "he had known Lukacs for five years, had met her several times, and had auctioned off several of her works without incident in 1953," the court declared, adding that "there was no evidence that she was acting with unusual haste."[57] Her assertion "that they were an old Viennese family possession was plausible, given that she had lived in Austria and seemed relatively well off," and though she provided no ownership documents, "there is no evidence that such documentation was customary for an art sale at that time."[58] Under these circumstances, the gallery owner's actions did not fall short of Swiss due diligence requirements, as the court understood them.

---

[52] *Id.*, at *7. As discussed earlier, that rule is subject to the exception that "if the object had been lost or stolen, the owner who previously lost the object retains the right to reclaim the object for five years." *Id.* The exception was inapplicable because the Galerie Gutekunst acquired the drawing fifty years before the litigation commenced.

[53] *Id.*

[54] *Id.*

[55] *Id.*

[56] *Id.*

[57] *Id.*, at *8.

[58] *Id.*

Moreover, the court stated, "[e]ven assuming that the situation required Kornfeld to conduct a more comprehensive investigation into the Drawing's provenance, it would have been highly unlikely that he would have been able to conclude that the Nazis, or anyone else, had taken the Drawing from Grünbaum."[59] Even now it was uncertain what had happened to Grünbaum's collection after his arrest. After more than two years of pretrial discovery and the benefit of archival research unavailable in 1956, declared the court, the heirs had "not produced any concrete evidence that the Nazis looted the Drawing or that it was otherwise taken from Grünbaum."[60] The art could have followed any of several lawful paths into Mathilde Grünbaum's possession:

> The Drawing could have been one of the 417 [artworks] Elisabeth Grünbaum possibly exported through Schenker in 1938. Alternatively, the Drawing could have been one of the three drawings Lukacs's husband exported through Schenker – or even one of the three watercolors he exported, since the Drawing's gouache medium is often confused for watercolor. Lukacs's brother-in-law Berthold Reis also exported three watercolors in 1938, and any of those could have been the drawing.[61]

"Nor," continued the court, "did the research by Sotheby's into the Drawing's provenance in 2004, which included consultations with two independent art researchers and a genealogist working for a potential Grünbaum heir, turn up any evidence that the Nazis stole it."[62] Accordingly, "there is no reason to think a more extensive inquiry by Kornfeld over fifty years ago would have led him to any different conclusion."[63]

Bakalar was therefore the legitimate owner of the drawing, the court concluded. "Because Kornfeld purchased the Drawing in good faith, he acquired good title to it and had the authority to pass that title to Galerie St. Etienne," and when Bakalar purchased it from the latter in 1963 "he gained ownership to it with all accompanying property rights."[64]

9.4.3 Title Under New York Law

The court of appeals, as we saw above, ruled that the district court had erred in applying Swiss law to the ownership dispute, and remanded the case with instructions to apply New York law instead. Rather than holding a new trial, the district court relied on the evidence and factual findings adduced in the earlier trial, this time construing their significance under the substantive law of New York.

---

[59] *Id.*

[60] *Id.*

[61] *Id.*

[62] *Id.*

[63] *Id.*

[64] *Id.*, at *9.

Following the lead of the court of appeals, the district court emphasized two features of New York law: "absent other considerations an artwork stolen during World War II still belongs to the original owner, even if there have been several subsequent buyers and even if each of those buyers was completely unaware he was buying stolen goods," and if the Grünbaum heirs make "a threshold showing that they have an arguable claim to the Drawing, New York law places the burden on Bakalar, the current possessor, to prove that the drawing was not stolen."[65]

The court began its analysis by reiterating its view, expressed in the earlier decision, that there was no "concrete evidence" that the Nazis had stolen the drawing.[66] "This Court previously found that the Drawing was possessed by Grünbaum prior to his arrest in 1938 and by Lukacs in 1956," it noted.[67] "The most reasonable inference to draw from these facts is that the Drawing remained in the Grünbuam family's possession," it declared, adding that the "alternative inference – that the Drawing was looted by the Nazis and then returned to Grünbaum's sister-in-law – is highly unlikely."[68] Thus, "what little evidence exists," the court concluded, "suffices to establish by a preponderance of the evidence that the Drawing was not looted by the Nazis."[69]

Nonetheless, it did not follow that Mathilde Lukacs was the rightful owner of the drawing, or had authority to transact on the owner's behalf, when she sold it in Switzerland in 1956. It was possible that she received the drawing as a gift from Grünbaum's heirs, but this was pure conjecture. Such a gift would have to be shown "by clear and convincing evidence," the court stated, which was impossible because "there is simply no evidence as to how Lukacs acquired the Drawing."[70] It was also possible that Lukacs herself was an heir entitled to inherit part of Grünbaum's estate, but it was undisputed that no intestacy proceeding was conducted in Austria before the 1956 sale; without an appropriate court order distributing the estate, Lukacs "was not lawfully entitled to dispose of the Drawing under Austrian law."[71]

Under New York law, Bakalar had therefore failed, in the court's view, to discharge his burden of proving he was the legitimate owner of the drawing. Because he could not "establish that Lukacs held title to the [drawing] at the time it was sold to Galerie Gutekunst," he could not establish that he himself had acquired title as an indirect purchaser of the work.[72]

[65]*Bakalar*, 819 F. Supp.2d at 298 (brackets and quotation marks omitted). Here the district court was quoting the court of appeals opinion in *Bakalar I*, 619 F.3d at 141, 147.

[66]*Bakalar*, 2008 WL 4067335, *8.

[67]*Bakalar*, 819 F. Supp.2d at 299.

[68]*Id.*

[69]*Id.*

[70]*Id.*

[71]*Id.* at 301. The court added that the conclusion was the same under the intestacy law of New York.

[72]*Id.*

9.5 The Claim's Timeliness

Having ruled in the heirs' favor on the question of title, the district court turned to Bakalar's assertion that the heirs' claim to the drawing was nonetheless barred by the doctrine of laches.[73]

9.5.1 The Doctrine of Laches

As we saw above, the court had earlier held that New York law supplied the applicable version of the laches doctrine.[74] The doctrine is, as the court put it, "an equitable defense based on the maxim *vigilantibus no dormientibus aequitas subvenit* (equity aids the vigilant, not those who sleep on their rights)."[75] It holds that an otherwise valid claim to recover property may be barred if the claimants "were aware of their claim" and "inexcusably delayed taking action," and if the possessor "was prejudiced as a result."[76] The doctrine may apply even if the claimants did not have "actual knowledge of the claim; rather, it is sufficient that [they] *should have known*," the court emphasized.[77] In addition, the doctrine "focuses not only on efforts by the party to the action, but also on efforts by the party's family," according to the court.[78] "In the context of claims of lost or stolen works of art or cultural artifacts," stated the court, "the doctrine of laches safeguards the interests of a good faith purchaser of lost or stolen art by weighing in the balance of competing interests the owner's diligence in pursuing his claim."[79]

By way of illustrating the doctrine, the district court gave the examples of two recent decisions of its own judges, *Greek Orthodox Patriarchate of Jerusalem v. Christie's, Inc.*,[80] and *Sanchez v. Trustees of the University of Pennsylvania*.[81] In *Greek Orthodox Patriarchate*, which we encountered earlier, a medieval manuscript disappeared from a monastery in the early twentieth century, found its way into a French purchaser's hands sometime in the 1920s, and was put up for auction

---

[73]The court had earlier declined to grant Bakalar summary judgment on this issue, holding that the evidentiary record was insufficiently developed.

[74]See Section 9.3.2 above.

[75]*Bakalar*, 2006 WL 2311113, *3 (internal quotation marks omitted). The court was quoting Ivani Contracting Corp. v. City of New York, 103 F.3d 257, 259 (2d Cir.), cert. denied, 520 U.S. 1211 (1997). On laches doctrine, see generally Fort (2009) and Vaquer (2006).

[76]*Bakalar*, 819 F. Supp.2d at 303.

[77]*Id.* (italics in original).

[78]*Bakalar*, 2006 WL 2311113, *3, quoted in *Bakalar*, 819 F. Supp.2d at 303.

[79]Greek Orthodox Patriarchate of Jerusalem v. Christie's, Inc., 1999 WL 673347, *7 (S.D.N.Y. 1999), quoted in *Bakalar*, 819 F. Supp.2d at 303.

[80]1999 WL 673347 (S.D.N.Y. 1999).

[81]2005 WL 94847 (S.D.N.Y. 2004).

in 1998, at which time the monastery came forward for the first time to claim it. Because the monastery had done nothing until then to investigate the manuscript's disappearance, the court found its claim barred by laches, holding that "the question of whether the Patriarchate was sufficiently diligent in searching for [the manuscript] to defeat [the] laches defense is easily answered. The Patriarchate was not diligent at all."[82] And in *Sanchez*, a collection of pre-Columbian art belonging to the plaintiffs' grandfather was stolen around 1920 and eventually came into the possession of a university. Holding that the plaintiffs' 2003 claim against the university was barred by laches, the court observed that there was no evidence that the grandfather "undertook any search or made any effort whatever to recover the Collection," and that the "desultory effort [the plaintiffs] engaged in between 1970 and the present are not remotely enough to satisfy the requirements of a diligent search."[83]

9.5.2 *The Heirs' Delay*

With those cases as reference points, the district court considered the actions of the Grünbaum heirs. The court began by rejecting the heirs' argument that the laches defense "cannot apply because they were unaware of any claim against Bakalar and did not know of the Drawing's whereabouts until 2005."[84] For laches to apply, it was not necessary that the heirs "have been aware of a claim against Bakalar specifically; it is enough that they knew of—or should have known of—the circumstances giving rise to the claim, even if the current possessor could not be ascertained."[85] In addition, the heirs "did not need to have specific knowledge of the Drawing" for laches to apply; rather, the doctrine asks whether the owner has shown "a lack of diligence with respect to the collection as a whole, rather than the individual items."[86]

One of the heirs, Vavra, "was aware since childhood of both Grünbaum's substantial art collection and his death in a concentration camp," yet "prior to being contacted by an attorney in 1998, he made no effort to locate or claim title to any Grünbaum property," the court observed.[87] His grandmother, Fritz Grünbaum's sister, "displayed a similar lack of diligence," there being "no indication that she ever attempted to pursue a claim to Grünbaum's art collection, despite being aware of Grünbaum's art collection and her potential intestate rights, as evidenced by her correspondence with an Austrian lawyer concerning Grünbaum's music

[82]*Greek Orthodox Patriarchate*, 1999 WL 673347, at *10.

[83]*Sanchez*, 2005 WL 94847, at *3.

[84]*Bakalar*, 819 F. Supp.2d at 304.

[85]*Id.*

[86]*Id.*, at 304–5.

[87]*Id.* at 305.

royalties."[88] As for the other heir in the case, Fischer, his "parents and grandparents remained in close contact with [Mathilde] Lukacs for years," and "Fischer and his parents even visited her in Switzerland in 1959."[89] The "Fischers therefore had ample opportunity to inquire about Fritz Grünbaum's property, yet to Fischer's knowledge, neither he nor any of his predecessors made any such inquiries or claims."[90]

The court then balanced the equities. "However laches is applied in this case," stated the court, "it will work a certain inequity on the losing party, and this Court is 'in the unenviable position of determining who gets the artwork, and who will be left with nothing despite a plausible claim of being unfairly required to bear the loss.'"[91] On one hand, "a finding of no unreasonable delay would deprive Bakalar of property he purchased in good faith almost fifty years ago"; on the other hand, "a ruling for Bakalar will deprive Grünbaum's rightful heirs of a Drawing that, but for the atrocities of the Holocaust, might have remained in the family until today."[92] Nonetheless, the doctrine weighed in favor of the current possessor in the present case, for several reasons. First, Vavra and Fischer's "ancestors were aware of—or should have been aware of—their potential intestate rights to Grünbaum property, and Vavra and Fischer are bound by the knowledge of their respective families."[93] Second, while some delay in seeking the art collection would have been excusable in the turmoil after the war, "no such efforts were made by any member of their families" at any point in the intervening sixty years.[94] Third, the delay had been prejudicial to Bakalar, depriving him of the evidence needed to establish his title; it has "resulted in deceased witnesses, faded memories, lost documents, and hearsay testimony of questionable value."[95] Most important in this respect was "the death of Mathilde Lukacs in 1979, perhaps the only person who could have elucidated the manner in which she came to possess the Drawing, or indeed, whether she owned it at all."[96] The district court accordingly entered judgment for Bakalar.

In a brief unpublished opinion the court of appeals affirmed, discerning "no clear error" in the district court's findings that the heirs and their families had been insufficiently diligent and that Bakalar's ability to defend himself had been prejudiced as a result.[97] The case came to an end when the Supreme Court denied review.

---

[88] *Id.*

[89] *Id.*

[90] *Id.*

[91] *Id.* (quoting United States v. Davis, 648 F.3d 84, 86 (2d Cir. 2011)).

[92] *Bakalar*, 819 F. Supp.2d at 305.

[93] *Id.*

[94] *Id.* at 306.

[95] *Sanchez*, 2005 WL 94847, at *3, quoted in *Bakalar*, 819 F. Supp.2d at 306.

[96] *Bakalar*, 819 F. Supp.2d at 306.

[97] *Bakalar II*, 500 Fed. Appx. at *9. The court of appeals also rejected the heirs' contention that the district court had given them insufficient time to gather expert testimony.

9.6 Epilogue

Schiele's *Seated Woman with Bent Left Leg (Torso)* was sold at Sotheby's to a private collector in 2015. Later that year, the Grünbaum heirs filed suit against a New York dealer, seeking to recover two other Schiele works that were sold to the Bern gallery in 1956.[98] That case is still pending.

References

American Law Institute. 1971. *Restatement (Second) of Conflicts of Law*. Philadelphia, PA: American Law Institute.

Arnbom, Marie-Theres, and Christoph Wagner-Trenkwitz. 2005. *Grüss mich Gott! Fritz Grünbaum, 1880-1941. Eine Biographie*. Vienna: Christian Brandstätter Verlag.

Bergman, Carol. 2015. Egon Schiele, My Father, and Me. *Forward*, February 15.

Cohan, William D. 2017. A Suit over Schiele Drawings Invokes New Law on Nazi-Looted Art. *New York Times*, February 27.

Feliciano, Hector. 1997. *The Lost Museum: The Nazi Conspiracy to Steal the World's Greatest Works of Art*. New York: Basic Books.

Fort, Kathryn E. 2009. The New Laches: Creating Title Where None Existed. *George Mason Law Review* 16: 357–401.

Petropoulos, Jonathan. 2014. Inside the Secret Market for Nazi-Looted Art. *ARTnews*, January 29.

Schnabel, Gunnar, and Monika Tatzkow. 2007. *Nazi Looted Art: Handbuch Kunstrestitution weltweit*. Berlin: Proprietas-Verlag.

Smale, Alison. 2013. Report of Nazi-Looted Trove Puts Art World in an Uproar. *New York Times*, November 4.

Turner, Michelle I. 1999. The Innocent Buyer of Art Looted During World War II. *Vanderbilt Journal of Transnational Law* 32: 1511–1548.

van Woudenberg, Nout. 2012. *State Immunity and Cultural Objects on Loan*. Leiden: Martinus Nijhoff.

Vaquer, Antoni. 2006. Verwirkung Versus Laches: A Tale of Two Legal Transplants. *Tulane European and Civil Law Forum* 21: 53–72.

Cases

Bakalar v. Vavra, 2006 WL 2311113 (S.D.N.Y. 2006); 237 F.R.D. 59 (S.D.N.Y. 2006); 550 F. Supp.2d 548 (S.D.N.Y. 2008); 2008 WL 4067335 (S.D.N.Y. 2008), vacated, 691 F.3d 136 (2d Cir. 2010), on remand, 819 F. Supp.2d 293 (S.D.N.Y. 2011), aff'd, 500 Fed. Appx. 6 (2d Cir. 2012), cert. denied, 133 S. Ct. 2038 (2013)

Bournias v. Atlantic Maritime Co., 220 F.2d 152 (2d Cir. 1955)

Curley v. AMR Corp., 153 F.3d 5 (2d Cir. 1998)

Greek Orthodox Patriarchate of Jerusalem v. Christie's, Inc., 1999 WL 673347 (S.D.N.Y. 1999)

Guaranty Trust Co. of New York v. York, 326 U.S. 99 (1945)

---

[98]Reif v. Nagy, No. 161799/2015 (N.Y. Sup. Ct., filed Nov. 16, 2015). See Cohan (2017).

In re Holocaust Victims Assets Litigation, 105 F. Supp.2d 139, 159 (E.D.N.Y. 2000), aff'd, 413 F.3d 183 (2d Cir. 2005)
Istim, Inc. v. Chemical Bank, 581 N.E.2d 1042 (N.Y. 1991), cert denied, 539 U.S. 904 (2003)
Ivani Contracting Corp. v. City of New York, 103 F.3d 257, 259 (2d Cir.), cert. denied, 520 U.S. 1211 (1997)
Karaha Bodas Co., LLC v. Perusahaan Pertambangan Dan Gas Bumi Negara, 313 F.3d 70 (2d Cir. 2002), cert. denied, 539 U.S. 904 (2003)
Klaxon Co. v. Stentor Electric Manufacturing Co., 313 U.S. 487 (1941)
Kunstsammlungen Zu Weimar v. Elicofon, 536 F. Supp. 829 (E.D.N.Y. 1981)
Oberster Gerichtshof, Supreme Court of Austria, Apr. 1, 2008, Docket No. 5 Ob 272/07x
Sanchez v. Trustees of the University of Pennsylvania, 2005 WL 94847 (S.D.N.Y. 2004)
Schultz v. Boy Scouts of America, Inc., 480 N.E.2d 679 (N.Y. 1985)
Solomon R. Guggenheim Foundation v. Lubell, 550 N.Y.S.2d 618, 624 (A.D. 1990), aff'd, 569 N.E.2d 426, 427, 429 (N.Y. 1991)
United States v. Davis, 648 F.3d 84 (2d Cir. 2011)
Warin v. Wildenstein & Co., Inc., 2001 WL 1117493 (N.Y. Sup. 2001), aff'd, 746 N.Y.S.2d 282 (A.D. 2002)

Chapter 10
Museum of Fine Arts, Boston v. Seger-Thomschitz

10.1 Background

Oskar Reichel (1869–1943) was a physician and well-known art collector in Vienna, with a particular interest in Austrian modernist painting. An early patron of the expressionist painter Oskar Kokoschka, he purchased many of the artist's works, including *Two Nudes (Lovers)* (1913), which portrays the artist's troubled affair with Alma Mahler.[1] In 1924, and again in 1933, Reichel loaned the painting along with other works for exhibitions at the Neue Galerie in Vienna, authorizing the gallery to sell them if there was an interested buyer.

Following the Anschluss in 1938 Reichel and his family, being Jewish, became the target of Nazi persecution. In 1939, he sold five Kokoschka works, including *Two Nudes*, to Neue Galerie owner Otto Kallir, also Jewish, who by then had fled to Paris following the aryanization of his gallery. Reichel died in 1943, having lost both his business and his house to the Nazis. His wife Malvine was sent to Theriesenstadt and survived the war. Two of their sons escaped Austria and settled abroad; a third was deported and murdered at the Lodz death camp.

Kallir emigrated to America with his inventory in late 1939, and opened the Galerie St. Etienne in New York, which would play a major role in introducing Austrian expressionism to the American public.[2] He sold *Two Nudes* to another gallery in 1945. A private collector acquired the painting in 1947 and kept it for many years, eventually bequeathing it to the Museum of Fine Arts, Boston in 1973.

Reichel's son Raimund returned to Vienna in 1982 and died in 1997. He left everything to his friend Claudia Seger-Thomschitz, who thereby became the sole

[1]On Kokoschka, see generally Vergo (2015); Bruderlin (2014); Weidinger (1996). Reichel was also a patron of Egon Schiele, who painted his portrait in 1910. On Reichel's role in the cultural life of the era, see Harris (2008), p. 334.

[2]See Reagan (2007).

B.L. Hay, *Nazi-Looted Art and the Law*, DOI 10.1007/978-3-319-64967-2_10

surviving heir of Oskar Reichel.[3] In 2003, the city of Vienna returned to Seger-Thomschitz several paintings by Anton Romako, which Reichel had sold to the aryanized Neue Galerie in 1939. The gallery had later sold them to the city. A municipal document explained that the paintings were being returned because Reichel had sold them under duress as a result of Nazi persecution. Shortly afterward, Seger-Thomschitz learned that other artworks from Reichel's collection were located in the United States. In March 2007, she contacted the Museum of Fine Arts, Boston, asserting ownership of *Two Lovers* and requesting its return. Following a nine-month investigation by its curators, the museum informed her that it had decided it held good title to the painting and would not turn it over to her.

10.2 Proceedings

In January 2008, the Museum of Fine Arts filed suit against Seger-Thomschitz to establish its own title to *Two Nudes*, bringing the action in Massachusetts federal court on grounds of diversity of citizenship. In its complaint, the museum requested a judicial declaration that it held valid title to the painting and that Seger-Thomschitz had no claim to it. The museum's complaint made two sets of allegations in support of its position.[4]

First, it contended that Reichel's sale of the painting to Kallir in 1939 had been voluntary. The museum noted that Reichel had previously consigned the painting for sale at Kallir's gallery on two occasions, in 1925 and 1933. It also noted that in 1957, Reichel's surviving sons Hans and Raimund submitted a claim to Austrian authorities seeking compensation for property taken from the family during the Nazi era. The claim asserted that a large collection of paintings by Anton Romako had been sold under duress; however, the application made no mention of any works by Kokoschka. No one in the Reichel family, the museum asserted, ever challenged the sale of *Two Nudes* to Kallir.

Second, the museum contended that the action was time-barred. The painting's whereabouts, the museum stated, had been publicly available information for many decades. The collector who purchased *Two Nudes* in New York in 1947, Sarah Reed Blodgett, loaned it to a series of public exhibitions during the twenty-five years that she owned it. Since acquiring it from her, the museum had kept the work on continuous display as one of its principal modern paintings. The museum had also loaned it for public exhibitions at numerous institutions around the world. For this reason, asserted the museum, the statute of limitations and the equitable doctrine of laches had extinguished whatever claim Reichel's heirs might have had to the painting.

[3] Raimund's brother Hans had died in 1979, leaving everything to him.

[4] See Complaint (filed Jan. 22, 2008), Museum of Fine Arts, Boston v. Seger-Thomschitz, No. 08-cv-10097 (D. Mass.).

Seger-Thomschitz filed a counterclaim for replevin and conversion against the museum, seeking a declaration that she was the rightful owner of the painting and an order that the museum surrender it to her. In support of the claim, she alleged that Reichel had in effect been forced to sell the painting to Kallir.[5] In late 1938, her filing noted, the Nazis pushed Reichel out of the medical profession, closed the family's art gallery, dispossessed him and his family from their home, and ordered him to disclose his assets and to sell his art collection, with the proceeds to be deposited in a blocked account. The filing also noted that the Romako paintings restituted by Austria had been sold to Kallir's former gallery in Vienna at about the same time that the Kokoschkas were sold to Kallir in Paris. The painting's sale under these circumstances in early 1939 was not voluntary, her filing alleged, and title to it remained with Reichel's estate.

Before pretrial discovery had been conducted, the district court granted the museum's motion for summary judgment under the statute of limitations, writing an unpublished opinion.[6] The court ruled that under Massachusetts law, the appropriate limitations period was three years, and that the claim accrued when Reichel's heirs were given reasonable notice of its existence. Both of Reichel's sons had access to the information necessary to bring a claim during their lifetimes, the court opined; in addition, Seger-Thomschitz had access to such information after receiving restituted artworks from the city of Vienna in 2003. Under either measure, the limitations period had elapsed. The court declined the suggestion that it should disregard the statute of limitations on equitable grounds, stating that the 1939 sale may have been voluntary and that courts in other cases involving such "debatable" claims had granted declaratory relief to museums.

The First Circuit court of appeals affirmed the judgment in a published opinion.[7] The statute of limitations, the appeals court ruled, had expired three years after Seger-Thomschitz could reasonably have learned of their claim against the museum, which was no later than 2003. The court rejected Seger-Thomschitz's argument that the Massachusetts statute of limitations should be deemed preempted by federal law because of the museum's tax-exempt status or because of the matter's significance for foreign affairs. Noting the twin objectives of making "restitution" available to legitimate owners and providing current possessors with "repose" against stale claims, the court ruled that the Massachusetts rule struck a reasonable balance between the two. Summary judgment in the museum's favor was therefore proper, the court concluded.

The Supreme Court declined to hear the case.

[5]Answer and Counterclaim (filed May 29, 2008), Museum of Fine Arts, Boston v. Seger-Thomschitz, No. 08-cv-10097 (D. Mass.).

[6]Museum of Fine Arts, Boston v. Seger-Thomschitz, 2009 WL 6506658 (D. Mass. 2009).

[7]Museum of Fine Arts, Boston v. Seger-Thomschitz, 623 F.3d 1 (1st Cir. 2010).

10.3 The Statute of Limitations

The Massachusetts statute of limitations governing replevin and conversion claims provides that "actions of tort, actions of contract to recover for personal injuries, and actions of replevin, shall be commenced only within three years next after the cause of action accrues."[8] Three questions for the courts were first, whether the provision should be disregarded on equitable grounds; second, what constitutes "accrual" in cases of missing or stolen art; and third, when accrual had occurred in Seger-Thomschitz's case.

10.3.1 Law and Equity

For claims brought under the federal courts' diversity jurisdiction, as the district court noted, the applicable statute of limitations is generally the same one that would be applied by the state courts of the forum state.[9] Seger-Thomschitz argued for an exception to this rule on equitable grounds, urging the court to "displace the provincial Massachusetts limitation period with the equitable doctrines of laches and unclean hands."[10] Her argument was that in failing to promptly return the painting to her, the museum was effectively guilty of "aiding, abetting, encouraging and facilitating the illegal and intentional trafficking in stolen art and cultural property."[11] As a result, she argued, the court should employ its inherent equitable powers to prevent the museum (which itself was invoking the court's equitable jurisdiction to grant declaratory relief) from hiding behind the statue of limitations.

In the district court's view, however, the equities favored the museum for three reasons. First, as the court put it, "the alleged illegitimacy of the transfer of the Painting to Kallir in 1939 is not clear-cut."[12] Here the court was apparently impressed by the evidence adduced by the museum, which had taken pains in its motion for summary judgment to make the case that the sale had been voluntary. The museum emphasized that Oskar Reichel's sons Hans and Raimund long knew of the sale to Kallir and never suggested it had been involuntary. Hans, who settled in Illinois, was interviewed and photographed for a 1957 book about Kokoschka and other expressionist painters, which contained the name and location of the painting's owner at the time, Sarah Blodgett.[13] Raimund, who returned to Vienna

---

[8]Mass G.L. c. 260 §2A.

[9]*Seger-Thomschitz*, 2009 WL 6506658, at *5 (citing Molinar v. Western Electric Co., 525 F.2d 521 (1st Cir. 1975). This general rule derives from Guaranty Trust Co. of New York v. York, 326 U.S. 99 (1945).

[10]Quoted in *Seger-Thomschitz*, 2009 WL 6506658, at *5.

[11]*Id.* at *6 (quoting Answer and Counterclaim).

[12]*Seger-Thomschitz*, 2009 WL 6506658, at *6.

[13]Blodgett also owned a Kokoschka portrait of Hans, which had the same provenance as *Two Nudes*. See Section 10.5 below.

after several decades in Argentina, spoke with numerous art historians about his father's Kokoschka collection, and in a 1985 letter referred to *Two Nudes* as having "hung in our dining room." Recalling its sale, his letter continued:

> Before 1914, my father was quite well-to-do; he was laughed at and ridiculed for supporting the "crazy painter." Because of inflation during and after World War I, my father lost a lot of his wealth, e.g., a war bond of 800,000 crowns (gold crowns), etc. In 1938 he transferred his OK paintings (I think there were about ten) to Kallier [sic] when the latter was emigrating to the USA, exporting them was easy, since they were "degenerate," and my father made an arrangement with Kallier to provide the proceeds to my brother who was already over there – Around 1940 or 41 Kallier sent two-hundred-and-fifty dollars, and so my brother sent me half, $125. Some years later I spoke with Kallier in N.Y. in his Galerie St. Etienne, he told me that he lost his shirt for it![14]

Neither brother, the museum pointed out, had ever questioned the sale, despite having sought compensation for other Nazi-era losses. This and other evidence put forth by the museum was enough to persuade the court that the question of the 1939 sale's validity was not "clear cut."[15]

The second reason the equities favored the museum was that the long delay preceding Seger-Thomschitz's claim had deprived the museum, and the court, of information necessary to judge the voluntariness of the sale. Had Reichel's estate taken action earlier, witnesses with direct knowledge of the sale might have been available to describe what had happened. As things stood, the court pointed out, "all of the witnesses with first-hand knowledge of the transfer are now deceased."[16]

Third, the court pointed out, the museum had acted conscientiously when confronted with Seger-Thomschitz's claim, searching for what documentary evidence there was bearing on the validity of its title. "Upon being notified of [her] claim to the painting," the court stated, the museum "embarked upon an investigation into its provenance, with particular attention to Kallir, before asserting its ownership."[17] Here the court may have been impressed by the written report submitted by the museum's provenance curator, who had spent "over half [her] time over the past eighteen months researching the ownership and exhibition history of the Painting, including the history of the Reichel family during the Twentieth Century."[18] The report presented in detail the evidence the investigation had unearthed, including Oskar Reichel's long course of dealings with Kallir and repeated attempts to sell *Two Nudes*. Though the report was inconclusive about the circumstances of the 1939 sale, it may have persuaded the court that the museum

---

[14]Quoted in Memorandum of Points and Authorities in Support of Museum of Fine Arts, Boston's Motion for Summary Judgment (filed Sep. 19, 2008), Museum of Fine Arts, Boston v. Seger-Thomschitz, No. 08-cv-10097 (D. Mass.), at 6.

[15]*Seger-Thomschitz*, 623 F.3d at 6.

[16]*Seger-Thomschitz*, 2009 WL 6506658, at *6.

[17]*Id.*

[18]Declaration of Victoria Reed in Support of Museum of Fine Arts, Boston's Motion for Summary Judgment (filed Sep. 19, 2008), Museum of Fine Arts, Boston v. Seger-Thomschitz, No. 08-cv-10097 (D. Mass.), at 2.

had undertaken an exhaustive search for the available evidence and had presented it fairly.[19]

For these reasons, the court concluded that there were no equitable grounds for suspending or disregarding the statute of limitations in adjudicating the museum's request for declaratory relief. "I find no evidence," the court declared, "of bad faith, laches or unclean hands by the MFA that would justify setting aside the Massachusetts three-year limitations period."[20] The court of appeals did not comment on this aspect of the court's ruling.

10.3.2 The Massachusetts Discovery Rule

The problem for the courts in the Seger-Thomschitz case then became to determine when the three-year limitations period begins running in cases involving a claim for missing or stolen art. With some hesitation on the part of the court of appeals, they settled on the "discovery rule" established in other contexts by the state courts of Massachusetts.

10.3.2.1 The Massachusetts Cases

The leading Massachusetts ruling on the discovery rule is *Bowen v. Eli Lilly*,[21] in which the plaintiff sued in state court for injuries sustained as a result of her mother's ingesting the defendant's product during pregnancy. The plaintiff's mother had taken the anti-miscarriage drug DES, which turned out to be carcinogenic; fourteen years after contracting cancer as an adult, the plaintiff filed a claim against the drug's manufacturer for negligence. On appeal from the issuance of summary judgment in the defendant's favor on statute of limitations grounds, the state's highest court affirmed, holding that the claim had accrued when the plaintiff knew or should have known that she had been injured by the defendant. That point had been reached, according to the court, more than three years before suit was brought. In reaching this decision, the high court surveyed its earlier rulings and extended the reach of the state's discovery rule.

The court began by remarking on the unfairness that would result if a statute of limitations were held to have expired before the plaintiff knew, or even could have known, that she had suffered injury as a result of another's conduct. To avoid such

[19]The court also noted that in suing for declaratory relief rather than turning over the painting, the museum was following the lead of certain peer institutions. *Seger-Thomschitz*, 2009 WL 6506658, at *6 ("Other museums faced with similar claims in which the circumstances of a wartime transfer made the legitimacy of the transfer debatable have also refused to summarily return the artworks and, instead, sought declaratory judgments of ownership.").

[20]*Id.*

[21]557 N.E.2d 739 (Mass. 1990).

unfairness, the court explained, it had "developed (in the absence of a governing statute) a discovery rule for the purpose of determining when a cause of action accrues, and thus when the statute of limitations starts to run," which "prescribes as crucial the date when a plaintiff discovers, or any earlier date when she should reasonably have discovered, that she has been harmed or may have been harmed by the defendant's conduct."[22] The court had first embraced this discovery rule, it observed, in *Hendrickson v. Sears*,[23] involving a property purchaser's malpractice suit against a lawyer who had negligently conducted a title search that, if done properly, would have revealed a legal encumbrance on the property. Though more than three years had elapsed since the negligent search and resulting purchase, the plaintiff's suit against the lawyer was allowed to go forward. Because "the title defect was, in the circumstances, inherently unknowable by his clients," the court later explained, "their cause of action against him did not accrue until they discovered or should reasonably have discovered the attorney's misrepresentations concerning the record title."[24] In so holding the court "declined to apply the rule, then applicable to medical malpractice claims, that the statutory period began to run when the negligent act occurred, even if the plaintiff could not reasonably ascertain the harm until later."[25]

Shortly after the *Hendrickson* decision, the court noted, it applied the rule to a claim of fraudulent misrepresentation in a real estate transaction in *Friedman v. Jablonski*,[26] in which the claim was brought more than three years after the closing of the purchase. The court held that "when the plaintiffs claimed a misrepresentation concerning the existence of a right of way over other property, the plaintiffs had certain obligations of reasonable inquiry and that the decision whether any misrepresentation should reasonably have been uncovered had to be made in light of what reasonable inquiry would have disclosed."[27] As the court later explained, "[w]e concluded that by the time the plaintiffs took title to the property, reasonable inquiry would have shown that there was no right of way, and thus the statute of limitations began to run at that time."[28] And in *Franklin v. Albert*,[29] the court overruled its older decisions that a medical malpractice claim accrues at the time of the physician's negligence, even if the plaintiff could not have discovered it until later. Reasoning that the older decisions were out of step with its more recent rulings, which "recognize the principle that a plaintiff should be put on notice before his claim is barred," the court ruled that "[w]e now extend this principle to medical malpractice actions and hold that

[22] *Id.* at 741.

[23] 310 N.E.2d 131 (Mass. 1974).

[24] *Bowen*, 557 N.E.2d at 741.

[25] *Id.*

[26] 358 N.E.2d 994 (Mass. 1976).

[27] *Bowen*, 557 N.E.2d at 741.

[28] *Id.*

[29] 411 N.E.2d 458 (Mass. 1980).

these causes of action accrue when the plaintiff learns, or reasonably should have learned, that he has been harmed by the defendant's conduct."[30]

The *Bowen* case presented a slightly different problem. In the decisions just canvassed, the plaintiffs did not know they had been injured until more than three years had elapsed; the source of the injury was not in doubt. These cases focused, in the court's words, "on the question whether, in given circumstances, the plaintiffs should reasonably have discovered that they had been harmed," while "there was no significant doubt concerning the cause of the harm once the plaintiffs discovered it."[31] In *Bowen*, the situation was reversed, as it was not the fact of injury but its source that was unknown to the plaintiff for more than three years. "In this case," as the court put it, "the plaintiff was always well aware that she had suffered substantial physical harm," ever since being diagnosed with cancer; "[t]he question is whether she was sufficiently on notice as to the cause of her physical harm."[32] For the statute of limitations to begin running "we do not require that a plaintiff have notice of a breach of a duty," the court held, "but we do require that a plaintiff have (1) knowledge of sufficient notice that she was harmed and (2) knowledge or sufficient notice of what the cause of harm was."[33]

The court then examined the evidence concerning the information that had been available to the plaintiff in the period between 1969, when she contracted a rare form of cancer at the age of twenty, and 1983, when she filed suit against the defendant. In 1971, the plaintiff's mother received a letter from a medical researcher, which the plaintiff read, stating he had found a link between the ingestion of DES by pregnant women and the development of this rare cancer in their daughters. Enclosed with the letter was an academic article he had published on the subject, based in part on the study of her own illness, which the plaintiff read and understood to be "about me."[34] The next year the plaintiff began to keep a file about the emerging controversy over DES, which included a 1976 study, also read by the plaintiff, stating that it had become "clear that the culprit" was DES in numerous cases of the cancer type she had contracted.[35]

From this the court concluded that the trial court had properly entered summary judgment for the defendant, because "the prospect of a significant causal connection between DES and the plaintiff's cancer was brought to the plaintiff's attention more than three years before this action was commenced."[36] This was true even though the plaintiff had said that it was only in 1982, a year before filing suit, that she came to believe that the drug had caused her injuries. "The fact that it was not until June, 1982, that the plaintiff believed that DES caused her cancer does not aid her because we test

[30] *Id.* at 619.

[31] *Bowen*, 557 N.E.2d at 741.

[32] *Id.*

[33] *Id.* at 742.

[34] *Id.* at 743.

[35] *Id.*

[36] *Id.*

the accrual of her cause of action by what a reasonable person in her position would have known or on an inquiry would have discovered" in the years before then.[37] "In this case," the court declared, "the plaintiff was aware not only of numerous articles published in the popular media but also she knew of scientific opinion, based in part on the plaintiff's own circumstances, stating that there was the prospect of a causal link between DES and the rare vaginal cancer from which she suffered."[38] By the same token, the plaintiff could have determined that it was the defendant, as manufacturer of the drug, who was responsible for her injuries. "Evidence of the manufacturer's identity," the court stated, "had been readily available at all times through the pharmacist who sold the DES to the plaintiff's mother"; this was "a fact as to which the plaintiff had a duty of inquiry based on the information concerning causation that she had."[39]

10.3.2.2 Applicability to Missing Art Cases

The district court in Seger-Thomschitz's case treated it as uncontroversial that the discovery rule applied to her claim, perhaps because the parties did not dispute that issue. Seger-Thomschitz did argue that her case should be controlled by Massachusetts' six-year statute of limitation for contract actions rather than the three-year statute for tort actions, but the court rejected this out of hand, noting that she "did not allege the existence of any agreement" between herself and the museum; rather, her claim alleged "that the MFA wrongfully obtained property belonging to her and that she now seeks its return."[40] That claim, the court declared, "sounds clearly in tort, not contract, and thus is subject to the three-year statute of limitations period."[41] Under Massachusetts law, the court further stated, "the general rule is that causes of action in tort accrue when the plaintiff is injured. However, under the discovery rule exception, the limitations period does not begin to run in circumstances where 'the plaintiff did not know or could not reasonably have known that he or she may have been harmed by the conduct of another.'"[42]

The court of appeals was less certain about the matter, remarking that "the discovery rule is not the only possible way of measuring accrual in a missing art case," and that a "number of alternative approaches" had been proposed.[43] It noted in particular New York's adoption of the demand and refusal rule, under which a claim to recover stolen artwork from an innocent purchaser "does not accrue until there has been a demand for, and a refusal to surrender, the property."[44] Referring to

---

[37]*Id.*

[38]*Id.*

[39]*Id.*

[40]*Seger-Thomschitz*, 2009 WL 6506658, at *6.

[41]*Id.*

[42]*Id.* (quoting Koe v. Mercer, 876 N.E.2d 831, 836 (Mass. 2007) (other citations omitted)).

[43]*Seger-Thomschitz*, 623 F.3d at 7, citing Hawkins et al. (1995) and Bibas (1994).

[44]*Seger-Thomschitz*, 623 F.2d at 7 n. 7, citing Solomon R. Guggenheim Foundation v. Lubell, 569 N.E.2d 426 (N.Y. 1991). See generally chap. 8 above.

a series of authorities on the subject of conversion, the court of appeals expressed the view that the "case law suggests that such a rule could potentially be applied in Massachusetts as well."[45] But neither Seger-Thomschitz nor the museum had raised the issue, and the court decided not to pursue the matter on its own. Because "the parties do not contest the district court's decision to apply it here," stated the court, "[w]e therefore follow the district court's lead in applying the discovery rule to Seger-Thomschitz's counterclaims."[46]

10.3.3 The Claim's Tardiness

Having determined that the case was governed by the discovery rule, the courts next had to decide whether the museum was entitled to summary judgment on the ground that Reichel's heirs had notice of their claim more than three years before suit was filed in 2007. They answered in the affirmative, for a number of reasons.

First, Oskar Reichel's family had long known of the circumstances of the 1939 sale of *Two Nudes* to Kallir, including whatever element of duress or coercion was present in the transaction. "Here," the district court declared, "the evidence is undisputed that the members of the Reichel family had sufficient knowledge of Reichel's ownership and transfer of the Painting to put them on notice of a possible injury long before [Seger-Thomschitz] contacted the MFA."[47] Oskar's son Raimund later said, the district court noted, that in 1940 or 1941 he and his brother had received $250 from Kallir in connection from the sale, and "recalled visiting Kallir at his New York gallery after WWII and discussing the Painting and its sale with him."[48] Furthermore, the district court observed, "although the Reichel family never claimed compensation for any of the Kokoschka works that had been transferred to Kallir for sale, it did claim restitution for artwork and property that had been seized by the Nazis," receiving "compensation for the forced sale of [the family home], and both Raimund and Hans submitted applications for compensation for their father's Romako collection, which he was admittedly forced to sell."[49] Given this evidence, the district court concluded, and the court of appeals agreed, that Reichel's immediate family "had ample notice of any possible claim to the Painting decades before the filing of this lawsuit."[50]

Second, Seger-Thomschitz, who became the family's sole heir after Raimund's death in 1997, also had ample notice of any possible claim to the painting. "Even if

---

[45] *Id.* (citing Atlantic Finance Corp. v. Galvam, 39 N.E.2d 951 (Mass. 1942), In re Halmar Distributors, 968 F.2d 121 (1st Cir. 1992), and Keeton et al. (1984)).

[46] *Seger-Thomschitz*, 623 F.3d at 7.

[47] *Seger-Thomschitz*, 2009 WL 6506658, at *7.

[48] *Id.*

[49] *Id.*

[50] *Id.* at *8, quoted in *Seger-Thomschitz*, 623 F.3d at 8.

the limitations period was tolled during Raimund's lifetime for some reason," the district court stated, Seger-Thomschitz "is still barred because she waited more than three years to assert her claim after she was put on inquiry notice of her possible right to the Painting."[51] She "first learned that the Nazis had confiscated artworks from Oskar Reichel in the Fall of 2003 when the Museums of Vienna contacted her concerning their intent to return to her as the sole heir of Oskar Reichel four artworks in their collection by the artist Anton Romako," the court noted, and "[a]lthough she disclaims any specialized knowledge or familiarity with the art world, she understood that she had a claim to paintings formerly belonging to Reichel and, in fact, retained counsel in 2004, well within the limitations period, 'for all purposes relating to the restitution of artworks lost by Oskar Reichel due to Nazi persecution.'"[52] Referring to the property declaration the Nazis had extracted from Oskar Reichel in 1938, which had included the contents of his art collection, the district court further noted that the "Austrian government had made Property Declarations generally available in 1998; therefore, Reichel's declaration (showing his ownership of the Painting) was accessible in 2003."[53] Accordingly, in the district court's view, the "information necessary to pursue her claim was readily available to both [Seger-Thomschitz] and her counsel at that time."[54] The court of appeals agreed, remarking that Austria's 2003 restitution of Romako's paintings "put her on notice that she might have a claim to other artworks that were previously owned by Dr. Reichel."[55]

Third, information concerning the whereabouts of *Two Nudes* had been readily available for many years. "In contrast to many missing art cases," the court of appeals stated, echoing the district court, "the location of the Painting has been no secret in this case."[56] Raimund Reichel remained in touch with Kallir after the latter sold the painting in New York in the mid-1940s, and could easily have tracked down the subsequent owners; the painting had been lent out for numerous public exhibitions, including one in Vienna after Raimund had resettled there. Since its acquisition by the museum in 1983 the painting had been on nearly continuous public display there, and from 2000 onward had been listed on the museum's website together with information concerning Oskar Reichel's previous ownership of it. In addition, several books and catalogues raisonnés of Kokoschka's works, and other resources such as the online Getty Provenance Index, indicated the work's provenance and current owner. "Although the availability of these sources may not have been obvious to Seger-Thomschitz, who is a nurse with no specialized training in Nazi-era art claims, that fact does not excuse her delay," the court of appeals ruled, adding that it "was her burden under Massachusetts law to discover from the

[51] *Seger-Thomschitz*, 2009 WL 6506658, at *8.

[52] *Id.* at 9 (quoting Answer and Counterclaim).

[53] *Seger-Thomschitz*, 2009 WL 6506658, at *9.

[54] *Id.*

[55] *Seger-Thomschitz*, 623 F.3d at 8.

[56] *Id.* at 7.

relevant professional communities" the whereabouts of Reichel's former collection and whether she had a claim to any of its contents.[57]

Finally, summary judgment was appropriate, in the courts' view, because there was no real dispute between the parties on the foregoing facts. In opposition to summary judgment, Seger-Thomschitz contended that there should be a jury trial on the statute of limitations issue, with the jury instructed to determine whether her claim had accrued more than three years before the claim was filed. Determining the time of accrual, she argued, requires weighing the evidence concerning what information was available to the Reichel heirs and when; "because the discovery rule is fact intensive," she continued, "juries—rather than the court—should determine when plaintiffs knew or should have been aware of their claims."[58] But the court of appeals, again echoing the district court, rejected this argument, noting that while a jury trial is often required in cases involving conflicting evidence, "summary judgment may be granted on a limitations defense if there is no *genuine* dispute about the material facts, and the record evidence would not permit a reasonable jury to return a verdict for the nonmoving party."[59] That was the situation here, in the court of appeals' view. "Any reasonable jury confronted with the [evidentiary] record," it declared, would conclude that Seger-Thomschitz's causes of action accrued no later than the fall of 2003, "when she learned that the Nazis had confiscated artworks from Dr. Reichel, and could then, with reasonable diligence, have discovered her claim to the Painting."[60] For this reason, the court concluded, there was no need for a jury trial on the matter, and the district court had properly entered summary judgment in the museum's favor.[61]

10.4 Federal Common Law Time Limits

An additional question considered by the court of appeals was whether the state statute of limitations should be deemed preempted by federal law, to be replaced by a federal common law rule of laches. Contending that the federal courts "enjoy special common law authority to fashion appropriate rules of decision when the rights and duties of federally chartered or supported institutions are at issue," Seger-Thomschitz urged the court of appeals to deem the state limitations preempted on the basis of the museum's status as a charitable organization exempt from federal taxation.[62] Her argument was that the federal government has a strong interest in

[57] *Id.* at 9.

[58] Quoted in *id.*

[59] *Id.* (emphasis in original).

[60] *Id.*

[61] The courts' conclusions are criticized in Kreder (2012), pp. 110–114.

[62] Brief of Defendant-Appellant, Museum of Fine Arts, Boston v. Seger-Thomschitz, No. 09-1922 (1st Cir. Sep. 30, 2009), at 46.

ensuring that charitable organizations act in such a way as to produce the public benefits for which they are subsidized with tax exemptions, and that by failing "to take reasonable precautions against acquiring stolen artworks or other illicit contraband in their public collections," the museum and its peer institutions were engaged in behavior that "undermines their role as public trustees and the prescribed 'public benefit' that their exempt activities might otherwise confer," making "taxpayer-supported museums repositories of untold quantities of stolen art and illicit cultural property," and fueling "the thriving international criminal commerce in stolen art, cultural property and antiquities."[63] These federal interests were compromised, she argued, by reliance on a state statute of limitations that insulated the museum from suit.

The court of appeals rejected this argument, relying primarily on recent pronouncements by the Supreme Court that "the judiciary should create special federal common law rules in 'few and restricted' cases,"[64] because "[w]hether latent federal power should be exercised to displace state law is primarily a decision for Congress, not the federal courts."[65] Though the federal courts do have the power in appropriate circumstances to promulgate rules of their own devising to displace state law, the court of appeals emphasized that to "justify the application of a federal common law rule, the proponent must typically show that there is a 'significant conflict between some federal policy or interest and the use of state law.'"[66] Seger-Thomschitz, the court determined for reasons to be explored here, failed to demonstrate the existence of the necessary conflict.

10.4.1 The Jurisprudence of Federal Common Law

The court of appeals took its bearings from two recent Supreme Court decisions concerning the promulgation of federal common law rules, the first being *O'Melveny & Myers v. Federal Deposit Insurance Corporation*.[67] In that case, the Federal Deposit Insurance Corporation (FDIC), an independent agency of the federal government, took control of an insolvent savings and loan institution in California and placed it in receivership. As receiver, the agency brought suit in federal court against the law firm that had worked for the savings and loan, accusing it of committing malpractice and breach of fiduciary duty by failing to prevent certain fraudulent acts by the corporation's officers. In its defense, the law firm

[63] *Id.* at 49.

[64] *Seger-Thomschitz*, 623 F.3d at 10 (quoting O'Melveny & Myers v. FDIC, 512 U.S. 79, 87 (1994)).

[65] Atherton v. FDIC, 519 U.S. 213, 218 (1997), quoted in *Seger-Thomschitz*, 623 F.3d at 10 (internal quotation marks omitted).

[66] *Id.* at 10 (quoting Wallis v. Pan American Petroleum Corp., 384 U.S. 63, 68 (1966)).

[67] 512 U.S. 79 (1994).

invoked a principle of California corporate law according to which a corporate officer's knowledge of his own actions is imputed to the corporation; applying this principle to the case would mean that the savings and loan (and hence its receiver) was estopped, or barred, from bringing the malpractice suit. In response, the FDIC argued that federal common law, not California law, should determine whether the knowledge of a corporate officer acting against the corporation's interests should be imputed to the corporation.

The case eventually reached the Supreme Court. In a rather derisive opinion, the Court ruled that the imputed knowledge issue should be governed by California law, not by a court-fashioned rule of federal common law. In suing the defendant for malpractice and breach of fiduciary duty, the Court began by observing, the FDIC was bringing claims based on California law; the case did not arise under, or involve enforcement of, any federal statute. This meant, under the familiar precept that "[t]here is no federal general common law," that questions of substantive law, including corporate law questions concerning imputed knowledge, must ordinarily be governed by state law.[68] The exception to this rule, according to the Court, comes when the otherwise applicable state law rule conflicts significantly with a federal policy or interest, in which case courts can displace state law with a "special federal rule."[69] "Our cases," it stated, "uniformly require the existence of such a conflict as a precondition for recognition of a federal rule of decision."[70]

The Court was unconvinced by the FDIC's arguments that such a conflict was created by the California imputation rule. It rejected the agency's contention that the state rule should be disregarded for the sake of national uniformity in the agency's work, responding that if state laws could be set aside on that basis then "we would be awash in 'federal common-law' rules," because variation in state law is a characteristic feature of the federal system.[71] It also rejected the agency's argument that the California rule should give way for the sake of the financial soundness of the federal deposit insurance fund, which the Court dismissed as "a broad principle indeed, which would support not just the elimination of the defense at issue here, but judicial creation of new, 'federal common-law' causes of action to enrich the fund."[72] The courts have no authority to do that, the Court declared, "because there is no federal policy that the fund should always win."[73] Finally, the Court rejected the agency's contention that applying the state rule would harm federal interests by insulating attorney malpractice from liability, responding that the regulation of legal services "involves a host of considerations that must be weighed and appraised," a task for which federal judges are ill-equipped and "is

[68] *O'Melveny & Myers*, 512 U.S. at 83 (quoting Erie Railroad. Co. v. Tompkins, 304 U.S. 64, 78 (1938)).

[69] *O'Melveny & Myers*, 512 U.S. at 87.

[70] *Id.*

[71] *Id.* at 88.

[72] *Id.*

[73] *Id.*

more appropriately for those who write the laws, rather than for those who interpret them."[74] The agency's case against the law firm, the Court concluded, "is not one of those extraordinary cases in which the judicial creation of a federal rule of decision is warranted."[75]

The Court confronted a related issue a few years later in a second case, *Atherton v. Federal Deposit Insurance Corporation*.[76] There the FDIC took over a failed savings and loan in New Jersey and, acting as receiver, sued its officers and directors in federal court for breaching their duty to the bank by making a series of imprudent loans. One question that arose in the case concerned the standard of care applicable to the defendants' behavior: in particular, the question was whether their actions should be judged according to a simple negligence standard, a gross negligence standard, or some other measure of culpability. On this question, the FDIC took the position that, rather than letting state law supply the governing standard of care, the judiciary should fashion its own federal common law standard. The court of appeals for the Third Circuit accepted the FDIC's argument, holding that in breach-of-duty cases brought against officers and directors of federally chartered savings institutions, the applicable standard of care should be furnished by federal common law rather than state law.

The Supreme Court reversed. In an opinion more thoughtful and nuanced than the one it had issued in the *O'Melveny* decision, it explored the possible rationales for federal common law making and concluded that they did not, in the circumstances of the case, warrant displacing the applicable state laws concerning the duties of corporate officers and directors. The central question, the Court stated, was "whether the application of state-law standards of care to [federally chartered savings associations] would conflict with, and thereby significantly threaten, a federal policy or interest."[77] The considerations raised by the FDIC in support of a judge-made federal standard did not meet this threshold, in the Court's view. The first such consideration was the need for uniform treatment of savings institutions, which was undermined by a patchwork system of divergent state legal standards. To this the Court replied that the value of uniformity was easily overstated, and that "our Nation's banking has thrived despite disparities in matters of corporate governance."[78] State-chartered savings institutions, were subject to divergent standards of care for their directors and officers, some facing liability only for willful or reckless misconduct, others for simple negligence; these disparities had hardly created havoc in the financial system. Indeed, the Court noted, federal regulators themselves allow "considerable disparity in the standard of care" applicable to financial institutions other than savings banks of the type at issue in the present case.[79]

---

[74]*Id.* at 89 (quoting Northwest Airlines, Inc. v. Transport Workers, 451 U.S. 77, 98 n. 41 (1981) (internal quotation marks omitted)).

[75]*O'Melveny & Myers*, 512 U.S. at 89.

[76]519 U.S. 217 (1997).

[77]*Id.* at 219.

[78]*Id.* at 220.

[79]*Id.* at 221.

The fact that certain savings institutions were federally chartered, the Court stated, did not warrant creation of special federal common law rules for them. Earlier in the nation's history there might have been some justification for federal common lawmaking, given that before the civil war federally chartered banks were rare and often "encountered hostility and deleterious state laws,"[80] leading the Court in *McCulloch v. Maryland*[81] to impose strict limits on state jurisdiction over them. After the civil war, however, federally chartered institutions became much more common, and "thereafter this Court held that federally chartered banks are subject to state law."[82] In a long series of decisions, the Court noted, it had held that states could regulate such institutions, provided that the laws in question were "general and undiscriminating" and did not "conflict with the letter or the general objects and purposes of Congressional legislation,"[83] did not "interfere with the purposes of [the federally chartered banks'] creation,"[84] and did not "impose an undue burden on the performance of the banks' functions."[85] The lesson of these decisions, the Court stated, was that "[t]o point to a federal charter by itself shows no conflict, threat or need for 'federal common law.'"[86]

Nor, in the Court's view, would effective federal regulation of savings institutions be impaired by allowing states to set standards of care applicable to breach-of-duty lawsuits against their directors and officers. The FDIC called the Court's attention to the "internal affairs doctrine," a "conflict of laws principle which recognizes that only one State should have the authority to regulate a corporation's internal affairs," because "otherwise a corporation could be faced with conflicting demands."[87] This doctrine did not demonstrate "a need to create federal common law," in the Court's view, because "it seeks only to avoid conflict by requiring that there be a single point of legal reference"; though it calls for a single source of law setting forth management's duty of care, "[n]othing in that doctrine suggests that the single source of law must be federal."[88] For these and other reasons, the Court could "find no significant conflict with, or threat to, a federal interest" requiring the displacement of state law by federal common law.[89]

---

[80] *Id.* at 221.

[81] 4 Wheat. 316 (1819).

[82] *Atherton*, 519 U.S. at 222.

[83] Davis v. Elmira Savings Bank, 161 U.S. 275, 290 (1896), quoted in *Atherton*, 519 U.S. at 223.

[84] First National Bank in St. Louis v. Missouri, 263 U.S. 640, 656 (1924), quoted in *Atherton*, 519 U.S. at 223.

[85] Anderson National Bank v. Luckett, 321 U.S. 233, 248 (1944), quoted in *Atherton*, 519 U.S. at 223.

[86] *Id.*

[87] Edgar v. MITE Corp., 457 U.S. 624, 645 (1982), quoted in *Atherton*, 519 U.S. at 224.

[88] *Id.*

[89] *Id.* at 225.

10.4.2 The Court of Appeals Decision

Following the lead of the *O'Melveny* and *Atherton* decisions, the court of appeals found that Seger-Thomschitz had not made the case for substituting a federal common law rule for the state statute of limitations. Her argument, as the court summarized it, was that "the federal government has a compelling interest in 'ensuring that charitable organizations that operate as tax exempt entities provide the public with the benefits for which their tax exemptions were granted,'" and that museums "have 'undermined the rationale for their tax exemptions' by consistently failing to investigate the provenance of the artworks they acquire, thereby facilitating commerce in stolen artworks and other contraband."[90] Because statutes of limitations such as that of Massachusetts enable museums to shield stolen art from recovery by the rightful owners, she argued, the federal courts "are empowered to formulate appropriate rules of accrual in lawsuits seeking to reclaim Nazi-confiscated artworks in the possession of U.S. tax-exempt museums that will encourage these museums to operate lawfully."[91]

The court was not persuaded. "On this record," it declared, "Seger-Thomschitz's argument asks too much of the federal courts and the federal tax code."[92] The court noted that tax-exempt organizations, like non-exempt organizations, are pervasively regulated by state law, for example by the application of state antidiscrimination laws to their employment activities. In the case of a museum, it observed, its trustees were bound by common law fiduciary duties—not unlike those at issue in the *O'Melveny* and *Atherton* case—to avoid the types of wrongdoing of which Seger-Thomschitz accused the museum in the present case. By an act of "legislative grace," the federal government has decreed that nonprofit institutions such as the museum are not required to pay federal tax on their income.[93] Though the federal tax code does require an organization to adhere to certain standards to qualify for tax-exempt status, the court stated, "those standards do not justify a free-ranging superintendence by the federal courts" of the organization's activities.[94] If a tax-exempt organization fails to satisfy its obligations under the tax code, its tax-exempt status can be revoked and, in extreme cases, its operators may be subject to federal civil or criminal penalties. These protective devices, in the court's view, sufficed to safeguard the "federal interest in ensuring that tax-exempt organizations 'demonstrably serve and be in harmony with the public interest.'"[95] Because it could "perceive no need to create additional federal common law rules to punish and deter bad behavior by tax-exempt organizations, as Seger-Thomschitz

---

[90] *Seger-Thomschitz*, 623 F.3d at 10 (quoting appellant's brief) (internal brackets omitted).

[91] *Id.* (quoting appellant's brief).

[92] *Id.*

[93] IHC Health Plans, Inc. v. Commissioner of Internal Revenue, 325 F.3d 1188, 1193 (10th Cir. 2003), quoted in *Seger-Thomschitz*, 623 F.3d at 10.

[94] *Id.* at 11.

[95] Bob Jones University v. United States, 461 U.S. 574, 592 (1982), quoted in *Seger-Thomschitz*, 623 F.3d at 11.

proposes," the court ruled that it would "decline her invitation to replace, on that basis, the Massachusetts limitations period with a federal common lawlaches defense."[96]

10.5 Foreign Affairs Preemption

Seger-Thomschitz also argued that the state statute of limitations should be disregarded on the ground that it conflicted with the foreign policy of the United States government. The strict three-year limitations period was preempted, she argued, by the Holocaust Victims Redress Act of 1998, a federal statute; and also by three international conventions adopted by the federal government, the Washington Conference Principles on Nazi-Confiscated Art, the Vilnius Forum Declaration, and the Terezín Declaration on Holocaust Era Assets and Related Issues.[97] Her argument rested on *American Insurance Association v. Garamendi*,[98] in which the Supreme Court held that a California law designed to facilitate Holocaust-related claims against insurance companies conflicted with, and was therefore preempted by, some international accords on the subject entered into by the federal government.

The court of appeals rejected the argument. The *Garamendi* case stands for the proposition, declared the court, that a "'state law must give way' when it is in 'clear conflict' with an 'express federal policy' in the foreign affairs context."[99] That principle was "inapposite" to the Massachusetts statute of limitations, in the court's view, for two reasons: first, in contrast to the federal compensation accords that preempted the California legislation in *Garamendi*, there was no "comparably express federal policy bearing on" the matter of limitations periods for bringing suit; and second, "even if there were such a policy, the Massachusetts statute of limitations would not be in clear conflict with it."[100]

Federal Policy The federal documents relied on by Seger-Thomschitz for her preemption argument, the court stated, "are, for the most part, phrased in general terms evincing no particular hostility toward generally applicable statutes of limitations," such as that of Massachusetts.[101] The Holocaust Victims Redress Act of

[96]*Id.*

[97]This was related to but distinct from the argument, rejected a few years earlier by the Ninth Circuit in *Orkin v. Taylor*, 487 F.3d 734, 739–41 (9th Cir. 2007), that federal law created an independent cause of action for the recovery of art lost to Nazi persecution. See Section 5.3 above.

[98]539 U.S. 396 (2003).

[99]*Seger-Thomschitz*, 623 F.3d at 11 (quoting American Insurance Association v. Garamendi, 539 U.S. 396, 421 (2003)).

[100]*Seger-Thomschitz*, 623 F.3d at 12.

[101]*Id.* Here the court implicitly distinguished the case from Von Saher v. Norton Simon Museum of Art at Pasadena, 592 F.3d 954 (9th Cir. 2009), in which the a state statute of limitations that singled out Nazi-looted art claims was found invalid under the foreign affairs preemption doctrine. See Section 6.3 above.

1998, in the court's view, "merely expresses the 'sense of the Congress' that 'all governments should undertake good faith efforts to facilitate the return' of Nazi-confiscated property."[102] The Washington Conference Principles on Nazi-Confiscated Art "state that when Nazi-confiscated artwork is identified, 'steps should be taken expeditiously to achieve a just and fair solution, recognizing this may vary according to the facts and circumstances surrounding a specific case.'"[103] The Vilnius Forum Declaration "'asks all governments to undertake every reasonable effort to achieve the restitution of cultural assets looted during the Holocaust' and recognizes that 'solution may vary according to the differing legal systems among countries and the circumstances surrounding a specific case.'"[104] The court could "discern no express federal policy disfavoring statutes of limitations in the general language of those documents."[105]

A more colorable argument for preemption could be found in the Terezín Declaration, according to the court. The signatories to the Declaration, including the United States, took the position that looted art claims should be resolved on the basis of their "facts and merits" with an eye toward achieving "just and fair solutions" based on consideration of "all the relevant documents" and "all relevant issues":

> [W]e urge all stakeholders to ensure that their legal systems of alternative processes, while taking into account different legal traditions, facilitate just and fair solutions with regard to Nazi-confiscated and looted art, and to make certain that claims to recover such art are resolved expeditiously and based on the facts and merits of the claims and all the relevant documents submitted by all parties. Governments should consider all relevant issues when applying various legal provisions that may impede the restitution of art and cultural property, in order to achieve just and fair solutions, as well as alternative dispute resolution, where appropriate under law.[106]

Though this statement "reflects a clear preference that Nazi-era art disputes should be resolved 'based on the facts and the merits' rather than legal technicalities," the court of appeals stated, its language was nevertheless "too general and too hedged to be used as evidence for an express federal policy disfavoring statutes of limitations."[107] The signatories' "preference for the resolution of claims on the merits does not mean that all time limitations should be abandoned"; moreover, "the Terezín Declaration recognizes that 'various legal provisions that may impede the restitution of art and cultural property' will continue to be applied," for which the

[102]*Seger-Thomschitz*, 623 F.3d at 12–13 (quoting Holocaust Victims Redress Act, Pub. L. No. 105-158 § 202, 112 Stat. 15, 17–18 (1998)).

[103]*Seger-Thomschitz*, 623 F.3d at 13 (quoting U.S. Dept. of State, The Washington Conference on Holocaust Era Assets, Washington Principles on Nazi-Confiscated Art (Dec. 3, 1998)).

[104]*Seger-Thomschitz*, 623 F.3d at 13 (quoting Vilnius International Forum on Holocaust-Era Looted Cultural Assets, Vilnius Forum Declaration (Oct. 5, 2000)).

[105]*Seger-Thomschitz*, 623 F.3d at 13.

[106]Prague Holocaust Era Assets Conference, Terezín Declaration (June 30, 2009), quoted in *Seger-Thomschitz*, 623 F.3d at 13.

[107]*Id.*

"proposed solution is for governments applying such provisions to 'consider all relevant issues ... in order to achieve just and fair solutions,'" the court stated.[108] "None of this language," it concluded, "is sufficiently clear and definite to constitute evidence of an express federal policy against the applicability of state statutes of limitations to claims for the recovery of lost, stolen, or confiscated art."[109]

State Law Even if the above federal documents were read to contain "an express federal policy disfavoring overly rigid timeliness requirements," continued the court of appeals, "the Massachusetts statute of limitations would not be in 'clear conflict' with that policy."[110] The *Garamendi* decision indicated, the court observed, "that it is appropriate to 'consider the strength of the state interest, judged by standards of traditional practice, when deciding how serious a conflict must be shown before declaring the state law preempted.'"[111] So viewed, according to the court, the interests of Massachusetts in having its limitations period enforced were considerable. "The enactment of generally applicable statutes of limitations is a traditional state prerogative, and states have a substantial interest in preventing their laws from being used to pursue stale claims," the court stated.[112] "In that sense," it continued, "the statute in this case is unlike the law in *Garamendi*, which 'effectively singled out only policies issued by European companies, in Europe, to European residents, at least fifty-five years ago.'"[113]

In addition, the court stated, the state's statute of limitations was compatible, rather than in conflict, with the policy aims set forth in the Terezín Declaration and other federal documents it had described. In its view, "the Massachusetts statute of limitations, as tempered by the discovery rule, is flexible and sensitive to the facts of each case," and "strikes a reasonable balance between restitution and repose, permitting a claimant who has diligently pursued her rights to have her day in court."[114] The Massachusetts rule's attentiveness to circumstances eliminated the rigidity that Seger-Thomschitz attributed to it. "Indeed," the court declared, "because a claimant in a missing or confiscated art case may be able to defeat [a statute of limitations defense] by demonstrating that she diligently pursued her property, the Massachusetts discovery rule may not be that different in practice from the federal common lawlaches defense that Seger-Thomschitz would like us to apply."[115] The court accordingly concluded that the "Massachusetts statute of limitations is not preempted under *Garamendi*."[116]

---

[108] *Id.*

[109] *Id.*

[110] *Id.*

[111] *Id.* (quoting *Garamendi*, 539 U.S. at 420).

[112] *Seger-Thomschitz*, 623 F.3d at 13–14.

[113] *Id.* (brackets omitted) (quoting *Garamendi*, 539 U.S. at 425–26).

[114] *Seger-Thomschitz*, 623 F.3d at 14.

[115] *Id.*

[116] *Id.*

Final Remarks The court closed its opinion by asserting the justice of the result, emphasizing the salutary function of time limits. "Statutes of limitations defenses, even when tempered by a discovery rule, may preclude otherwise meritorious claims," it remarked, and by their nature "are somewhat arbitrary in their choice of a particular time period for asserting a claim."[117] And yet such rules "cannot be fairly characterized as technicalities," for they "are found and approved in all systems of enlightened jurisprudence, represent[ing] a pervasive legislative judgment that it is unjust to fail to put the adversary on notice to defend within a specified period of time and that the right to be free of stale claims in time comes to prevail over the right to prosecute them"; statutes of limitations are built on the recognition that "search for truth may be seriously impaired by the loss of evidence, whether by death or disappearance of witnesses, fading memories, disappearance of documents, or otherwise."[118]

But the court also had a note of caution for museums. "Although we make no judgment about the legality of the MFA's acquisition of the Painting in 1973," it stated, "we note the MFA's own disclosure that, when confronted with Seger-Thomschitz's claim, it initiated a provenance investigation for the Painting that it had not done before."[119] The museum's delay in examining the provenance of *Two Nudes* "may have been legally inconsequential in this case," it stated.[120] "However," the court declared, "for works of art with unmistakable roots in the Holocaust era, museums would now be well-advised to follow the guidelines of the American Association of Museums: 'museums should take all reasonable steps to resolve the Nazi-era provenance status of objects before acquiring them for their collections—whether by purchase, gift, bequest, or exchange.'"[121] The passage of time, the court seemed to warn, would not necessarily bar future lawsuits.[122]

10.6 Epilogue

Concurrently with the proceeding in Boston, Seger-Thomschitz sought to recover another Kokoschka painting, *Portrait of Youth* (1910), from a collector in New Orleans. The painting, which depicts Oskar Reichel's son Hans, formed part of the

---

[117] *Id.*

[118] *Id.* (quoting United States v. Kubrick, 444 U.S. 111, 117 (1979)).

[119] *Seger-Thomschitz*, 623 F.3d at 14.

[120] *Id.*

[121] *Id.* (quoting American Association of Museums 1999).

[122] In the Holocaust Expropriated Art Recovery Act of 2016, enacted several years after this case came to a close, Congress determined that to "further United States policy as set forth in the Washington Conference Principles on Nazi-Confiscated Art, the Holocaust Victims Redress Act, and the Terezín Declaration," state statutes of limitations would be preempted by a federal limitations period beginning with a claim's actual discovery by the claimants. Holocaust Expropriated Art Recovery Act, Pub. L. 114–308 (Dec. 16, 2016), § (3)(1). See Chap. 15.

1939 transfer to Kallir, and was purchased at his New York gallery by the collector's mother in 1946. The collector brought an action for declaratory relief in federal district court in Louisiana, which ruled that Seger-Thomschitz's claim was untimely under Louisiana's law of prescriptive ownership. On appeal, the Fifth Circuit rejected Seger-Thomschitz's arguments that the Louisiana prescription period should be deemed preempted by federal law, writing a short opinion whose reasoning was similar to the First Circuit's ruling that the Massachusetts statute of limitations was not preempted.[123]

Kokoschka's *Two Nudes (Lovers)* remains in the Rabb Gallery of the Museum of Fine Arts, Boston.

References

American Association of Museums. 1999. Recommended Procedures for Providing Information to the Public About Objects Transferred in Europe During the Nazi Era. Accessed July 1, 2017. http://www.aam-us.org/docs/default-source/professional-resources/nepip-recommended-procedures.

Bibas, Steven A. 1994. The Case against Statutes of Limitations for Stolen Art. *Yale Law Journal* 103: 2437–2470.

Bruderlin, Markus. 2014. *Oskar Kokoschka: Humanist und Rebell.* Munich: Hirmer Verlag.

Harris, Constance. 2008. *The Way Jews Lived: Five Hundred Years of Printed Words and Images.* Jefferson, NC: McFarland.

Hawkins, Ashton, Richard A. Rothman, and David B. Goldstein. 1995. A Tale of Two Innocents: Creating an Equitable Balance Between the Rights of Former Owners and Good Faith Purchasers of Stolen Art. *Fordham Law Review* 64: 49–96.

Keeton, W. Page, Dan B. Dobbs, Robert W. Keeton, and David G. Owen. 1984. *Prosser and Keeton on Torts.* 5th ed. Saint Paul, MN: West Publishing.

Kreder, Jennifer Anglim. 2012. Fighting Corruption of the Historical Record: Nazi-Looted Art Litigation. *Kansas Law Review* 61: 75–137.

Reagan, Gillian. 2007. Dealer with the Devil. *Observer*, September 11.

Vergo, Peter. 2015. *Art in Vienna 1898-1918: Klimt, Kokoschka, Schiele and Their Contemporaries.* 4th ed. New York: Phaidon.

Weidinger, Alfred. 1996. *Kokoschka and Alma Mahler: Testimony of a Passionate Relationship.* New York: Prestel.

Cases

American Insurance Association v. Garamendi, 539 U.S. 396 (2003)

Anderson National Bank v. Luckett, 321 U.S. 233 (1944)

Atherton v. FDIC, 519 U.S. 213 (1997)

Atlantic Finance Corp. v. Galvam, 39 N.E.2d 951 (Mass. 1942)

Bob Jones University v. United States, 461 U.S. 574 (1982)

[123]Dunbar v. Seger-Thomschitz, 615 F.3d 574 (5th Cir. 2010).

Bowen v. Eli Lilly, 557 N.E.2d 739 (Mass. 1990)
Crosby v. National Foreign Trade Council, 530 U.S. 363 (2000)
Davis v. Elmira Savings Bank, 161 U.S. 275 (1896)
Dunbar v. Seger-Thomschitz, 615 F.3d 574 (5th Cir. 2010)
Edgar v. MITE Corp., 457 U.S. 624 (1982)
Erie Railroad. Co. v. Tompkins, 304 U.S. 64, 78 (1938)
First National Bank in St. Louis v. Missouri, 263 U.S. 640 (1924)
Franklin v. Albert, 411 N.E.2d 458 (Mass. 1980)
Friedman v. Jablonski, 358 N.E.2d 994 (Mass. 1976)
Guaranty Trust Co. of New York v. York, 326 U.S. 99 (1945)
Hendrickson v. Sears, 310 N.E.2d 131 (Mass. 1974)
IHC Health Plans, Inc. v. Commissioner of Internal Revenue, 325 F.3d 1188 (10th Cir. 2003)
In re Halmar Distributors, 968 F.2d 121 (1st Cir. 1992)
Japan Line, Ltd. V. County of Los Angeles, 441 U.S. 434 (1979)
Koe v. Mercer, 876 N.E.2d 831 (Mass. 2007)
Molinar v. Western Electric Co., 525 F.2d 521 (1st Cir. 1975)
Museum of Fine Arts, Boston v. Seger-Thomschitz, 2009 WL 6506658 (D. Mass. 2009), aff'd, 623 F.3d 1 (1st Cir. 2010)
Northwest Airlines, Inc. v. Transport Workers, 451 U.S. 77 (1981)
O'Melveny & Myers v. FDIC, 512 U.S. 79 (1994)
Solomon R. Guggenheim Foundation v. Lubell, 569 N.E.2d 426 (N.Y. 1991)
United States v. Kubrick, 444 U.S. 111 (1979)
United States v. Pink, 315 U.S. 203 (1942)
Von Saher v. Norton Simon Museum of Art at Pasadena, 592 F.3d 954 (9th Cir. 2009)
Wallis v. Pan American Petroleum Corp., 384 U.S. 63 (1966)

Chapter 11
Schoeps v. Museum of Modern Art

11.1 Background

Paul von Mendelssohn-Bartholdy (1875–1935) was a banker and philanthropist in Berlin who, with his wife Elsa née Lavergue-Peguilhen (1899–1986), maintained a distinguished art collection. Though elevated to the aristocracy by Kaiser Wilhelm I, Paul faced persecution as a Jew, and was ejected from various professional associations after the Nazis came to power. In 1933, he shipped five Picasso paintings to Switzerland, and sold them about a year afterward for an unknown price. Paul died in Berlin in 1935; Elsa later settled in Switzerland, where she lived for many years after the war.

The purchaser of the Picassos, art dealer Justin Thannhauser, sold one of them, *Boy Leading a Horse* (1906), to American collector William Paley, who donated it to the Museum of Modern Art in New York in 1964. Thannhauser kept another of the Picassos, *Le Moulin de la Galette* (1900), and following his wartime emigration to the United States, donated it to the Guggenheim Museum in New York in 1963.

In 2007, lawyers for Julius Schoeps, grandson of one of Paul Mendelssohn-Bartholdy's brothers, contacted the two museums and claimed ownership of the two paintings. Schoeps contended that the sale of the paintings to Thannhauser had been made under duress, and that as Paul's heir he was entitled to their return. After conducting an investigation the two museums concluded that the sale of the paintings had been voluntary, and refused the demand.[1] Anticipating a lawsuit,[2] the museums went to court seeking declaratory relief.

---

[1]See Museum of Modern Art and Guggenheim Museum (2007). See also Guggenheim Museum (2009), which sets forth the museums' findings in more detail. For journalistic accounts of the case and the surrounding history, see Feuer (2007), Vogel (2007), Lacayo (2009), and Sontheimer (2011).

[2]In 2006, Schoeps had brought a lawsuit for another one of the five Picassos sold to Thannhauser, which was dismissed on the ground that he had not been properly appointed to sue on behalf of

B.L. Hay, *Nazi-Looted Art and the Law*, DOI 10.1007/978-3-319-64967-2_11

11.2 Proceedings

In December 2007, the Museum of Modern Art and the Guggenheim Museum jointly filed suit in federal district court in New York, naming Schoeps as a defendant, with jurisdiction based on diversity of citizenship. In their complaint, they sought a declaration that Schoeps had no claim on the merits because the sale of the Picassos to Thannhauser had not been made under duress. They also sought a declaration that Schoeps' claim was untimely, and in addition that he was not a proper claimant because the paintings had been the property of Elsa, to whom he was unrelated.[3] Following an initial ruling allowing the case to go forward,[4] two of Elsa's heirs joined the litigation.

The district court denied the museums' motion for summary judgment in January 2009.[5] In its ruling, the court held that there were issues of fact in the case requiring trial, particularly with respect to the circumstances of the sale to Thannhauser.[6] It held that German substantive law would be applied to determine whether that sale was the product of duress, and in addition that New York substantive law would govern the availability of a "good faith purchaser" defense with respect to the subsequent 1936 sale of one of the Picassos. Finally, it held that it would take evidence on the museums' defense of laches concurrently with the trial on the merits of the case.[7]

In February 2009, on the day that trial was scheduled to begin, the parties announced that they had reached a settlement. Upon learning that the settlement agreement contained a confidentiality provision, the court asked the parties for their consent to make the terms of the settlement public. In response, the heirs, but not the museums, refused to consent. Thereafter, the court published an opinion in which it ruled that, given the heirs' position, it could not disclose the terms of the settlement.[8] The court criticized the parties for including a confidentiality term in the settlement of a case of such public interest, and urged the heirs to change their mind and unseal the agreement. This brought the case to a close.

Mendelssohn-Bartholdy's estate. Schoeps v. Andrew Lloyd Webber Foundation, 851 N.Y.S.2d 74 (Sup. 2007).

[3]The museums took the position that Paul had made a gift of the art collection to Elsa upon their marriage in 1927, and that the art was therefore not part of his estate when he died in 1935.

[4]Museum of Modern Art v. Schoeps, 549 F. Supp.2d 543 (S.D.N.Y. 2008).

[5]Schoeps v. Museum of Modern Art, 594 F. Supp.2d 461 (S.D.N.Y. 2009). In this ruling, the court repositioned the parties, making the heirs the plaintiffs and the museums the defendants.

[6]Another triable issue, in the court's view, was whether the paintings had belonged to Paul or Elsa at the time of the sale, which would determine whose heirs could claim the paintings.

[7]In a separate ruling, the court denied a television network's request to broadcast the trial proceedings on the ground that the presence of cameras might affect jurors' impartiality. Schoeps v. Museum of Modern Art, 599 F. Supp.2d 532 (S.D.N.Y. 2009).

[8]Schoeps v. Museum of Modern Art, 603 F. Supp.2d 673 (S.D.N.Y. 2009).

11.3 Sale Under Duress

The heirs' claims rested on the assertion that Paul and Elsa von Mendelssohn-Bartholdy's sale of the Picassos was made under duress as a result of Nazi persecution. The assertion raised two legal issues: which state's law would supply the applicable definition of duress, and whether there was sufficient evidence of duress to warrant a trial.

11.3.1 Applicable Law

Applying the *Klaxon* principle,[9] the district court noted that it must follow the forum state's choice-of-law rules and, as we saw in the previous chapter, that the New York courts follow an "interest analysis" approach in which, generally speaking, the law of the state with the greatest interest in the dispute applies.[10] "The New York Court of Appeals," continued the court, "has laid down five factors to be considered in determining which forum's law will govern a contract dispute, including the place of contracting, the place of negotiation, the place of performance, the location of the subject matter of the contract, and the domicile or place of business of the contracting parties."[11] Without discussing, the court declared that "[a]ll five of these factors plainly support the application of German law to the issue of whether the transfer of these German-held Paintings in 1935 was a product of Nazi duress or the like."[12]

The appropriate German legal rule to apply, the court further concluded, was the German Civil Code, or Bürgerliches Gesetzbuch. The court rejected the heirs' contention that it should instead apply the Military Government Law imposed by the Allies during the postwar occupation, which instructed allied tribunals to treat property as presumptively confiscated if it was transferred during the period of Nazi rule by a member of a persecuted group. That military law, declared the court, "did not displace the German Civil Code," but rather "established a limited regime under which claims brought in a particular tribunal, which no longer exists, and by a given deadline, which has passed, were entitled to a special presumption, which is no longer available."[13] The military law therefore "neither applies to this case nor precludes the claim here asserted," stated the court.[14]

[9]Klaxon Co. v. Stentor Electric Manufacturing Co., 313 U.S. 487 (1941), holding that in diversity cases federal courts should apply the same law that state courts of the forum would apply.

[10]*Schoeps*, 594 F. Supp.2d at 465. On choice of law in the New York courts, see Section 9.3.1.2 above.

[11]*Id.* (citing Zurich Insurance Co. v. Shearson Lehman Hutton, Inc., 642 N.E.2d 1065 (N.Y. 1994)).

[12]*Id.*

[13]*Id.* at 466.

[14]*Id.*

11.3.2 Questions of Fact

The code provisions pertinent to a claim of duress were Bürgerliches Gesetzbuch section 123 and 138, according to the court. The first of these provides, in the court's words, that "a party may rescind a contract if he or she entered into it because of a threat."[15] The second provides, in the court's words, that "a contract may be declared void *ab initio* if it is entered into when one party is at a distinct disadvantage in bargaining—for example, if that party is in 'dire need'—and its terms lopsidedly favor the other party."[16]

There was sufficient circumstantial evidence, in the court's view, to warrant a jury trial on the question whether the sale to Thannhauser was voidable under either of these provisions. "While the record regarding the transfers of these Paintings is meager, it is informed by the historical circumstances of Nazi economic pressures brought to bear on 'Jewish' persons and property, or so a jury might reasonably infer," declared the court.[17] Given that historical context, "the Court concludes that Claimants have adduced competent evidence to create triable issues of fact as to whether they have satisfied the elements of a claim under BGB § 138 and/or § 123," it continued.[18] Without elaborating, the court stated that the heirs "have adduced competent evidence that Paul never intended to transfer any of his paintings and that he was forced to transfer them only because of threats and economic pressures by the Nazi government."[19] Summary judgment is "therefore not appropriate," the court concluded.[20]

11.4 Additional Issues

Several other issues required the court's attention before trial: the timeliness of the claims; the heirs' standing to bring the claims; the availability of a good-faith-purchaser defense; and the advisability of televising the trial.

11.4.1 The Claims' Timeliness

Because the case was brought under the federal courts' diversity jurisdiction, questions of timeliness were governed by the law of the forum state.[21] A defense

[15]*Id.* (citing expert report on German law).

[16]*Id.*

[17]*Id.*

[18]*Id.*

[19]*Id.*

[20]*Id.*

[21]This general rule is based on Guaranty Trust Co. of New York v. York, 326 U.S. 99 (1945).

based on the statute of limitations was unavailable to the museums because, under New York law, the three-year limitations period applicable to claims for stolen or converted property begins to run only after a demand has been refused[22]; in the Schoeps case, that did not occur until 2007. The museums contended, however, that the claims were barred by the equitable doctrine of laches, which, as we saw in the previous chapter, may be applied when a property claimant "inexcusably delayed taking action" and the current possessor "was prejudiced as a result."[23] The court refused to grant summary judgment on this defense, holding that "genuine questions of fact exist as to, *inter alia*, whether Elsa knew she had a potential claim to the Paintings during her lifetime and whether the Museums, as Claimants argue, had reasons to know that the Paintings were misappropriated and so are barred from invoking laches by the doctrine of 'unclean hands.'"[24] The court accordingly held that "the fact-intensive question of whether laches bars Claimants' action will be the subject of an evidentiary hearing conducted by the Court simultaneously with the jury's trial of the merits of the case."[25]

11.4.2 The Heirs' Capacity to Sue

The museums unsuccessfully contended that the heirs could not bring their claims because they had not been formally appointed to represent the estates of Paul and Elsa.[26] The district court rejected this assertion on the ground that they had become heirs under German inheritance law, which did not recognize the existence of "estates" in the way that American law did. "It is true," explained the court, "that under New York law, a cause of action possessed by the decedent at the time of his or her death may be brought subsequently by a representative of the decedent only if the plaintiff has been appointed personal representative of the decedent's estate by the New York surrogate."[27] Nonetheless, "when under the relevant foreign inheritance law there is no estate but rather property passes immediately by operation of law to the decedent's heirs, this requirement does not apply."[28]

---

[22]See Guggenheim Foundation v. Lubell, 569 N.E.2d 426 (N.Y. 1991). On the demand-and-refusal rule, see Section 8.4 above.

[23]Bakalar v. Vavra, 819 F. Supp.2d 293, 303 (S.D.N.Y. 2011). See Section 10.4.1 above.

[24]*Schoeps*, 594 F. Supp.2d at 468. On the doctrine of laches, see generally Fort (2009). On the doctrine of unclean hands, which allows a court to deny equitable relief to a party that has behaved inequitably, see Anenson (2010).

[25]*Schoeps*, 594 F. Supp.2d at 468.

[26]As noted earlier, a claim brought by Schoeps against a possessor of another Picasso sold to Thannhauser was dismissed on this ground. Schoeps v. Andrew Lloyd Webber Foundation, 851 N.Y.S.2d 74 (Sup. 2007).

[27]*Schoeps*, 594 F. Supp.2d at 466.

[28]*Id.* at 466–67.

11.4.3 Good-Faith Purchase Defense

The Museum of Modern Art also raised a defense based on Thannhauser's sale of *Boy Leading a Horse* in 1936 to William Paley, who later donated it to the museum. Even if Thannhauser had acquired the painting unlawfully, argued the museum, Paley was unaware of this fact; Paley was thus a "good-faith purchaser" and therefore acquired good title to the painting under the law of Switzerland, the place where he purchased it. Having acquired title, the argument continued, Paley passed it on when he made his gift to the museum. The heirs countered with the argument that Paley's rights to the painting should be governed not by Swiss law but by the law of New York, which, as we have seen, generally denies title to possessors of stolen or misappropriated art, including innocent purchasers.[29]

The question for the court therefore was whether "the validity and legal effect of the sale of *Boy* to Paley in 1936" was to be governed by the substantive law of Switzerland or New York.[30] Applying New York's "interest analysis" approach to choice-of-law problems, the district court first observed that the place of a property sale was not necessarily the state with the greatest interest in its regulation. "In disputes over transfers of personal property, interest analysis will often lead to the conclusion that the law of the forum where the transfer took place applies"; but "such a result is not inevitable, and where another forum has a more significant relationship to the parties and the property, that forum's law will apply," it explained.[31] "In particular," it elaborated, "when the parties did not intend that the property would remain in the jurisdiction where the transfer took place, that forum will have a lesser interest in having its law applied."[32]

With these observations, the court decided that New York law should govern the validity and effect of the sale to Paley. Though the sale took place in Thannhauser's Lucerne gallery, the painting "was immediately shipped to New York, where Paley lived, and the painting was paid for by a check made out to a New York bank."[33] Thannhauser was not a Swiss citizen, and neither were Paul and Elsa von Mendelssohn-Bartholdy, stated the court. Furthermore, "*Boy* has been in New York for over seventy years and is now the property of a major New York cultural institution that is also a party to this action," it declared.[34] "Under these circumstances," according to the court, "interest analysis leads to the conclusion that New York law applies to the sale of *Boy* to Paley, and the Claimants' claims as to *Boy* are therefore not barred by Swiss law."[35]

---

[29] See Section 9.3.1 above.

[30] *Schoeps*, 594 F. Supp.2d at 467.

[31] *Id.* at 468 (citing American Law Institute 1971, § 245).

[32] *Schoeps*, 594 F. Supp.2d at 468.

[33] *Id.*

[34] *Id.*

[35] *Id.*

11.4.4 Televised Coverage of the Trial

A final issue, appearing here for the first time in Nazi-era art restitution cases, was whether to grant a television station's request to broadcast the trial. Though the federal courts do not generally allow cameras in the courtroom, the local rules for the federal courts in New York leave the matter to the discretion of individual judges. "The undersigned is among those who have [allowed television broadcasts], in the belief that, in general, audio-visual coverage of court proceedings that do not involve a jury should be freely allowed," stated the court, adding that the "country has a long tradition of making court proceedings and documents open to the public," and television coverage "is simply another way in which the public can keep abreast of public proceedings in the courthouse."[36] Special concerns, however, arose with jury trials, for "broadcasting does raise the spectre of potential interference with jurors' own sense of privacy and anonymity, which is so central to their ability to be scrupulously impartial," declared the court, explaining its decision to deny the television station's request.[37] "In the instant case," it stated, "involving very sensitive issues concerning allegations of Nazi coercion and 'looted art,' the potential risks to jury impartiality were, in the Court's view, sufficient to deny broadcasting in this case."[38]

11.5 Settlement Confidentiality

On the morning that trial was to begin, the parties informed the court that they had agreed to a settlement, according to which the museums would keep the paintings in exchange for a sum of money. The parties indicated that the settlement agreement contained a confidentiality provision prohibiting disclosure of the agreement's terms, and moved to dismiss the action. The court granted the motion but requested a sealed copy of the agreement, and asked the parties for their written views on whether the court could make the document public.

The museums stated that they had no objection to the proposed disclosure, but the heirs insisted that the agreement be kept secret. The court then published a rather extraordinary opinion announcing that it would keep the settlement agreement confidential, while voicing its disapproval both of the parties for having chosen secrecy, and of the law for honoring their choice.[39]

"At the heart of this action," the court began, "are issues of considerable public import."[40] The heirs "claim that two of New York's foremost cultural institutions

---

[36]*Schoeps*, 594 F. Supp.2d at 534.

[37]*Id.*

[38]*Id.*

[39]See *Schoeps*, 603 F. Supp.2d at 674–76. On confidentiality provisions in settlements, see generally Anderson (2006) and Moss (2007).

[40]*Id.* at 674.

turned a blind eye to the fact that great works of art in their collections," namely the two Picassos, "were sold by [Paul] against his will because of Nazi duress in the 1930s."[41] For their part, the museums, seeking "to clear their names (or so they said)," had filed suit for declaratory relief in order to "combat what they alleged, in effect, was an effort by [the heirs] and their counsel to use the façade of Nazi iniquities to extort monies from public institutions that were vulnerable to bad publicity."[42] Yet on the day that a public trial was to be held that would bring the available evidence to light, the parties had agreed to shield the matter behind a wall of silence.

The confidentiality agreement was "against the public interest," continued the court, and represented "a troubling reversal of the parties' previously stated positions on this issue."[43] From the beginning, the parties on both sides had "portrayed this lawsuit as of considerable public interest because of the importance of establishing the truth concerning the sensitive issues involved."[44] The museums had "portrayed themselves as institutions dedicated to serving the public by enriching its cultural life" and in seeking equitable relief had assured the court that they were "committed to transparency," stated the court.[45] "Despite these protestations, and despite the fact that the Museums are not-for-profit corporations who, by their own admission, hold their collections for the public trust," the museum had agreed, "for reasons that remain entirely unexpressed," to keep the resolution of the case from public view.[46] "Yet it was only being pressed by the Court," it observed, "that the Museums retreated from their position" and "stated that they no longer oppose disclosure."[47]

As for the heirs, during the litigation they had "claimed loudly throughout that they were vindicating a historical injustice."[48] Now, however, "for reasons wholly unexplained and seemingly no more compelling than concealing the amount of money going into their pockets," they insisted on a shroud of secrecy.[49] The court acknowledged that the heirs, being citizens of other countries, "may be somewhat unfamiliar with the transparency typical of United States courts."[50] Even so, having

[41]*Id.*

[42]*Id.*

[43]*Id.* at 675.

[44]*Id.*

[45]*Id.*

[46]*Id.* Had they been public agencies, the court noted, the museums likely would have been obliged by freedom-of-information laws to disclose the settlement's terms. See *id.* (citing Washington Post Co. v. New York State Insurance Dept., 463 N.E.2d 604 (N.Y. 1984)). "It is hard to see why institutions that proclaim their public status and that seek and receive public support should view themselves as not owing a similar obligation, even if one is not imposed by law," the court stated. *Schoeps*, 603 F. Supp.2d at 675.

[47]*Schoeps*, 603 F. Supp.2d at 675.

[48]*Id.*

[49]*Id.*

[50]*Id.*

"repeatedly sought to clothe themselves as effectively representatives of victims of one of the most criminal political regimes in history," the heirs must surely have understood the public significance of the litigation.[51] That the heirs "should believe that there is any public interest in maintaining the secrecy of their settlement," the court stated, "baffles the mind and troubles the conscience."[52]

Regrettably, continued the court, the law of the Second Circuit, of which the New York federal courts are a part, required it to respect the parties' decision. The law's inflexibility on this subject, in the court's view, was a mistake, inasmuch as it failed to take account of cases in which the public interest might strongly favor disregarding the parties' preference for secrecy. A case such as this, involving questions of great historical and cultural importance, was "very different, in many respects, from the ordinary case that courts of the Second Circuit have had in mind when they have enforced confidentiality provisions in settlement agreements," it stated.[53] The Third Circuit, it noted with approval, had proclaimed that "the broad brush of confidentiality should be applied in a more nuanced way," lamenting that too many courts enforce confidentiality provisions "without sufficiently inquiring into the potential public interest in obtaining information concerning the settlement agreement."[54] Unfortunately, the law of the Second Circuit "admits of no such distinctions," but instead "strongly endorses the confidentiality of settlement agreements in virtually all cases" as a means of facilitating the negotiated resolution of lawsuits.[55]

Given the prevailing law, "the Court has no choice, therefore but to preserve the confidentiality of the settlement agreement," it declared.[56] It closed with an appeal to the heirs, urging them to consider "their public responsibilities, not just to the Courts of the United States that have made judicial processes so freely available to them, but to the public generally."[57] The court announced that it would keep a copy of the settlement agreement under seal, "in that the [claimants], after they have had a greater opportunity to reflect" on their responsibilities, "may yet move to unseal it."[58] The heirs did not honor the request.

---

[51] *Id.*

[52] *Id.* at 675–76.

[53] *Id.* at 676.

[54] *Id.* (quoting Pansy v. Borough of Stroudsburg, 23 F.3d 772, 785–86 (3d Cir. 1994)). On the debates over confidentiality provisions, see the symposium introduced by Anderson (2006).

[55] *Schoeps*, 603 F. Supp.2d at 676.

[56] *Id.*

[57] *Id.*

[58] *Id.*

11.6 Epilogue

In March 2013, the heirs again filed suit in New York federal court, seeking to recover another of the five Picassos that Paul von Mendelssohn-Bartholdy had sold to Justin Thannhauser in 1934. The painting, *Madame Soler* (1903), was sold by Thannhauser in 1965 to the Bavarian Ministry of Culture and Education, which placed it in the Neue Pinakothek museum in Munich. The heirs named the State of Bavaria as the defendant, and sought return of the painting on the ground that von Mendelssohn had sold it under duress. The case was assigned to the same judge who had presided over the heirs' case against the Museum of Modern Art and the Guggenheim.

The court dismissed the heirs' action in June 2014, ruling—in an opinion that barely concealed the judge's anger toward the heirs—that the suit was barred by foreign state immunity. The court caustically rejected the heirs' contention that the case fell within the Foreign Sovereign Immunities Act's "commercial activity" exception, which generally lifts immunity for suits based upon a foreign state's commercial activities if they have a sufficient connection to the United States.[59] "In no real sense is this suit even 'based upon' Bavaria's acquisition of *Madame Soler*," declared the court; and even if it were, the acquisition had no meaningful connection to the United States.[60] Bavaria's purchase occurred "entirely outside the United States," nothing of any "legal consequence" took place here, and the heirs' assertions to the contrary were "factually unsupported" and rested on "dubious legal contentions."[61] Their argument that the purchase caused a "direct effect" in the United States was "balderdash."[62] The court concluded by instructing the clerk's office "to enter judgment and close this case."[63]

Picasso's *Boy Leading a Horse* and *Le Moulin de la Galette* remain, respectively, at the Museum of Modern Art and the Guggenheim in New York.

References

American Law Institute. 1971. *Restatement (Second) of Conflicts of Law*. Philadelphia, PA: American Law Institute.

Anderson, Joseph F., Jr. 2006. Secrecy in Litigation: The Healthy Debate Continues. *Chicago-Kent Law Review* 81: 301–304.

Anenson, T. Leigh. 2010. Limiting Legal Remedies: An Analysis of Unclean Hands. *Kentucky Law Journal* 99: 63–118.

---

[59]Foreign Sovereign Immunities Act, 28 U.S.C. § 1605(a)(2). See Section 4.3 above.

[60]Schoeps v. Freistaat Bayern, 27 F. Supp.3d 540, 544 (S.D.N.Y. 2014).

[61]*Id.* at 545–46.

[62]*Id.* at 546.

[63]*Id.* The heirs did not appeal.

Feuer, Alan. 2007. A Lawsuit Will Determine the Fate of 2 Picassos. *New York Times*, December 18.
Fort, Kathryn E. 2009. The New Laches: Creating Title Where None Existed. *George Mason Law Review* 16: 357–401.
Guggenheim Museum. 2009. Guggenheim Museum Settles Litigation and Shares Key Findings. Press Release, March 25. https://www.guggenheim.org/news/guggenheim-settles-litigation-and-shares-key-findings (visited June 15, 2017).
Lacayo, Richard. 2009. Settled Question? *Time*, February 3.
Moss, Scott A. 2007. Illuminating Secrecy: A New Economic Analysis of Confidential Settlements. *Michigan Law Review* 105: 867–912.
Museum of Modern Art and Guggenheim Museum. 2007. Statement from the Museum of Modern Art and the Solomon R. Guggenheim Foundation Regarding Claims on Two Picasso Paintings in Their Collections. Press Release, December 7. http://press.moma.org/wp-content/press-archives/news/Schoeps_FinalLetter.pdf (visited June 15, 2017).
Sontheimer, Michael. 2011. One Jewish Family's Battle with a Munich Museum. *Spiegel Online*, October 18.
Vogel, Carol. 2007. Two Museums Go to Court over the Right to Picassos. *New York Times*, December 8.

Cases

Bakalar v. Vavra, 819 F. Supp.2d 293 (S.D.N.Y. 2011)
Guaranty Trust Co. of New York v. York, 326 U.S. 99 (1945)
Guggenheim Foundation v. Lubell, 569 N.E.2d 426 (N.Y. 1991)
Klaxon Co. v. Stentor Electric Manufacturing Co., 313 U.S. 487 (1941)
Museum of Modern Art v. Schoeps, 549 F. Supp.2d 543 (S.D.N.Y. 2008); restyled Schoeps v. Museum of Modern Art, 594 F. Supp.2d 461 (S.D.N.Y. 2009), 599 F. Supp.2d 532 (S.D.N.Y. 2009), 603 F. Supp.2d 673 (S.D.N.Y. 2009)
Pansy v. Borough of Stroudsburg, 23 F.3d 772 (3d Cir. 1994)
Schoeps v. Andrew Lloyd Webber Foundation, 851 N.Y.S.2d 74 (Sup. 2007)
Schoeps v. Freistaat Bayern, 27 F. Supp.3d 540 (S.D.N.Y. 2014)
Washington Post Co. v. New York State Insurance Dept., 463 N.E.2d 604 (N.Y. 1984)
Zurich Insurance Co. v. Shearson Lehman Hutton, Inc., 642 N.E.2d 1065 (N.Y. 1994)

Chapter 12
De Csepel v. Republic of Hungary

12.1 Background

Mór Lipót Herzog (1869–1934) was a Jewish banker and industrialist in Budapest who, together with his wife Johanna Herzog de Csete (1874–1940), assembled one of the most renowned art collections in Europe, which upon their deaths was inherited by their children, Erzsébet, András, and István.[1] Following the arrival of Nazi occupying forces in March 1944, the Hungarian government seized the collection, giving some of it to Adolf Eichmann for shipment to Germany and placing the rest in the Museum of Fine Arts in Budapest, which prompted the museum's director to boast that its holdings now rivaled the Prado in Madrid. Erzsébet Herzog fled the country with her children and settled in the United States, later acquiring the name Elizabeth Weiss de Csepel. Her brother András was deported and died in a Nazi forced-labor camp, while his children escaped to Argentina and eventually settled in Italy. The third sibling, István, narrowly escaped deportation to Auschwitz, and survived the war by hiding in a safe house owned by a foreign embassy in Hungary.

Following the war, the surviving Herzog family members began a long, unsuccessful attempt to recover the collection from the Hungarian government.[2] The government temporarily returned some artworks to the family in the late 1940s, but seized them again when the family tried to take them out of the country. Other works remained in the government's custody because the family failed to pay exorbitant fees for their return. Following the collapse of communism in 1989, Elizabeth Weiss de Csepel, then eighty-nine years old, managed to persuade the government

[1]On the Herzog family and their collection, see Applebome (2008), Dempsey (2010), McCagg (1972), and Vogel (2010).

[2]Some of the works transported by Eichmann back to Germany were recovered by American forces and transferred to the Hungarian government after the war. Much of the collection is believed to have been taken by Soviet troops back to Russia.

B.L. Hay, *Nazi-Looted Art and the Law*, DOI 10.1007/978-3-319-64967-2_12

to return seven minor pieces, but the prize items of the collection, including El Greco's *Christ at the Mount of Olives* (ca. 1610) and other masterworks, remained in Hungarian museums. Following her death in 1992, her daughter Martha Nierenberg took up the negotiations, and in 1999 filed suit in Budapest to recover twelve artworks. The Hungarian judiciary initially ruled in the Herzog family's favor, but after extensive legal maneuvering reversed itself in 2008 and ordered only one artwork returned to the family, ruling that the Herzogs' remaining claims had been extinguished by a 1973 agreement between Hungary and the United States, and also that the government had acquired title to the collection by adverse possession.

12.2 Proceedings

In July 2010, David de Csepel, Angela Herzog, and Julia Herzog, acting on behalf of the Herzog family, filed suit in federal district court in the District of Columbia, naming as defendants the Republic of Hungary and several state-owned Hungarian museums, and basing jurisdiction on diversity of citizenship.[3] The complaint asserted that the defendants held at least forty Nazi-looted works from the Herzog collection, and had breached bailment agreements under which they held the works in trust for the heirs after the war. Advancing theories of conversion and related common-law claims, the complaint sought a declaration that the heirs were the rightful owners, along with an order to return the works or pay damages. The defendants denied the claims on the merits, and also sought dismissal on various procedural and jurisdictional grounds.

The district court ruled on the defendants' motion to dismiss in September 2011.[4] The court rejected their defense of sovereign immunity, holding that the case fell under the "expropriation" exception to immunity under the Foreign Sovereign Immunities Act. It also rejected the defendants' positions that the action was barred by international treaty, by the statute of limitations, and by the doctrines of act of state, political question, and forum non conveniens. The court agreed with the defendants, however, that part of the action was barred by the doctrine of international comity, dismissing the action with respect to the eleven artworks that Martha Nierenberg had unsuccessfully sought in the Hungarian courts.

Both parties took an immediate appeal. In April 2013, the court of appeals ruled for the plaintiffs, reinstating the part of the action that had been dismissed and upholding the district court's refusal to dismiss the rest of the action.[5] On the question of sovereign immunity, the court declined to consider whether the case fell within the Foreign Sovereign Immunities Act's "expropriation" exception to

---

[3]The museums were the Hungarian National Gallery, the Museum of Fine Arts, the Museum of Applied Arts, and the Budapest University of Technology and Economics.

[4]De Csepel v. Republic of Hungary, 808 F. Supp.2d 113 (D.D.C. 2011).

[5]De Csepel v. Republic of Hungary, 714 F.3d 591 (D.C. Cir. 2013).

state immunity; instead, it concluded that the plaintiff's complaint brought the case within the Act's "commercial activity" exception to immunity. The court agreed with the district court's rejection of the defendants' other proposed grounds for dismissal. The court of appeals disagreed, however, with the district court's dismissal of part of the action on international comity grounds; here it held that the complaint had adequately alleged that the Hungarian proceedings had violated due process and were therefore not entitled to deference.

On remand, the case proceeded to pretrial discovery. In March 2016, the district court made further rulings on its authority to hear the case.[6] It held that in light of the evidence that had emerged since the court of appeals decision, the case no longer fell within the Foreign Sovereign Immunities Act's commercial activity exception to immunity. It further held, however, that the evidence did not change its earlier conclusion that the case fell within the Act's expropriation exception to immunity.

The defendants again appealed, challenging the district court's new ruling denying sovereign immunity. In mid-2017, that appeal was still pending.

12.3 Foreign State Immunity

As we have seen in earlier chapters,[7] the Foreign Sovereign Immunities Act generally allows suits against foreign states and their instrumentalities for claims seeking property expropriated in violation of international law, as well as in certain cases arising out of the commercial activities of the defendant. Because the Herzogs' claims involved contracts with Hungary as well as Nazi looting, both exceptions furnished potential grounds for jurisdiction in the case.

12.3.1 Expropriation Exception

The expropriation exception lifts a foreign state's immunity in cases "in which rights in property taken in violation of international law are in issue," if an agency or instrumentality of the foreign state owns or operates the property and engages in some commercial activity in the United States.[8] The district court held that the Herzog claims satisfied these requirements, a conclusion that required consideration of several issues.

[6]De Csepel v. Republic of Hungary, 169 F. Supp.3d 143 (D.D.C. 2016). In a 2014 decision, the district declined to rule on the defendants' renewed motion to dismiss until discovery was complete. De Csepel v. Republic of Hungary, 75 F. Supp.3d 380 (D.D.C. 2014).

[7]See Sections 3.5, 4.4, and 7.3 above. On foreign state immunity in American and international law, see generally Nanda and Pansius (2011), Yang (2012), Fox and Webb (2013).

[8]Foreign Sovereign Immunities Act, 28 U.S.C. § 1605(a)(3).

Taking in Violation of International Law A taking of property is committed in violation of international law, the district court began its analysis by noting, "if: (1) it was not for a public purpose; (2) it was discriminatory; or (3) no just compensation was provided for the property taken."[9] The Herzogs' complaint plainly met this standard, in the court's view, because it asserted discriminatory and uncompensated takings by "the Hungarian government, in collaboration with the Nazis," which confiscated the family's art collection "as part of a larger campaign of asset seizure and genocide against Hungarian Jews."[10]

The court rejected the defendants' assertion that, because the Herzogs were Hungarian citizens when their property was taken, the seizure did not violate international law. The court acknowledged that it was "well-settled that a state's taking of the property of its own citizens, no matter how egregious, does not constitute an international law violation."[11] The principle was inapplicable to the Herzogs' claim, however, because by 1944 Hungary had "*de facto* stripped [the Herzog family] and all Hungarian Jews of their citizenship rights."[12] The court also rejected the defendants' argument that the Herzogs had in effect received "just compensation" for the expropriation as a result of postwar compensation legislation enacted in Hungary during and after the Soviet era. The Herzogs had in fact received nothing under those laws, according to the court, and the laws did not purport to resolve all outstanding claims against the state.[13]

The court also rejected Hungary's argument that the heirs' claims should be dismissed because they had failed to seek compensation in the Hungarian courts for the taking of the collection. "When a case involves a basic expropriation claim," the court acknowledged, "it is plausible that no international law violation has occurred until the plaintiff has sought compensation in a domestic forum."[14] But Holocaust-era property seizures from Jews were genocidal in nature: such expropriations "did more than effectuate genocide or serve as a means of carrying out genocide," but were "*themselves genocide*," because they were designed to deprive Jews "of the resources needed to survive as a people" and were "undertaken for the purpose of bringing about a protected group's physical destruction."[15] Such genocidal takings, the court noted, violated international law regardless of whether compensation was paid. "The violation is the genocide itself, which occurs at the moment of the

---

[9]*De Csepel*, 808 F. Supp.2d at 128. Here the court relied on the formulation of Siderman de Blake v. Republic of Argentina, 965 F.2d 699 (9th Cir. 1992), discussed in Section 3.5 above, and also in American Law Institute (1987), § 712.

[10]*De Csepel*, 808 F. Supp.2d at 129.

[11]*Id.*, citing *Altmann v. Republic of Austria*, 317 F.3d 954, 968 (9th Cir. 2002).

[12]*De Csepel*, 808 F. Supp.2d at 130.

[13]*Id.* at 131.

[14]*De Csepel*, 169 F. Supp.2d at 168.

[15]Simon v. Republic of Hungary, 812 F.3d 127, 142–43 (D.C. Cir. 2016) (emphasis in original), quoted in *De Csepel*, 169 F. Supp.3d at 163. This idea is also developed, as the district court noted, by the Seventh Circuit's opinion in Abelesz v. Magyar Nemzeti Bank, 692 F.3d 661, 675 (7th Cir. 2012).

taking, whether or not a victim subsequently attempts to obtain relief through the violating sovereign's domestic laws."[16]

Finally, the court rejected the defendants' argument that the plaintiffs' claims should be dismissed because they were not based on the 1944 Nazi seizure, but rather were based on the Hungarian government's breach of postwar "bailment agreements" in which the government undertook to hold the collection for the Herzog family. In the district court's view, the factual basis for jurisdiction under the Act need not fully "overlap with a plaintiff's substantive claim."[17] Here it relied on a recent decision in another case in which the D.C. Circuit "found jurisdiction under the expropriation exception even though plaintiff's substantive claims against Hungary for acts during the Holocaust were not based on takings."[18] In that case, *Simon v. Republic of Hungary*, the court of appeals held that victims of Nazi persecution could proceed even though they were "plead[ing] a 'violation of international laws' only to 'give rise to jurisdiction' under the FSIA's expropriation exception, not to establish liability on the merits" of their claims, which were "common-law causes of action such as conversion, unjust enrichment, and restitution."[19] Relying on *Simon*, the district court held that the Herzog heirs could go forward even though their claims concerning postwar bailment of Nazi-looted property was not a "straightforward takings claim."[20]

Remaining Elements The district court also found that all of the Hungarian museums named in the compliant were government "instrumentalities," defined by the Act as "'an organ of a foreign state' or an entity that is majority-owned by the foreign state."[21] In addition, the court noted that the Hungarian museums made art loan exchanges with American museums, engaged in tourism advertising in the United States, and sold books and prints featuring the Herzog collection to American consumers. These contacts with the United States, the court concluded, were "more than sufficient" to satisfy the Act's expropriation exception.[22]

12.3.2 Commercial Activity Exception

The courts also considered whether the Herzogs' claims fell within the Act's commercial activity exception, which lifts a foreign state's immunity for claims that are based "upon an act outside the territory of the United States in connection

[16]*Simon*, 812 F.3d at 149, quoted in *De Csepel*, 169 F. Supp.3d at 168.

[17]*De Csepel*, 169 F. Supp.3d at 163.

[18]*Id.*

[19]*Simon*, 812 F.3d at 141, quoted in *De Csepel*, 169 F. Supp.3d at 163.

[20]*De Csepel*, 169 F. Supp.3d at 163.

[21]*Id.* (quoting 28 U.S.C. § 1603(b)).

[22]*Id.* at 132.

with a commercial activity of the foreign state elsewhere," if "that act causes a direct effect in the United States."[23]

Commercial Activity In their complaint, the Herzog heirs asserted that "Hungary nominally 'returned' portions of the Herzog Collection that had been looted during WWII," but that the Herzog family "had no choice but to re-deliver possession, or to consent to [Hungary's] retention of possession of those portions of the Herzog Collection."[24] Hungary's "possession or re-possession" of the collection after the war, the complaint asserted, "constituted an express or implied-in-fact bailment contract for the benefit of plaintiffs," which Hungary had breached by refusing to return the collection.[25] According to the court of appeals, these allegations made out a claim that Hungary's actions constituted commercial activity. To determine the commercial character of an action, the court noted, courts ask "not whether the foreign government is acting with a profit motive," but rather "whether the particular actions that the foreign state performs (whatever the motive behind them) are the type of action by which a private party engages in trade and traffic or commerce."[26] In the court of appeals' view, "Hungary's alleged breach of bailment agreements easily satisfies this standard," because a "bailment is a form of contract, and a foreign state's repudiation of a contract is precisely the type of activity in which a 'private player within the market' engages."[27]

In response, Hungary argued that its handling of the collection was sovereign, not commercial, in character, because it was done pursuant to postwar diplomatic accords. "As Hungary sees it," the court of appeals summarized, "the bailment obligations alleged by the family arise from a World War II Peace Treaty with the Allied Powers that requires Hungary to restore or provide compensation for certain property expropriated during the Holocaust."[28] Any breach of its obligations was sovereign rather than commercial in character, according to this argument, because a country's violation of the reparations requirements of a peace treaty does not qualify as commercial activity.[29] The flaw in the argument, in the appeals court's view, was that the Herzog heirs were alleging that the family and the Hungarian government "directly agreed to a bailment relationship"; though "the complaint refers to the Peace Treaty, it nowhere alleges that the Treaty is the source of the bailment obligations," and "provides no basis for converting the commercial act of

---

[23]Foreign Sovereign Immunities Act, 28 U.S.C. § 1605(a)(2). On the commercial activity exception, see generally Foster (2014) and Nanda and Pansius (2011), § 3:5.

[24]Complaint, de Csepel v. Republic of Hungary, No. 10-Civ.-1261 (D.D.C.), ¶ 99.

[25]*Id.*, ¶ 100.

[26]Republic of Argentina v. Weltover, Inc., 504 U.S. 607, 614 (1992) (emphasis in original), quoted in *de Csepel*, 714 F.3d at 599.

[27]*De Csepel*, 714 F.3d at 599 (quoting Saudi Arabia v. Nelson, 507 U.S. 349, 360 (1993)).

[28]*De Csepel*, 714 F.3d at 599 (citing Treaty of Peace between Hungary and the Allied Powers art. 27 (Feb. 10, 1947), 61 Stat. 2065, 41 U.N.T.S. 135).

[29]*Id.*

contract repudiation into the sovereign act of 'treaty participation,' as Hungary urges."[30]

Direct Effect in the United States The remaining issue was whether Hungary's challenged actions had produced a "direct effect" in the United States. Here the critical question, in the court of appeals' view, was whether "Hungary promised to perform specific obligations in the United States."[31] If the heirs could prove that the bail agreements implicitly or explicitly required the return of the art "to be directed to members of the Herzog family Hungary knew to be residing in the United States," the direct-effect requirement would be satisfied.[32] If, instead, Hungary had made no such undertaking, then the commercial activity exception would be inapplicable for the same reason it had been inapplicable in the *Westfield* case, where "Nazi Germany's seizure of a German resident's artwork caused no 'direct effect' in the United States" because Germany had not "promised to deliver the art collection to the United States."[33] The court of appeals found that the Herzog heirs' complaint made the necessary allegations to satisfy the direct-effect requirement, and remanded the case to determine whether there was supporting evidence.

Following discovery, the district court ruled against the plaintiffs. "There is no question," declared the court, "that plaintiffs have presented evidence of express and implied bailments between the Herzogs and Hungary, some of which involve Herzogs residing in the United States."[34] There was, however, no evidence that the agreements required Hungary to deliver the collection to the United States. None of the bailment documents specified a place of delivery, and those parts of the collection that Hungary had returned over the years were delivered to Herzog representatives in Budapest. "The D.C. Circuit's prior ruling in this case rested on the inference that the bailment agreements required Hungary to return the artwork to owners in the United States," stated the court.[35] "But the evidence soundly refutes that inference, so the Court cannot find subject matter jurisdiction under the FSIA's commercial activity exception."[36]

12.3.3 Effect of International Agreements

The Foreign Sovereign Immunities Act specifies that its provisions are "[s]ubject to existing international agreements" to which the United States was a party at the

[30]*Id.* at 599–600 (quoting Hungary's brief).

[31]*Id.* at 600–1.

[32]*Id.* at 601.

[33]*Id.* (quoting Westfield v. Federal Republic of Germany, 633 F.3d 409, 415 (6th Cir. 2011) (brackets omitted)).

[34]*De Csepel*, 169 F. Supp.3d at 162.

[35]*Id.* (brackets omitted).

[36]*Id.* at 163.

time of the Act's 1976 enactment. This means, the court of appeals explained in the Herzog litigation, that if there is a conflict between the Act and an international agreement in existence at the time of its enactment, "the agreement prevails."[37] Relying on that principle, Hungary unsuccessfully argued that lifting its immunity under the Act conflicted with two prior international agreements.

1947 Peace Treaty The treaty with the allies required Hungary to restore or provide compensation for property taken "on account of the racial origin or religion" of people within its jurisdiction, and provided that unsettled disputes should be referred to allied diplomatic missions.[38] These provisions, argued Hungary, foreclosed the Herzogs from bringing their claims in the American courts. The court of appeals disagreed, holding that the claims "fall outside the Treaty's scope" because they involve "breaches of bailment agreements formed and repudiated after the war's end."[39] The court therefore concluded that "the Peace Treaty presents no conflict with Hungary's amenability to suit under FSIA."[40]

1973 Property Accord In 1973, Hungary entered into an agreement with the United States settling certain claims of American nationals for property that had been nationalized or expropriated by the Hungarian government.[41] Noting that "the 1973 Agreement had been consistently interpreted by both signatories to only bar claims against Hungary by U.S. citizens who were citizens at the time their claims arose," the district court held that "the Agreement could therefore only plausibly govern claims by Erzsébet Herzog (Elizabeth Weiss de Csepel) and her American heirs for takings that occurred between 1952 and 1973."[42] It "would not," according to the district court, "govern confiscations that occurred during the Holocaust, when no Herzog was a U.S. citizen."[43] The court of appeals took a different approach, emphasizing that the Herzog heirs were alleging bailment contracts with Hungary that were only recently breached. Because the 1973 Agreement only purported to settle claims that arose before its enactment, "it has no application to bailment agreements allegedly repudiated in 2008," when the Hungarian courts refused to return the collection.[44]

[37]Moore v. United Kingdom, 384 F.3d 1079, 1085 (9th Cir. 2004), quoted in *De Csepel*, 714 F.3d at 601.

[38]Treaty of Peace between Hungary and the Allied Powers art. 27, 40 (Feb. 10, 1947), 61 Stat. 2065, 41 U.N.T.S. 135.

[39]*De Csepel*, 714 F.3d at 602.

[40]*Id.*

[41]Agreement between the Government of the U.S. and the Government of the Hungarian People's Republic Regarding the Settlement of Claims (March 6, 1973), 24 U.S.T. 552.

[42]*De Csepel*, 169 F. Supp.3d at 167. Elizabeth de Csepel became an American citizen in 1952.

[43]*Id.*

[44]*De Csepel*, 714 F.3d at 603.

12.4 Additional Jurisdictional Issues

Hungary raised several other challenges to the courts' authority that, in the court of appeals' words, they could "easily dispose of."[45]

12.4.1 Political Question

Referring again to the 1947 Peace Treaty and the 1973 Agreement discussed above,[46] Hungary argued that the Herzog heirs' action was barred by the political question doctrine.[47] The argument, the appeals court noted, was "based entirely on the notion that plaintiffs' claims are addressed and settled by" those two accords.[48] But that premise was false, because the heirs were asserting "that Hungary has breached certain agreements regarding specific artwork in a manner that does not implicate existing international compensatory frameworks at all."[49] For that reason, concluded the court, "the family's claims raise no 'separation-of-powers concerns that would justify invocation of the political question doctrine.'"[50]

12.4.2 Act of State

Hungary also asserted that its refusal to return the art was insulated from judicial challenge by virtue of the act of state doctrine, which "requires American courts to presume the validity of an official act of a foreign sovereign performed within its own territory."[51] The doctrine was inapplicable to the case against Hungary, ruled the court of appeals, because "it applies only to 'conduct that is by nature distinctly sovereign, *i.e.*, conduct that cannot be undertaken by a private individual or entity.'"[52] Because the heirs' complaint sought relief for Hungary's breach of bailment contracts, continued the court of appeals, "the district court got it just right: their claims challenge 'not sovereign acts, but rather *commercial* acts' entitled to no 'deference under the act of state doctrine.'"[53]

---

[45]*Id.* at 604.

[46]See Section 14.3.3.

[47]On the political question doctrine, see generally Choper (2005).

[48]*De Csepel*, 808 F. Supp.2d at 143, quoted by the appeals court in *de Csepel*, 714 F.3d at 604. The court of appeals adopted the district court's reasoning as its own.

[49]*De Csepel*, 808 F. Supp.2d at 144, quoted by the appeals court in *de Csepel*, 714 F.3d at 604.

[50]*De Csepel*, 714 F.3d at 604 (quoting the district court in *de Csepel*, 808 F. Supp.2d at 144).

[51]Republic of Austria v. Altmann, 541 U.S. 677, 713 (2004), quoted in *De Csepel*, 714 F.3d at 604.

[52]*De Csepel*, 714 F.3d at 604 (quoting McKesson Corp. v. Islamic Republic of Iran, 672 F.3d 1066, 1073 (D.C. Cir. 2012)). On the doctrine, see generally Harrison (2016).

[53]*De Csepel*, 714 F.3d at 604 (quoting the district court in *de Csepel*, 808 F. Supp.2d at 143).

12.4.3 *Forum Non Conveniens*

Hungary also invoked the doctrine of forum non conveniens, which allows a court to dismiss an action if "an adequate alternative forum is available" and "a balancing of private and public interest factors strongly favors dismissal."[54] The district court assumed for purposes of argument that an adequate alternative forum existed in Hungary, but concluded that Hungary had failed to discharge its burden of showing that "the balance of private and public factors" strongly favored dismissal.[55] Observing that the plaintiffs did not reside in Hungary, the court reasoned that convenience to the witnesses and similar considerations, while they might weakly support resort to the Hungarian courts, did not overcome "the 'strong presumption' in favor of plaintiffs' choice of forum."[56] The court of appeals upheld that decision, ruling that the district court had not abused its discretion in finding that the scales tipped against dismissal.[57]

12.5 Statute of Limitations

It was undisputed that the case was governed by the District of Columbia's three-year limitations period for claims seeking "the recovery of personal property or damages for its unlawful detention."[58] The three-year period commences "when the plaintiff demands the return of the property and the defendant refuses, or when the defendant takes some action that a reasonable person would understand to be either an act of conversion or inconsistent with a bailment," according to the District of Columbia judiciary.[59]

"In order to trigger the statute of limitations," the courts noted in the Herzog litigation, "a defendant's refusal to return the property 'must be absolute and unconditional.'"[60] The critical question for the courts, therefore, was whether Hungary had "absolutely and unconditionally" refused the heirs' demands more than three years before the current proceedings began in 2010. In its motion to dismiss,

---

[54] Agudas Chasidei Chabad of U.S. v. Russian Federation, 528 F.3d 934, 950 (D.C. Cir. 2008), quoted in *de Csepel*, 714 F.3d at 605. On forum non conveniens, see generally Nanda and Pansius (2011), § 6:1.

[55] *De Csepel*, 808 F. Supp.2d at 138.

[56] *Id.* (quoting Piper Aircraft Co v. Reyno, 454 U.S. 235, 255 (1981)).

[57] *De Csepel*, 714 F.3d at 606.

[58] D.C. Code § 12-301(2). As the court of appeals noted, actions brought under the Foreign Sovereign Immunities Act are controlled by the forum state's time limits. *De Csepel*, 714 F.3d at 603.

[59] Malewicz v. City of Amsterdam, 517 F. Supp.2d 322, 335 (D.D.C. 2007), quoted in *De Csepel*, 714 F.3d at 603. The *Malewicz* decision relied on In re McCagg, 450 A.2d 414, 416 (D.C. 1982).

[60] *De Csepel*, 714 F.3d at 603 (quoting *Malewicz*, 517 F. Supp.2d at 335); accord *de Csepel*, 808 F. Supp.2d at 141.

Hungary took the position that its definitive refusal had occurred, and the clock had started running, no later than 1999, when Martha Nierenberg filed her suit in the Hungarian courts.

Both the district court and the court of appeals rejected this argument. The heirs' complaint, they noted, alleged that the defendant had continued negotiations throughout the Hungarian proceedings.[61] The "complaint alleges that Hungary's refusal of the family's demand for the Collection did not occur until January 2008, when 'Hungary issued its final decision that it would not honor its obligation to return the Herzog Collection to the Herzog Heirs'"; it was only then "that Hungary 'made clear that any further demand by the Herzog Heirs for restitution of any portion of the Herzog Collection would be futile.'"[62] Evidence might later emerge, the court of appeals acknowledged, to indicate that the heirs' claim had accrued at an earlier date. "But at the motion to dismiss stage," it explained, "we look only at the complaint, in which we see nothing that conflicts with the family's allegation that their bailment claims accrued in January 2008."[63]

12.6 International Comity

Hungary also argued that the action was precluded by the earlier litigation in the Hungary courts, filed in Budapest by Martha Nierenberg in 1999, which had resulted in a judgment against her in 2008. The district court accepted this argument in part: noting that the Hungarian courts' judgment "applied only to eleven paintings," it held that the judgment "cannot have preclusive effect as to the pieces of art not at issue in that litigation."[64] With respect to those eleven paintings, however, the district court concluded that the Hungarian judgment should bar further litigation. Here it relied on the principle of international comity, which "teaches that, when possible, the decisions of foreign tribunals should be given effect in domestic courts."[65] The Herzog heirs furnished no reason, in the court's view, to disregard the Hungarian court's "sixteen-page decision," which had "examined the factual circumstances surrounding each of the eleven paintings" and "determined that Ms. Nierenberg's claim had been extinguished by the 1973 Agreement and that additional defendants had acquired title through adverse possession."[66]

[61]The district court deemed the statute of limitations to have been "equitably tolled" during the Hungarian proceedings. The court of appeals found it unnecessary to reach that question, concluding instead that the claim had not accrued until the conclusion of those proceedings. See *De Csepel*, 714 F.3d at 603.

[62]*De Csepel*, 714 F.3d at 604 (quoting complaint).

[63]*Id.*

[64]*De Csepel*, 808 F. Supp.2d at 144.

[65]Laker Airways Ltd. V. Sabena, Belgian World Airlines, 731 F.2d 909, 931 (D.C. Cir. 1984), quoted in *de Csepel*, 808 F. Supp.2d at 145. On international comity, see generally Dodge (2015).

[66]*De Csepel*, 808 F. Supp.2d at 145.

The court of appeals disagreed. In their complaint, the plaintiffs had alleged that the Hungarian proceedings had not been conducted "in accordance with internationally recognized standards of due process or in accordance with international law."[67] They should, stated the court of appeals, be given the chance to prove those allegations, which presented "fact-intensive issues" that could not be resolved at the pleadings stage.[68] Moreover, according to the court, international comity was an affirmative defense, meaning that the plaintiffs were not required to give a detailed refutation of it in their complaint. "Because nothing in the complaint contradicts the family's claims of due process violations, dismissal at this stage was inappropriate."[69] The court added that it was expressing "no opinion as to whether the due process violations alleged by the family actually occurred," or whether they were sufficiently serious "as to require non-recognition of the Hungarian judgment."[70] Those issues, it explained, "are properly addressed at summary judgment or trial."[71] It accordingly remanded for further proceedings.

12.7 Epilogue

The defendants took an immediate appeal of the district court's 2016 ruling that denied them immunity under the Foreign Sovereign Immunities Act.[72] The appeal was still pending in mid-2017.

References

American Law Institute. 1987. *Restatement (Third) of the Foreign Relations Law of the United States*. Saint Paul, MN: American Law Institute.

Applebome, Peter, 2008. Footprints of Holocaust in a Battle for Lost Art. *New York Times*, January 13.

Choper, Jesse H. 2005. The Political Question Doctrine: Suggested Criteria. *Duke Law Journal* 54: 1457–1523.

Dempsey, Judy. 2010. Roadblocks Remain in Case of Paintings Lost to Nazis. *New York Times*, October 28.

---

[67]Complaint, de Csepel v. Republic of Hungary, No. 10-Civ.-1261 (D.D.C.), ¶ 79, quoted in *de Csepel*, 714 F.3d at 607.

[68]*De Csepel*, 714 F.3d at 607.

[69]*Id.*

[70]*Id.*

[71]*Id.* at 608.

[72]Like other circuits, the D.C. Circuit has held that under the collateral order doctrine, a court's refusal to grant foreign state immunity is immediately appealable. See Foremost-McKesson, Inc. v. Islamic Republic of Iran, 905 F.2d 438, 443 (D.C. Cir. 1990).

Dodge, William S. 2015. International Comity in American Law. *Columbia Law Review* 115: 2071–2104.

Foster, George K. 2014. When Commercial Meets Sovereign: A New Paradigm for Applying the Foreign Sovereign Immunities Act in Crossover Cases. *Houston Law Review* 52: 361–414.

Fox, Hazel, and Philippa Webb. 2013. *The Law of State Immunity*. 3rd ed. Oxford: Oxford University Press.

Harrison, John. 2016. The American Act of State Doctrine. *Georgetown Journal of International Law* 47: 507–571.

McCagg, William O. 1972. *Jewish Nobles and Geniuses in Modern Hungary*. New York: Columbia University Press.

Nanda, Ved P., and David K. Pansius. 2011. *Litigation of International Disputes in U.S. Courts*. 2nd ed. Saint Paul, MN: Thomson/West.

Vogel, Carol. 2010. Hungary Sued in Holocaust Art Claim. *New York Times*, July 27.

Yang, Xiadong. 2012. *State Immunity in International Law*. Cambridge: Cambridge University Press.

Cases

Agudas Chasidei Chabad of U.S. v. Russian Federation, 528 F.3d 934 (D.C. Cir 2008)

De Csepel v. Republic of Hungary, 808 F. Supp.2d 113 (D.D.C. 2011), aff'd in part and rev'd in part, 714 F.3d 591 (D.C. Cir. 2013), on remand, 169 F. Supp.3d 143 (D.D.C. 2016), appeal docketed, No. 16-7042 (D.C. Cir. Apr. 12, 2016)

Foremost-McKesson, Inc. v. Islamic Republic of Iran, 905 F.2d 438 (D.C. Cir. 1990)

In re McCagg, 450 A.2d 414 (D.C. 1982)

Laker Airways Ltd. V. Sabena, Belgian World Airlines, 731 F.2d 909 (D.C. Cir. 1984)

Malewicz v. City of Amsterdam, 517 F. Supp.2d 322 (D.D.C. 2007)

Moore v. United Kingdom, 384 F.3d 1079 (9th Cir. 2004)

Piper Aircraft Co v. Reyno, 454 U.S. 235 (1981)

Republic of Argentina v. Weltover, Inc., 504 U.S. 607 (1992)

Republic of Austria v. Altmann, 541 U.S. 677 (2004)

Siderman de Blake v. Republic of Argentina, 965 F.2d 699 (9th Cir. 1992), cert. denied, 507 U.S. 1017 (1993)

Simon v. Republic of Hungary, 812 F.3d 127 (D.C. Cir. 2016)

Westfield v. Federal Republic of Germany, 633 F.3d 409 (6th Cir. 2011)

Chapter 13
Detroit Institute of Arts and Toledo Museum of Art v. Ullin

13.1 Background

Martha Nathan *née* Dreyfus (1875–1958) and her husband Hugo Nathan (1861–1922) owned an extensive art collection at their home in Frankfurt, which Martha inherited upon Hugo's death. She emigrated to Paris to escape anti-Semitic persecution in 1937 and, returning to Frankfurt the following year to collect her belongings, was forced to surrender six paintings to the Nazis. In late 1938, she sold to a Paris-based group of dealers several artworks she had previously moved to Basel, including Paul Gauguin's *Street in Tahiti* (1891) and Vincent van Gogh's *The Diggers* (1889). Shortly afterward, the dealers sold the Gauguin to the Toledo Museum of Art, and sold the van Gogh to an American collector who later bequeathed it to the Detroit Institute of Arts.[1]

Nathan settled in Switzerland in 1939. After the war, she filed claims in Germany for the six paintings seized by the Nazis, as well as for the loss of her house in Frankfurt. She did not seek compensation for the art in Basel that she had sold in 1938, including the Gauguin and the van Gogh. Following her death in 1958, her brother Willy Dreyfus became executor of her estate, and pursued additional claims in the 1970s for losses that the family's banking business had sustained at Nazi hands. Like Martha, Willy (who lived until 1977) never filed a claim with respect to the Gauguin or the van Gogh.

In 2004, Nathan's heirs approached both the Detroit and Toledo museums with a request that they return the two paintings. The heirs argued that Nathan had sold the paintings under duress in order to finance her escape from Nazi Germany and her survival in exile. Though the dealers she sold them to were not connected to the Nazis, indeed were also Jewish, she had been forced by the threat of Nazi persecution to sell the works for well below their market value, according to the heirs; they

[1] For this and other background information, see Martinez (2015) and Micucci (2006).

B.L. Hay, *Nazi-Looted Art and the Law*, DOI 10.1007/978-3-319-64967-2_13

pointed out that the amount she sold them for, $16,000, was only one-third of their insured value, and that the dealers had quickly resold them for $59,000.

After investigating the matter, the museums turned down the heirs' request, announcing in a joint press release that their research showed "that Mrs. Nathan voluntarily chose to sell the paintings, that she received fair market value, and that, in choosing not to pursue any restitution of these paintings, she recognized that she had rightfully sold them to their new owners."[2] The museums stated that the prices that Nathan received in the 1938 sale were "consistent with prices for comparable works sold voluntarily in Europe at that time," and noted that for several years after the sale Nathan continued to lend works for exhibition by one of the Parisian dealers who had purchased the two paintings.[3] Nathan "had an appropriately strong sense of justice, as evidenced by her energetic and successful post-war restitution claims," the museums stated, "and we find it telling that the paintings by van Gogh and Gauguin were not subjects of these claims," adding that "we are proud to preserve Mrs. Nathan's legacy through our continued stewardship of these paintings."[4]

13.2 Proceedings

In January 2006, the Detroit and Toledo museums simultaneously filed suit, respectively, in federal district court in Michigan and Ohio, naming the Nathan heirs as defendants and invoking the courts' jurisdiction based on diversity of citizenship. The complaints in the two suits, which were essentially identical, requested a declaration that the Detroit museum owned *The Diggers* and that the Toledo museum owned *Street in Tahiti*, and an order quieting title to that effect. The heirs jointly filed an answer stating that Martha Nathan's transfer of the paintings had been involuntary, and asserting counterclaims against the museums for restitution of the paintings.

The museums filed motions for judgment on the pleadings, contending that the heirs' claims to the paintings were time-barred. In December 2006, the federal district court in Ohio granted the Toledo museum's motion, ruling that the heirs' claim to the Gauguin was barred by Ohio's four-year statute of limitations.[5] In March 2007, the federal district court in Michigan, in an unpublished opinion, granted the Detroit museum's motion, ruling that the heirs' claim to the van Gogh was barred by Michigan's three-year statute of limitations.[6]

The heirs did not appeal, and the proceedings ended there.

---

[2]Detroit Institute of Arts and Toledo Museum of Art (2006), p. 2.

[3]*Id.* at 3.

[4]*Id.* at 2.

[5]Toledo Museum of Art v. Ullin, 477 F. Supp.2d 802 (N.D. Ohio 2006).

[6]Detroit Institute of Arts v. Ullin, 2007 WL 1016996 (E.D. Mich. 2007).

13.3 The Courts' View of the Merits

Though resting their decisions on the statute of limitations, the district courts in both cases left little doubt that they accepted the museums' version of events, and did not believe the heirs had a sound claim to the paintings. Both pointed out that Martha Nathan had sold the paintings to a group of three Jewish dealers, two of whom she had known for years and were themselves refugees from the Nazis,[7] and that neither she nor her brother (acting as her estate's executor) ever challenged the sale. "In short, this sale occurred outside Germany by and between private individuals who were familiar with each other," the court in the Toledo museum case observed, adding that the purchasers "like her, were Jews who suffered during Nazi-era Germany."[8] "The Painting was not confiscated or looted by the Nazis; the sale was not at the direction of, nor did the proceeds benefit, the Nazi regime," and the painting was conspicuously absent from the items as to which Nathan and her estate had sought "restitution and damages for wartime losses that resulted from Nazi persecution."[9]

If she had in fact been the victim of duress or other wrongdoing, the courts rather clearly thought, Martha Nathan would have pressed a claim long ago. To such reasoning it might be objected, of course, that it never occurred to Nathan that the law would provide redress for such a sale, in which wartime conditions may have led her to part with the paintings for less than their market value. Like many others who never pursued legal relief for wartime losses, she may have believed a judicial remedy was hopeless. Be that as it may, the courts put a great deal of weight on the fact that she chose not to pursue the matter after the war. As in other cases we have looked at, then, the courts may have viewed dismissal under the statute of limitations as a sort of shorthand merits ruling, avoiding protracted litigation of what they viewed—again, rightly or wrongly—as claims of doubtful merit.[10]

13.4 The Claims' Timeliness

13.4.1 Conflicts of Law

The initial decision confronting the courts was which statute of limitations to apply. Under the *Guaranty Trust* decision,[11] state law supplies the statute of limitations to

[7]Two of the dealers, Alexander Ball and Justin Thannhauser, were Germans whose galleries had been seized by the Nazis. The third, George Wildenstein, was French.

[8]*Toledo Museum v. Ullin*, 477 F. Supp.2d at 805, 807.

[9]*Id.* at 805. For comparable language in the Detroit museum case, see *Detroit Institute v. Ullin*, 2007 WL 1016996, *1–2.

[10]For criticism of the decisions, see Kreder (2012).

[11]Guaranty Trust Co. v. York, 326 U.S. 99 (1945).

claims heard under the federal court's diversity jurisdiction; and under the *Klaxon* decision,[12] the forum state's choice-of-law rule selects the applicable state law. Following these principles, the district court in the Toledo case found that Ohio choice-of-law rules required application of the forum's own statute of limitations; on that basis, the court held that the Ohio statute of limitations governed the suit over the Gauguin. This was so, the court concluded, whether or not Ohio law governed other substantive issues in the case.[13] By the same reasoning, the district court in the Detroit case found that Michigan choice-of-law rules required application of the forum's statute of limitations, and concluded that the Michigan statute of limitations governed the dispute over the van Gogh.[14]

13.4.2 Timeliness Under Ohio Law

The heirs' claim to the Gauguin, the district court held in the Toledo case, was subject to Ohio's four-year limitations period for actions seeking "the recovery of personal property."[15] The Ohio courts, the district court noted, apply a "discovery rule" to determine when the clock starts for this purpose, holding that a claim accrues under this provision when the claimant "discovers or, in the exercise of reasonable care, should have discovered the complained-of injury."[16]

Applying this rule, the court took the view that the heirs' claims accrued well over four years before the case was filed. First, the court reasoned, Martha Nathan's own knowledge is imputed to her estate; and she had all the information necessary to make a claim if there was one to make. "If she believed she had a claim to the Painting, she could have investigated and brought suit back then," the court stated; yet "[u]p to her death in 1958, twenty years after the alleged sale, she did not challenge the art dealers' purchase of the subsequent sale to [the Toledo museum]," which "did not try to hide its possession of the Painting."[17] Any "fraud, duress or wrongdoing would or should have been known at the time the art dealers acquired the Painting," in the court's view, and "[e]ven if, for some unexplained reason, she could not discover any wrongdoing at that time, once the chaos of World War II Europe subsided, a reasonable and prudent person would have made further inquiry into the terms of her sale to the art dealers."[18]

[12]Klaxon Co. v. Stentor Electric Manufacturing Co., 313 U.S. 487 (1941).

[13]*Toledo Museum v, Ullin*, 477 F. Supp.2d at 806.

[14]*Detroit Institute v. Ullin*, 2007 WL 1016996, *2.

[15]Ohio Revised Code § 2305.09(B), quoted in *Toledo Museum v, Ullin*, 477 F. Supp.2d at 806.

[16]*Toledo Museum v, Ullin*, 477 F. Supp.2d at 807, citing Investors REIT One v. Jacobs, 546 N.E.2d 206 (Ohio 1989), Hambleton v. R.G. Barry Corp., 465 N.E.2d 1298 (Ohio 1984), and Copeland v. Delvaux, 623 N.E.2d 569 (Ohio App. 1993).

[17]*Toledo Museum v, Ullin*, 477 F. Supp.2d at 807.

[18]*Id.*

Second, the court continued, even if Nathan's knowledge were not imputed to her heirs, "they too should have made inquiry into the Painting's provenance well before 2002."[19] Congress held numerous hearings on the subject of Nazi-era artwork in this country in 1998, the court stated, and "the public debate surrounding Nazi-era assets should have led the Nathan heirs to inquire into the location of her former assets."[20] The heirs "knew she was persecuted by the Nazis and sustained wartime losses," which "would have led a reasonable person to make further inquiries" that "would have revealed the sale of the Painting in 1938."[21] Thus, "by 1998, at the latest, [the heirs] had sufficient notice to alert them to the possibility of wrongdoing surrounding the painting."[22] Even on the most lenient application of the discovery rule, then, the claim had expired years before the claim was filed.[23]

13.4.3 Timeliness Under Michigan Law

The district court's terse unpublished opinion in the Detroit case followed the same lines as its Ohio counterpart. Michigan law gives claimants three years to bring suits to recover personal property, the court declared, and a claim accrues "at the time the wrong upon which the claim is based was done."[24] For commercial conversion claims, the court stated, the Michigan courts have held the "discovery rule" inapplicable; the claim begins to run when the conversion occurs, regardless of whether the claimant knows about it.[25] Applying that principle to the case before it, the court held that the heirs' claims "accrued on the date that Mrs. Nathan sold the Painting to the three European art dealers in 1938," and therefore expired in 1941.[26] And even if a discovery rule did apply to the heirs' claims, the court continued, their claim would be untimely: "In 1973, the executor of Mrs. Nathan's estate [i.e., her brother Willy Dreyfus] made claims in addition to those previously asserted by Mrs. Nathan, for his family's wartime losses," and at that point "Mrs. Nathan's heirs, 'through the exercise of reasonable diligence should have discovered' that they had

---

[19] *Id.*

[20] *Id.*

[21] *Id.*

[22] *Id.* at 807–8.

[23] The court rejected the heirs' argument that the Toledo museum had "waived" the statute of limitations by including (in compliance with American Association of Museums guidelines) the Gauguin on a website listing works that had left Europe during the Nazi era and urging people with possible claims to such works to come forward. *Id.* at 808–9.

[24] Michigan Compiled Laws § 600.5827, quoted in *Detroit Institute v. Ullin*, 2007 WL 1016996, *3.

[25] *Detroit Institute v. Ullin*, 2007 WL 1016996, *3.

[26] *Id.*

a possible cause of action to recover the painting."[27] At the latest, the court thus reasoned, the Nathan estate's claims had expired in the 1970s.

13.5 Epilogue

Congress singled out the Detroit case when it voted to enact the Holocaust Expropriated Art Recovery Act of 2016, which created a new federal statute of limitations for Nazi-era art restitution claims.[28] The Act's authors expressed concern that laws such as Michigan's were insufficiently responsive to the "unique and horrific circumstances of World War II and the Holocaust" and the challenges facing heirs who must "painstakingly piece together their cases from a fragmentary historical record ravaged by persecution, war, and genocide."[29]

Gauguin's *Street in Tahiti* remains in the Toledo Museum of Art, and van Gogh's *The Diggers* remains in the Detroit Institute of Arts.

References

Detroit Institute of Arts and Toledo Museum of Art. 2006. Detroit and Toledo Museums Present Research Findings on Nazi-Era Provenance for Two Paintings in Their Collection. Accessed June 1, 2017. http://www.toledomuseum.org/wordpress/wp-content/uploads/Provenance_Research.pdf.

Kreder, Jennifer Anglim. 2012. Fighting Corruption of the Historical Record: Nazi-Looted Art Litigation. *Kansas Law Review* 61: 75–137.

Martinez, Alanna. 2015. Museums Respond to Biting Report on Nazi-Looted Art. *Observer*, July 2.

Micucci, Dana. 2006. Of Museums, Heirs and Lawsuits. *New York Times*, April 21.

Cases

Brennan v. Edward D. Jones & Co., 626 N.W.2d 917 (Mich. App. 2001)
Copeland v. Delvaux, 623 N.E.2d 569 (Ohio App. 1993)
Detroit Institute of Arts v. Ullin, 2007 WL 1016996 (E.D. Mich. 2007)
Guaranty Trust Co. v. York, 326 U.S. 99 (1945)
Hambleton v. R.G. Barry Corp., 465 N.E.2d 1298 (Ohio 1984)
Investors REIT One v. Jacobs, 546 N.E.2d 206 (Ohio 1989)
Klaxon Co. v. Stentor Electric Manufacturing Co., 313 U.S. 487 (1941)
Toledo Museum of Art v. Ullin, 477 F. Supp.2d 802 (N.D. Ohio 2006)

---

[27] *Id.* (quoting Brennan v. Edward D. Jones & Co., 626 N.W.2d 917, 920 (Mich. App. 2001)).

[28] See Chap. 15 below.

[29] Holocaust Expropriated Art Recovery Act, Pub. L. 114–308 (Dec. 16, 2016), § 2(6).

Chapter 14
Vineberg v. Bissonnette

14.1 Background

Max Stern (1904–1987) was the owner of the Galerie Julius Stern, an art dealership in Düsseldorf. The gallery was founded by his parents in 1913, and inherited by Stern upon his father's death in 1934.[1] Following the passage of the Nuremburg laws, the Reich Ministry of Fine Arts ordered Stern to close the gallery and liquidate its inventory. In September 1937, after his appeals of the order were rejected, he consigned hundreds of works from the inventory and his private collection to Kunsthaus Mathias Lempertz in Köln, which shortly afterward auctioned them off. The Nazis froze the proceeds of the sale, along with the rest of Stern's assets, following his flight to Paris in December 1937; later his citizenship was revoked and his remaining German assets confiscated. Stern joined his sister Gerda in London prior to the outbreak of the war, and eventually settled in Montreal, where he became a prominent art dealer and collector.

Following the war, Stern made extensive efforts to recover the art he had lost to the Nazis, placing newspaper advertisements seeking information about its whereabouts and traveling to Europe on numerous occasions to search for it. Most of the art was untraceable, in part because the Lempertz auction house's sale records had been destroyed during the war. He managed to recover about a dozen works in the 1950s, and in 1964 a German court awarded him compensation for his losses. Discouraged by its lack of progress Stern gave up his search, filed away the documents he had assembled, and never mentioned the matter to his associates in Montreal. Upon his death in 1987, he bequeathed his assets to a foundation for the benefit of several universities.

[1]On the Stern family members and their activities in the art world, see Moreault (2004), Roussow (2006), and Schmidt (2005). See also the information collected at the website of the Max Stern Art Restitution Project at Concordia University.

B.L. Hay, *Nazi-Looted Art and the Law*, DOI 10.1007/978-3-319-64967-2_14

In the early 2000s, the Stern estate's executors resumed the search for the lost art after finding the evidence Stern had put in his files, including the Nazi liquidation orders and the catalog from the auction of his collection. A list of the missing works was placed on the Art Loss Register, which notified the estate in January 2005 that one of them, Franz Xaver Winterhalter's painting *Girl from the Sabine Mountains* (1835), had surfaced on the art market. The painting was being sold by Maria-Louise Bissonnette, the daughter of Karl Wilharm, a Nazi party member and SA officer who had purchased it at the 1937 Lempertz auction. Bissonnette had kept the painting at her home in Rhode Island since relocating there from Germany in the 1950s.

The Stern estate contacted the Holocaust Claims Processing Office of New York, a division of the state's Banking Department that assists claimants of Nazi-era assets.[2] The office sent a letter to Bissonnette requesting that the painting be returned to the estate, which led to fifteen months of negotiations between the parties. Upon learning in 2006 that Bissonnette had shipped the painting back to Germany, the estate filed suit against her in the American courts.

14.2 Proceedings

The Stern estate, represented by Robert Vineberg and two other trustees, sued Bissonnette in May 2006, bringing the action in Rhode Island federal court under the diversity jurisdiction. The complaint asserted claims of replevin and conversion, and sought recovery of the painting along with a declaration that the foundation had valid title to it. The defendant's answer denied the claims on the merits, and also challenged their timeliness.[3] The court enjoined the defendant against further movement of the painting, which had been brought back to the United States.

Following pretrial discovery, the court granted summary judgment to the Stern estate.[4] Applying the substantive law of Rhode Island, the court ruled in the estate's favor on the replevin claim, holding that Stern was the painting's rightful owner, that it had been unlawfully taken from him, and that Bissonnette was in wrongful possession of it. The district court also ruled in the estate's favor on the defense of laches, holding that Stern and the estate had acted with reasonable diligence to locate the painting, and that Bissonnette had not been prejudiced by the delay in the filing of suit. The court declined to address whether the action was timely under the applicable statute of limitations, holding that Bissonnette had waived that defense.

---

[2]On the office's work, see generally Dugot (2001).

[3]The answer also asserted that because Stern had recovered compensation in the German courts, the present suit was barred by the doctrines of res judicata and collateral estoppel. Bissonnette abandoned this position when the estate sought summary judgment.

[4]Vineberg v. Bissonnette, 529 F. Supp.2d 300 (D.R.I. 2007).

The First Circuit court of appeals upheld the grant of summary judgment in November 2008.[5] On appeal, Bissonnette did not challenge the district court's ruling on the merits of the case, but argued that she should have prevailed on the laches defense. The court of appeals disagreed. The court did not address the question whether Stern and the estate were insufficiently diligent in searching for the painting. The court ruled, however, that Bissonnette was not harmed by their delay in bringing the action, because the delay had not deprived her of evidence or otherwise prejudiced her ability to defend herself in the case.[6] The court accordingly affirmed the judgment, which brought the case to an end.

14.3 Title to the Artwork

The paper trail in the Vineberg case was sufficiently clear that the district court deemed a trial unnecessary, and ruled that the Stern estate was entitled to summary judgment on the question of title to the painting.

The district court applied the substantive law of Rhode Island, which the parties agreed should govern the case.[7] That state's replevin statute creates a cause of action for the recovery of property "unlawfully taken or unlawfully detained from the owner or from the person entitled to possession thereof."[8] To recover the painting, according to the court, "the Stern Estate must show that (1) it is the lawful owner of the Painting, (2) the Painting was taken from Dr. Stern unlawfully, that is, without his permission, and (3) Defendant is in wrongful possession of the Painting."[9]

The undisputed evidence presented by the estate easily satisfied these requirements, in the court's view. First, the 1937 Lempertz catalog for the sale of Stern's gallery inventory "identified the Painting as being part of the auction," and the German court that awarded Stern compensation for his losses in 1964 listed the painting as part of the inventory.[10] Therefore, declared the court, the "Stern Estate is the lawful owner of the painting."[11]

Second, there was no question that Stern's "relinquishment of his property was anything but voluntary," because "the Nazi government forced Dr. Stern to

---

[5]Vineberg v. Bissonnette, 548 F.3d 50 (1st Cir. 2008).

[6]The court also rejected Bissonnette's contention that the district court had abused its discretion in refusing to extend the calendar for pretrial discovery after she replaced her lawyer.

[7]The Stern estate urged application of Rhode Island law, and Bissonnette raised no objection. The court accordingly ruled that it "need not engage in an extensive choice of law analysis and will apply Rhode Island law." *Vineberg*, 529 F. Supp.2d at 305.

[8]R.I. Gen. Laws § 34-21-1, quoted in *Vineberg*, 529 F. Supp.2d at 306.

[9]*Vineberg*, 529 F. Supp.2d at 306.

[10]*Id.* at 307.

[11]*Id.*

liquidate inventory in his art gallery and controlled the manner of the forced sale."[12] Indeed, in the 1964 compensation proceeding "the German restitution court found that the [Lempertz] auction was a 'distressed sale which Dr. Stern was forced to participate in for reasons of persecution,'" the district court noted.[13] "The Nazi party's actions in this instance are therefore properly classified as looting or stealing," the court stated.[14] "The Court concludes that the Painting was taken unlawfully from Dr. Stern," it continued.[15]

Third, though "Bissonnette acquired the Painting through no wrongdoing on her part," she had no rights to it.[16] The person from whom she inherited it, having purchased the painting at the Lempertz auction, "did not acquire good title to the Painting," declared the court, for "[w]here pillage has taken place, the title of the original owner is not extinguished."[17] Bissonnette "cannot lay valid claim to ownership," and is therefore "in wrongful possession of the Painting," the court concluded.[18]

Bissonnette did not challenge this determination on appeal.

14.4 The Claim's Timeliness

Bissonnette initially suggested that the estate's claim was barred by the statute of limitations, but did not argue the question when the estate moved for summary judgment, leading the district court to declare she had waived the statute of limitations defense.[19] Bissonnette's defense of laches was therefore the only timeliness issue adjudicated in the case.

14.4.1 The District Court Ruling

The laches doctrine is applicable, in the district court's words, when a claimant's "unexplained and inexcusable delay cause prejudice to the defendant."[20] In the formulation of the Rhode Island courts, which is typical of other jurisdictions and was followed without objection from the parties, a "court applying the doctrine

[12] *Id.*

[13] *Id* (quoting German court).

[14] *Id.*

[15] *Id.* at 308.

[16] *Id.*

[17] *Id.* (quoting Menzel v. List, 267 N.Y.S.2d 804, 811 (Sup. Ct. 1966)).

[18] *Vineberg*, 529 F. Supp.2d at 308.

[19] *Id.* at 305.

[20] *Id.* at 308–9.

applies a two-part test: (1) there must be negligence on the part of the plaintiff that leads to a delay in the prosecution of the case, and (2) the delay must prejudice the defendant."[21]

The district court ruled that Bissonnette had failed to establish either element of the defense. It held, first, that both Max Stern and the executors of his estate had been sufficiently diligent in looking for the painting. "The record reflects that Dr. Stern took significant steps in attempting to make public the fact that the inventory of his gallery was taken by the Nazi party," it stated, noting that immediately upon the war's end Stern "used diplomatic channels, post war procedures, the press, and personal finances to locate the lost artwork."[22] In addition, stated the court, the Winterhalter painting "has been in the private collection of Defendant and her family for nearly seven decades," and therefore "was not readily 'susceptible to discovery' as it was not 'drifting in the art community.'"[23] The court concluded that "based upon the highly unusual set of circumstances in this matter, Dr. Stern took the appropriate steps and made reasonable efforts in attempting to publicize his loss and locate the inventory of his gallery."[24] The court further concluded that "the Stern Estate, Dr. Stern's successor in interest, had made reasonable efforts to locate the Painting," having listed it with the Art Loss Register and notifying Bissonnette of its claim within one month of learning the painting was in her possession.[25]

Second, the "claim of laches also fails," the court continued, "because she cannot show prejudice."[26] Bissonnette, the court reasoned, had failed to show how she had been harmed by the delay, or how her position would have been improved if the claim had been brought sooner. The court rejected her contention that the "expense and inconvenience" of litigation constituted the "prejudice contemplated by the doctrine of laches."[27] It also rejected her assertion that her "inability to sell the property due to the pending lawsuit" rose "to the level of material prejudice."[28] Bissonnette's "laches argument," concluded the district court, "is unavailing."[29]

---

[21]*Id.* at 309, citing Hyszko v. Barbour, 448 A.2d 723 (R.I. 1982), and Fitzgerald v. O'Connell, 386 A.2d 1384 (R.I. 1978).

[22]*Vineberg*, 529 F. Supp.2d at 310.

[23]*Id.* (quoting Erisoty v. Rizik, 1995 WL 91406, *11 (E.D. Pa. 1995) (ellipses omitted)).

[24]*Vineberg*, 529 F. Supp.2d at 310.

[25]*Id.*

[26]*Id.*

[27]Lin Ron, Inc., v. Mann's World of Arts and Crafts, Inc., 624 P.2d 1343, 1345 (Colo. App. 1981), quoted in *Vineberg*, 529 F. Supp.2d at 311.

[28]Junkins v. Spinnaker Bay Condominium Association, 2002 WL 337780, *12 (Ohio App. 2002), quoted in *Vineberg*, 529 F. Supp.2d at 311 (brackets omitted).

[29]*Vineberg*, 529 F. Supp.2d at 311.

14.4.2 The Court of Appeals Ruling

The court of appeals found it unnecessary to decide whether Stern and the estate had been sufficiently diligent in searching for the painting, because it agreed with the district court that, reasonable or not, the resulting delay had not harmed Bissonnette. "Typically," the court of appeals noted, "the kind of prejudice that will support a laches defense arises out of a loss of evidence, the unavailability of important witnesses, the conveyance of the property in dispute for fair market value to a bona fide purchaser, or the expenditure of resources in reliance upon the status quo ante."[30] Bissonnette, it stated, "fails to point to any particular witnesses (or types of witnesses) whom she might have consulted or to any particular documents (or types of documents) she might have located but for the delayed commencement of the action," and "has not explained how the acquisition of further testimony might assist her defense."[31] Because she has "chosen not to contest ownership of the Painting," and cannot "identify any other controverted issue to which difficult-to-locate witnesses might be pertinent," the delay in filing suit had not compromised her ability to defend herself.[32] "Laches, in legal significance," noted the court, borrowing the words of a nineteenth-century Rhode Island decision, "is not mere delay, but delay that works a disadvantage to another."[33]

The court of appeals concluded with a word of approval for the outcome of the case, as well for the legal system that had brought it about. "A de facto confiscation of a work of art that arose out of a notorious exercise of man's inhumanity to man," it declared, "now ends with the righting of that wrong through the mundane application of common law principles. The mills of justice grind slowly, but they grind exceedingly fine."[34]

14.5 Epilogue

Following the court of appeals judgment, Winterhalter's *Girl from the Sabine Mountains* was returned to the Stern estate in 2008 and shortly afterward was displayed at the Montreal Museum of Fine Arts.[35] The Düsseldorf City Museum has announced an exhibition, scheduled for 2018, to commemorate the Galerie Julius Stern.

[30] *Vineberg*, 548 F.3d at 57.

[31] *Id.* at 58.

[32] *Id.* at 58.

[33] Chase v. Chase, 37 A. 804, 805 (R.I. 1897), quoted in *Vineberg*, 548 F.3d at 58.

[34] *Vineberg*, 548 F.3d at 58–59.

[35] Cooper (2009). On other works recovered by the estate in Europe and the United States without litigation, see Barron and Chan (2009), Clément (2010), and O'Connor (2013).

References

Barron, James, and Sewell Chan. 2009. After 70 Years, Painting Seized by the Nazis Is Returned. *New York Times*, April 21.

Clément, Eric. 2010. Une toile volée par les nazis arrive à Montréal. *La Presse*, December 9.

Concordia University. Max Stern Art Restitution Project. http://www.concordia.ca/arts/max-stern.html (visited June 13, 2017).

Cooper, Russ. 2009. Stern Paintings Unveiled at MMFA. *Concordia Journal*, May 21.

Dugot, Monica. 2001. The Holocaust Claims Processing Office's Handling of Art Claims. *Fordham International Law Journal* 25: 133–138.

Moreault, Michel. 2004. *Max Stern: Montreal Dealer and Patron*. Montreal, QC: Montreal Museum of Fine Arts.

O'Connor, Joe. 2013. Lost Treasures from a Dark Era. *National Post*, March 6.

Roussow, Henk. 2006. In Pursuit of an Art Dealer's Dream. *Chronicle of Higher Education*, June 2.

Schmidt, Herbert. 2005. *Der Elendsweg der Düsseldorfer Juden, Chronologie des Schrecken, 1933-1945*. Düsseldorf: Droste.

Cases

Chase v. Chase, 37 A. 804 (R.I. 1897)

Fitzgerald v. O'Connell, 386 A.2d 1384 (R.I. 1978)

Hyszko v. Barbour, 448 A.2d 723 (R.I. 1982)

Junkins v. Spinnaker Bay Condominium Association, 2002 WL 337780 (Ohio App. 2002)

Lin Ron, Inc., v. Mann's World of Arts and Crafts, Inc., 624 P.2d 1343 (Colo. App. 1981)

Vineberg v. Bissonnette, 529 F. Supp.2d 300 (D.R.I. 2007), aff'd, 548 F.3d 50 (1st Cir. 2008)

Chapter 15
Conclusion

In December 2016, Congress enacted the Holocaust Expropriated Art Recovery Act, which created a new federal statute of limitations for Nazi-era art restitution claims in both state and federal courts. The Act replaces state limitations periods with a six-year period that generally begins upon a claim's "actual discovery" by the claimants, not counting any time that they were unable to bring the claim due to a state statute of limitations.[1] Congress's rationale for the law, set forth in the preamble that we alluded to in an earlier chapter,[2] is worth quoting in full.

> (1) It is estimated that the Nazis confiscated or otherwise misappropriated hundreds of thousands of works of art and other property throughout Europe as part of their genocidal campaign against the Jewish people and other persecuted groups. This has been described as the "greatest displacement of art in human history."
>
> (2) Following World War II, the United States and its allies attempted to return the stolen artworks to their countries of origin. Despite these efforts, many works of art were never reunited with their owners. Some of the art has since been discovered in the United States.
>
> (3) In 1998, the United States convened a conference with 43 other nations in Washington, DC, known as the Washington Conference, which produced Principles on Nazi-Confiscated Art. One of these principles is that "steps should be taken expeditiously to achieve a just and fair solution" to claims involving such art that has not been restituted if the owners or their heirs can be identified.
>
> (4) The same year, Congress enacted the Holocaust Victims Redress Act, which expressed the sense of Congress that "all governments should undertake good faith efforts to facilitate the return of private and public property, such as works of art, to the rightful owners in cases where assets were confiscated from the claimant during the period of Nazi rule and there is reasonable proof that the claimant is the rightful owner."
>
> (5) In 2009, the United States participated in a Holocaust Era Assets Conference in Prague, Czech Republic, with 45 other nations. At the conclusion of this conference, the participating nations issued the Terezín Declaration, which reaffirmed the 1998 Washington

[1] Holocaust Expropriated Art Recovery Act, Pub. L. 114–308 (Dec. 16, 2016), § (5).

[2] See Section 8.7 above.

B.L. Hay, *Nazi-Looted Art and the Law*, DOI 10.1007/978-3-319-64967-2_15

Conference Principles on Nazi-Confiscated Art and urged all participants "to ensure that their legal systems or alternative processes, while taking into account the different legal traditions, facilitate just and fair solutions with regard to Nazi-confiscated and looted art, and to make certain that claims to recover such art are resolved expeditiously and based on the facts and merits of the claims and all the relevant documents submitted by all parties." The Declaration also urged participants to "consider all relevant issues when applying various legal provisions that may impede the restitution of art and cultural property, in order to achieve just and fair solutions, as well as alternative dispute resolution, where appropriate under law."

(6) Victims of Nazi persecution and their heirs have taken legal action in the United States to recover Nazi-confiscated art. These lawsuits face significant procedural obstacles partly due to State statutes of limitations, which typically bar claims within some limited number of years from either the date of the loss or the date that the claim should have been discovered. In some cases, this means that the claims expired before World War II even ended. (See, e.g., *Detroit Institute of Arts v. Ullin.*) The unique and horrific circumstances of World War II and the Holocaust make statutes of limitations especially burdensome to the victims and their heirs. Those seeking recovery of Nazi-confiscated art must painstakingly piece together their cases from a fragmentary historical record ravaged by persecution, war, and genocide. This costly process often cannot be done within the time constraints imposed by existing law.

(7) Federal legislation is needed because the only court that has considered the question held that the Constitution prohibits States from making exceptions to their statutes of limitations to accommodate claims involving the recovery of Nazi-confiscated art. In *von Saher v. Norton Simon Museum of Art*, the United States Court of Appeals for the Ninth Circuit invalidated a California law that extended the State statute of limitations for claims seeking recovery of Holocaust-era artwork. The Court held that the law was an unconstitutional infringement of the Federal Government's exclusive authority over foreign affairs, which includes the resolution of war-related disputes. In light of this precedent, the enactment of a Federal law is necessary to ensure that claims to Nazi-confiscated art are adjudicated in accordance with United States policy as expressed in the Washington Conference Principles on Nazi-Confiscated Art, the Holocaust Victims Redress Act, and the Terezín Declaration.

(8) While litigation may be used to resolve claims to recover Nazi-confiscated art, it is the sense of Congress that the private resolution of claims by parties involved, on the merits and through the use of alternative dispute resolution such as mediation panels established for this purpose with the aid of experts in provenance research and history, will yield just and fair resolutions in a more efficient and predictable manner.[3]

Though it does not allow claimants to reopen cases that have reached a final judgment, the Act's "actual discovery" rule of accrual will permit future claims that would otherwise be barred by the rulings in the *Orkin*, *Grosz*, *Seger-Thomschitz*, and *Ullin* cases, and avoids the constitutional problems that led the *von Saher* court to strike down similar California Holocaust restitution legislation. Future claimants will thus have an easier time insisting on a trial on the merits, as well as having greater leverage in settlement negotiations. Many of the complexities that pervade these cases will probably nonetheless remain.

[3]Holocaust Expropriated Art Recovery Act, Pub. L. 114–308 (Dec. 16, 2016), § (3) (citations omitted).

"Vincent van Gogh is said to have reflected that 'paintings have a life of their own that derives from the painter's soul,'" the court remarked in *Orkin v. Taylor*.[4] "The confused and perhaps turbulent history of his painting *Vue de l'Asile et de la Chapelle de Saint–Rémy*," added the court, speaking of the work at issue in that case, "may prove the truth of his observation."[5] And so perhaps of this restitution litigation in the American courts, which may have a life of its own for some time to come.

[4]Orkin v. Taylor, 487 F.3d 734, 736 (9th Cir.), cert. denied, 552 U.S. 990 (2007).
[5]*Id.*

Index

B.L. Hay, *Nazi-Looted Art and the Law*, DOI 10.1007/978-3-319-64967-2

Printed by Printforce, the Netherlands